INSIGHT G

Canada

Part of the Langenscheidt Publishing Group

ABOUT THIS BOOK

Editorial

Project Editor
Jane Hutchings
Editorial Director
Brian Bell

Distribution

UK & Ireland
GeoCenter International Ltd
The Viables Centre , Harrow Way
Basingstoke, Hants RG22 4BJ
Fax: (44) 1256-817988

United States
Langenscheidt Publishers, Inc.
46–35 54th Road, Maspeth, NY 11378
Fax: (718) 784-0640

Canada
Thomas Allen & Son Ltd.
390 Steelcase Road East
Markham, Ontario L3R 1G2
Tel: (905) 475-9126. Fax: (905) 475-6747

Worldwide
Apa Publications GmbH & Co.
Verlag KG (Singapore branch)
38 Joo Koon Road, Singapore 628990
Tel: (65) 865-1600. Fax: (65) 861-6438

Printing

Insight Print Services (Pte) Ltd
38 Joo Koon Road, Singapore 628990
Tel: (65) 865-1600. Fax: (65) 861-6438

This guidebook combines the interests and enthusiasms of two of
the world's best known information
providers: Insight Guides, whose titles
have set the standard for visual travel
guides since 1970, and Discovery
Channel, the world's premier source
of nonfiction television programming.

The editors of Insight Guides provide practical advice and general
understanding about a destination's history, culture and people.
Discovery Channel and its website,
www.discovery.com, help millions of
viewers explore their world from the
comfort of their home and encourage
them to explore it firsthand.

How to use this book

Insight Guide: Canada is
structured to convey an
understanding of the country

and its culture and to guide readers
through its major sights:

◆ To understand Canada today, you
need to know something of its past.
The first section covers the country's
History, culture and **People** in lively,
authoritative **Features**.
◆ The main **Places** section provides
a full run-down of all the attractions
worth seeing. The principal places
of interest are coordinated by number with full-color maps.
◆ The **Travel Tips** listings section
provides a convenient point of reference for information on travel,
hotels, restaurants, sports
and festivals. Information
may be located quickly by
using the index printed on
the back cover flap – and
the flaps are designed to
serve as bookmarks.

◆ **Photographs** are chosen not only to illustrate geography and attractions but also to convey Canada's moods and the activities of its people.

The contributors

This new edition was supervised by **Jane Hutchings**, one of the series' regular editors, and builds on the original edition produced by **Andrew Eames** and **Hilary Cunningham**.

Joanna Ebbutt played a major part in updating this edition. A long-time resident of Toronto, she wrote the chapter on that city and the feature on living with snow. Ebbutt also fully revised the guide for the 2000 update, and wrote the new chapter on Nunavut.

Michael Algar, an author of Canadian travel books, lives in Toronto. He compiled the Travel Tips as well as contributing features on Canadian sport, Alberta's rodeo, West Coast flora and fauna, and whale-watching.

The author of the History chapters, **Hilary Cunningham** is a native of Toronto and graduate of the University of Toronto and Yale University.

Other contributors include the culinary columnist and illustrator **Colette Copeland**, author of the Food and Drink chapter. **Charles Foran** tackled the thorny problem of French/English relations. Canada at Work is by **John Duffy**, who has worked as a government adviser and speech writer. Duffy says that sometimes Canada feels like New York run by the Swiss, and sometimes Pittsburgh run by the Russians. **Geoff Hancock**, editor-in-chief of *Canadian Fiction Magazine*, wrote about Art and Performance.

The progeny of a small Ontario town, **Patrick Keyes** contributed the account of the Inuit and those of Canada's Yukon and Northwest Territories. Writer and cartoonist **Philip Street** wrote the Montréal chapter and teamed up with **Malcolm MacRury** to write about Ontario. **Matthew Parfitt**, who arrived in Montréal at the age of eight on one of the last passenger liners, has written about Québec.

In Newfoundland **John Lucas** found a special sense of humor; **Anne Matthews** discovered the smallest province, Prince Edward Island; **Diane Hall** supplied her impressions of New Brunswick and Nova Scotia; and **John Loonam** – a native of New York State who was spellbound by British Columbia – contributed the chapters on this province and Vancouver. The Prairie section is by **David Dunbar**, who says that the diversity of Canada's Texas "never fails to surprise" him.

Map Legend

—— --	International Boundary
-----	Province
⊖	Border Crossing
▪—▪	National Park
-----	Ferry Route
Ⓜ	Metro/Subway
✈	Airport
🚌	Bus Station
P	Parking
❶	Tourist Information
✉	Post Office
♁	Church/Ruins
☾	Mosque
✡	Synagogue
♜	Castle/Ruins
∴	Archaeological Site
∩	Cave
★	Place of Interest

The main places of interest in the Places section are coordinated by number with a full-color map (e.g. ❶), and a symbol at the top of every right-hand page tells you where to find the map.

INSIGHT GUIDE
Canada

CONTENTS

EXPLORE YOUR WORLD
Discovery
CHANNEL

Brass band on
a raft at
Whistler's
Classical
Music Festival

Travel Tips

Insight on...

Information panels

Places

HOPE AND PROMISE

Charles Dickens once described Canada as a land of "hope and promise." Today it is that and more: a land of exuberant cities, breathtaking scenery and diverse cultures

The writer George Woodcock said, a couple of decades ago, "The national voice of Canada is muted," and this is certainly true. Canadians are among the last people to sing the praises of their exceptionally fine land, and proclaiming its attractions has usually been left to foreigners.

"I saw a great and wonderful country; a land containing in its soil everything that a man desires; a proper land, fit for proper men to live in and to prosper exceedingly," observed British Field-Marshal Lord Montgomery in 1946. More than 100 years earlier, another traveler from Great Britain, Charles Dickens, was equally enthusiastic: "Few Englishmen are prepared to find out what it is. Advancing quietly; old differences settling down, and being fast forgotten; public feeling and private enterprise alike in a sound and wholesome state; nothing of flush or fever in its system, but health and vigour throbbing in its steady pulse; it is full of hope and promise."

This "hope and promise" can be seen the entire length of Canada's 5,500-km (3,400-mile) border, from Montréal, with its old-world charm and new-age outlook, to Toronto, teeming with street energy, theaters and ethnic restaurants, to Vancouver on the far west coast, where individuality is a valued trait and the pioneer spirit of a young culture pervades every aspect of life. The increasing assertiveness of French-Canadians in Québec has given a new dynamism to French culture in the province, although it has also introduced a note of bitterness and accusation into the politics of a country which had hitherto valued politeness and moderation.

In between, and north of the big cities, lies some of the most beautiful landscape in the world. There are over 40 national parks, home to wild birds and grizzly bears, three national marine conservation areas and 28 rivers totaling more than 6,000 kilometers (3,750 miles) in the Canadian Heritage Rivers System. Over half the countryside is forest, and trees soaring to a height of more than 60 meters (200 ft) are not uncommon.

Theaters, art, restaurants, breathtaking scenery. Time to put all modesty aside, because Canada has a great deal to shout about.

PRECEDING PAGES: the ferry from Vancouver to Victoria, British Columbia; the Rockies; fall begins in New Brunswick; Raymond Mason's "Illuminated Crowd" sculpture on McGill College Avenue, Montréal. **LEFT:** trading post, Saskatchewan.

Decisive Dates

THE FIRST CANADIANS

70000–12000 BC during the Ice Ages waves of proto-Mongolian peoples cross the Bering Strait to America via a land-bridge, and live as hunter-gatherers.

CIRCA 8000 BC several Indian cultures develop on Canadian territory: Northern Algonquin (Micmac, Beothuk, Cree and Ojibwa) to the northeast; further south, Iroquois and Huron; west of the Great Lakes, Plains (Blackfoot) Indians; further north, Athepask Indians (Slave, Chipewyan); and in the west, Tlingit, Kwakiutl, and Haida.

CIRCA 6000 BC the Inuit arrive in Canada by crossing the Bering Strait.

CIRCA AD 1000 Vikings sail from Iceland to Newfoundland and Labrador and establish coastal settlements.

EUROPEAN EXPLORERS

1497 the Venetian John Cabot is sent by the British to seek out the elusive Northwest Passage, and arrives on Canada's east coast, believing it to be the northeast coast of Asia.

1534 Jacques Cartier explores the Gulf of St Lawrence and reaches the Iroquois village of Hochelaga (today's Montréal). Cartier claims Canada for France.

THE RISE OF NEW FRANCE

1608 cartographer, mariner and trader Samuel de Champlain founds Québec, capital of the colony of New France. He soon establishes a network of trading routes across the interior.

1609–33 French ally themselves with the Huron against the Iroquois.

1642 Montréal is founded, and soon becomes a beaver pelt trading center.

1670 the Hudson's Bay Company, the largest fur trading company in the world, is founded. England begins to compete with France in North America, and several skirmishes occur.

ENGLISH DOMINATION

1713 England conquers Newfoundland, New Brunswick and Nova Scotia.

1755 English deport Acadians from Nova Scotia.

1759 Battle of Québec, New France becomes a British colony.

1774 under the terms of the Québec Act, England deprives the French in Canada of the right to speak their own language, to practise the Catholic religion and to apply French civil law.

1775-83 American Revolution results in an influx of Loyalists to Québec, Ontario and New Brunswick.

1791 colony is divided into two parts: English Upper Canada (later Ontario) and French Lower Canada (Québec).

1793 Alexander Mackenzie becomes the first person to cross the continent to the Pacific.

1812 war with the United States, which is eager to gain control of the Great Lakes. In 1818 an agreement is reached, establishing the southern border along the 49th parallel.

1840 Upper and Lower Canada unite, creating the Province of Canada.

1857 gold is discovered in the Fraser River, British Columbia. One year later Britain declares British Columbia a crown colony in order to stave off American greed. After the gold rush of 1862 in the Caribou Mountains, many miners remain in Western Canada as farmers and ranchers.

CONFEDERATION

1867 the British North America Act establishes the state Canada. The colonies of Ontario, Québec, Nova Scotia and New Brunswick collectively form the Dominion of Canada.

PRECEDING PAGES: Montréal's maritime past.
LEFT: Samuel de Champlain, founder of Québec.

1869 Rupert's Land, owned by the Hudson's Bay Company, is sold to Canada. The sale enrages the Métis people and sparks an uprising, led by Louis Riel, against the government.
1870 Manitoba is created from parts of Rupert's Land and joins the confederation. The Northwest Territories is formed.
1871 British Columbia announces that it will join the confederation on condition that a continental railway line is built.
1873 Prince Edward Island decides to join the confederation.
1881–85 the Canadian Pacific Railroad is built. The stations along its route become the starting points for future settlement.

GOLD RUSH AND MINERAL WEALTH
1898 gold is discovered in the Klondike River, prompting the biggest gold rush in history.
From 1900 2.4 million new settlers arrive in the country in several waves of immigration, and very soon transform the prairies into a corn belt. Rich mineral resources are found beneath the Canadian Shield.
1905 the provinces of Alberta and Saskatchewan are created from the North West Territory and join the confederation.
1914 oil is discovered in Alberta.

WAR-TIME CONFLICTS
1914–18 World War I; Canada sends troops to support Britain. The old rift between English and French Canadians opens up again during the debate on national conscription.
1931 the Statute of Westminster elevates Canada to the status of a sovereign state within the British Commonwealth.
1939–45 World War II; Canadian troops suffer heavy losses. Debate about conscription.

POST-WAR GROWTH
After 1945 a new wave of immigration sets in. Economic prosperity, largely due to close co-operation with the United States, brings a strong economic dependence in its wake, and the US exerts a great deal of influence on Canadian culture. New oil finds are made in Alberta, which grows very wealthy as a result.
1949 Newfoundland joins the confederation.
1959–62 two new transport routes stimulate Canada's economy: the St Lawrence Seaway and the

RIGHT: Immigrants from Europe disembarking in search of a new life, 1903.

7,821-km (4,850-mile) long Trans-Canada Highway. Toronto begins to emerge as the most important industrial center in Canada, pushing Montréal into second place.

CAMPAIGN FOR SEPARATISM
1960 the separation crisis begins with the "Quiet Revolution" in Québec. Supporters of the Parti Québécois call for independence from federal Canada.
1980 in a first referendum, the majority of Québecois decide to remain part of Canada.
1982–92 Canada Act ends British control of Canadian affairs. Canada receives a new constitution, under the terms of the Constitutional Act. Québec agrees only

on condition that an amendment to it (the Meech Lake Accord), emphasising the cultural and linguistic independence of the province, is upheld. The amendment fails to be ratified in the provincial parliaments and in a nationwide referendum. Canada once again threatens to fall apart politically.
1989 Free Trade Agreement between Canada and the USA (NAFTA).
1992 the founding of a self-governing homeland for the Inuit, called Nunavut Territory, is agreed.
1995 Québecois vote by a wafer-thin majority to remain part of Canada.
1999 On 1 April 1999 the Northwest Territories are divided, creating the territory of Nunavut, covering one-fifth of Canada's landmass.

A NATION IN THE MAKING

The steady population of Canada began around 20,000 years
ago with the arrival of the Inuit

The first settlers to arrive in Canada long before the Europeans were nomadic bands wandering from Siberia across the Bering Strait. These robust and courageous souls sought a new life in the frozen wilds of northern Alaska and Yukon. They are thought to have arrived some 20,000 to 40,000 years ago. Their reception was not a warm one. Facing bitter temperatures and hostile winds, it is a wonder that they survived in such an unfriendly climate. These first "Canadians" developed a remarkable subsistence technology suited to the brutal environment and traces of their ancient culture linger. They have come to be known as the Inuit.

The Inuit peoples

The ancestors of contemporary Inuit needed both intelligence and imagination to thrive in their new continent. If one word can describe the theme of life in their culture, it is survival.

The Arctic Inuit are noted because of the simplicity of their hunting and cooking utensils. Bows and arrows made with tips of flint, ivory or bone were the main means of catching the family dinner. They also created special tools to accommodate the seasonal needs of hunting – and many of these practices remain today. Archaeologists celebrate the Inuit for their ingenious winter ice-spears. The spears have tiny feathers or hairs attached to one end which the hunter holds over a hole in the ice waiting for movement that would indicate the presence of an animal. This often involves sitting over a hole in the freezing cold for several hours.

Food was a major obsession. Blubber, meat and fish were staples and always eaten raw (when they are most nutritious). Partially digested lichen found in a caribou's stomach was considered a delicacy and sometimes created a little diversity in a meal. When natural food supplies ran out, families would move to another area, usually on sleds made of frozen fish or hides – these could be eaten if necessary.

Inuit are often associated with dome-like snow huts or igloos. Without trees (and therefore timber) the prospects of constructing even a simple hut were poor – and snow was a readily available resource. Igloos, dwelling structures that are still used by contemporary Inuit, are made of snow blocks – the result looks much like a ski torque. The house consists of one or two interconnecting rooms. Inside, a platform for sleeping or working stands across from the entrance way; an area for animal carcasses and a heating lamp completes the layout.

The early Inuit had nearly 100 words for snow but no word for chief or ruler; theirs was a different understanding of power and authority. In these nomadic bands authority resided with the group and the underlying theme to Inuit life was a principle of harmony within the group.

Existing in a harsh and rugged world, the Inuit developed a religion that reflected their feelings about their cold, hard life. Living people needed "luck" to exist in a world full of malevolent spirits – when a person died, their "luck" had run out. Yet today's Inuit, living almost an identical lifestyle when undisturbed by colonialism, are noted for their cheerful, fun-loving natures. As many Inuit will say, even today: "If you knew of the dangers I live through each day, you would understand why I am so fond of laughter."

West Coast tribes

As people traveled to other parts of Canada and spread into the plains and woodlands, many distinct languages and cultures flourished.

Throughout Canada today, one finds evidence of a remarkably rich and varied Indian history – a cultural heritage that was largely destroyed through the process of colonization. The West

> ### THE EARLY INUIT
> The Inuit had nearly 100 words for snow, but no word for chief ... authority resided with the group

LEFT: portrait of Chief Joseph. Indians inhabited Canada many thousands of years before the arrival of the Europeans.

Coast supported several Indian populations; among these were the Kwakiutl, Bella Coola, Nootka, Haidas, and Tlingit Indians. These groups found the Pacific coast to be extremely abundant in natural resources. The sea provided cod, halibut, salmon and edible kelp; water animals were used as furs; and the forests yielded deer, beaver and bear.

Unlike the Inuit, the Northwest Coast Indians were able to make extensive use of timber: they are known for their huge dug-out canoes usually stretching to 20 meters (66 ft) in length and their wooden huts 80 meters (270 ft) long. The ancestral fishing grounds that still lie along the

motifs, like European crests, became associated with particular lineages and came to represent rank, wealth and status.

The material wealth and artistic skills of the Northern Coastal cultures engendered a lively system of trade among tribes – this network was later to become very important to the fur trade in Canada. Nootkas specialized in whale products while the Haidas "mass manufactured" ceremonial canoes. Slaves were also traded. The result was a fairly sophisticated practice of interchange.

Not surprisingly, the West Coast Indians show a marked preoccupation with what colonial offi-

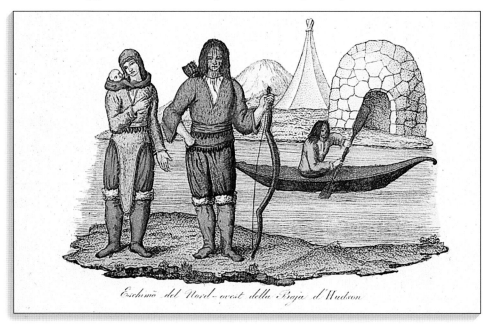

Eschimo del Nord-ovest della Baja d'Hudson

rugged Pacific Coast were the sites of much activity and often a few weeks of hard work yielded enough food for the year.

Given the bounty of food and building materials, Northwest Coast cultures were able to devote ample time to the creation of objects. Many of their styles and techniques remain in use today and travelers to the museums and craft reserves note the omnipresence of animals, mythical creatures with protruding canines; and strangely painted human forms. Found on totem poles, houses, canoes and bowls, the beings depicted are said to be supernatural ancestors who have revealed themselves to certain artists so that they might be painted. These figure

cials considered to be "private property and material wealth".

Travelers to this area of Canada will undoubtedly hear of the famous potlatches. These were exchange ceremonies given by a chief and his local group to another chief and his followers. During the ceremony, huge quantities of gifts were given to each guest. Much feasting was followed by lengthy speeches. These celebrations usually marked a change in the status of a member of the hosting group such as the movement of an inheritor into an inheritance. Frequently if two men were eligible to inherit one position, a series of rival potlatches were held. These often involved the destruction of property by burning or demolition – sometimes the slaying of a slave was a part of the procedure. The potlatches continued until one contester was "broken" financially and relinquished his claim.

Plains tribes

Inhabiting yet another area in Canada's broad geographical milieu were the Plains Indians: the Blackfoot, Sarcee and Assiniboine tribes. Each group possessed a distinctive language so incomprehensible to the other that sign language was used to facilitate trade. Yet each tribe

member of the group – a herd was chased toward an enclosure erected around a pit. One person covered himself with a buffalo hide and imitated the animal's movements in the hope of drawing the herd towards the pit. Once inside the enclosure the buffalo toppled into the pit. They were then shot with arrows, butchered and later eaten.

Dependency on the buffalo made the Plains peoples nomadic. Such mobility demanded a transportable house; it is from this that the origin of the teepee can be traced. A conical-

was bound to the other through their dependency on the buffalo. The buffalo was the nucleus of life. From the buffalo came pemmican (a protein-concentrated food carried by Indians on the trail); skins that were used as blankets, clothes and tent coverings; and buffalo hair that was dried and either woven into rope or used to stuff moccasins. Before the arrival of the horse in the late 18th century, buffalo were hunted on foot, often by stampeding the beasts into a compound. This procedure, referred to as "buffalo jumping", involved every

LEFT: 19th-century Inuit family in front of their "snow home". **ABOVE:** an example of West Coast Inuit art.

shaped hut with an aperture at the tip for smoke, the teepee was not only practical but sacred. The floor represented the earth of mortal life and the peak the sky of the gods. The roundness of the tent symbolized the sacred circle of life.

Until the coming of the "White Man" and firearms, Plains people remained fairly loosely organized – the competition created by the fur trade changed all this. Originally the political unit of the band was a leader: when several of these bands united, a council was formed of all the leaders. During trading ventures, wars, and celebrations the council acted as a guiding body.

One of the most famous festivals associated with the Plains Indians was their Sun Dance. A sacred pole was erected to the Great Spirit and offerings tied to it. The bands danced around the stake, recited war deeds, and prayed for guidance in their hunt of the buffalo. Practising their own brand of "machismo", Plains youths would perform acts of self-mutilation, one of which involved piercing the chest with skewers tied to the pole with leather thongs, the idea being that self-inflicted torture would arouse the compassion and benevolence of the Great Spirit.

Woodland tribes

Perhaps the best known, next to the Inuit, of Canada's native peoples are the Indians of the

eastern woodlands. As early as 1000 BC eastern Canada began to be settled by semi-nomadic tribes. It is here that one discovers the contrasting lifestyles of the peaceful Huron, the fierce Iroquois, and the entrepreneurial Algonquin.

Like the rest of the Indians of Canada, the people of this area made maximum use of their environment. The Huron of southern and central Ontario are noted for being a horticultural society. Living in longhouses within pallisaded villages, the Huron cultivated the land and subsisted on staples of squash, beans, and maize: the "Three Sisters." It is the Huron who first met and baffled French missionaries to Canada. The French discovered a people who demonstrated an unusual equality between the sexes and a consensus rather than authoritarian government.

Walking through the woods of lower Ontario, it is easy to speculate where buried Huron and Iroquois sites might lie. These Indians chose locations for their villages on the basis of four criteria: access to water, nearness to forests for timber, nearness to rich soil for cultivation, and strategic placement for defense.

Life within the pallisaded compound is difficult to picture, although the Jesuits and other explorers vividly describe their horror at the living conditions within the camp. Samuel de Champlain, aghast at what he perceived to be filth and disorder, wrote of the longhouses in which two or three dozen people lived. The smoke from each fire in the house, he wrote, "circulates at will, causing much eye trouble, to which the natives are so subject that many become blind in their old age." Indian notions of communal sharing and sanitation offended the Europeans, yet despite their lack of "proper sanitation" Indians rarely died of disease until they became exposed to European viruses.

By way of contrast to the Huron, the Iroquois were a fiercer group of people and more inclined to warfare. They were the only Indians of Canada to believe in two Great Spirits, one good and the other evil. In Iroquois religion, the two deities were constantly at odds with one another and their myths are most frequently incidents of clashes between the good and evil gods. Before the arrival of the Europeans the Iroquois had sown the seeds of a great Empire: they had established a confederacy of several nations of tribes, they had developed a unified system of currency (*wampum*) that regulated trade, and they had organized the confederacy for warfare against enemy tribes. Perhaps if Europe had discovered North America a century later, it would have encountered a highly sophisticated and politically unified culture of Indians. But it did not. Although the history of Canada is in part a history of burgeoning European society, for the Indians it is a tale of exploitation, strife and eventual extinction.

Such is the stage setting, so to speak, for the arrival of the first Europeans: a vast land inhabited by highly differentiated Indian groups, each adapted to a particular lifestyle.

LEFT: "Miss One Spot". RIGHT: Chief Duck and the Blackfoot family.

VOYAGES OF DISCOVERY

The early explorers dreamed of finding gold and gemstones; instead they found timber and waters teeming with fish

The history of Canada is not carved in stone, nor is the land steeped in the blood of conquering civilizations. While the histories of European nations usually include colorful tales of the rise of great civilizations, the construction of vast cities, and the stratagems and spoils of conquest, Canada's history is a humbler story of wilderness, of hardship and determination, of disappointment and dreams.

The first visitors to encounter Canada after the crossing of the nomadic hunters were the Vikings, whose ancestors had traveled from Norway to Iceland. From Iceland, the Vikings moved westward when Eric the Red discovered and settled Greenland. A fierce and hardy people, the Vikings were great sailors and often took to the seas in search of food and adventure. On one such voyage a seaman, Bjarne Herjolfsen, caught sight of North America and returned home to tell of the unknown land. Around AD 1000, Eric the Red's son, Lief, set out to find the new continent. The Viking sagas tell of Lief's strange adventures and his discoveries of Helluland (Baffin Island), Markland (Labrador), and Vinland. In 1961 an archaeologist, Helge Ingstad, stumbled upon the remains of a Norse settlement in L'Anse aux Meadows and decided that Vinland was probably Newfoundland.

For Lief, Vinland was a land of great marvels: the sagas recount his amazement at the succulent grapes and enormous salmon. One year after the expedition, Lief's brother Thorvald returned to North America hoping to make contact with Vinland's natives. Legends tell of how "Skraelings" attacked Thorvald and his crew with bows and arrows. In other tales the illegitimate daughter of Eric the Red, Freydis the Brave and Cruel, defends the Vikings by rushing towards the Skraelings and frightening them with her wild eyes and gnashing teeth.

Who were the Skraelings? The Viking sagas describe them as dark-skinned people who wore

their hair in a strange fashion. Historical anthropologists have speculated that they may have been Algonquins. Whoever they were, they prevented the Vikings from establishing permanent settlements on the mainland. It is possible that the Vikings returned to northern Canada. The tall, blond "Copper Eskimos", so named by the

explorer Vihjalmun Stefannson in 1910, have led some to suggest that the Norse people interbred with the Inuit of Baffin Island.

Cabot and Cartier

The 15th century marked a new beginning in the consciousness of humankind, a consciousness that was to have profound significance for Canada. The dream of discovering a route across the Atlantic to the spices, jewels and silks of the Orient became the fantasy of kings and merchants. As improvements in ship building occurred, the dream became a possibility. John Cabot is the first explorer to have "officially" discovered Canada and claimed it for a king.

LEFT: the Vikings reached Canada from Iceland around AD 1000. **RIGHT:** Martin Frobisher, the 16th-century explorer, set out in search of the Northwest Passage.

An Italian navigator, Cabot was known for his imaginative flights of fancy and adventuresome spirit. In 1496 he persuaded Henry VII to give him leave to find a route to the Indies and claim it for England. On Tuesday, 2 May, 1497, Cabot boarded the *Matthew* with 18 men and set sail for the Americas. After 52 weary days at sea, the *Matthew* sighted Cape Breton Island where Cabot landed on 24 June. Cabot unfurled the British flag and, planting it firmly in the soil, claimed the country to be under the sovereignty of Henry VII. But where was all the gold?

Cabot soon discovered that the soil was extremely fertile and the climate warm and

friendly. He was convinced that he had found the northeast coast of Asia; further investigation could only lead him to the precious silks and gems of which he had so often dreamed. Cabot found neither, but he did report banks of teeming fish and a great abundance of timber.

Upon Cabot's return, Henry VII, who had wanted gold, was singularly unimpressed with the explorer's tales of fish and paid him £10 for his efforts. The king told Cabot to try another expedition – this was realized in 1498. This time Cabot reached Newfoundland. Cabot finally returned to England where he died aged 48. Many explorers set out after Cabot but were not successful until Jacques Cartier, who was sent

by Francis I of France, ventured to North America in 1534. His expedition marks the origin of French and British competition for control of North America.

On his first trip, Cartier traveled inland until he found the Gulf of St Lawrence. Assured that the river was a water route to the Orient, Cartier sailed up the St Lawrence until he came to the Iroquois villages of Hochelaga and Stadacona (the sites of modern Montréal and Québec City respectively). Here the Indians were so friendly and hospitable that he took two back with him to France. Like Henry VII, Francis I was disappointed but Cartier mollified him by telling the king that he had erected a cross on Gaspé Peninsula in his name and had called the country New France.

The Arctic expeditions

While the early explorers devoted their time to discovering a new route to the Orient, 50 years after Cartier others became obsessed with the Northwest Passage. One such man was Martin Frobisher. With a reputation as a daredevil, Frobisher was sent by Elizabeth I to find an ice-free route to the Americas. Despite Frobisher's inability to produce anything of consequence for British history, he remains, even to this day, a cherished folk hero. No less than 300 years after Frobisher's voyages, the explorer Charles Hall discovered the relics of a structure Frobisher's crew had built. Hall wrote that in 1861, three centuries later, the native peoples spoke of Frobisher as if he had just visited them.

Henry Hudson was another man drawn to the excitement of exploration. Hoping to open a passage to China, Hudson made several trips to North America, his last one ending tragically. In 1609 the *Discovery* froze in the ice of James Bay and the boat and its crew went into "winter quarters." After a long, tense winter aboard the vessel, Hudson quarreled with a member of his crew, John Greene, who later led his shipmates into mutiny. Hudson was set adrift in the Bay with his son and seven others loyal to him, and nothing was ever heard of him again.

Following on Hudson's heels was Thomas James (1631) – after whom James Bay is named – who wrote vividly of his excursions in a travel

LEFT: the early settlement of Québec. **RIGHT:** in 1778 Captain James Cook set ashore on the Pacific coast to look for a river route through the continent.

account titled *The Dangerous Voyage of Captain Thomas James*. The writings of his log later became the material upon which Coleridge based his famous poem *The Rime of the Ancient Mariner*. After James, Edward Parry, a British naval officer, pushed through the northern icebergs to reach Melville Island in 1819 – he had come the farthest yet.

Perhaps the most heart-wrenching story of all the explorers is that of John Franklin, a British rear-admiral and explorer. In 1819 Franklin was put in charge of an exploration that was to mark out a route from Hudson Bay to the Arctic Ocean. He made a second trip in 1825 after the success of his first voyage and returned to North America a third time in 1845. On his last expedition, Franklin was sure he would find the Northwest Passage. He was accompanied by a Captain Crozier who had served with Edward Parry. His ships, *Erebus* and *Terror*, were last seen on 26 July, 1845. Years later a rescue mission discovered their skeletal remains and a diary of the last days of the journey. Franklin, only a few miles from success, had died of exhaustion and exposure.

It wasn't until 1906 that Norwegian explorer Roald Amundsen finally conquered Canada's merciless north and opened up the Northwest Passage. In only a few centuries, Canada's relentless North had claimed several European "sacrificial lambs."

Travelers to the west

The West Coast of Canada was yet another site of interest for the ever curious Europeans. In 1778 Captain James Cook landed here in the course of his Pacific explorations. Cook volunteered to find a waterway through North America originating in the west but finally had to conclude that it did not exist. George Vancouver followed in 1791–95 and discovered the outlet of the Bella Coola River. Seven weeks later, a fiery Scotsman, Alexander Mackenzie, ended up at the same spot.

Such is the early history of Canada. For the Europeans, it yielded neither gold nor gems and was, for the most part, a disappointment. With resignation the rulers of France and England began to make plans for the colonization of the New World.

RIGHT: exploration and trade: traveling up the West Coast rivers of Canada in search of furs.

THE RISE AND FALL OF NEW FRANCE

The 17th century witnessed the development of a flourishing fur trade, continuing exploration, and bitter differences between settlers and tribes

Colonizing the New World was no easy task for the rulers of Europe in the 17th century. Cold, barren and unexplored, Canada held little appeal for the people of England, France and Spain. Those, however, who did venture to Canada encountered a burgeoning system of trade between the Europeans and the Indians and soon realized that the economic potential of settling in Canada was very attractive.

The fur trade

Curious and for the most part friendly, the Indian tribes that met French and British settlers in Canada became enamored of European metalware which, for them, represented a massive technological improvement over their crude stone and wooden utensils. As a result the Indians developed a dependency on the Europeans – a dependency that was to change their lives.

At first the Indians had little to offer in return for the highly valued knives and axes, and the Europeans complained bitterly of the relative uselessness of their handcrafted canoes and snowshoes. By the late 1600s, however, the Indians had begun to trade furs with the settlers, particularly luxury furs. When the hatmakers of Europe obtained beaver pelts from Canada they engendered a rage for beaver hats which they claimed were the warmest and most durable in the world, and thereby created an immense and ongoing market for furs in the new colony. The Indians, never quite understanding the "white man's" infatuation with the beaver, became the main suppliers to the fur merchants and continued to receive various European-manufactured wares for their pelts. Marc Lescabot, a 17th-century French writer, noted that the Indians became awed by the beaver for the little creature had mysteriously brought them kettles, axes, knives and gave them food and drink without the trouble of cultivating the land. By the early 1700s the fur trade in Canada was boom-

ing and competition for the monopoly of the fur market in North America had begun.

Father of Canada

The man who was in many ways responsible for expanding the fur trade in Canada was the French explorer Samuel de Champlain. An

idealist with a passion for exploration, Champlain is probably the most frequently cited "Father" of Canada and is often honored because of his wish to found Canada upon principles of justice and compassion.

Acting on behalf of the French monarchy, in 1604 Champlain established the first French colony in North America in Acadia (Nova Scotia). Acadia became mythologized as an idyllic French settlement where peace and prosperity reigned and its tiny villages set in the picturesque Maritimes became the subject of many folktales and poems.

Champlain's Acadian village of Grand Pré was immortalized in Henry Wadsworth

---

LEFT: trading pelts for export to meet the demands of European fashion (1758). **RIGHT:** Samuel de Champlain, one of Canada's many progenitors.

Longfellow's epic poem *Evangeline*, the tale of a town's Utopian existence crumbling under the cruel administration of the British and the separation of two lovers. Of Acadia and Acadians, Longfellow wrote:

> *Thus dwelt together in love*
> *these simple Acadian farmers...*
> *Neither lock had they to their doors,*
> *nor bars to their windows*
> *But their dwellings were as open as*
> *day and the hearts of the owners;*
> *There the richest was poor and the*
> *poorest lived in abundance.*

After Acadia, Champlain continued his explorations into the interior of Canada and on 3 July, 1608, on the site of an old Indian settlement called Stadacona, Champlain founded Québec. Though momentous for Canada's history as a whole, the founding of Québec for him was quite unextraordinary and, as he indicated in his diary, a location he chose more for convenience than historical importance: "When I arrived there [Québec] on July 3, I looked about for a suitable place for our buildings, but I could not find any more convenient or better situated than the point of Québec, so called by the savages, which is filled with nuts and trees...near this is a pleasant river, where formerly Jacques Cartier passed this winter." The "pleasant river" turned out to be the mighty Gulf of St Lawrence, which later became an important passageway for the export of furs to Europe.

The Hurons

One year after Champlain's settlement of Québec, a group of Indians came down from the northwest to trade their pelts with the French. Upon their arrival the Frenchmen were astonished by the appearance of their half-shaven heads and the tufts of hair that grew perpendicularly to their scalps. Likening the Indians' hair to the bristles on the back of an enraged boar (*la hure*), the French called them the Hurons. Thus began a long and tragic relationship.

One of Champlain's main objectives while in Canada was to control the flourishing fur trade and to establish stricter management of the Indians. Already allied with the Hurons, Champlain failed to see that the fur trade was exacerbating already existing hostilities among Indian tribes. Animosities of a ritualistic nature had always existed between the Huron and the Iroquois Confederation. With the fur trade the disputes

acquired a mercenary element. When Champlain established an alliance between the French and the Huron, he immediately became the Iroquois' enemy.

On his famous expedition to Ticonderoga with 60 Huron warriors and three armed French men, Champlain officially initiated open warfare between the Iroquois and French. The skirmish began without gunfire, but Champlain's firearms massacred 300 Iroquois. The event inspired a deep and lasting hatred among the Iroquois and marked the beginning of a series of ferocious raids on French trading posts.

While Champlain was organizing settlements

and repelling hostile Iroquois, other colonists, mostly men from France, began to appear.

The pioneers

These early settlers, who became known as the *coureurs de bois*, or woodsmen, looked to New France as an escape from a life of drudgery – many had exchanged prison sentences for emigration papers. The *coureurs de bois* became the backbone of Canada's trading system. Trapping animals for a living, which involved not only a precarious existence in the bush, but also fighting off Indians, the voyagers were the intrepid entrepreneurs of Canada's early days. Described as bold, boisterous, daring fellows in French

THE RISE AND FALL OF NEW FRANCE ◆ 35

Canadian folklore, these men became the employees of large European companies seeking trade monopolies in the New World. By the 1750s Canada had become an economically prosperous investment for France, and Britain began to take a closer look at a country she had virtually ignored for almost half a decade.

When Samuel de Champlain and other explorers ventured to Canada in the early 17th century, their plans for the settlement of the new colony, although the dreams of imaginative men, were essentially

CONVERTING THE INDIANS

Samuel de Champlain's aim was to create a land made for "the glory and praise of God and France"

ical acquisition. It was a very real place, empty and enormous. And at times, life was so very hard. On claiming Canada for France, Samuel de Champlain's first task was to regularize the fur trade. His second task was to set about Christianizing the native population so that the continent could truly become a land made for "the glory and praise of God and France". The years 1632 to 1652 are often referred to as the "golden years" for the missions in Canada… a somewhat misleading phrase because, although it captures a

expressions of the grandiose visions of European monarchs. For them Canada was merely an addition to the ever-expanding empires of England and France. Canada was a valuable piece of property on the "Monopoly board" the super powers of the 17th and 18th centuries ruthlessly fought to claim. But for the others who journeyed to Canada – the farmers and fishermen, the women and children, the missionaries and even the reckless *coureurs de bois* – Canada was much more than just a geograph-

sense of intense religious activity in Canada during this time, it fails to express the low success rate (in terms of conversions).

The missionaries arrive

The first missionaries brought to Canada by Champlain were four Récollets, strict Franciscans who enthusiastically plunged into the bush in search of the "heathen savages". The Récollets patiently began to work on saving Indian souls – but with little success. Not long after, the Jesuits were invited to join the Canadian missions, and in 1625 Fathers de Brébeuf and de Noue left France to begin converting the Iroquois and Huron. The Jesuits, like most Euro-

---

LEFT: smallpox threatens a shipload of immigrants.
ABOVE: Jean de Brébeuf, a Jesuit priest who worked among the Huron, is tortured to death by the Iroquois.

peans, failed to understand the Indian way of life. Communally oriented, lacking hierarchical structures and methods of authority, openly polytheistic and possessing different concepts of diet and sanitation, the Indians seemed to the Jesuits "barbaric".

Summing up this attitude, Champlain wrote of the Indians in 1609: "There is an evil tendency among them to be revengeful, and to be great liars, and one cannot fully rely upon them, except with caution and when one is armed... [they] do not know what it is to worship God and pray to Him, but live like beasts, but I think they would soon be converted to Christianity if

came...took our village and seized Father Brébeuf and his companion; and set fire to all the huts. They proceeded to vent their rage on these two fathers, for they took them both and stripped them naked and fastened them each to a post. They tied both their hands and feet together. They beat them with a shower of blows from cudgels... there being no part of their body which did not endure this torment."

The unfortunate priests endured other horrific tortures. The account states that despite his suffering, Brébeuf continued to preach to the Indians until they cut off his tongue and lips. After his slow and painful death, the Iroquois were so

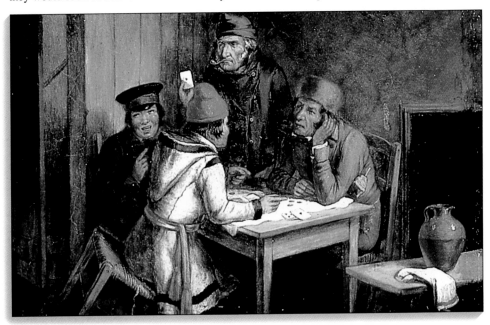

some people would settle among them and cultivate their souls, which is what most of them wish." Needless to say, the Jesuits were not always welcomed into Indian communities and many of them, given the name of "black robes" by the Iroquois, became symbols of evil and misfortune. Despite their ethnocentric attitudes, some of the Jesuit missionaries were men of great courage. Many suffered horrible deaths and became the first martyrs of Canada. Such is the story of Father Jean de Brébeuf, a Jesuit who worked among the horticultural Huron.

Brébeuf's martyrdom on 16 March, 1649, was recorded by a contemporary, Christophe Regnault, in *Jesuit Relations*: "The Iroquois

impressed by his fortitude that they ate his heart, believing that by so doing they would become as brave as Brébeuf.

First French-Canadians

In the early annals of Canadian history, there were two types of settlers who traveled to the New World, the *coureur de bois* and the *habitant*, the French colonist who settled the fertile shores of the St Lawrence River and cultivated the land. From the very beginning these two lifestyles were radically different. To the *habitant* the fur traders were as treacherous and vengeful as the despised Iroquois, while the farmer frightened away their game and pushed the *coureur de bois* farther into the wilderness. Although the *coureurs de bois* are often portrayed as the more robust of the two, life for the *habitant* was also very difficult. Clearing the tree-infested lands of the St Lawrence shores demanded arduous labor, crops were slow to start and a year's food could be ruined instantly by bad weather. Wild beasts and hostile Indians were constant worries.

Early homes in New France were wooden huts crudely built of rough logs; in the winter,

PROSPEROUS TIMES

By the 1630s the settlements of Québec and Montréal had become bustling commercial centers.

There were rewards to be reaped as well. Soon the wooden shelters gave way to houses built of stone with steep roofs and large heat-yielding fireplaces. As the forests were cleared, as settlements became towns, and as farmers prospered on their strips of land (called *seigneuries*), families of New France eventually enjoyed higher standards of living than their European counterparts.

For the farmer of early Canada, tenant dues and church tithes were low, no taxes were paid, fertile land was available for

water for the household had to be drawn from a hole in the ice. Of the icy weather in early Canada, the poet Standish O'Grady wrote:

Thou barren waste, unprofitable strand
Where hemlocks brood on
    unproductive land,
Whose frozen air on one bleak
    winter's night
Can metamorphose dark brown hares
    into white.

LEFT: a favorite pastime of the *habitants*, card playing, was strictly forbidden by the Catholic Church.
ABOVE: Cornelius Krieghoff's portrait of the life of a French-Canadian family in the 19th century.

the asking, food was bountiful, and everyone possessed the right to hunt and fish. By the 1630s the little settlements of Québec and Montréal had burgeoned into bustling centers of commerce and become bastions of French sovereignty. The French clergy, so unsuccessful among the Indians, had founded schools, hospitals and even a university (Jesuit College founded in 1636, one year before Harvard). An elaborate system of courts and litigation procedures was implemented.

In 1640 New France had 240 inhabitants – by 1685 the population had swelled to 10,000. Montréal and Québec had become lively and popular colonial capitals. The artist Cornelius

Krieghoff, one of the most insightful chroniclers of early Québecois culture, portrays the French Canadians as hardworking but cheerful people. The winter, when fields slept under layers of snow and warehouses were fully stocked, was the time when the Québecois "played."

Extremely fond of their children, the French-Canadians socialized mainly through family gatherings, card playing, dancing, and drinking parties. (By 1749 drunken horse-driving had become so serious in Québec that a strict law fining inebriated drivers six *livres* – about six dollars – came into effect.) The only ominous presence seems to have been the clergy, who

in France, blockaded the St Lawrence River for three years and wrested the fur trade from France's charter: The Hundred Associates. At the same time Acadia (Nova Scotia) was claimed for James VI of Scotland by Sir William Alexander. Various disputes ensued until 1632 when Canada and Acadia were restored to France under the Treaty of Saint-Germain-en-Laye.

Government in New France

Bitter complaints about New France were constantly arising from the colonists – one of which was the lack of a central, authoritative govern-

sternly disapproved of dancing, cards, jewelry and even hair ribbons. In 1700 Bishop Laval furiously chastised Québecois women for their elaborate coiffures and scandalous wardrobes.

Settlements and skirmishes

While the Jesuits continued to proselytize Catholicism and French colonists resolutely set down roots, Samuel de Champlain and other French officials were faced with the problem of maintaining control over the new colony. Several skirmishes with other governments over territory had already occurred.

In 1627 the notorious Kirke brothers, English adventurers who supported the Huguenot effort

ment. As a result, in 1647, a council consisting of a governor, the religious superior of the Jesuits, and the Governor of Montréal was instituted. Although the council's role was to monitor economic activities in the colony, this model proved inefficient. Consequently New France was officially made a ward of the Crown (under Louis XIV) in 1663.

Two men in particular were instrumental in bringing a strong, centralized government to French Canada. The first was Jean Baptiste Colbert, an ambitious finance minister, who endeavored to recast French colonial policy by establishing a new administrative system. Colbert sought to make New France a province with a government similar to that of France. To this end he implemented a new structure which consisted of a governor-general, an intendant and a superior council. The Bishop of New France was made a member of the council but was more often than not engaged in bitter argument with the reigning governor.

One of New France's more colorful governors was the Comte de Frontenac, a man of great personal charm who was also extravagant and unscrupulous. From the beginning of his career, Fron-

> **EAST-WEST RELATIONS**
>
> Colbert's neglect of the western regions enabled the British to gain a firmer hold on the New World

Hudson's Bay Company in the west and underestimated its importance in Canada's future.

Jean Colbert's reorganization of the colony gave New France a firmly centralized government that could efficiently deal with day-to-day problems. Jean Talon, the first intendant of Colbert's model, quickly set about reorganizing the settlement and was able to bring in thousands of new colonists, including women. Most of the population flocked to three towns, Montréal, Québec and Trois-Rivières. Colbert and Talon hoped

tenac set himself in opposition to the most influential clergymen in Canada. He wrote of the Jesuits: "Another thing displeases me… this complete dependence of the grand vicar and seminary priests on the Jesuits, for they never do the least thing without their order."

Frontenac complained that the Jesuits exerted unreasonable control over the colonists. He scandalized New France by his disrespectful attitude toward them. Meanwhile, he overlooked the aggressive presence of the British

that settlers would establish permanency along the St Lawrence, but many traveled inland.

The transient nature of the population was a major obstacle in the settling of New France – Colbert, feeling that mobility was deleterious to French interests, subsequently forbade colonists to leave the central settlement and confined the fur trade to the areas of Montréal, Trois-Rivières and Tadoussac. Colbert's neglect of the western regions merely enabled the British to gain an even firmer foothold in the New World.

Anglo-French rivalry

In the 1660s two malcontent trappers, Médard des Groseilliers and Pierre Radisson, decided

LEFT: a *habitant* urges his horse to greater speed over the ice. **ABOVE:** a *calèche* meanders through the frosty streets of modern Québec city.

they were going to do something about the high costs of hauling furs back to Québec (as ordered by the colonial government) and the exorbitant taxes they were paying on fur pelts. They fled to New England and were escorted to Britain. In London Groseilliers and Radisson persuaded a group of London merchants to assume control over the fur trade in the middle of Canada by forming the Hudson's Bay Company – the company claimed exclusive trading rights in all territories draining into Hudson Bay.

New France suddenly found herself in an awkward position: to the south were the Dutch and English-supported Iroquois and to the north

was the expanding Hudson's Bay Company. Fearful of losing their new colony, New France's militia began to launch expeditions to throw the English out of Hudson Bay.

By the time the 18th century began, hostilities had increased, especially in the east where New England farmers began to covet Acadia. For several years New France was kept active by repelling new settlers and engaging its armies in ruthless, devastating raids.

Agreement, however, was reached in 1713 when the Peace Treaty of Utrecht was signed and North America was carved up among the European powers. The French gave up much of their land. Acadia and Hudson Bay were ceded

to the British and Article 15 of the treaty recognized British sovereignty over the Iroquois people and permitted them to trade with western Indians in traditionally French domains.

Years of peace

Despite France's reluctance to honor the treaty, three decades of peace reigned. Canada began to prosper – the fur trade flourished; the population increased from 19,000 in 1713 to 48,000 by 1739; agriculture and fishing blossomed, and lumbering began to develop.

English imperialist economic aspirations, however, soon emerged and fighting broke out between the colonial powers again in 1744. A series of small battles followed until in 1756 a war was finally declared between France and Britain which was to prove decisive.

France, characteristically nonchalant in her attitude towards the new colony, sent the Marquis de Montcalm with meager reinforcements to Québec. Lack of soldiers and food supplies made defeat seem almost inevitable. In addition, France did not wish to risk sending her fleets to North America since it would leave the mother country in a vulnerable position. New France's frontier was long and lightly guarded – how could Montcalm hope to defend it?

The fall of New France

Québec seemed (to both nations) to be the deciding factor in the war. In 1759 a force under General James Wolfe began an advance. Montcalm, relying upon the strategic position of the city atop formidable precipices, let the invaders come to him. After several unsuccessful frontal attacks, one of Wolfe's men suggested that he should try a flank attack. On the night of 12 September, Wolfe and his troops crossed the St Lawrence River under the cover of darkness and scaled the cliffs. Unprepared, the French repelled the British but panicked and hastily retreated (not knowing that their attackers too had panicked and were about to retreat).

Wolfe was killed in the exchange and Montcalm was mortally wounded. After the fall of Québec it was only a matter of time before the rest of New France fell to the British. By 1763, under the Treaty of Paris, France lost her lands in Canada to England.

LEFT: the death of General Wolfe at the siege of Québec (1759). **RIGHT:** Wolfe's troops attack the city.

ARRIVAL OF THE BRITISH

While Britain established control over the country, its attempts to anglicize
70,000 French-Canadians proved somewhat over-ambitious

When Canada was ceded to the British, few tears were shed in France. New France, what Voltaire had called "a few acres of snow", had become a gnawing irritation for French officials and its removal from France's empire was met more with relief than regret. It became ever clearer that the *habitants* who had originally settled Canada for France were to be left to their own devices.

Britain's victory in Canada began to produce major changes on the continent; one such was the shift in control of the fur trade from French hands to British ones. Although glowing from its recent economic advancement in Canada, Britain was still faced with one serious problem: the vast majority of its newly acquired colony were people of foreign descent.

From the first Britain planned to extirpate French culture from its colony. British colonial officers hoped that American settlers would eventually move into the region and outnumber the nearly 70,000 French Canadians. For the French *habitants* the prospect of cultural defeat only added further to their already traumatized condition – they felt themselves abandoned by France and, although not cruelly treated by Britain, in the hands of an insensitive and arrogant administration.

Britain's attempts to anglicize Québec proved futile. More than 99 percent of the white population in Canada were French – it was blatantly unrealistic to expect a sudden transformation of Catholic *françaises* into English-speaking Anglican subjects of King George III. It soon became clear that a compromise with the French was necessary, and could be advantageous.

Governor Sir Guy Carleton was one of the administrators who recognized the importance of securing the fidelity of the French Canadians. Acutely aware of the rebellious rumblings to the south, Carleton urged Britain to negotiate with the French else it might find itself faced with continental insurrection. Under Carleton's

guidance, the Québec Act 1774 which granted the Québecois cultural, political and economic protection, was passed. Under the Act, British criminal law was retained but French civil law restored; the Catholic Church retained the right to levy tithes and prosecute the recalcitrant; lastly, Franco-Catholics were no longer

excluded from public office. The decree pacified most *Canadiens*.

The American Revolution

Carleton proved to be perspicacious in his treatment of the Québecois for, as American disenchantment with Britain climaxed, it became apparent that French settlers might favor English interests. Carleton's Québec Act, however, only served to accommodate the interest of the *habitants* and consequently alienated and angered British subjects. These tensions were brought to the surface with the advent of the American Revolution. The rebellion itself was, to some extent, engendered by the Québec Act –

LEFT: Britain soon imposed its own traditions on French Canada. **RIGHT:** toe-tapping amusement in 1840.

irritated by the extensions of French-protected trapping regions (which encroached upon traditionally American lands), the American Continental Congress instituted a plot of revenge against the British in 1775. The first act of the Congress was not to declare independence from England but to invade Canada.

In British North America (formerly New France) sentiments about the war were mixed. The intervention of France on the American side briefly raised hopes among the Québecois. English merchants continued to sulk over what they perceived to be a betrayal of their government. The arrival of British regulars, however, in

1776, seemed to convince French and British dissenters alike that to side with England would be the most prudent course.

The American Revolution served to cement British rule in Canada in several ways. The relative weakness and disorganization of the invaders convinced British businessmen that it was in their economic interests to support the imperial struggle.

In Nova Scotia the experience of the American Revolution possessed a more distressing component. Settlers here identified themselves with New England and found themselves caught between contradictory loyalties. The Americans, however, recognized the foolhardi-

ness of dividing the colony and decided not to invade Nova Scotia – George Washington named these settlers "neutral Yankees". In the end the war strengthened ties between Britain and Nova Scotia, again for economic reasons.

Another significant effect of the American Revolution was the influx into Canada of 60,000 United Empire Loyalists, men and women who did not support American grievances. Most Loyalists were from New York State, and had fled to Nova Scotia in search of British protection; in Canada they were granted indemnity and land. The Loyalists radically altered the composition of Canada's population; their presence created a cultural dualism that contained all the pronounced differences existing between the French and British peoples.

Upper and Lower Canada

The aftermath of the American Revolution brought with it a renewed bitterness among the British over what they perceived to be pro-French policies in the colony. The Loyalists wanted a representative government (something denied by the Québec Act). Still dependent upon British patronage, French leaders became uneasy and realized that confrontation with the Anglos was inevitable. Carleton, newly named Lord Dorchester, returned to Québec to rectify what had become "a delicate situation", the result being the Constitutional Act of 1791.

Under its directives the colony was to have an elected assembly that would exercise legislative authority in conjunction with a legislative council appointed by the king. Most importantly the Constitutional Act divided the St Lawrence Valley into two colonies: one named Upper Canada and the other Lower Canada. This development marked a new dawn in the emergence of French-Anglo rivalries and ushered in another act in the drama of British North America.

After the Revolution, hostilities between the British and Americans flared up in 1812 when American rebels attempted to invade Canada. They were finally routed during the Battle of Queenston Heights. Although Britain lost some of its territories to the fledgling nation, the War of 1812 formalized British North America's right to remain part of the British empire.

LEFT: a town crier in Halifax. **RIGHT:** General Gates leads his army during the American Revolution (1775–83).

CONFEDERATION CANADA

Disenchantment with British rule and rebellions calling for an elected assembly led to the emergence of a unified Dominion of Canada

The aftermath of the War of 1812 brought with it a new sense of vigor and self-determination among Canadians. As the economy flourished, Upper Canada settlers began to evaluate the political and economic role of Britain in the colonies. In Lower Canada, similar questions were being raised, although for different reasons: widespread unemployment and growing poverty engendered bitter criticism of the British among French Canadians.

Canadian settlers were mainly disenchanted with the political structure of their colony. Although the Assembly was an elected body, a Council appointed by the king of England held executive powers and frequently overruled resolutions passed in the elected legislature. Frustrated by patronage, corruption and privilege, Canadians began to call for Responsible Government, in particular, an elected Council.

The rebellions

In Québec the Council (called the *Château Clique*) received the brunt of its criticisms from the acerbic Louis-Joseph Papineau, the founder of the Patriote Party. The *patriotes* drew up a list of 92 resolutions and demanded the elimination of the appointed Council.

Britain refused to accommodate their wishes. Eventually pushed beyond the point of polite discussion, the *patriotes* took to the streets in October 1837 and clashed with British soldiers. After several deaths, the uprising was quelled and the party was left without a leader when Papineau fled to the United States.

In Upper Canada the fight for Responsible Government was spearheaded by William Lyon Mackenzie, a fiery Scotsman who was the publisher/editor of a local newspaper. Mackenzie, known for his lacerating attacks against the Family Compact (the name for the appointed Council in Upper Canada), had been elected to

the Assembly in 1828 but expelled from it in 1831 for libel.

In 1837 Mackenzie rallied several hundred angry protestors in Montgomery's Tavern on Toronto's Yonge Street. After a few shots of whiskey, discontent began to turn into active dissent and the group of rebels marched towards

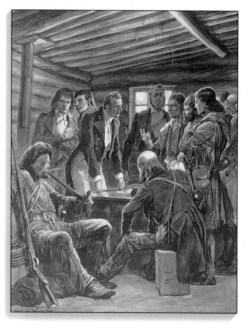

the government buildings. They were met by a group of 27 armed militiamen. When a colonel shot at the rebel blockade, he was killed by return fire. The mishap so flustered the protestors that they fled in panic, Mackenzie going to the United States.

Britain adopted a severe stance against the rebellions although many Canadians shared the sentiments of the insurgents. When two leaders of the Upper Canada rebellion were hanged, vexation with the British way of governing heightened.

John Ryerson said of the execution: "Very few persons present except the military and ruf scruf of the city. The general feeling is total

LEFT: the radical William Lyon Mackenzie, who campaigned for "Responsible Government" in Upper Canada. **RIGHT:** Sir George Simpson establishes a council to administer British Columbia (1835).

opposition to the execution of these men."

Britain, however, recognized the need to reform the colony's outmoded constitution. A royal commission was established to investigate the problems. The man chosen to direct the inquiry was a politician from one of the wealthiest families in England, Lord Durham, nicknamed "Radical Jack" by his colleagues. A man of dour intensity and a violent temper, Durham was appointed Governor General.

Following six short months of investigation, Durham returned to England to prepare his report on the "Canada issue". In the document, Durham complained that the five colonies were

granted Responsible Government. Adopting, but modifying, some of Durham's suggestions, Britain united Canada West and Canada East and awarded each sector equal representation in a new joint legislature. In 1849 the new legislature formed an administration for the Province of Canada (Upper and Lower Canada).

The beginnings of Confederation

The feeling that American or British domination would always threaten Canada while the colonies remained separate geographic units pervaded political thought in the 1850s and early 1860s. Confederation, a notion that had

stagnating and that in order to exist alongside the dynamic and aggressive United States, Canada would have to develop a viable economy. Such an economy, he believed, could be realized through the unification of the colonies into a single province.

Durham also believed that such a union would relieve the tension between the English and French settlers by drawing the latter into mainstream British culture. French culture (which Durham privately thought was essentially backward), the report explained, had been retarded by French colonial policies.

Despite the glaring ethnocentrism of the report, it did recommend that Canadians be

been discussed for nearly a century, suddenly reappeared as a viable possibility.

After self-government was achieved, politics became sectional in Upper and Lower Canada. Issues such as the importance of developing an intercolonial railway and the need to acquire new territories were neglected because of conflicting party interests.

Political deadlock finally contrived in 1864 to bring together a coalition of rival parties united on the one issue of Confederation. At the same time similar discussions were also taking place in the Maritime provinces. A conference of provincial ministers was held and in 1867 the British North America Act was passed by Parliament in England creating a confederated Canada comprising Ontario and Québec (formerly Upper and Lower Canada), New Brunswick and Nova Scotia under the title "Dominion of Canada" (see page 50).

The unlikely midwife of a unified Canada was Sir John A. Macdonald, a man who had originally opposed the concept of Confederation when the Liberal newspaper magnate George Brown had proposed it, but who was to become the dominion's first prime minister. Born in Scotland, in

JOHN A. MACDONALD

Macdonald introduced a crucial qualification for a prime minister: wit, articulate attack and rebuttal

But what he lacked in demeanor and appearance, he compensated for through his sharp intelligence and keen powers of insight. Never one to be lost for words, Macdonald introduced to Canadians a crucial qualification for a prime minister: wit, articulate attack and rebuttal.

Despite this polished exterior, Macdonald's life was tragically fraught with misfortune. He had married his cousin Isabella Clark, whom he met on a trip to Scotland, but soon afterwards her health failed. Macdonald's first years as a politi-

the year of Napoleon's Waterloo, and brought to Kingston, Ontario, when still a small boy, Macdonald was perhaps the most improbable person in public life to nurture a fledgling Canadian territory.

Macdonald, a tall, gangly figure with a careless but stinging sense of humor, didn't seem to fit the mold of a Canadian prime minister. An audacious alcoholic and a bit of a dandy, he lacked the prim reserve of a British politician.

FAR LEFT: Scottish-born John A. Macdonald, the dominion's first prime minister, and **(LEFT)** his wife, Baroness Macdonald. **ABOVE LEFT:** Louis Riel, hanged for treason. **ABOVE RIGHT:** Métis rebels on the march.

cian fluctuated between attending heated arguments in the Assembly during the day and returning home at night to watch his wife slowly die. Nine years after Isabella's eventual death Macdonald married Susan Agnes Bernard, who gave birth to a mentally handicapped daughter. Influenced by the attitudes of the times, Macdonald was scarred by the event for the rest of his life.

The Métis rebellion

Confederation, once approved by London, was not distinguished by a smooth transition. One of the first omens of trouble to come was the acquisition of Rupert's Land from the Hudson's

The Dominion of Canada is born

Throughout the early 1800s the idea of uniting the five British colonies in North America was discussed on both sides of the Atlantic. Unification, it was argued, would not only strengthen the economy, it would provide a solid force against any future aggression by the United States.

A joint legislative Assembly for Upper and Lower Canada had been established in Ottawa in 1849. But rather than tackling major issues, activity cen-

tred around petty political bickering. Governments lasted a few months, then a few weeks, until in 1864 political deadlock emerged.

Towards confederation

With the American Civil War raging to the south, Canadians were chilled by the prospect of renewed Anglo-American conflict. Confederation seemed to be a timely way to get the colonies going again. In the same year as the deadlock, an unlikely coalition of rival parties (the Blues led by George Étienne Cartier, the Conservatives headed by John A. Macdonald and the Liberals by the powerful newspaper magnate, George Brown) was formed. Their union was based upon a platform of Confederation.

In the Maritimes a similar discussion of uniting the coastal provinces had surfaced. The provinces had called for a conference to draw up a strategy for Confederation, when the governments of Upper and Lower Canada heard of their plans. A delegation consisting of John A. Macdonald, George Brown and six other ministers decided to "crash" the conference and push for their own proposals.

Awash with Champagne

The *Queen Victoria* was chartered in Québec City and, loaded with $13,000 worth of champagne, set sail for Prince Edward Island.

Although somewhat disconcerted by the fact that they were met by only one official in an oyster boat, the delegation was able to persuade the Maritime governments that Confederation should include Upper and Lower Canada. The rough terms of Confederation were drawn up at "the great intercolonial drunk" (as one disgusted New Brunswick editorial described it) and received ratification a few weeks later at the Québec Conference.

The new nation

On 1 July, 1867, Confederated Canada became a reality when the British North America Act divided the British Province of Canada into Ontario and Québec (formerly Upper and Lower Canada) and united them with New Brunswick and Nova Scotia (Prince Edward Island and Newfoundland dropped out at the last minute). The new nation was called the Dominion of Canada.

The founding act

An extract from the act read as follows:
Whereas the provinces of Canada, Nova Scotia and New Brunswick have expressed their Desire to be federally united into One Dominion under the Crown of the United Kingdom of Great Britain and Ireland, with a Constitution similar in Principle to that of the United Kingdom;

And whereas such a Union would conduce to the Welfare of the Provinces and Promote the interests of the British Empire;

And whereas on the Establishment of the Union by Authority of Parliament, it is expedient, not only that the Constitution of the Legislative Authority in the Dominion be prepared for, but also that the Nature of the Executive Government therein be declared;

And whereas it is expedient that Provision be made for the eventual Admission into the Union of other parts of British North America.

ABOVE: the fathers of Confederation in debate.

Bay Company for £300,000. Unwisely, the government regarded the territory as the sole property of the company and neglected to take into account the indigenous population living there, namely the Métis of the Red River Colony. Trouble soon followed. The Métis, who spoke French and practised Catholicism, were homesteaders who had long thought of themselves as a sovereign but autonomous nation of neither European nor Indian extraction, but one of both. When Rupert's Land was acquired without their

LOUIS RIEL

"He shall hang though every dog in Québec should bark in his favor," said Prime Minister Macdonald

oner court-martialled and shot. Much to Macdonald's dismay, Scott had been a citizen of Ontario; worse, he was a Protestant murdered by a Catholic. Predictably the affair became politically "delicate". It was finally settled when the colony entered the Confederation as the province of Manitoba. Riel fled to the United States. Despite its promises, the Canadian government did not respect the integrity of the Métis community and over a decade after the first rebellion, Riel returned to begin a second one, this time in

FORT GEORGE, OR ASTORIA, COLUMBIA RIVER.—THE HUDSON'S BAY COMPANY'S ESTABLISHMENT.

consultation, the Métis organized under the leadership of Louis Riel, a man of charismatic eloquence. They seized Fort Garry, a British outpost, and set up a provisional government. No blood was shed during the insurrection.

Supported by an American fifth column of infantrymen, the Métis were in a strong position and the Macdonald government knew it. Negotiations had commenced and all might have ended peacefully if a young upstart, Thomas Scott (who had been captured by the Métis), had not tried to throttle Louis Riel. Riel had the pris-

Saskatchewan. Eventually captured by British troops, Riel was put on trial for treason. Perhaps the blackest stain on Macdonald's otherwise illustrious career was his decision to have Louis Riel hanged. Responding to indignant French cries of opposition, the Prime Minister remarked: "He shall hang though every dog in Québec should bark in his favor." Riel's death only served to entrench the old, bitter hatred between the French and the English.

The railway scandal

A second slight on Macdonald's political record occurred through the Pacific Railway scandal By the time a second election was due in

ABOVE: Hudson's Bay trading post. The company's sale of Rupert's Land to the government enraged the Métis.

Canada, Prince Edward Island, the Prairies and the Pacific Coast had been added to the Confederation. The problem of connecting the provinces became a major issue in the elections of 1872. A national railway stretching from coast to coast seemed to be the natural solution.

The Canadian-Pacific Railway was a project proposed by Macdonald's party and was organized by Sir Hugh Allan, a prominent Montréal shipping magnate. The railway was backed by large American investments and Macdonald bluntly told Allan that foreign capital must be eliminated from the project. Allan agreed, but deceived Macdonald by retaining his American partners and keeping them in the background.

Six weeks before the election day, Macdonald found himself desperate for campaign funds; he asked Hugh Allan for support. Mysteriously, $60,000 appeared; another $35,000 soon followed. In a moment of fatal foolhardiness Macdonald wired Allan for a final amount: "I must have another ten thousand. Will be the last time of calling. Do not fail me."

Macdonald's ticket won the election. At the moment of his relief, however, others were planning his demise. The offices of Sir Hugh Allan's solicitor were ransacked and stolen documents were sold to ministers of Macdonald's rival party, the Liberals, for the sum of $5,000.

The Liberals exposed the scandal: it seemed that Prime Minister Macdonald had given Hugh Allan the Canadian Pacific Railway project in exchange for election funds. Eventually forced to resign, Macdonald left office in disgrace. The railway was later completed but it would always lack the luster of accomplishment of which Macdonald had dreamed.

The close of a century

When Macdonald left office the task of shaping Canada's future was taken up by Alexander Mackenzie. Macdonald later returned as prime minister, then others followed: Sir John Abbott, Sir John Thompson, Sir Mackenzie Bowell, Sir Charles Tupper. By 1900 Canada was well on its way as a nation. Continually facing new challenges and reconciling divergent interests, Canada saw the advent of the 20th century as the beginning of a future of golden promise.

RIGHT: the coming of the railways was – despite this storybook representation – fraught with hardship and scandal, which led to the prime minister's resignation.

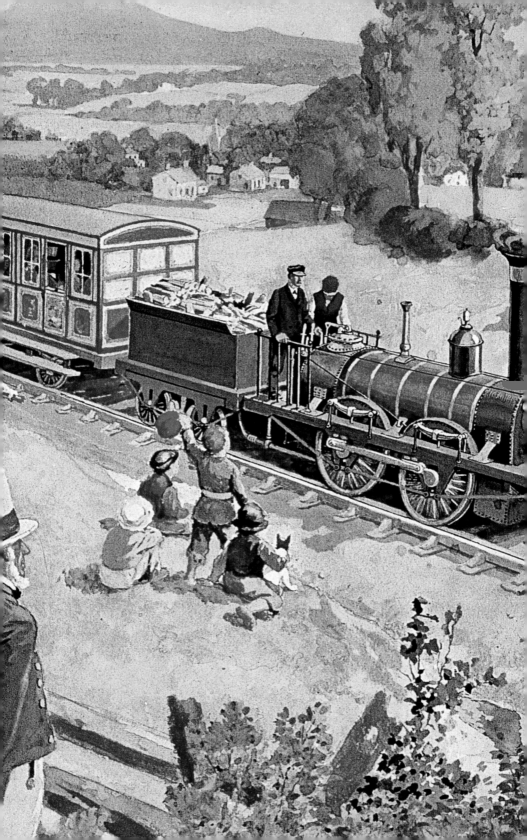

SETTLEMENT AND WAR

The Canadian government is obliged to back British war efforts,

but the Canadian people are not convinced

A tentative prosperity and progress ushered Canada into the 20th century. Under Prime Minister Wilfrid Laurier's government railway construction continued apace and by 1914 the Canadian-Pacific extended from one coast to the other. Although diplomatic relations began to be forged with the rest of the world, most international ties were organized through Britain, and Canadians began to grumble about being ruled by a tiny island thousands of miles away. Further resentment erupted over the "Alaska Boundary Fiasco."

To settle a dispute between the US and Canada over the Alaska/Yukon boundary a commission of three Americans, three Canadians and one British minister was formed. The Americans issued a proposal that was overwhelmingly in their own favor. Lord Alvertone, for Britain, voted with the US, which was seen by Canada as a betrayal of their interests and further evidence of British duplicity.

Britain was also contributing to the burgeoning influx of Europeans. Canada's immigration policy favored Anglo-Saxon migrants, but the influx was not enough and the west, in particular, loomed large and empty.

Laurier's Minister of the Interior, Clifford Sifton, initiated a widespread advertising scheme designed to attract other European settlers to the Prairies. Advertisements reading: THE LAST BEST WEST; HOMES FOR MILLIONS; 160-ACRE FARMS IN WESTERN CANADA; FREE, were distributed throughout Europe. The result was the mass migration of Ukrainians, Czechs, Slovaks, Poles, Hungarians and Serbs to Alberta and Saskatchewan (provinces created in 1905). Sifton believed that Slavic immigrants, because of their farming backgrounds, were ideal settlers for Canada's west. When criticized for bringing "inferior breeds" to Canada, Sifton replied: "I think a stalwart peasant in a sheepskin coat… with a stout wife and half a dozen

children, *is* good quality." For a fee of $10 and a promise to remain on the farm for six months of the year for three years, newcomers received 160 acres of prairie grass.

Like the French *habitants*, prairie homesteaders faced difficult beginnings. The tough Prairie scrub had to be cleared and soil, dried

for thousands of years under a blazing sun, had to be plowed. Winter temperatures so cold they could freeze human flesh within five seconds and torrid summers were difficulties offset only by successful harvests. As folksongs recounted, many left in search of a kinder environment:

> *So farewell to Alberta,*
> *farewell to the west*
> *It's backward I'll go*
> *to the girl I love best*
> *I'll go back to the east*
> *and get me a wife*
> *And never eat cornbread*
> *the rest of my life.*

Canada's unique brand of democratic socialism

PRECEDING PAGES: Toronto's Yonge Street, June 1901.

LEFT: celebrating progress and prosperity.

RIGHT: Poster encourages British families to emigrate.

was born of the rugged lives of prairie farmers struggling to survive in the early 20th century. It is from this era that one discovers the roots of populist, radical and progressive movements in Canadian politics.

Women had a voice, too. Nellie McClung and Emily Murphy led a movement in the famous "Persons Case". The frontier women objected to the chauvinistic interpretation of the "persons clause" in the British North America Act which specified that "persons" could be nominated to the Senate. The Canadian parliament understood this to mean men only. McClung's and Murphy's petition was turned down by the

Supreme Court but its decision was overruled by an executive committee in London. As a result, the Senate was opened to both sexes in 1929.

The rise of industrialism

With the development of new businesses and industries, many Canadians experienced radical changes in their lifestyles: for the entrepreneur, commercial development meant assured affluence, but for many others it meant a life of drudgery and exploitation.

In the east, the factory became the oppressive environment of the urban immigrant. Twelve-hour days, six-day weeks, and low wages were standard practices. The hiring of women and children at lower rates of pay was also common.

When questioned by a Labor Commission in 1910 about the appropriateness of brutally whipping six-year-old girls in his textile factory, one Montréal merchant replied that just as training a dog required strict forms of punishment, so, too, did the hiring of children necessitate rigorous discipline. In 1905 David Kissam Young, a writer for the *Industrial Banner*, described the Canadian factory owner's creed as: "Suffer little children to come unto me; For they pay a bigger profit than men you see."

This led to the rise of trade unions and labor organizations. In 1908 Ontario passed the first child-labor law in Canada – the minimum age at which a child could work was 14 years.

World War I

The 1914–18 war in Europe had profound consequences for Canada. Still considered a loyal subject of the British Empire, Canada felt duty-bound to enter the war in support of Britain. The decision was not without its own advantages. When Russian wheat exports were hindered by fighting, Canada became the main agricultural supplier of Britain and its allies. Canadian munitions industries sprang up overnight and fortunes were made. But these economic benefits were gained at the expense of many lives.

Robert Borden was prime minister of Canada for the duration of World War I, and his main task was to ensure that Canada found the 500,000 men it had promised in support of Britain.

Efforts to actively support the war in Europe began to pervade Canadian society. Appeals to civic pride were made by political leaders, ministers preached of Christian duty, army officials advertised the glamor of wearing complete highland regalia, and women wore badges reading "Knit or Fight".

French-Canadians were reluctant to join the war effort. Unmoved by loyalty to either France or Britain, Québec inhabitants responded cynically to the government's patriotic propaganda. Tensions eventually led to anti-conscription riots in 1918. In one skirmish, soldiers from Toronto opened fire on crowds in Québec and killed four civilians. Ottawa warned that future rioters would be conscripted on the spot.

Borden's administration took an increasingly harsh attitude. A War Tax Measure, burdening already precariously balanced household budgets, was passed; anti-loafing legislation (which stated that any males between the ages of 16 and 60 not gainfully employed would be jailed) was issued; all "radical" unions were suppressed, and all publications printed in enemy languages were outlawed.

On 18 August, 1918, Canadian and Australian troops broke through a German battalion near Amiens. The German soldiers were pushed farther back until the final day at Mons on 11 November when the

EMANCIPATION

Women shed several pounds of clothing, cut their hair and fought for new gender identities

America of any "suspected or real communists". The movement never made any serious headway in Canada. Radical parties in the prairies, union organizers and the handful of self-avowed communists experienced mild to severe harassment, but Canada lacked the fanatic allegiance to "democracy" of the US.

Like Americans, Canadians were thrilled by the glamorous Toronto-born Mary Pickford and flocked to see Douglas Fairbanks and Rudolph Valentino in their latest silent films: women shed pounds of

German army was defeated. By the time the war was over, Canada had lost 60,611 lives – thousands of others returned home severely and permanently mutilated, both physically and mentally.

The purring Twenties

If the 1920s roared in the United States, they at least purred in Canada. In the States a modern equivalent of the Inquisition, the Big Red Scare, swept across the country and sought to purge

FAR LEFT: registering immigrants. **ABOVE:** Canadian soldiers during World War I. Around 60,000 Canadian troops lost their lives in the war in Europe.

clothing, cut their hair and fought for new gender identities; Canadians politely marveled at the athletic ability of Babe Ruth... but Canada was still a land of small towns. As such, it bolstered a small town conservative attitude – an attitude given a literary form in Stephen Leacock's *Sunshine Sketches* (1914) – subtly arrogant but at the same time self-remonstrating.

There were new Canadian directions to be taken as well, early in the century. In the arts, the Group of Seven created a stunning but scandalously different visual image of the Canadian landscape. Using the techniques of Cézanne, the Impressionists and Art Nouveau, Lawren Harris, A.Y. Jackson, Arthur Lismer, Frederick Varley, J.E.H. MacDonald, Franklin Carmichael and Frank Johnston re-explored Canada as bold iconoclasts – their works distinguished Canada internationally and had a lingering effect on the country's visual arts for many decades.

Grain drain

When the Depression hit Canada in 1929, it hit hard, exacerbated by the collapse of the world grain market – a wheat glut had made it more economical for Canada's clients to buy from Argentina, Australia or the Soviet Union.

R.B. Bennett's Conservative government quickly rallied to address the problems of a fal-

tering economy. Relief programs and social services (which became expert at detecting "fraud and waste") were soon established.

Callous in their lack of understanding of the hardship the Depression caused, politicians claimed that "jobs were there to be found", and they created work camps in British Columbia for single men. Hundreds of workers either froze to death on the trains or were murdered on their way to find work. Those who made it to the camps were paid 20 cents a day. Widespread unemployment sent men and women into the streets. In Toronto a team of men would shovel snow from the driveway of a wealthy Rosedale family for seven hours, only to be paid 5 cents.

Nowhere was destitution greater than on the prairies. Out west it seemed as if the forces of nature had collaborated with the vagaries of the economy to make life as miserable as possible. In 1931 raging winds swept away the fertile top-soil; in 1932 a plague of grasshoppers devoured the crops; and 1933 marked the beginning of a series of droughts, hailstorms and early frosts.

Even Newfoundland, barely surviving itself, sent prairie families dried cod cakes. (Not sure what to make of the cod, some westerners used it to plug up holes in their roofs.) Prairie hardship influenced the development of the Cooperative Commonwealth Federation (CCF), a farmers' labor movement that was later to become Canada's socialist party, the NDP (New Democratic Party).

As the Depression deepened throughout Canada, radio sets became the main means of escape and, in what the government claimed was an attempt to allay the misery of millions, the Canadian Radio Broadcasting Commission was set up. Sports events, radio dramas, the lively commentaries of Gordon Sinclair, and reporting of events such as the Dionne quintuplets born in Calendar, Ontario, served as diversions for many Canadians. When the Depression ended, millions of citizens were left scarred – a decade of hardship had produced a thrifty generation.

World War II

Five days before Britain declared war on Germany, the front page headline of one influential Canadian paper, *The Toronto Star*, read: "WOUNDED FATHER AND SON ROUT THREE GUNMEN." No mention was made of Adolf Hitler's seizure of Czechoslovakia, Germany's non-aggression pact with the Soviet Union, or the invasion of Poland. *The Star's* headline was indicative of the mood pervading Canadian society at the time: a belief that the war would just go away. But on 3 September, 1939, Canadians had their heads pulled out of the sand. Newspaper headlines this time read: "BRITISH EMPIRE AT WAR – HIS MAJESTY CALLS TO BRITONS AT HOME AND OVERSEAS."

Canada's involvement was complicated by the fact that in 1931 the Statute of Westminister had made it an autonomous community within the British Empire. Legally Canada could remain out of the war – but morally there seemed to be no alternative but to enter it..

In French Canada the politician Maurice Duplessis challenged the government's right to speak for *all* of the people of Canada. Québec, Duplessis argued, ought to remain independent of any European struggles. Then, in the spring of 1940, when the German *blitzkrieg* began, Duplessis' calls for neutrality were lost amid the scrambling of French Canadians to register for overseas service. Prime Minister Mackenzie King maintained support for the war by promising that conscription would never be thrust upon

CONSCRIPTION

The Québecois voted against conscription and a fierce nationalist movement rose up to resist the draft

conscription, through a national plebiscite. The majority of voters agreed, but the vast majority of Québecois voted against conscription and a fierce nationalist movement rose up to resist the draft; in its ranks was the young Pierre Elliott Trudeau, later to become one of Canada's most popular prime ministers. Fortunately for King, it was not necessary to conscript soldiers until the final months of the war.

By the time the fighting was over, Canada had lost 45,000 lives. The troops had fought bravely

them. Soon the country was spending $12 million a day on the war effort; by 1943, 1.5 million were employed in munitions factories.

When Japan attacked Pearl Harbor in 1941, Canada, in recognition of the growing bonds being forged between itself and the US, promptly declared war on Japan.

As the war raged on, Britain began to experience severe manpower problems. King decided to see if the Canadian people would agree to

LEFT: settlers travel west on the Canadian-Pacific (1915). **ABOVE:** the Depression, compounded by freak weather conditions, almost destroyed life on the prairie homesteads in the 1930s.

and had played a vital role in the war's deciding battles. But like other nations, Canada's record was not unblemished. Using the pretext that angry neighbors might harm Japanese-Canadians, the government had interned 15,000 in camps and had auctioned off their property. Under Minister of Justice Ernest Lapointe, Canada refused to admit all but a few Jewish refugees, both during and after the war. Lapointe's "none is too many" sentiment received support from influential anti-Semites across the country. With these blots to its copybook, and with a returning army of displaced and tired soldiers, the Canadian nation set about the daunting task of building a new future.

LE DEVOIR

FAIS CE QUE DOIS

Rédacteur en chef : Omar HÉROUX

Directeur : Gérard FILION

MONTRÉAL, VENDREDI, 1er JUILLET 1949

ME LX — No 151

A. Gall, évêque
BEAU ET CHAUD

FIN DE LA GRÈVE DE L'AMIANTE

Augmentation de 10 cts; pas de représailles

L'entente a été signée tôt ce matin après une assemblée des grévistes — Le juge Thomas ...blay présidera le tribunal d'arbitrage — Le retour ...cienneté sera respecté — La production se continuer ...à demain pour se ...la production et Foster

...ER ROY

Les instituteurs sont en fave... subsides fédéraux à l'édu...

A la condition que soit respecté... l'autonomie provinciale

Recherches interrompues à Val-d'Or

Val-d'Or (P.C.) — Les ...cherches entreprises pour ...ver bien les fillos Gray ...ver bien les fillos Gray ...ont été momentanément inter...pues, mais les moustiques et les ...tières et les moustiques qui ha...saient les hommes.

Le jeune homme est disparu ...re, un dimanche de trois hom...le dimanche de trois ...raire, un samedi après un re...fin la semaine de la ...l'on a intimé hier de le ...de surveillance le ...le Québec pour fins ...

POSTWAR PROSPERITY

The conclusion of World War II left Canada in a position of relative strength and its standard of living soared

World War II, along with integrating Canada's investment and trading systems into the North American grid, had brought to new levels of success the old "National Policy" of Sir John A. Macdonald, which used federal policy to promote central Canada's industrial development through harnessing the resources of the country's regions. The result was a spectacular continent-wide prosperity.

At the same time, the federal government's power increased to historic highs. Armed with taxing and spending powers gained from the provinces during the crisis of the war, the Liberal government of Mackenzie King laid the foundations of the Canadian welfare state. Old age pensions were increased, unemployment insurance was expanded and federal-provincial welfare programs grew rapidly.

Throughout the 1950s, the basics of Canadian public life remained stable. A seemingly-permanent Liberal government in Ottawa, now under the stewardship of Québec's Louis St-Laurent, continued to win elections with a coalition anchored in Québec and the West. US investment combined with Canadian enterprise to expand industry and resource sectors rapidly. Future prime minister Lester Pearson levered Canada's international status to give it a voice in international bodies such as the United Nations. His proposal for the first use of UN peacekeeping troops – the now familiar "blue helmets" of the world's hot spots – in the 1956 Suez Crisis, won him the Nobel Peace Prize.

Powerful forces were reshaping Canadian society. The population increased by 50 percent between 1946 and 1961, to 18 million people, with 2 million coming in the greatest immigration in the nation's history. The face of urban Canada began to change, as Mediterraneans and Eastern Europeans transformed dull cities. The

A BURGEONING NATION

The face of Canada began to change as its population increased by 50 percent between 1946 and 1961

country became one of the world's most urbanized nations, with 77 percent of Canadians living in towns by 1961. Television and other mass-communications, mass-merchandising and suburbanization were accelerating social and cultural mobility. Women's roles were changing, with a significant increase in female participation in the workforce.

The political and cultural upheavals of the 1960s were pre-figured by the upset victory of John Diefenbaker's Progressive Conservatives in 1957. His minority-government election, based on eroding Liberal support in urban Ontario and the west, became a majority triumph a year later, when Québec's right-wing provincial government delivered the province to Diefenbaker, creating a national landslide. Although Diefenbaker's period in office, which lasted until 1963, was unable to reorder the political dynamics of Canada, it was a harbinger of an accelerating transformation.

The Quiet Revolution

In 1960, a pivotal provincial election in Québec brought to power a new Liberal government with a new vision of the province.

For decades, Québec's political development had followed its own path, in many respects separate from the currents of change afoot throughout the Western world. The pillars of Québec society – a parochial government, a powerful Catholic Church, and a dominant Anglo-Saxon business elite – were to be dramatically transformed in what became known as *la révolution tranquille*. With the slogan, "*maîtres chez nous*" (masters in our own house), the government of Jean Lesage transferred responsibility for the health and education systems from the church to the provincial government, and promoted the development of a French-speaking state sector as a competitor to the Anglo business establishment.

The social energies released by the Quiet Revolution ran in two opposing directions, both

LEFT: industrial disputes such as this one in 1949 were a feature of development.

with deep roots in Québec's political tradition. Some sought to parlay Québec's self-assertion into a greater role in national politics, to bring "French Power" to the federal government in order to secure for Québec all of the benefits of the modern Canada rising around it. Montréal intellectual Pierre Trudeau, who abhorred what he saw as the inward-looking character of Québec nationalism, would become the exemplar of this current. Others saw Canadian federalism as incapable of responding to Québec's unique imperatives of cultural survival, and sought to fulfill Québec's aspirations through the growth of a separate nation-state.

The separatist movement began among radical intellectuals and traditionalist folk singers, but would gain credibility as more powerful adherents joined, most notably René Lévesque, who had a been a minister in the Lesage Government and would become the first separatist premier of Québec from 1976 to 1983. This crystallization of the federalist and separatist tendencies in Québec politics dominates the life of the province to this day.

The growing assertiveness of Québec clashed with the increasing activism of the federal government, Liberal once again under Lester Pearson from 1963 to 1968 and ambitious to continue building the welfare state through such initiatives as a national medicare system. A major conflict erupted in 1965 over whether the government would provide public pensions to Québecois. The province won the day, opting out of the national income tax collection and pension systems and using its new pension fund to invest in Québec companies and promote francophone business interests.

Québec's social ferment was perhaps more politicized than that of the rest of Canada during the early 1960s. Through much of the decade, English-speaking Canada – along with the United States – reveled in sustained prosperity and a growing sense of sophisticated modernity. This culminated in two events: 1967's world's fair in Montréal at which a 100-year-old Canada played host to an approving world; and, in 1968, the election as prime minister of the urbane, even hip Trudeau. Simultaneously, the current of philosophical discontent that coursed through the western world in the mid-to-late 1960s found fertile ground in Canada. Student radicalism, the sexual revolution, widespread divorce, the awakening of fem-

inism – Canada participated fully in the rambunctious "cultural revolution" of the period.

The key popular music figures of the period in Canada were singer-songwriters such as Joni Mitchell, Leonard Cohen and Neil Young – not as loud as, say, Jimi Hendrix or Janis Joplin, but more reflective and, notably, still alive.

As elsewhere, the ferment culminated in tragedy, when radical separatists, the *Front de la Libération du Québec*, kidnapped a British diplomat, James Cross, and Québec's Minister of Labour, Pierre Laporte in October, 1970. The federal government responded by declaring martial law – a move widely supported at the

time and seemingly vindicated when Laporte was found murdered, but since believed by many to have been a panicked over-reaction. The episode concluded with the release of Cross and flight of the terrorists to Cuba. Throughout Canada there was a genuine sense of innocence lost as the legacy of the "October Crisis".

The cracks widen

The 1970s were a pivotal decade for Canada. "Stagflation" (low growth, high inflation and unemployment) was just one manifestation of what seemed to be an unfair alteration of the ground rules under which Canada had grown. The social transformations of the 1950s and upheavals of the 1960s left Canada – as they did other western countries – with a pervasive sense of directionless unease throughout the decade.

While politicians and pundits argued such topics as "the limits of growth", the "revolution of rising expectations" and Trudeau's aggrandizement of the state, public tastes rummaged furiously through a wild assortment of fads. American imports, such as the truckstop culture of Citizens' Band radio, the gentrification-and-renovation of former slums in urban centers, and,

OIL BOOM

In the 1970s the rising oil and gas-rich western provinces began to challenge national policies

very existence. The first was the oil shock of 1973, and the end of the "Long Boom" that had transformed the country and the world in the postwar years.

The Canadian economy slowed through the 1970s, distorted by double-digit inflation. Chronic unemployment began. This weakened an underpinning of Canadian politics – the seemingly unlimited power of governments to tax and spend in order to redistribute wealth and invest in improving the quality of life. Taxes continued to rise, as did

above all, the *soignée* "decadence" of the coke-blown discotheque, all found a ready market among Canadians. The national longing for the Big Time seemed bizarrely fulfilled when Margaret Trudeau, the Prime Minister's wife, abandoned her first lady role for a glam-ish life of frolic with the likes of Keith Richards and the environs of New York's Studio 54.

Three crucial events shaped and echoed this sense of dislocation, cracking the basic pattern of Canada's national life and threatening her

LEFT: Pierre Trudeau led the nation, while his wife Margaret (**ABOVE**) created national scandal. **RIGHT:** René Lévesque, leader of the separatist Parti Québécois.

spending, but a gap began to appear between governments' revenues and expenditures, which has continued to widen to this day. In time, this reversed the field on which the ongoing struggle between federal and provincial governments took place. Whereas since the war they had jockeyed for the political credit from introducing new programs, federal-provincial politics became a contest over who could shift the blame for declining service levels and chronic budgetary deficits.

The second critical development came with the oil shock. The rise of Western Canada, for generations an economic hinterland, fundamentally altered the nation's politics. Oil and gas-rich western provinces challenged the old National Policy of Macdonald, with its preference for central Canadian industry. Politically, the western provinces began to join with a still-more assertive Québec in a drive to transfer powers to the provincial governments. Prime Minister Trudeau was adept at out-maneuvering these demands by appealing to citizens' sense of Canada as a whole, and through the adroit use of his immense personal standing in an increasingly restive Québec.

The third key event of the 1970s was the election, in November of 1976, of a separatist Parti Québécois government in Québec under René

Trudeau used it to fashion a Constitution Act that was proclaimed in 1982. However, the Act was put through over the angry protests of Québec, which had been isolated in the federal-provincial maneuvering that led to repatriation.

On his resignation in 1984, Trudeau could reflect with satisfaction on some important achievements in his 16 years of power. However, his desired legacy of a strong federal government with a united country seemed farther away than ever. Federal-provincial relations were rancorous, westerners increasingly alienated from national affairs, and Québec sullen over its exclusion from the constitutional deal.

Lévesque. While the PQ was elected on a good government platform that downplayed separatism, Lévesque pressed ahead with a province-wide referendum in May 1980. The result seemed conclusive: while 41 percent of voters cast a *"Oui"* ballot, 50 percent said *Non* to the government's request for a mandate to negotiate separatism.

Trudeau campaigned actively in the referendum contest, promising Québecois a "renewed federalism" if they would remain in Canada. His promise took the form of a crusade to "repatriate" the Canadian Constitution so that it could be amended without British consent, and add to it a Charter of Rights and Freedoms. This proposal carried considerable popular support, and

Moreover, the Canadian economy had stagnated badly. The annual federal budget deficit had grown to a nearly uncontrollable size, dramatically limiting the strength of the federal government and its ability to make choices.

Prosperity and provincialism

The disastrous financial performance of the last Trudeau government was largely due to the recession which rocked the Canadian economy in 1981 and 1982. This worldwide downturn did not spare Canada, where unemployment reached 11 percent. The recession sealed the fate of the Liberals, who had ruled as Canada's "natural governing party" for 42 of the previous 49 years.

English Canada turned to the Progressive Conservatives under their new leader, Québecois Brian Mulroney. What made Mulroney's victory inevitable was a historic shift in Québec, where the Tories had been marginal since the 1890s. Mulroney appealed to Québecois' sense of betrayal over the constitutional accord of 1981, promising amendments to the Constitution which would allow Québec to "re-enter the Canadian family… with honour and enthusiasm". The result was the greatest federal election victory in

THE SEPARATIST ISSUE

Mulroney promised Québec constitiutional amendments to allow it to "re-enter the Canadian family with honor"

Optimism was sufficient, however, for the Mulroney Government to win re-election on a platform of free trade with the United States.

The 1988 campaign became a pitched battle between economic and cultural "nationalists" who divided their votes between the Liberals and the socialist New Democratic Party, and "free traders" in Québec, the West and in industrial Ontario who, in concert with major business interests, secured a renewed 168-seat majority for the Tories.

Canadian history, with 211 out of 295 seats in the House of Commons going Conservative.

The boom of the 1980s allowed Mulroney great scope to tackle Canada's deficits. For most of the country, the classic images of the 1980s were smart cars, chic restaurants and soaring property values. But for many Canadians the boom never really happened. Unemployment remained considerable, rural and Atlantic Canada stayed in decline, and in the cities, homeless people became a feature of urban life.

Harmony and conflict: French style in the Frontenac Hotel, Québec (**LEFT**), and British style in the parliament buildings in Ottawa (**ABOVE**).

Although it never became a campaign issue in 1988, many Canadians were also growing insecure with Mulroney's Québec policy. His promise to amend the constitution had been, it seemed, fulfilled in the April 1987 Constitutional Accord signed at Meech Lake in Québec. At Meech Lake, all 10 premiers and the federal government had agreed to amend the constitution to meet five specific demands of Québec, including legal recognition of the province as a "distinct society". The federal and provincial legislatures were given until 23 June, 1990 to ratify the Accord, but trouble arose as new governments were elected – in New Brunswick, Manitoba and Newfoundland – expressing reservations. Also, women feared their rights would be compromised. Natives complained that their constitutional issues had been ignored. Recent immigrants, who now made up one-third of Canada's population, worried that their rights would be undermined. Then, in 1989, Premier Bourassa bowed to nationalist pressures in Québec and introduced a law banning the use of English on signs. This was a catalytic event in crystallizing opposition to the Accord. Thousands of English Canadians, normally uninterested in constitutional minutiae, expressed their belief that Meech Lake would "Balkanize the country" and "give too much to Québec".

In this troubled context, Québec reacted angrily to the failure of the Meech Lake Accord. Premier Bourassa embarked his government on a two-year process of reviewing Québec's political options, including separation. Slowly, however, the elements of a new deal emerged. For the west, the appointed Senate would be replaced with an elected body designed to enhance the power of regions over the national government. For Québec, a modified version of its five Meech Lake demands would be included. Rights of immigrant Canadians and women would be explicitly reconfirmed, while the issue of self-government for natives would be tackled as well.

A new deal for the nineties

If the brinkmanship and backroom deals of the Meech Lake process soured the national mood, the economic events of 1990 curdled it. A recession longer and deeper than any since the Great Depression engulfed the country's economy. The impact of free trade on weaker sectors of the economy, a high-interest rate policy to combat the inflation of the late 1980s, the introduction of a confidence-crippling value-added tax in 1990, and a worldwide restructuring of industrial economies combined with enormous force, particularly in the central Canadian industrial heartland. Unemployment soared to 11 percent, property values tumbled and businesses folded.

This ambitious project culminated in a second Accord, in August of 1992 at Charlottetown, PEI. The Accord was submitted to a national referendum in October, needing majority support in all provinces to pass. Six provinces passed it; four, including Québec, rejected it. In the wake of the defeat, all talk of constitutional amendment was abandoned, and Brian Mulroney resigned.

He advised his successor, Kim Campbell: "You need the hide of a bloody rhinoceros, and don't ever let the polls get in the way of your objectives." However, when Campbell led the party into the next general election after just four months as leader, her defeat, which left the Progressive Conservatives with just two seats instead of 153, went into the record books as the worst ever suffered by a ruling party.

The Liberals, under Jean Chrétien, took power, with the separatist Bloc Québécois the second largest party. The result boosted the fortunes of Lucien Bouchard, a former Progressive Conservative minister who had quit over the failure of Meech Lake and founded the Bloc Québécois. Although a Québecois, Jean Chrétien underestimated the strength of the separatist movement and was given a shock when, in a 1995 referendum, the

> ## CANADA'S STRENGTH
>
> Building a prosperous, humane society on such unpromising ground was a formidable achievement

proposal to grant Québec independence was defeated by a margin of 1.12 percent. The turnout of 93 percent of voters proved the strength of feeling on both sides, and the government in Ottawa had to come to terms with the fact that half of Québec was seriously discontented. How long would it be before the next referendum? Bouchard's answer was unequivocal: "Keep hope," he told a dejected rally, "because the next time will be ours."

Things have not proved so simple. After the 1995 referendum, the leader of the PQ, Jacques

Parizeau, resigned, and Lucien Bouchard switched from the federal to the provincial arena to take over the reins of the PQ. While the PQ won in the 1998 provincial election by 75 votes to 48, the provincial Liberal party won the popular vote. Bouchard's election campaign included a promise to create "winning conditions" for sovereignty. He has since focused on paying down Québec's deficit, which has entailed battling with the mostly separist-inclined trade unions.

On the wider political stage, much of the traditionally liberal Canada seemed to be following the United States in moving to the right. Ontario elected Mike Harris as its premier in 1995 after the former golf and ski instructor had campaigned on a platform of tax and spending cuts, welfare reform and a balanced budget. Canada's old formula, once described as "Ontario bleeds the west, bribes Québec, and gives the Atlantic welfare" seemed to be breaking down. The national elections of 1997 re-elected Chrétien and the Liberal Party with a growing Reform Party in opposition.

Divided we stand

If there is a cause for optimism in assessing Canada's political and economic prospects, it probably lies in the country's historic ability to muddle through. There is a bedrock common sense to Canadians – including Québecois – that has made the country's political culture resistant to radicalism. As one commentator pointed out, the 1995 vote in Québec was in its way a vindication of the country's strong democracy since, in 90 percent of the world's countries, the leaders of such a forceful secessionist movement would have ended up in jail. Moreover, the last two recessions have taught Canadians some painful lessons about taking prosperity for granted. Those who wish the country to remain together in the future have at their disposal some powerful economic arguments.

For the rest of the world, the drama seems baffling. Why should Canadians be putting at risk what is an enviable prosperity? But the forces that tug at Canada's unity are, after all, part of the nation's heritage. Building a prosperous, humane society on the unpromising ground once described by Voltaire as *quelques arpents du neige* was a formidable achievement, and one that won't lightly be discarded.

LEFT: the Queen on a state visit: not always popular with the French (**ABOVE**).

REACHING NEW ARCHITECTURAL HEIGHTS

Today Canada stands at the forefront of modern architecture and its architects are sought after the world over for their flair and expertise.

From the log cabins of the frontiersmen to the vibrant skyline of modern Toronto, Canada has an eclectic array of architectural styles. In the early days of colonization, settlers simply built replicas of their home-country buildings. The French, for instance, erected the simple stone houses they had been familiar with in Normandy, while the Ukrainians constructed onion-domed churches across Manitoba.

Architects – sometimes military engineers – drew on their own design heritage and by the late 19th century a form of building etiquette had evolved: parliament buildings and churches tended to be designed in the Gothic style, banks and railway stations were Classical, legislative buildings looked to the Renaissance, the French château-style was reserved for hotels, while houses, particularly in the Atlantic provinces, drew on English Georgian influences.

FUTURISTIC DESIGN

As the 20th century progressed, Canadian design began to take on its own distinct identity. Montréal's Expo '67, with Moshe Safdie's "Habitat" of stacked dwellings, and the 1976 Montréal Olympics, characterized by Roger Taillibert's circular stadium, attracted international recognition.

Since then the country hasn't been afraid to commission buildings on a large scale, and a number of influential architects have emerged including Moshe Safdie (National Gallery of Canada, Ottawa), Arthur Erickson (UBC Museum of Anthropology in Vancouver), Douglas Cardinal (Musée Canadien des Civilisations, Hull, Québec), Patricia and John Patkau (Canadian Clay and Glass Gallery, Kitchener, Ontario), and in the Maritime provinces Brian MacKay-Lyons is making an impact with his

▽ **VANCOUVER**
Shimmering on the water's edge, Vancouver harbors a number of architectural highlights, including the not-to-be-missed UBC Museum of Anthropology, by Arthur Erickson. Below, the MacMillan Planetarium dominates the skyline and offers visitors a close-up view of the universe.

▷ **CN TOWER, TORONTO**
Built in the 1970s, Toronto's landmark, the 553-meters (1,815-ft) high telecommunications tower is the tallest free-standing structure in the world.

◁ NEW BRUNSWICK
Fredericton, the elegant provincial capital, was founded by Loyalists in 1784. The Lieutenant-General's house, left, is typical of early colonial architecture in eastern Canada.

▽ TORONTO
Award-winning Humber River Bicycle Pedestrian Bridge, by Montgomery and Sisam Architects, 1994: an enlightened civic project that put the needs of Toronto's residents first.

STYLE MAKER OF THE MUSEUMS

For an architect who was asked to withdraw from his architectural studies at university, partly because his designs were thought too radical, Douglas Cardinal has not done too badly. He now ranks among the world's top practitioners.

After graduating with honors from the University of Texas in the 1960s, Cardinal practiced in his home town of Red Deer, Alberta, and then in Edmonton, pioneering the use of the computer in structural calculations with his award-winning St Mary's Church, and gradually gaining recognition for his distinctive approach.

In 1983 he won the prestigious commission to build the Musée Canadien des Civilisations in Hull, Québec (pictured above) to house the nation's collection of native artifacts.

Combining both nature and technology, Cardinal describes the museum's curving shape as symbolizing the emergence of a continent sculpted by winds, rivers and glaciers.

Following on from the success of this project, Douglas Cardinal Architects are designing the Smithsonian's National Museum of the American Indian in the heart of Washington DC.

 YUKON
Design in a cold climate: Yukon Visitor Reception Center, Whitehorse, by Sturgess Architecture and FSC Manasc Architects. A winner in the annual Governor General's Awards for Architecture, 1997, the building was commended for creating a balance with its environment.

▽ BRITISH COLUMBIA
Barnes House, by Patkau Architects, on a rocky outcrop at Nanaimo. The Vancouver-based practice has won acclaim for its projects, including a school for native children on the west coast.

△ OTTAWA
Dominating the capital's skyline, the National Gallery of Canada, by Moshe Safdie, is a haven of spacious galleries and tranquil courtyards. It contains a reconstructed 19th-century chapel.

▷ DOUGLAS CARDINAL
The architect Douglas Cardinal was born in Red Deer, Alberta, in 1934. His father, a wildlife warden, was half Blackfoot. In his work, Cardinal combines his passion for native culture with his skill for high-tech design.

SEARCHING FOR AN IDENTITY

With the history of its peoples spanning thousands of years and a multitude of cultures, the quest for a national identity for Canadians is elusive

For the native peoples, the Canadian identity stretches thousands of years into the past – their search is a struggle to retain elements of their ancient culture. From a colonial perspective, the traditions which surface in Canadian culture seem to be born of an earlier time, of different origins and places, of anti-

alists fled the American Revolution and journeyed to Canada in support of British sovereignty; others found their way to Canada because of poverty and persecution.

In short, many of the earliest Canadians were fugitives, clinging to their culture and customs in the hope that they might be able to reproduce

quated rituals and customs. Unlike the far more tangible character of the United States, Canada's identity is more reclusive and subtle.

The sense of antiquity and elusiveness in Canadian culture is perhaps the product of its unusual history. As the late Northrop Frye, a noted Canadian intellectual, once observed, the vast majority of early Canadians (with the exception of the Indians) were people who did not wish to be in Canada. The French, abandoned by France after 1763, were left "high and dry" in Québec; the Scottish and Irish were pushed off their lands through the Highland clearances in the 16th, 17th and 18th centuries and were shipped to Canada; thousands of Loy-

in Canada what they had possessed at home. In Canada one experiences echoes of different pasts, all harmonized into a Canadian score.

This is not to say that Canada has not had its own peculiar effect on its inhabitants. The cold, the hostile environment, the bounty of food, the availability of land – all combined to make Canada both a haven and a hell for its first immigrants. Songs, poems, paintings of early Canada celebrate its compassion and callousness. Yet underlying these themes of survival is the notion of multiculturalism.

From coast to coast, there is no one thing that will mark a person Canadian except perhaps for the ubiquitous "eh?" everyone seems to use without reservation as in "It's cold outside, eh?" or "The Prime Minister's not talking any sense these days, eh?"

Within each region – North, East, West and Central – there are definite qualities that demarcate Prairie folks from Maritimers, Ontarians from Québecois. The Canadian identity is an odd mixture of assertive regionalism and resigned nationalism.

Summing up the constant tension which exists between the federal and provincial aspects of the Canadian personality, Henri Bourassa, a well-known journalist and politician, once remarked: "There is an Ontario patri-

of Sikhs, Hindus, Buddhists, Muslims and Jews attest to this). Canada's international image is promoted as a "mosaic" not a "melting pot".

Canada's multifaceted identity is also reflected in its diverse political system. Elections in Canada tend to be times of competing and compromising interests, of identities exerting and reshaping themselves.

As a national ideology, the notion of a mosaic neatly fulfills Champlain's original wishes to found Canada on principles of justice and compassion. As an implemented process, however, it falls short of success. John Porter, in his classic *The Vertical Mosaic*, harshly denounced the

otism, a Québec patriotism or Western patriotism, but there is no Canadian patriotism."

In 1970, multiculturalism became an official government policy in Canada. The policy was designed to reflect one of the original principles of Confederation: that Canada become a system of coordination among different but equal parts. As a result there is a certain toleration for ethnic and religious plurality (the growing number

Canadian mosaic as a highly differentiated, hierarchical structure that forced certain ethnic groups into occupational ghettos. Other critics have claimed that the cultural mosaic has only served to obscure the fact that Canada remains a rigidly class-divided society.

There is much truth to be found in these statements. Statistics indicate that the financial, political and cultural interests in Canada are controlled by a group of only 2,000 people, none of whom are women or native peoples. About 80 percent of this group are of British origin and 90 percent are Protestant. The elite of Canada is very much a WASP elite.

The question of a Canadian identity, then,

PRECEDING PAGES: Native Canadians celebrate their heritage; a Nova Scotian and a young gent.
ABOVE, LEFT TO RIGHT: Huron Chief; "new wave" Canadian, Vancouver; young entrepreneurs, Manitoba; a seasoned captain from Prince Edward Island.

emerges as a complex, multidimensional issue. The questions of "what is my culture?", "what is my heritage?" surface at one time or another in the lives of all Canadians. The endeavor to articulate a culture concept in Canada continues.

Native peoples

Perhaps as long ago as 40,000 years, Canada's first inhabitants crossed the Bering Strait to settle the frozen regions of the north. For many millennia Indian life flourished in Canada. This, however, was drastically altered when European explorers, greedy for the riches of the Orient, stumbled across the New World and began to

Reserves are often places of severe poverty and a deathly lethargy; cheap hotels and broken-down bars almost inevitably house the inner city Indian alcoholic or drug addict. Canada's native groups are caught between two worlds and, without a place in either, they struggle with an alienation that no other Canadian shares.

Other images abound. Across Canada colorful ceremonies and festivals attest to the fierce fighting spirit of many native peoples and their determination to carve out a just existence for themselves in Canada. Eloquent and powerful leaders have arisen in an attempt to synthesize divergent backgrounds and interests into a uni-

colonize North America. Disease, death by gunfire and forced settlement severely reduced the number of Canada's aboriginal population.

Comprising less than one percent of the total population, Canada's Indian, Inuit and Métis peoples continue to struggle against policies which seek to stigmatize them as "non-people". Communities of Indians that have been forced to live on reserves find themselves in semi-colonial territories where government handouts, "white" schools and running water are supposed to be accepted as improvements over a previously primitive way of life.

Visitors to Canada will frequently encounter a certain tragic pathos in the native peoples here.

fied political entity. Increasingly, Indian groups have pressed for more economically valuable land claims – some, like the Dene, have demanded their own nation – and have made some headway with a government whose patronage has ultimately ghettoized them. No longer submissive, the Canadian native peoples have emerged as a force to be reckoned with.

French-Canadians

When Jacques Cartier established a settlement along the St Lawrence at the sites of Hochelaga and Stadacona, little did he know that his fledgling community would become Canada's "black sheep of the family". Abandoned early on by

France and reluctantly adopted by Britain, French Canada continues to embody a fierce ethnic pride, a distinct cultural identity and a tenacious traditionalism, especially in Québec.

A British-dominated Canada has often treated Québécois demands for cultural autonomy as the cries of a spoilt child. But like dousing an already well lit bonfire with gasoline, nothing seems to irk French-Canadians more than trivializing the issue of French ethnicity in Canada. As a result, *Canadien* attitudes towards *les*

English attempt to understand and respect each other's differences.

Biculturalism overshadows the quest for a cultural mosaic. For the French-Canadians it is not just a matter of being a part of the puzzle but rather being recognized as a primary part, as a founding partner of the nation. As one parent put it: "I want my children to grow up in a French culture which has spoken French for many years. I detest the American television and music which has been the diet of our youth for so many years. The rest

> **RECOGNITION**
>
> For the French-Canadians it is a matter of being recognized as a founding partner of the nation

anglais (which is just about everybody else) range from a stern disapproval to outright racial hatred. Most English-speaking Canadians are capable of showing the same range.

There are still some places in Québec where a few words in English will only get one stony and silent stares. There are still places in Ontario where the introduction of French classes into a high school will produce hordes of angry parents threatening to transfer their children. There are, however, places where the French and the

ABOVE FROM LEFT TO RIGHT: women from Manitoba; a Dene native; a Greek-Canadian ready to dance; and a Scottish highlander.

of Canada is English, why should we be English too?" Québec's separatists lost the 1995 referendum – but by just over one percent of the vote, and the quest for French integrity within Canada is far from being a settled issue.

English, Scottish and Irish

Canada is predominantly a "British" nation. The pomp and ceremony of public events, the ubiquitous portraits of the royal family in hallways and antechambers, the presence of a parliamentary government – all are suggestive of an English ancestry.

The history of Anglo-Saxons in Canada is much more piebald in nature than British traditions might acknowledge. In addition to those immigrants who traveled directly from England, Canada received many of its British inhabitants via the United States. Loyalist "Yankees" fleeing the American War of Independence entered Canada in droves during the latter part of the 18th century and tipped the scales in favor of an Anglo-dominated population.

English immigrants were joined by Irish refugees (many of whom were victims of the potato famine) who had come across the Atlantic in search of food and employment. Similarly, Scottish immigrants, pushed off their lands to make room for sheep farms, ventured

been named after a favorite spot or person in the British Isles: Prince Edward Island, Queen Charlotte Islands, New Glasgow, Oxford, Windsor, Caledonia, Liverpool.

Germans and Scandinavians

Next to the French and British, peoples of Germanic stock were the earliest European settlers. Germans came to Nova Scotia as early as 1750 and founded the town of Lunenburg in 1753. This tiny metropolis eventually became a thriving center of Maritime shipbuilding. German Loyalists also immigrated to Upper Canada and established a (still-existing) community in a

to Canada. The combination of Irish Catholics and Protestant Scots was rarely compatible and riots, usually occurring during one of the annual parades, were common in the 19th century. Not surprisingly some of the tension still persists.

Today, cultural images of the Irish, English and Scottish are almost everywhere in Canada, whether it be in the opening session of parliament or in a neighborhood pub. Highland games, Irish folk festivals and political ceremonies (which seem strangely imitative of Buckingham Palace's changing of the guard) are common sights in each of the provinces.

A glance across a map of Canada will also reveal that many of the towns and cities have

town they named Berlin, which was later changed to Kitchener during World War I, owing to fear of anti-German sentiments.

Swedes, Norwegians and Finns have also established settlements in the west that have retained their original ethnic flavor. A group of Icelanders fostered the prairie town of Gimli, "a hallway of heaven", and have managed to thrive on the successful commercial production of two Canadian delicacies: goldeye and whitefish.

Ukrainians

The 18th century saw the influx of thousands of Ukrainians – "the people of sheepskin coats" as popular journalism of the time named them.

Attracted by free farms in the west and undaunted by prairie fields, Ukrainians first settled in Manitoba, Saskatchewan and Alberta. They were later joined by Polish, Czech, Slovak and Serbo-Croatian immigrants.

Next to French-Canadians, Ukrainians have perhaps the most vocal and assertive sense of a national identity. Recognition of their ethnic heritage is pursued aggressively through powerful organizations, daily and weekly Ukrainian newspapers, and political groups that have spearheaded

UKRAINIAN SETTLERS

Next to French-Canadians, Ukrainians have the most vocal and assertive sense of a national identity

human. Some established roots in Canada and through sheer endurance and a knack for frugality, they eventually prospered in the face of racist government policies (one of which was the imposition of a "head tax").

The success of the Chinese in developing lucrative commercial enterprises led to the Chinese Immigration Act of 1923 – sparked by the jealousy of white merchants – which effectively barred the immigration of Asians to Canada until the 1960s when immigration policies were relaxed. Pow-

the struggle to give languages other than French and English official status in Canada.

The Chinese

Abandoning the exhausted goldfields of California, the Chinese first came to British Columbia as miners. Others arrived in the 1880s, recruited to work in the railway gangs that built the Canadian-Pacific.

Laboring under duress and in dangerous conditions, many Chinese died in the service of a country that considered them to be less than

Left: the Salvation Army meets today's generation in Toronto. **Above:** keeping cool in Elora, Ontario.

erful in small commerce and visible as doctors, lawyers, professors and engineers, Chinese-Canadians have emerged as a new voice in the debate about ethnic identity.

Summing up the feelings that most minority Canadians experience in possessing a hyphenated heritage, one Chinese-Canadian has commented: "The assumption is that there is a given culture and that there are add-on ethnic groups who are somehow second-class citizens… We must encourage equality among Canadians through a mixing of experience, exposure to each other and participation in our culture. We need to establish areas where there is a similarity or a shared experience."

THE FRENCH AND THE ENGLISH

Historically the relationship between the French and English speaking peoples has been uneasy, if not explosive. But bridges are being built across the cultural divide

Eight hundred kilometers (500 miles) separate Québec City from Toronto. Situated between these two cities are cosmopolitan Montréal and loyalist Kingston; in between these two cultural focal points lie 300 years of Canadian history, tradition and circumstance. Québec City is archetypically French, politi-

cally resistant, insular, its visual splendor and old worldliness reminding one of Europe, of the ancient towns in Normandy or along the Rhine. Toronto is both typically English Canadian and North American. The city serves as an economic center for the entire country. Everything from its skyline, waterfront, endless suburban sprawl, down to its professional baseball team locates Toronto squarely in the mode of a North American urban center. These two cities share in common a vast country called Canada. But what else do they share? What does inner-city Québec – the narrow lanes lined with cafés and bistros, the sheer cliff face edging the town from the St Lawrence River to Place Royale – share

in common with the silver and black skyscrapers of downtown Toronto? One city communicates in French, the other in English. One city looks to France for its cultural heritage, to the French for much of its music, film and literature. The other city combines the vestiges of British custom, an indigenous literary community, with strong leanings towards American popular culture.

The Confederation of Canada in 1867 did not guarantee that these two worlds would unite. Economically, Québec and English Canada do communicate on a regular basis. The St Lawrence Seaway, the Trans-Canada Highway, the tourist charms of Montréal and Québec City serve to maintain a steady flow of traffic between the two communities. Economic ties, along with political commitments (through the federal government in Ottawa), remain strong. Canada is a country – a viable and functioning nation noted for its size and natural wealth. Yet a fragmentation exists. Once beyond economic and political considerations, the ties between the French and English grow more tenuous, more problematic. Eventually a difficult question must be asked; culturally, spiritually, what do these two worlds share in common?

The weight of history

Any understanding of French-English relations today must begin deep in North American history. There one finds the ancient animosities between England and France carried over to the New World, dividing settlers, forcing those who should have united in a hostile environment to isolate themselves and create boundaries on a continent so immense that such artificial divisions should have been unnecessary.

The weight of history was upon the New World from its inception. North America was a battleground for the English and French to wage imperial war. In Canada the French arrivals tended to settle along the banks of the St Lawrence, in the area now known as Québec, with the English establishing themselves farther inland, initially in the Great Lakes region. By the 1750s, less than 100 years after the first influx of population, the lines were already drawn between French and English areas. With the rapid growth of the English community to the south, which was soon to be called the United States of America, the French were in a very real way already isolated and defeated.

The population of New France was less than a tenth of that of the English colonies. From the very beginning the French in North America were a visible minority. What consolation they found derived largely from the "safety net" of mother France, watching over their interests. After 1759, however, this too disappeared. The English subsequent military possession of Québec virtually ruled out hope of reconciliation between the two communities.

The British were the victors, the conquerors; the Québécois the defeated. French settlers were abandoned by their country and left to fend for themselves on an English continent. A pattern emerged in 1759 which persists to this day; a largely English-speaking government dictating to a largely French-speaking population.

By 1867 a fairly rigid socio-economic relationship had developed. The English in Québec were the bankers, businessmen, the power brokers; the French were the workers, farmers, the *paysans* who created and sustained a rich folk culture. In other words, the English continued to play the role of victors, and to reap the spoils.

What Confederation gave Québec was a political framework for change – the provincial government. The decentralized nature of the agreement, allotting considerable power to each province, should have provided the Québécois with a means to reassert themselves. For many reasons this did not really happen for almost 100 years. The seeds were planted, however, the very same day the country was born.

English bosses

The first half of this century saw little overt change in the situation. English Canada expanded, solidified its borders, with Ontario coming quickly to dominate the economic scene. Naturally the markets of Montréal and Québec City were worth preserving. Statistic after statistic from this period suggests basic

---

FAR LEFT: Toronto theatrical thinks it's all a bit of a laugh, while **(RIGHT)** the hauteur of a French-descended Québecois shows disdain for the English.

problems: companies located in Québec with an entirely French-speaking work staff but entirely English-speaking management; blatant instances of discrimination against the natives; English-Canadian businessmen earning huge profits from the province without reinvesting it in the economy.

Provincial politicians – especially the looming figure of Maurice Duplessis – found themselves supporting English hierarchies to maintain their political lives, seeking outside investment, inadvertently suppressing the aspirations of the Québécois to strengthen the province's financial status.

In English Canada the French were seen as backward, remote, a society of Catholic farmers and blue-collar workers with little to offer the rest of the country except the brilliant hockey players of the Montréal Canadiens. English was simply not spoken in most parts of the province. Even in Montréal, where the anglophone community ignored the Québécois culture around them, the majority of the inhabitants were unable to function in the economic and political language of Canada. Ottawa and Toronto controlled the lives of most Québécois, dictated their social and economic position, yet had relatively little to do with their day-to-day existence.

In 1964 Montréal writer Hugh MacLennan published his novel *Two Solitudes*, a bleak if honest account of relations between the two communities. MacLennan portrayed both English and French Canada as inward looking, defensive, unwilling to take the necessary step to end the "solitude" in which each exists.

This phrase, "two solitudes", has come to be an important part of the Canadian vocabulary. To some extent the term is as applicable today as it was 40 years ago. Yet the period between 1955 and 1980 saw a remarkable change in the fabric of both groups. In particular, the cultural and political awakening in Québec has altered into the Separatist Movement of the 1970s, had its root in cultural change is important. These artists were demanding that the Québécois take pride in their culture, their language, themselves. Québec was something quite different from the rest of Canada, it needed to be vigilant and protective of its identity.

The October Crisis

From the enlightened leadership of premiers Jean Lesage and Daniel Johnson, to the rise of René Lévesque and the Parti Québécois, the movement's political wing grew in prominence. A dark manifestation of this impulse, the ter-

completely the dynamics of the relationship. In the last 30 years tremendous upheaval has come close to dissolving the Canadian experiment.

A quiet revolution

In the late 1950s a group of artists, journalists, and political figures – Pierre Trudeau among them – began to assert the cause of Québec. Known in retrospect as the *révolution tranquille*, this movement sought to create an autonomy entirely known as Québec, by strengthening the cultural fabric of the society. Song writers, poets, playwrights, painters, film-makers, historians all rallied around the concept. That the *révolution tranquille*, which developed rorist group FLQ, gained much attention in the English Canadian press. While Albertans or Torontonians were oblivious to the cultural excitement in Québec, to the music of Gilles Vigneault, the writing of Hubert Aquin or Jacques Godbout, they were more than well aware of the bombings in Montréal. For them Québec's struggle for selfhood consisted of denunciations of English Canada, cries for independence, and a terrorist group running amok. This distortion was disastrous to the cause of French-English relations.

The assassination of Pierre Laporte in 1970 – the so called "October Crisis" – proved to be a decisive moment. For a few days English

Canadians witnessed with horror a brief and extremely exaggerated period of social unrest.

Suddenly all the news reports were filled with images of soldiers, of house-to-house searches, and of army checkpoints, not in Northern Ireland or Chile but in Québec, Canada.

These media images, the image of Prime Minister Pierre Trudeau declaring a state of emergency from Ottawa, did more to bring the cause of Québec's self-assertion to the surface than did any of the more positive events of the

DIVIDE AND RULE

Québec's growing pains forced people to examine their priorities. What if Québec separated?

a mind of its own and, because of the nature of provincial governments, a mandate within the Confederation to exert considerable control over its internal affairs. In a sense the gauntlet had been thrown at the feet of English Canada. During the years of the *révolution tranquille* the remainder of the country had been experiencing changes of its own, more quiet, peaceful changes, but ones sufficiently strong to demand a kind of self-examination. Immigration to urban centers, in particular Toronto and

previous 20 years. The October Crisis was indeed a baptism of fire.

The proud province

The remainder of the decade saw the strengthening of the Parti Québécois, their assumption of power in 1976, and the referendum on sovereignty-association of 1980. By the summer of that year, Québec, while apparently unwilling to sever its ties with the rest of Canada, had emerged as a force to be reckoned with. Assertive, self-possessed, the province now had

LEFT: *calèche* drivers in Québec. ABOVE: socializing in Montréal, a French-style café bar.

Vancouver, had altered the social make-up.

The "WASP" (White Anglo-Saxon Protestant) dominance of commerce in central Canada, while still unquestionable, was being flavored by new influences, new faces. Just as Montréal was no longer simply English controlled and French populated, so was Toronto no longer simply "hogtown" – city of the English money, and Anglo-Saxon temperament. Québec's growing pains greatly affected the economics of Canada. They also forced people to examine their priorities, their sense of self. What if Québec separated? Would Canada survive? The prospect of collapse was ludicrous and unthinkable, yet it was also very possible. Canada lurched quietly under a weight of implications. Québec's struggle had initiated a kind of collective debate on the nature of its national being.

After the close-run referendum of 1995, Québec remains a partner in Confederation. At times difficult economic conditions have relegated questions of independence to a secondary position, but the issue will not go away and the final outcome is far from certain. To some extent the Québecois' point has been made; ownership of business is again largely internally (or US) controlled, French is the language of commerce and politics, while the cultural life of the province continues to thrive. But relations the considerable wall which already existed between itself and English Canada.

What then is there to be said of Canada's bilingual experiment? At first glance one might be tempted to pronounce it an outright failure. The fate of Pierre Trudeau's official bilingualism policies of the 1970s – a symbolic attempt at presenting a unified front – seems indicative of the reality of the situation. Why should someone in Calgary be expected to learn French? Why should Manitoba have its laws written in French as well as in English? Québec – the "French" part of Canada – is many miles away and disinterested if not hostile towards the rest

between English Canada and Québec have been further strained during the implementation of many of these policies.

The exodus from Montréal of many English-language businesses offered – for the media, anyway – graphic representation of the isolation of the communities. Legislation brought in by the Parti Québécois, especially the controversial language bill 101, has left a bitter taste in the mouths of non-French speakers in Québec, along with frequent charges of discrimination against the government. Indeed many of the policies have had the effect of further entrenching the country's "two solitudes." In its bid to fortify, Québec has seemingly added bricks to of the country. English Canada's roots lie in Britain. England's queen is Canada's queen; the governor general, a representative of the throne, still offers nominal approval of all bills passed in parliament.

Culturally and economically the affinities are with the United States. Québec, now that much of the fuss about independence is in abeyance, remains more or less an excellent vacationing spot – exotic, foreign, yet still safely within the arms of Confederation.

Québec's culture is all but ignored. English Canada has had almost no exposure to the wealth of literature, film and visual art which has emerged in the past 20 years. One cannot overstate how much language can divide. Yet there is room for optimism. Perhaps the most constructive way of viewing the recent events in Canada is with an understanding of their necessity in forging a genuine relationship between the two communities. English Canada can no longer patronize Québec. It can no longer view the Québecois as impoverished and backward.

Likewise, French Canada can no longer complain of subjugation and inequality. No longer can they view English Canada as distant

A NOTE OF OPTIMISM

While English Canada can no longer patronize Québec ...French Canada can no longer complain of inequality

the Rideau Canal and the Ottawa River, one has a fine view of the twin city on the far shore – Hull. The far shore in this instance signifies not only the Ontario-Québec border, but also the cultural borders within the country. Hull is a typical small Québécois city. Low income, working-class streets of row houses with front porches, grocery shops and cafés open until late, the town possesses a definite charm. A half dozen bridges connect it with Ottawa. In the evenings, citizens of the larger city might cross one of the bridges to take

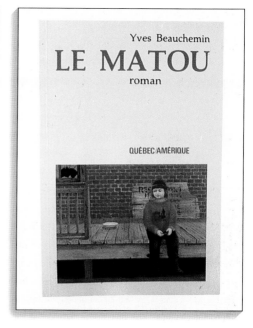

employers, selfish and indifferent to their needs. The communities are equal, siblings in a difficult experiment in nationhood.

Across the bridge

A visitor to Ottawa cannot help but be startled by the contrasts embodied there. The city itself is regal, stately, a miniature of an old English town. Home to the country's parliament, and to a number of British political institutions, Ottawa seems the quintessence of English Canada. From the parliament building, gazing out over

LEFT AND ABOVE LEFT: in Québec signs in French are the norm. ABOVE RIGHT: literary evidence of bilingualism.

advantage of the extended bar hours in Québec. Hull is a lively night out, a night away from the pressures of working in the decision-making center of all Canada. Otherwise, the two cities have relatively little to do with each other. On these bridges languages suddenly change, perspectives alter, biases and stereotypes come to the surface. On these bridges one is confronted with the reality of Canada's "two solitudes".

For the most part commerce-laden trucks comprise the largest percentage of traffic. Business is as usual. Little else is that way, however. Contact between the communities remains infrequent, tenuous, ill at ease. But the bridges are there. Anyone is free to cross over them.

THE INUIT

For 5,000 years the Inuit and their predecessors have inhabited the Arctic region.

Only now is their culture and way of life earning the respect it deserves

It was just a few years ago that Canadians living south of the 60th parallel were surprised to learn that Eskimos have always called themselves Inuit, the "only people". The name is quite apt when you consider that the Inuit were the only people who had lived in the Arctic for thousands of years. The "Eskimo" is not Inuit but Indian, meaning "eaters of raw meat".

It is hardly a name that fairly describes these resilient soft-spoken people. The fact that for so long Euro-Canadians called the Inuit "Eskimo" speaks volumes of the silence that has existed between the two.

The Arctic environment has not always been static; it has undergone both warming and freezing trends with a variety of life living in the region at different periods. The north's nomadic inhabitants have had to adapt accordingly.

The first group to live in the north migrated across the Bering Strait during a relatively warm period. This nomadic group, known as the pre-Dorset, spread north into the Arctic Archipelago and east to Greenland. These people hunted seals and fished the waters of the Arctic Ocean.

Around 1500 BC a cooling trend began in the north that forced them to move south onto the mainland. It was during this period that the pre-Dorset culture evolved into the indigenous Dorset culture. These people now stalked the caribou herds instead of hunting on the sea ice. Their cultural links with their cousins west of the Bering Strait were broken.

Yet the Dorset are not the direct ancestors of the Inuit. Starting in AD 900 another warming trend began that heralded the migration of the Thule from Alaska. The Thule hunted sea mammals. With the retreat of the permanent ice pack on the mainland, the whales, seals and walruses swam through the Bering Strait and into the Beaufort Sea. The Thule were quick to follow.

The Thule differed from the Dorset in several respects: one was that they lived in fairly large settlements along the coastline, unlike the

Dorset, who lived in small family groups. Secondly, the Thule were technically more sophisticated hunters. Ironically, about AD 1500, the Thule found themselves in a position similar to that of the Dorset 3,000 years earlier; yet another mini-ice age had set in. This period saw the ice pack grow so large that the number of

sea mammals passing through the Bering Strait to the Arctic Ocean decreased and the migration patterns of the caribou shifted southward. The Thule adapted; they broke into smaller groups and became more nomadic. It is these people who are called the Inuit.

Arctic home

The Inuit chose to make the Arctic their home, in spite of the adversity they encountered. Their history, culture and language are unlike that of the Indians, who moved south soon after crossing the Bering Strait.

In that harsh unforgiving land they perfected the building of igloos and airtight kayaks; they

LEFT: Arctic entertainment – a community trampoline.
RIGHT: an Inuit boy peeps out for the camera.

became experts in tracking polar bear and seal on the Arctic ice. Although they suffered from famines and exposure, the Inuit stayed.

Forged with their innate ability for innovation was a humility that made the Inuit a tolerant, stoic society, who accepted their limitations in a land where darkness reigns for six months of the year. The fact the Inuit have endured for centuries becomes even more remarkable when one considers that despite the technological sophistication that Euro-Canadians have brought with them, they still encounter tremendous emotional upheaval in adjusting to the isolation of northern climes. The Inuit do not have that sense of iso-

stowed him away, like booty, in the hold. After the search for gold and the passage both proved fruitless, Frobisher returned to England, where the north's "ambassador" was put on display for royalty. The grief-stricken man soon died in captivity of European disease, and ever since the Inuit have traditionally distrusted foreign involvement in their affairs.

Apart from Frobisher's expedition, the Inuit of the high Arctic seldom had contact with any Europeans until 1818, with the arrival of whaling vessels in the eastern Arctic Ocean. These whalers risked navigating through the treacherous iceberg-laden Davis Strait in search of the

lation; for them the wind, the snow, the seasons of light and darkness are a part of their life.

European contact

In 1576 the isolation of the Inuit ended when Martin Frobisher, an Elizabethan explorer and privateer, sailed into a large bay on Baffin Island in search of gold and the Northwest Passage to India. He was met by Inuit who circled his vessel in their kayaks. In a bid to coax them closer he rang a bell, the sound of which had probably never been heard in the Arctic before.

One curious Inuit was close enough to reach for the bell. Frobisher, with both hands, pulled the man and kayak up and into the ship and

bowhead whale. In the 1830s there were a series of whaling disasters, with vessels becoming trapped by the Arctic ice.

A solution to these problems was to establish whaling stations. In the 1840s William Penny, a typically shrewd Scottish whaling captain, began to employ local Inuit at his station on Baffin Island. He found that they were exceptional whalers, hardly surprizing when you consider that the Inuit had been whaling for centuries. Soon Penny and other astute whalers began to adopt the warm clothing, harpoons and other paraphernalia of Inuit technology.

Unfortunately, because the whaling proved so successful by the 1880s, the bowhead whale population in the Arctic was greatly reduced. In spite of the decline in the whaling industry, the contact with the southerners, or *Kabloonat*, continued because of the growing presence throughout the Arctic of the Hudson's Bay Company, Canada's largest fur-trading company. Although the Inuit maintained their semi-nomadic life, they began to rely upon trapping and trading to provide for themselves.

This shift away from living solely off the land to a barter and then cash-based economy pro-

DECLINE IN POPULATION

Penny noted on his arrival in Baffin Island in the 1840s there were 1,000 Inuit, but by 1858 there were only 350

how alone they were. While the Inuit economy was collapsing, missionaries were filing reports to medical authorities that tuberculosis and influenza epidemics were annihilating the Inuit.

William Penny noted in his journals that on his arrival on Baffin Island in the 1840s there were 1,000 Inuit, but by 1858 there were only 350. One anthropologist studying at Coronation Gulf found in the 1920s that 30 percent of the Inuit population had died from influenza over a 14-year period. Similarly in Coppermine

vided them with guns, butter, cooking utensils and foodstuffs. For some, the Hudson's Bay stores became a base or second home.

However, this arrangement changed when, in the 1840s, the price of furs fell dramatically. Suddenly they could no longer purchase ammunition or other goods that had become essential. On Baffin Island, two-thirds of the Hudson's Bay stores closed their doors.

A long period of starvation and deprivation began. Except for missionaries who struggled to aid the Inuit, the "only people" discovered

LEFT: a spear-hunting expedition. **ABOVE:** captured on film beside the Great Whale River (*circa* 1920).

in 1931, 19 cases of TB among a population of 100 were found.

The government intervenes

For the most part until the late 1940s the Canadian government had ignored the Inuit. However, after prodding from the churches, it began to take action. In 1950 medical authorities ordered 1,600 Inuit, or 14 percent of their population, to sanitoriums in Edmonton and Montréal. This action, though medically necessary, was devastating for the Inuit, the vast majority of whom had never left the north. As well as treating tuberculosis, the health authorities were startled by the high rates of infant mortality. In

1958 infant mortality was at 257 per 1,000 live births. By 1970 it had dropped to 100 per 1,000, and in 1981 it was 21 per 1,000.

The federal government introduced more than a medical plan for the Inuit; they coupled together policies that would rocket the Inuit into Canadian society. The central tenet of all these policies was to encourage them to abandon their nomadic life and move into government-built permanent settlements. These artificial communities provided housing, medical facilities, churches and schools.

However well-intentioned policy-makers were, they failed to understand that the Arctic began to rediscover the Inuit's remarkable skill in carving and other traditional crafts, and funding was made available to develop these skills.

As a result the Inuit co-ops have flourished, receiving international recognition for their work in several mediums, including stonecut prints, stencil, sculpture and carving.

The co-op system has evolved to become more than enclaves for artists. In many communities it manages hunting expeditions, municipal services and trading posts. The philosophy behind the co-ops reflects the Inuit concept of community and what western thinking might call egalitarianism. In abstract terms the

tundra and ocean is home for the Inuit. From the beginning of this resettlement period the Inuit struggled to retain their identity. The first step was made in 1959; in that year the Cape Dorset Artists Co-op was formed on Baffin Island.

A sense of community

Over the centuries the Inuit have worked with ivory, stone, bones and skins to make clothing, utensils, hunting tools, toys and religious amulets. Often intricate designs were patterned onto these objects. When whalers arrived trading began to take place, with the resourceful Inuit even manufacturing ivory cribbage boards for trade. It was in the 1950s that southerners

Inuit co-op is the synthesis of a traditional social matrix being placed within a capitalist framework. Such a configuration can bewilder outsiders. One example is a community in the Arctic that has for several years run a successful polar-bear hunt for visiting southerners. According to territorial law, dog teams must only be used for the hunt, not snowmobiles.

One year, the man chosen for the role of hunt leader by the co-op was not a particularly adept dogsledder. Another man, who had a reputation as a skillful traditional hunter, was not considered. Consequently, after a two-week expedition, the party failed to shoot a bear. The big game hunters were somewhat dissatisfied. The reasoning the co-op gave for hiring the poorer hunter was that he had no steady employment, while the best hunter already held a wage-paying position. This was perceived to be of more importance than providing the best service to the high-spending tourists.

The attitude of the community was not that they were penalizing one individual over another but that they were maintaining a communal harmony. For the same reason Inuit town meetings tend to be excruciatingly long, and are filled with long meditative silences.

COMMUNITY LIFE

The Inuit have developed into a self-sacrificing people who are remarkably tolerant of community goals

encouraged to have many children; many start from puberty and still bear children into their mid-forties. If it happens that for whatever reason the parents of a child are unable to support it, the child will be adopted by the grandparents, or by some other member of the family. There is less of a taboo attached to illegitimacy here than in the south, which is partly attributable to a sense of communal responsiblity for children. In the 1960s the Inuit were baffled when social workers first attempted to formalize adoption proce-

Generally, the Inuit will not leave a local meeting before a well thought-out consensus has been forged. Because of the relative isolation of the villages the Inuit have developed into a self-sacrificing people who are remarkably tolerant and respectful of community goals.

The next generation

The importance of children in a society where the line between nuclear family, extended family and community is blurred, cannot be overestimated. Traditionally, Inuit women are

dures. Social workers were equally puzzled when they attempted to unravel whose children belonged to whom.

Within the Inuit community there is clearly a different set of values operating from those in the south. The pursuit of personal wealth is for the most part played down. The respect one can earn in the eyes of the community is important. For men this respect has traditionally been earned through becoming a good hunter or trapper, although this is now changing. Carving, despite its lucrative nature, is not regarded as such a worthy occupation.

It is this intrinsic relationship to the land that has made the Inuit, particularly the older Inuit,

LEFT: Inuit women passing the time of day. **RIGHT:** the younger generation taking a picture on the ice.

ambivalent towards higher education and the learning of "southern skills". Mandatory school attendance was seen by the Inuit as a method of either forcing them to follow their children in to government-built communities, or to separate them from their children by sending them away to school. Many Inuit questioned the relevance and importance of their children learning subjects like English, science and math.

The federal government has attempted to integrate the educational system into the community. A program was introduced to recruit and train Inuit to become teachers. It failed in part because few Inuit were willing to leave their

community for eight months at a time to train.

Over the past 15 years it has been the young adult Inuit population that has been the most affected by the complications of living in a world with two divergent cultures. These Inuit are the product of a "baby boom" that swept across the Arctic in the 1950s and 1960s. This boom was in part created by the lowering of infant mortality and generally improved health.

The question that faces this group of people is how they will support themselves in the coming years. As part of government policy many left home to attend regional high schools. That isolation had a disorienting effect. They failed to learn, as their parents had, how to live off the

land, how to keep warm while out in the cold, how to build an igloo. Knowledge of survival techniques forms the basis of their culture. Yet, if the young are not familiar with traditional skills and their implicit philosophy, they also have not acquired the skills necessary to compete for management positions in government or in industry.

The continuity in passing down the knowledge and communal values from one generation to another has been broken. The resulting problems have manifested themselves in alcoholism, vandalism and suicide.

Adopting new technology

There can be little doubt that technology has brought about a safer and more comfortable life for the Inuit. They ride on snowmobiles, watch TV with VCR attachments and hunt with high-powered rifles. They have running water. They no longer live in snow houses. The question that many would ask is: has technology made the Inuit more or less Inuit? Yet these modern tools by themselves are not the issue.

The Inuit have traditionally been eager to adopt new technology. In their environment they had to be great innovators. It is what the technology represents that bothers the Inuit. Recall the first encounter of Frobisher. It was not the bell that trapped the Inuit but the unscrupulous intentions of the bell ringer.

The challenge for the Inuit is to make technology their own; then they will be rulers in their own land. In adopting this technology, the Inuit must look to their knowledge of how they lived in the past if they are to avoid becoming strangers in their own land.

For more than 5,000 years the Inuit and their predecessors have politically, aesthetically and socially been building and rebuilding a society that has allowed them to live independently in an environment where others could not bear the physical and psychological pressure.

It is their unique culture that has allowed them to make the north their home. If the young are not permitted to capture that spirit, if they are overwhelmed and bullied by western society, then they will no longer be Inuit. And Canadian society will lose a fragment of its colorful mosaic.

LEFT: an Inuit with his young daughter. RIGHT: bags packed and "ready to go".

ART AND PERFORMANCE

*Canadians have worked with great determination to create a vibrant artistic,
dramatic and literary scene that reflects the talents of its multicultural population*

Although artistically Canada is a young nation, its contribution to the arts world is impressive. It has renowned writers, respected literary events and drama festivals, and the third largest English-language publishing industry in the world. It is in the forefront of new music, and has much-admired theater and dance. Its French films have won accolades and it vies for the title of Hollywood North.

Creative Canadians have had to struggle to get their voices heard: against strict Catholicism and the narrow Protestantism which to this day encourages writers to list other occupations on their dust jackets, proof that they also know how to work at a real job. They have also had to make themselves heard above the clamor of their much louder neighbor.

Given that most Canadians live within 240 km (150 miles) of the United States border, with saturation from North American cable television, newspapers, books and magazines, fast food and shopping mall franchises, the lure of America has always been strong. A quick browse through the daily papers makes one doubt Canadian culture even exists.

Canadian cultural advocates argue their distinctions loudly, making frequent front page announcements of breaches in international contracts and improprieties in the sale of publishing houses to foreign investors. Since World War II, artists' efforts to develop a sense of identity have been backed by government protection of "cultural industries" in any negotiations with the Americans.

In spite of this intervention, after the war most serious Canadian artists went abroad, to England, France, and America. That changed in the 1960s, thanks to Canada's anti-American sentiment amplified by the Vietnam War, when Canada was identified with the distinctive voices of Leonard Cohen, Joni Mitchell and Neil Young. Generous government grants at that time changed the attitude of the audience and made it possible for the next generation of artists to have successful careers at home.

Regional strengths

The search for a cultural identity is also an attempt to unify a vast land. Canada's most

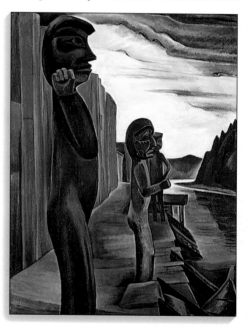

popular authors and artists are often identified with specific regions: Montréal with the work of Mordecai Richler and Gabrielle Roy; Halifax with Hugh MacLennan; Manitoba with Margaret Laurence; British Columbia with Emily Carr and Ethel Wilson; and rural Ontario with Stephen Leacock and Alice Munro.

Early Canadian society, with its long winters and agricultural industrial base, presented many limitations and few opportunities. Nineteenth-century artists in a sparsely populated country were isolated and without an audience. In the colonial period, Canadians turned to France, Britain and the US for inspiration and approval. This trend continued in the 20th century. In a

---

PRECEDING PAGES: West Coast totems. **LEFT:** the singer k.d. lang. **ABOVE RIGHT:** *Blunden Harbour, circa* 1928-30, by Emily Carr, who painted in British Columbia.

country suspicious of the arts, Canadians found fuller expression of their talent, and public recognition, abroad.

The tough, demanding industries such as mining, forestry, and fishing ("rocks, logs, and fish", as the poets say) and hardships of the pioneers left them little time for artistic creativity. Pioneering writers such as Susannah Moodie considered that escape was to be found only in the grave. Even today many writers and artists continue to dwell on the subject matter provided by their ancestral pasts, their immigrant backgrounds, and the pioneering days of their forebears.

copies around the world. The short stories of Morley Callaghan, the pioneer novels of Frederick Philip Grove, and the struggle of pioneering artists in the poems of E.J. Pratt; tales of shipwrecks and seal hunts, and epics of rail building and missionaries were serious efforts at describing the Canadian experience.

Policy changes

Since the 1960s, when Prime Minister Lester Pearson gave the country a flag, it has been easier to be a creative artist in Canada. The Centennial in 1967, and the famed Expo fair in Montréal, "Man and His World", generated a

But nowhere is the difference of experience more defined than between the English speakers and the French speakers of Québec, the "two solitudes" as the novelist Hugh MacLennan decribed it. The constant tension between the two communities has given a demanding dynamic to the country, which can be seen reflected in the arts.

Such 19th-century movements as the Canada First Movement, the Confederation Poets (or Maple Leaf school) drew inspiration from the landscape. Lucy Maud Montgomery's (1874–1942) still popular *Anne of Green Gables* novels and Mazo de la Roche's 16 impossibly romantic *Jalna* (1927) novels would sell millions of

new-found nationalism, which in turn stimulated a cultural revolution.

Since 1957, the Canada Council budget has grown from $1.5 million to over $200 million for support of the arts, humanities, and social sciences. Although artistic subsidy has many critics, its supporters argue that the policy has enabled Canadian culture to grow across the entire spectrum of activities.

Theater

Ceremonials and ritual drama are central to aboriginal and Inuit social and religious activities, which use masks, costumes and properties to enhance dialogue. Great ritual drama, like the

Kwakiutl, takes five months to perform. Most Canadians are not familiar with these traditions. Native theater and dance companies and a Native Writing School are now addressing centuries of neglect.

Since the mushrooming of theaters in the 1970s, Canadian audiences have had a choice of regional theaters and the summer festivals that take place across the country.

The most prominent of these events is the Stratford Festival in Stratford, Ontario, founded in 1953. With an operating budget of over $30

Canadian musical, *Anne of Green Gables*, first performed in 1964.

It has taken time for Canadian plays to emerge. In the 1960s and 1970s some small alternative theaters opened, including Vancouver's Savage God, Toronto's Theater Passe Muraille, Factory Theater, Tarragon Theater and Halifax's Neptune Theater. They shifted the emphasis to Canadian plays and more controversial content.The formation of what was to become the Playwrights Union of Canada in 1972 led to the turnaround in the-

THE BARD PLAYS ON

The Stratford Shakespeare Festival in Ontario attracts an audience of 500,000 to its annual six-month season

million, and attendance of around 525,000 people, it presents a six-month season of Shakespeare's plays, a variety of musicals, and contemporary classics. Without Stratford, there would not be theater in Canada. As a training ground for performers, directors, and stage technicians, it sets the standards which other companies aspire to, or sometimes react against.

Next in prominence is the Shaw Festival, founded in 1962, which features the plays of George Bernard Shaw. Charlottetown, on Prince Edward Island, is home of the longest-running

LEFT: the disturbingly realistic art of Alex Colville.
ABOVE: Shakespeare at the Stratford Festival, Ontario.

ater and the publishing and production of hundreds of Canadian plays. Among the leading second generation of playwrights are Carol Bolt, Rex Deverell, Michael Cook, David Fennario, David French, Ken Mitchell, John Murrell, Rick Salutin, Judith Thompson, Ken Gass, Guy Sprung and George Walker.

A major challenge to the nearly 90 smaller theaters in Toronto has been the successes of the blockbuster international musicals, such as *Les Misérables* and *Phantom of the Opera*. The Princess of Wales Theater in Toronto was built especially for *Miss Saigon*.

In financially difficult times, special interest theaters have grown. Comedy cabarets, theaters for senior citizens, children, feminist and gay theaters, and experimental media such as Video-cabaret, demonstrated a lively approach. Toronto's comedy club acts are broadcast worldwide, and have nurtured such talents as Dan Ackroyd, John Candy and Martin Shortt.

Dance

The Canadian Ballet Festival movement, launched in Winnipeg in 1948 to give dancers a sense of what their colleagues were doing else-where in Canada, soon developed into a strong regional ballet movement across the country. Four years later the first experimental dance

company, Les Grand Ballets Canadiens, was established in Montréal, while Celia Franca established Toronto's National Ballet of Canada, developing international ballet stars such as Karen Kain and Veronica Tenant.

With freedom to create non-literal and abstract dance, modern dance experiment com-panies such as the Paula Ross Company and Anna Wyman Dance Theater of Vancouver, the Toronto Dance Theater, Robert Desrosiers of Montréal as well as dozens of independent choreographers challenged the classics of the larger companies and, by the 1980s, classical ballet and modern dance companies were eager to learn from each other.

Painting and sculpture

Prior to Confederation, documentary tradition dominated Canadian painting. Painters were usually inspired by European trends. But land-scape painting changed immeasurably in Canada in 1920 with the first exhibition of the modernist Group of Seven (1920–33). The painting tended to post-Impressionist manner-isms, with great dabs of mysticism. It caught the public interest, and their claim to be Canada's national painters aroused furious debate among critics. An associate of the group, Tom Thomson, became romanticized after his mysterious drowning in 1917. His paintings of pine trees and lakes are among Canada's most famous images.

Most painters, however, worked in isolation and were disregarded, experiencing success posthumously. Emily Carr (1871–1945) for example, worked on the west coast, painting forests, Indian villages and totem poles with bold strokes and color. David Milne (1882–1953) introduced modernist techniques and he, too, found success in his later years.

Montréal painters did not respond to the call of the Group of Seven. Alfred Pellan, Paul Emile Bordaus, and John Lyman returned from France inspired by the example of modern European art, especially cubism and surrealism and called themselves the Automatists, after their 1947 exhibition. The most prominent of the younger painters was Jean-Paul Riopelle. Québec painting would soon show the new dynamics of color, abstract expressionism, and non-figurative forms.

The painter Bordaus' 1948 manifesto *Refus Global* advocated spiritual and artistic freedom and attacked the repressive government and church in Québec culture. The manifesto affected change in all the artistic disciplines, including dance, music, theater, painting and sculpture. Despite his own personal hardships, Bordaus's paintings and manifesto represent one of the major achievements of Canadian art.

There was an unprecedented expansion in the visual arts after World War II. Professional artists, galleries, exhibitions, and art magazines multiplied, as did museums, public art galleries and artist-run spaces as well as fine arts depart-ments in colleges and universities.

Toronto dominated artistic expression in the 1950s. Jack Bush, Harold Town, William Ronald were the major painters of a group who took the name Painters Eleven and promoted the new American abstractions of the 1950s.

A new generation of Toronto painters centered around the Av Issac's gallery reflected wide interests, from Dada to abstract expressionism, Joyce Wieland, Robert Markle and Gordon Raynor.

The most original of these was Michael Snow, who soon proved himself master of a wide range of media, including photography, film, sculpture, painting and music. Many other Canadian artists likewise became key innova-

FIRST NATIONS ART

Since the mid-20th century the work of Inuit artists has begun to achieve the recognition it long deserved

ing is now being challenged as the leading edge of the visual arts by conceptual art, sculpture, video, performance and the work of the First Nations people.

Since the mid-20th century the work of Inuit artists has begun to achieve the recognition it long deserved, winning international acclaim, and becoming an important force in the country's culture. In the 1950s and 1960s, with the help of the Hudson's Bay Company and Canadian Handicrafts Guild, Inuit-owned co-operatives were set up in many Arctic

tors in experimental cinema. In London, a similar group began with Jack Chambers, Tony Urquhart, Paterson Ewen and the late Greg Curnoe. A small community, they spoke to the needs of regionalism as a powerful force especially in sculpture and installation work.

Today the dominant painter of the Atlantic region is Alex Colville, who has set a new standard for realistic art with his enigmatic images. In the west, Jack Shadbolt, Toni Onley, Gordon Smith, and the late Roy Kiyooka, experimented with a variety of styles and techniques. Paint-

communities, as much as a source of income for the people as to encourage local skills. One of the most prominent Inuit sculptors is David Ruben Piqoukun whose work in stone is inspired by his concern for the loss of his culture and the spiritual beliefs of his ancestors. Art galleries countrywide, including Québec's fine Musée Canadien des Civilisations in Hull, are devoting space to First People's art.

Music

From the classics to pop, the music scene in Canada has been consistently and extraordinarily varied. It has a strong lyric quality, and is never afraid of breaking new ground. Outdoor

LEFT: dancing in the street – open-air ballet in Ottawa.
ABOVE: the Montréal Symphony Orchestra warms up.

concerts are an important part of the summer in every part of the country.

The founding of the Canadian League of Composers in 1951 and the Canadian Music Center (1959) coincided with national cultural stirrings of the postwar period. The younger generation of musicians born in the 1930s are some of Canada's best known composers, such as John Weinzweig, Barbara Pentland, and Jean Papineau-Coutours.

After the 1967 Centennial a remarkable flourishing of compositions explored new directions; chance music, electro-accoustic music, with R. Murray Schafer pre-eminent among the *avant*

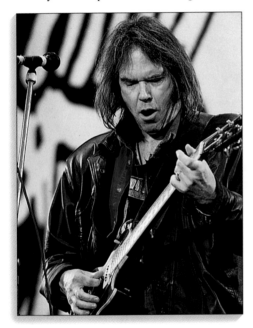

garde. Individual performers with worldwide reputations include classical pianist Glenn Gould, Teresa Stratas, Salome Bey, Jon Vickers, Maureen Forrester, and Steven Staryk. Among great 20th-century jazz artists, pianists Oscar Peterson and Paul Bley and the trumpeter Maynard Ferguson paved the way.

The opening of new concert halls, such as Roy Thomson Hall in Toronto, anticipated great success for serious music. Canada has more than 100 professional or community orchestras, although the classical orchestras face a difficult funding time, as they do in many parts of the world. In its intensity and diversity, the country's music has assumed astonishing propor-

tions. Toronto has become a center for new and alternative music in North America and a leader in Caribbean-influenced pop.

In the summer, live rock concerts feature the best of national and international performers. Canadian hard-rock groups such as Rush and The Tragically Hip and singers such as Bryan Adams or Céline Dion stage sell-out concerts. Every town in Canada has rock clubs and bars. The CRTC (Canadian Radio-Television and Telecommunications Commission) regulatory agency insures at least 35 percent of music played on the radio is Canadian and that 50–60 percent of broadcast television is of Canadian content – a policy that has helped to give many popular Canadian performers a start to their careers.

There is a long history of singer-songwriters who have found international fame since the 1960s, including Leonard Cohen, Paul Anka, Joni Mitchell, Neil Young, Rita MacNeil, Stompin' Tom Conners and k.d. lang. A national party station, MUCH-Music, takes popular music seriously, showcasing the political, social and artistic side of contemporary performers from English, French, and multicultural Canada. Though jazz clubs have short histories in most Canadian cities, the summer jazz and blues festivals have up to 25 acts criss-crossing the country. Even Cape Breton Island in Nova Scotia has a summer folk festival.

Modern writing

While prose and poetry has a long history in Canada, generally readership was small; most works were not published until accepted by a US or British company. Conservative tastes and puritanism limited subject matter. Some early publishing ventures such as First Statement and Contact Press attracted the *avant garde* of the 1940s and 1950s. The formation of the League of Canadian Poets (1966) and the Writers' Union of Canada (1973), the Playwrights Union of Canada, and Royal Commissions in 1971 and 1973 to investigate foreign ownership of the publishing industry encouraged writers of serious ambition to remain in Canada. By the 1970s sales of Canadian books rose to 25 percent of the billion dollar industry.

Not only did the audience for Canadian writers increase, but so did their self respect. Toronto's Harborfront Reading Series, founded by poet Greg Gatenby in 1974, is pre-eminent in the world for its festival of national and international literary celebrities. In the 1960s writing communities flourished coast to coast. By the 1970s, with federal and provincial government support, publishing houses were in every province. More than three dozen literary magazines are published out of every region, the most prominent being *Canadian Fiction Magazine*, *The Malahat Review*, *Liberté*, *Descant*, *Quarry*, and *Fiddlehead*. The Canadian Magazine Publisher's Association, an important lobby group, has around 400 titles on its membership list.

LITERARY OUTLOOK

Feminist, women of color, gay, lesbian and native writing are at the forefront of literary change in Canada

Atwood, Audrey Thomas, Gabrielle Roy and Mavis Gallant are widely read and part of the school curriculum. All have been deeply involved in the topics of women's roles and social change. Feminist writing, women of color, gay and lesbian writing, and native writing are at the forefront of change in literary Canada.

Film and television

Canada is considered part of the American domestic film market, and Canadian films have limited opportunities to be shown in Canadian

Major literary critics, such as George Woodcock, Marshall McLuhan, and Northrop Frye set new standards for the appreciation of Canadian letters. Toronto remains the place for writers to head for and, apart from its Harborfront reading Series, there is a year-round literary hub. This is home for Margaret Atwood, Michael Ondaatje and, until his death in 1996, the grand old man of Canadian letters, Robertson Davies.

In many ways, Canadian women writers attract the most interest overseas. Margaret Laurence, Adele Wiseman, Alice Munro, Margaret

LEFT: veteran rock star Neil Young. ABOVE: filming in a Canadian television studio.

theaters and on television. World War II changed the Canadian film industry, with the formation of the National Film Board, which began to train and develop Canadian film makers. The NFB is practically synonymous with quality documentary film. Beginning with documentary film needed for the war effort, the NFB expanded into areas of ethnic groups, Canadian art, and social problems. The 1974 development of a women's studio at the NFB led to the making of many good films on a variety of topics from a woman's perspective.

As film-makers began to turn their interest from educational and informative films to the fiction feature film, Hollywood moved to protect its interest. Despite complex talks of quota systems, there was virtually no feature film-making in English Canada until the 1960s. However, Canada did command worldwide respect for work in short film animation. Nearly all the films were produced by the NFB. Especially outstanding is the work of Norman McLaren, who dazzled millions around the world with such films as *Neighbours* which won an Academy Award (1952), and *Pas de Deux* (1969), with its haunting dance sequence developed with an optical printer.

The development of the 16mm camera and the influence of French "new wave" film-mak-

ing led to a more personalized cinema. By 1970 such films as Don Shebib's *Goin' Down the Road* and Gordon Pinsent's *The Rowdyman* were commercial and artistic successes. An important figure was David Cronenberg, whose low budget horror films created a cult following at home; he has since become a major international director with such films as *The Fly, M. Butterfly* and, most recently, eXistenZ. The 1967 development of the Canadian Film Corporation (now Telefilm Canada) was a significant step, with $10 million in production funds available. The 1970s however, put the emphasis on film as an industry and a tax shelter, not a cultural product. The result was considered a disaster.

Despite this, there were notable successes in the 1980s by such filmmakers as Anne Wheeler, Philip Boros, Patricia Rozema, and Atom Egoyan, who won a Director's Prize at Cannes. The world-famous Toronto International Film Festival held each September is considered as important as Cannes. In fact, it was recently polled in the *Los Angeles Times* as number one in the world. In 1999, its Perspective Canada program included 19 features and 37 shorts.

Québec film-making likewise has had its share of failures, but in recent years it has produced some exceptional prize-winning films: Denys Archand was twice nominated for an Academy Award for *Jesus of Montréal* and *The Decline and Fall of the American Empire*. Claude Jutra and Jean Beaudin made significant titles such as *Mon Oncle Antoine* and *J.A. Martin, Photographe*.

While the early 1990s saw the Québec film industry again in crisis, with less money and fewer productions, in the late 1990s there has been a significant resurgence. Almost half the films in the 1999 Toronto International Film Festival's Perspective Canada program were made in Québec, including features from veterans Jean Beaudin and Michel Brault. Director François Girard has earned critical acclaim internationally with his ambitious musical epic, *The Red Violin*.

If there have been hard times at home, actors have sought fame further afield. From Mary Pickford and Lorne Greene to Margot Kidder and Christopher Plummer, many well known Canadian actors, producers, and writers found success in Hollywood. Larger-than-life heroes Superman, Ghostbusters and Rambo originated from Canadian-born authors. Ottawa-born comedian Dan Aykroyd even made a tongue-in-cheek feature film about the Canadian plot to take over the Hollywood empire. Such figures are recognised internationally, just as many of Canada's writers and musicians have made their names outside the country. Sometimes it is a surprise to discover that such well-known people are Canadian, and not American after all. But their roots are the same as those who have stayed at home, where local arts are still active day after day. There is no lack of opportunity of attending a performance.

LEFT: Canadian actress Juliette Binoche in *The English Patient.* **RIGHT:** vibrant French-Canadian culture.

THE ANCIENT ART OF THE INUIT COMES OF AGE

Canada's galleries and museums are at last giving due recognition to its rich heritage of native art dating back to the Dorset peoples of 600 BC.

Traditionally there was no word for "art" in the Inukitut language. Early carvings tended to be functional – tools, weapons and utensils – or they were used for spiritual purposes, such as amulets and masks. The sculptures of animals, birds, sea creatures and human figures simply represented daily life.

The first people to produce what is now recognized as "art" belonged to the Dorset culture (*circa* 600 BC–AD 1000). They used ivory, bone and wood and, like today's artists, kept as close as possible to the original shape of the material. The items were often small and remarkably smooth.

INUIT ANCESTORS

Thule people, the ancestors of today's Inuit, migrated east from northern Alaska around AD 1000, and replaced the Dorset inhabitants. Their art was more feminine and less ritualistic. It consisted of decorated everyday items such as combs, needlecases, pendants and female figurines, harpoon toggles and gaming pieces. In the 16th and 17th centuries a colder climate led to the demise of the Thule culture. European exploration was beginning and the Inuit started to barter their carvings with the white man.

In the 1940s, the federal government began to encourage the developement of Inuit art in recognition of the much needed income it could bring to the isolated communities. With the help of the Hudson's Bay Company and the Canadian Handicrafts Guild, Inuit-owned co-operatives were set up across the Arctic.

Contemporary Inuit art has finally achieved international status, and across Canada museums and galleries are devoting space to its exhibition.

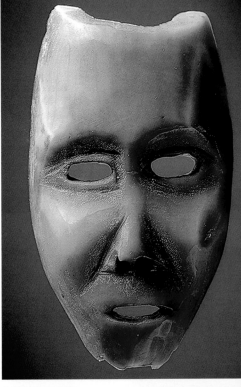

△ **HAUNTING FACE**
This miniature ivory mask is representative of the early Dorset culture in the Hudson Strait region, when carvings generally had spiritual connotations. It was probably one of the many items used in shamanic rituals.

◁ **BEAR FIGHT**
Animals, birds and fish are often the subject of Inuit sculptures. This small carving (8 cm/3 in tall) of two polar bears wrestling was made in the 19th century on the northwest coast.

▷ **MOTHER LOVE**
My Mother and Myself, Ovilu Tunnillie, dark green stone, 1990. Tunnillie is one of an acclaimed group of Cape Dorset artists, who as a child was taught to carve by her father.

CONTEMPORARY ARTISTS AT WORK

△ DECORATIVE WORK
Necklace with a carved pendant figure. Carvings were often made to be given as good luck charms.

△ CARVED AMULET
Amulets such as this Thule culture example in the form of a fish were one of the most common items of carving.

▽ EVERYDAY OBJECTS
This comb in the shape of a female figure, *circa* AD 1000, is an example of decorative Thule culture artwork.

BUYING WORK TODAY
Beware of imitations. Inuit artworks are much sought after and there has been a proliferation of cheap reproductions made from plastic, ceramics and "cast stone." To be sure of authenticity look for the "igloo tag" and the artist's incised signature.

▷ THE HUNTSMAN
Comb incised with an archer standing over a man and animals, *circa* 500 BC. Dorset hunters are thought to have brought bows and arrows to North America from Asia.

Inuit art comprises a great number of regional styles determined by tradition, available materials and the artists themselves.

Many of today's artists have experienced life away from their communities, and combine the various cultural influences in their work. David Ruben Piqtoukun, whose sculptures have been exhibited widely, was born in 1950 north of the Mackenzie River Delta. His father was a hunter and trapper. At the age of five Piqtoukun, like so many of his generation, was sent away to school and forced to come to terms with an English culture. His work has a strong spiritual element on the one hand, while also exploring the impact of outside influences on his culture. He lives in Toronto and regularly returns to his home community of Paulatuk.

Ovilu Tunnillie also experienced life in an alien world, which is reflected in her carving. She was born on Baffin Island in 1949. As a child she contracted tuberculosis and spent three years in hospitals in Manitoba. On her return she had to relearn both her language and way of life. Taught by her father, Tunnillie began carving in 1972. She now lives in Cape Dorset and her sculptures are exhibited worldwide.

CANADA AT WORK

A vigorous entrepreneurial capitalism and the realities of geography and language make for a business scene that is as diverse as the country itself

From the lakefront freeway into downtown Toronto, six major office towers dominate the skyline. Until recently, these represented the Canadian private sector: five banks and a regulated telephone monopoly.

Canadian business is compact, highly concentrated, and less sprawling than the American counterpart with which it is so closely integrated. The economy has been characterized by a high degree of oligopoly and either state regulation or out-and-out government ownership.

The origins of the country's business are in the fishing, fur trading and farming economies of the Atlantic, the "old Northwest" and New France. The first enterprises of consequence were the far-flung, paramilitarily-organized and highly paternalistic trading outfits such as the Hudson's Bay Company, which still exists as one of the country's largest department store firms, now known simply as The Bay. Canada's immense resources, her proximity to major markets, the demands of her vast distances, and the physical challenges of extracting wealth from a harsh land have created the basic characteristics of economic life. Resource extraction for export, conducted by large, stable enterprises, under close supervision or direct ownership by the state, is much of the story of business to this day. The power and size of its banks and insurance companies, railroad and transport firms, and mining and forestry conglomerates is a testament to the continuities of the country's economic life from its earliest beginnings.

Thinking big

Yet, as with so many other things Canadian, continuity with the past and a staid exterior obscures other traits. Canada is not without its audacious enterprisers. Whether it's Prime Minister Maconald and US railroad manager William Van Horne using state capital to build a transcontinental railway in the 1870s, Robert Campeau using junk bonds to acquire a chunk

of the American retailing industry in the 1980s, Paul and Albert Reichmann trading on the strength of their reputation to build London's Canary Wharf, or cable baron Ted Rogers using big banks' loans to compete with the telephone monopoly to build Canada's information highway, Canadian business has often dared to think

big. Of course, some of the bigness is imported. Southern Ontario's industrial economy is dominated by General Motors, Ford and Chrysler. Canada has higher percentages of foreign ownership than any other major industrialized economy. This causes the country's "economic nationalists" to wince, but foreign capital has played a major role in the transformation of Canada from a fishing ground into the world's seventh-largest industrial power.

The close integration of Canadian and US business is most evident in the Québec City-to-Windsor corridor, a string of urban areas including Montréal and Toronto which are connected by Highway 401, known euphemistically as

Traditional and contemporary industries: a mineworker (**LEFT**) and optical cables (**RIGHT**).

"Canada's Main Street". Along the highway itself, the only thing to remind travelers they are not in America is the appearance of Petro-Canada gas stations. Within the cities themselves familiar outlets abound, but often in close competition with home-grown companies. For urban casual clothing, the Gap competes in the same shopping malls with Toronto success story Roots. The hamburgers at Harvey's go head to head with the patties of McDonald's. And Clearly Canadian spring water will often edge Evian among discerning café *habitués*.

The basic feel of Toronto's business core is familiar to any who have turned the wheels of

Francisco and Los Angeles, Vancouver's offices fill up at 7am-ish to do business with Torontonians whose watches show it's 10am back East. Although to night-hawks in the city's burgeoning film and television industry (Vancouver makes a wonderful stand-in for a pricey American urban location shoot) this early rising smacks of Central Canadian domination, the coastal crowd takes its revenge by skipping out at 3.30pm to work the cellular phone on boats, or atop the ski slopes.

Yet Vancouver is surely the most Eastern of North America's west-coast cities, wired into a pattern of horizontal trade flows that underpin

commerce in Atlanta, Dallas, or Chicago. At 5pm on a Friday, the bars in the underground malls at King and Bay streets are filled with graying bankers in a haze of tobacco smoke, junior associate lawyers in high heels and mid-length skirts, and lager-swilling bond traders unsure of which table to slide up to. Little different from Québec City or Montréal, where civil servants and inductees into *la nouvelle élite du business Québécois* work the same groove.

The West Coast experience

The pattern of discrete but tangible variance with American neighbors is also evident in Vancouver. Like their fellow "left-coasters" in San

much of Canadian economics and politics. North America's natural trade flows are north-south, yet the country secured its existence through a deliberate government policy of moving Western raw material for manufacturing in Toronto and Montréal, rather than Chicago or New York.

The city's enormous prosperity (fueled to no small extent in the 1990s by Hong Kongers looking for a safe place just in case) and sun-drenched lifestyle mute the usual grousing about the economic clout of Toronto and Montréal. In the prairies and Atlantic Canada, however, the economic resentments are a lot closer to the surface. Calgary's oil patch players still smile at their embargo-threatening war-cry of 1975, "let the Eastern bastards freeze in the dark." And down East (*don't* ever call Newfoundland a Maritime province, it's part of "Atlantic Canada"), those with long memories can bend your ear in the club rooms of Halifax about the running down of Nova Scotia's steel and ship-building industries by Montréal and Toronto interests in the late 19th century.

Calgary's bright prosperity, based on some of the best oil and gas exploration companies in

FACING REALITY

Today one of the world's most comprehensive welfare states is undergoing a painful re-appraisal

been underway since the mid-1980s. Three fundamentals are changing rapidly. First, the system of horizontal trade flows – which built the industrial heartland of Ontario and Québec – is crumbling. With the advent of the Canada-US Free Trade Agreement (1988) and the North American Free Trade Agreement which included Mexico (1993), the tariff walls behind which trade moved east-west have fallen, making it easier for BC's wood and Alberta's gas to go to California, prairie wheat to bake the mid-West's

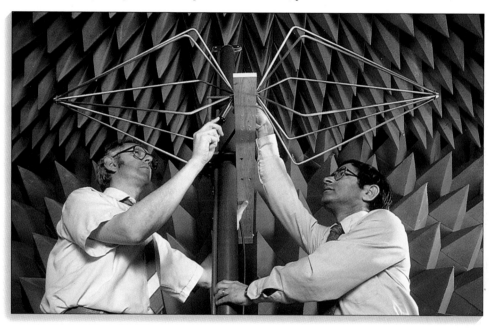

the world, and Wild-West chutzpah may make a visitor wonder what there is to be jealous of about business life in Ontario.

Change is in the wind

In the outports of Newfoundland, where 10 generations have jigged for cod and now the fishery has been closed because of local and foreign over-fishing, the collapse of a way of life can hardly be shrugged off. Nor can the immense restructuring of the Canadian economy that has

LEFT: moving pictures – here a scene from the TV series *Macgyver* – are big business in the West.
ABOVE: engineering research in Ottawa.

bread, and Ontario and Québec's auto parts to go to car plants in Ohio. This has spelt the end of Canada's postwar "branch-plant economy", forcing multinationals in Canada to compete for world product mandates, and home-grown businesses to take on the best in the world without a captive domestic market.

The twin free trade agreements have also forced Canada to address seriously its cost structures. For two generations, Canadian governments have erected one of the world's most comprehensive welfare states, with generous unemployment insurance, welfare rates and a universal system of 100 percent tax-supported medicare. The new realities of global competition, as well as the chronic indebtedness of Canadian governments, are forcing a painful reappraisal of the affordability of these programs.

New ways of working

A third foundation of Canada's economy, state enterprise, is also on the way out. Historically, Canadian governments have stepped in where private capital was unwilling to invest, funding the construction of the Canadian Pacific Railway in the last century, and directly owning anything from a national airline (Air Canada) to an oil company (PetroCan) and giant electrical utilities (Ontario Hydro and Hydro Québec).

The market revolution of the 1980s and the need for ready cash on the part of governments has reversed this historic trend. Air Canada is now 100 percent privately-owned; PetroCan has been privatized; some even toy with the idea of selling off the national television network, the Canadian Broadcasting Corporation. These "Crown Corporations", once touted as a uniquely "Canadian way" of generating wealth in the face of geography and size limitations, now seem destined for the history books.

The undermining of the east-west trading system, the welfare state and mixed enterprise is reflective of an even more profound change that is facing Canada and every other major trading nation. New technology has brought about the globalization that makes protected markets obsolete, forced countries to address their cost structures in a global context, and generated an information revolution that makes bureaucratic-style government enterprise uncompetitive. Canada is one of the most highly technologized economies in the world, with one of the finest telephone systems, densest broadcasting webs and highest rates of computer usage on earth.

As the world shifts towards a high-tech economy, Canada is adapting. The glamour investments on the Toronto Stock Exchange are not giant industrial concerns like Stelco, great mining conglomerates like Noranda, or forestry megaliths such as MacMillan Bloedel. Instead, companies like Bombardier (mass transit equipment), Corel (computer graphics software) and Newbridge (telephone switching devices) now fire the brokers' imaginations.

For Vancouver's TV producers, Calgary's natural gas marketers, Toronto's infotech innovators, and Montréal's computer animators, it is a brave new world. For others, like Hamilton's steelworkers, Faro's mine managers, or Newfoundland's dory fishermen, it is a world of bewildering, sometimes brutal change and loss. For the middle classes of Canada – its middle managers, civil servants, shopkeepers and health care workers – this world seems newly troubling, throwing shadows on areas of economic activity that always seemed secure.

To watch Canadian business life at the start of the 21st century is nothing less than to watch the drama of a very comfortable country that has received an abrupt wake-up call. Some are scrambling to get in the shower and get to work. Others try fitfully to roll over and sleep a little longer. Still others blame the messengers, and some simply lament the passing of time.

Five minutes' drive from the gleaming bank towers of Toronto's downtown lies a de-industrialized wilderness of weeded-over railroad and mothballed appliance factories. Inside the nearby converted warehouses, software designers, boutique securities dealers and urban development wizards log on to the pulses and rhythms of the new global economy. The beat of Canadian business – half dirge and half techno-pop – is on.

LEFT: Hydro Québec power cables. **RIGHT:** engineer for Bombardier, the mass transit specialists.

FOOD AND DRINK

Canadian cuisine is a coming together of a multitude of influences from the native peoples to recent immigrants, using the country's own abundant food resources

As Prime Minister Wilfrid Laurier said in 1905, "The 20th century is Canada's century," and nowhere is it so true as in the country's culinary development. Until then Canada had been made up of widely separate regions, where the early settlers had faced many challenges and Canadian cuisine consisted of eating what you could hunt, fish and forage – most of it learned from the native peoples, which saved many a fur trader and explorer from certain starvation.

As a result, there is no single cuisine that defines Canada, but one made up of several components: aboriginal, French, British, American, and the countless ethnic cuisines brought by successive waves of immigrants.

There are more than 80 cultural communities, and some 5,000 restaurants at any given time in a city such as Toronto alone, where the Italian population is the largest in any city outside Italy, and Chinatown is the second largest and busiest in North America. If the food or the ingredient exists, it's probably available somewhere in Canada, certainly in her large cities.

Foreign visitors can be forgiven if at first glance they think Canadian food is interchangeable with American; Canada is as much a hamburger/hotdog/taco culture, not least because of close geographical proximity, which also explains the similar, sometimes identical supermarket fare. American food trends quickly find their way across the border and the cuisines of the Southwest, California, and New Orleans have become part of the culinary landscape.

Eating to live

The present trend of eating for health is a difficult concept for most Canadians, who are more apt to think in terms of eating to live, especially during the long winters when the need for comfort food is at its height. Canadian food reflects

the country, which is not a homogeneous space. Cutting a long swath from east to west, from the Atlantic Provinces to the Prairies, to the West Coast and the Northern Territories, it defies the usual north-south ease of commerce and movement of most countries. Canada's secret is that it had a good, healthy diet millennia before being

discovered by white people: it was a country of abundant game, fish, corn, squash, beans, berries and greens. Much of the food eaten by settlers and colonials was an attempt to recreate food from the countries they had left behind; this not being practicable they began to adapt to the land and learn from the native people – and that ability to adapt is still there.

Food for all tastes

The sheer volume of immigrants brought with it all manner of food styles. The country is almost pathologically receptive to whatever is going on in the outside world, so what you can expect in Canada is a cuisine that's like an

---

LEFT: a Dene native at a Wilderness Camp in the Yukon demonstrates how to prepare salmon in the traditional way. **RIGHT:** Canada produces a rich variety of foods – here corn on the cob makes an eye-catching display.

orchestra, with native and colonial strands and a plethora of richly varied imports. Churrasco-style (Portuguese) barbecued chicken can coexist with Jamaican ginger beer, as can Armenian *lahmajoon* with Thai salad and real ale from a microbrewery. Here cuisines are ones that have come to stay. But in terms of melding them all into one distinct Canadian school of cookery, it has largely failed, unless you consider pubs serving linguini specials along with warm English beer and butter tarts for dessert a distinct Canadian experience.

Of course there are the regional specialties that the whole country enjoys: lobster, mussels, butter, brown sugar, corn or maple syrup and sometimes raisins or pecan nuts, are the subject of endless debates on whether they should be runny or chewy, use sugar or syrup alone, and who makes the best butter tarts in the country.

Creating a Canadian cuisine

Today Canada produces some of the finest chefs in the world, among them those who are practising what they describe as "market-inspired" cuisine, as they look less outside Canada for method and style, and more inwards, recognizing the excellence and abundance of the country's local ingredients, creating dishes with

oysters and fiddlehead greens from the Maritimes, and Prince Edward Island's famous potatoes; Quebec's maple sugar pie, Oka cheese and old-style bagels; Prairie beef, possibly the best on the continent; Manitoba wild rice, a nutty-tasting aquatic grass rather than a grain, and an aboriginal food long considered a delicacy; British Columbia salmon and Nanaimo bars; to say nothing of the beloved butter tarts.

Butter tarts are so uniquely Canadian, and so ubiquitous, that they deserve special mention. Their origins are unclear but one theory claims they are an adaptation of the southern US pecan pie or old-fashioned backwoods pies. These little pastry shells, filled with a sticky mixture of

PICK OF THE WINES

Ontario is Canada's largest wine producer, under a VQA (Vintner's Quality Assurance) appellation also adopted by British Columbia. Québec and Nova Scotia make wine on a smaller scale. Watch out for:

☞ Inniskillen, Stoney Ridge, Marynissen Estates and Pelee Island from Ontario
☞ Summerhill Estate, Mission Hill and Kettle Valley from British Columbia.

Canada is now the largest producer of Icewine, thanks to its consistent winters. This acclaimed nectar, made from grapes that are picked when frozen, is served as an apéritif or with dessert.

blueberries, fiddlehead greens, wild rice, maple syrup, bison, and seafood like sharkmeat. One well-known Toronto chef, Michael Stadtlander, even took to growing his own field of greens in the Ontario countryside, where he also serves dinner regularly.

Thanks to these chefs and the cookery book writers, Canadians have become more aware of their country's gastronomic resources, and are cultivating and using more homegrown foods.

The **Atlantic provinces** in eastern Canada

ter of British social life, German farmers settled in Lunenburg, and the Loyalists brought with them the flavors of New England and the South.

In the 19th century, Irish and Scottish immigrants introduced oatcakes, scones and shortbread. Some of North America's oldest culinary traditions are to be found in Newfoundland, settled by Irish, and English fishermen. Salt cod, salt beef and pork, pease pudding, molasses and root vegetables are staples, although these days the cod is more likely to be *gratinée*.

HOMEGROWN FOODS

Canadians have become aware of their gastronomic resources and are using more homegrown foods

saw four centuries of French settlement, where French cooking, combined with ways of using wild game, fish and maple syrup learned from the Micmac Indians, survives to this day. Although those settlers, the Acadians, were driven out by the British (and moved south where they settled in Louisiana, today's Cajuns), their influence is still evident in Nova Scotia and New Brunswick, in *galettes* (oatmeal and molasses cookies), *poutines* (baked fruit puddings) and sugar pies. Halifax became the cen-

Most of **Québec**'s early settlers came from northeastern France, some from the Charente-Maritime region south of Bordeaux. Their hardy rural background, combined with native methods such as tapping maple trees for syrup, served them well in the hard winters of New France. After the British conquest of 1759, Irish and Scottish immigrants introduced potato and oatmeal to the local cooking.

Today Québec's cuisine remains a mixture of its traditional fare, such as *tourtière* – a pie whose filling varies according to region, the most popular being ground pork simmered with garlic, onion, celery and seasonings – and contemporary French cuisine, including some of

LEFT: waffles and syrup, a Canadian breakfast speciality. **ABOVE:** on Prince Edward Island locals and visitors alike gather for celebratory lobster dinners.

France's specialties, such as foie gras, which is produced locally and shipped across Canada.

Southern **Ontario** is still a great agricultural centre, where long before the first settlers arrived, the Huron and Iroquois nations were cultivating corn, pumpkins and beans. Those first settlers were the United Empire Loyalists who came from America after the Revolution; they were mostly of British stock, with a number of people of German and other European ancestry, as well as Six Nations Indians. One of Ontario's earliest farmers, John McIntosh, developed the now-famous McIntosh apple. Among its best produce are peaches, corn and field tomatoes. The province's culinary contribution today rests on its agricultural produce, its wines from Niagara vineyards, and Toronto's unbelievable array of ethnic cuisines.

Manitoba, **Saskatchewan** and **Alberta** have come a long way since immigrant Scottish crofters to the prairies survived on little more than oatmeal, and the Métis cooked in the way of their Indian and French-Canadian heritage. Mennonites, Scandinavians from the Dakotas, and American ranchers moved north, and cowboys lived on steak, beans, flapjacks and raisin pies. Ukrainians, Eastern Europeans, Icelanders, European Jews and Chinese, with their own culinary traditions, contributed to shifting the emphasis from a heavily British one to a brave new multicultural world.

British Columbia came into being largely thanks to the gold rush. With that rush came countless roadhouses to feed the fortune-hunters, where beef stews and baked beans were popular fare. In the Okanagan Valley, orchards were planted; today the Okanagan also produces fine wines. Vancouver, once a meat-and-potatoes town, has turned gourmet, reflecting the West Coast culinary boom from Seattle and Los Angeles to the south.

British Columbia is the birthplace of the popular Nanaimo bar, a very sweet, layered, no-bake confection made of butter, cocoa, graham cracker crumbs, nuts, shredded coconut, and chocolate, whose recipe first surfaced in the *Vancouver Sun* in the 1950s.

The gourmet influence hasn't yet extended to the **Yukon** and **Northwest Territories**. These provinces cover one-third of Canada's landmass, but their population is sparse, mostly made up of Inuit and the Dene (native Indians of the northern prairies and northern British Columbia, as well as the Yukon and Northwest Territories), and outsiders working in government and business. Here the introduction of canned and packaged foods has resulted in the loss of many of the traditional ways of eating, such as caribou, moose, seal and wild fowl.

Café society

If the European-style café, complete with croissants and *pains-au-chocolat*, was once to be found only in Montréal, and the *espresso* bar in the Italian neighborhoods, cafés now dot the landscape, ripe enough even for the US coffee giant Starbucks to move in and settle down comfortably, despite that territory being occupied by its competitor, the homegrown Second Cup. *Caffe-latte* and *espresso* have become the norm, and *pain-au-chocolat* is a fast food.

RIGHT: Café life in Vancouver, the gourmet capital of the West Coast.

A QUICK GUIDE TO CANADIAN BEERS

Part of the Canadian stereotype is beer, along with back bacon, hockey and winter. But Canada has long had a brewing industry, until recently dominated by the Big Two: Molson and Labatts. There were some smaller regional breweries, but they were all brewing pretty much the same mainstream lager.

Things began to change in the mid-1980s, with the establishment of microbreweries, whose mission was to offer natural beers of distinction and taste, and brewpubs in every province and the Northwest Territories, producing an array of specialty beers, including various types of ale, stout, bitter and bock. This latest phase of Canada's brewing history seems, by all accounts, to be here to stay.

Among the labels to watch for are:

- Upper Canada
- Sleeman
- Conners
- Moosehead
- Les Brasseurs du Nord
- Great Western
- Drummond
- Arctic Brewing Company

PLACES

A detailed guide to the entire country, with principal sites cross-referenced by number to the maps

Canada is the second-largest country in the world, stretching over 5,500 km (3,400 miles) from the Atlantic Ocean to the Pacific and over 4,600 km (2,900 miles) from the northern tip of Ellesmere Island to the United States border.

This sprawling country is not, of course, fully inhabited: 89 percent of the land has no permanent population. In sharp contrast are the urban areas, where nearly 80 percent of Canadians live in large centers located within a few hours' drive of the southern border, mostly in Ontario or Québec.

The country is dominated by its three principal cities, Toronto, Montréal and Vancouver – places that have elicited comment for centuries. Toronto, for instance, invited the observation by Charles Mackay in 1859 that "there is a Yankee look about the place… a pushing, thrusting, business-like smart appearance." Montréal, on the other hand, "conveys the idea of a substantial, handsomely built European town, with modern improvements of half French, half English architecture." Vancouver is a different kind of place altogether, looking neither to America nor to Europe for its inspiration.

Rural Canada is divided into 10 provinces and three territories. Newfoundland is the most easterly province, bordering the North Atlantic; Prince Edward Island is the smallest; Nova Scotia is a peninsula; New Brunswick is nearly rectangular with a gentle, undulating surface; Québec's and Ontario's cities and high-octane profiles make them the best known; while the prairie provinces of Manitoba, Saskatchewan and Alberta are less exuberant.

Rudyard Kipling was particularly pleased with the clean air and pioneering spirit of British Columbia, observing in 1908 that "such a land is good for an energetic man. It is also not so bad for the loafer." Energy is certainly needed for exploring Canada's three territories: the Yukon, the Northwest Territories and, its newest one, Nunavut. You can loaf here, too. Or anywhere in Canada, for that matter.

PRECEDING PAGES: homeward bound at King's Landing, New Brunswick; along the tracks in Alberta; lonely waters in Lake Louise. **LEFT:** Rocky Mountain pass.

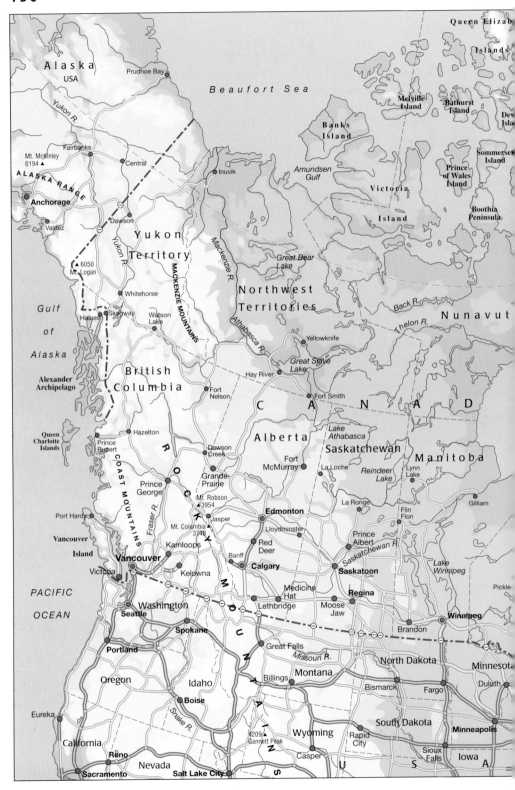

Queen Elizab
Islands

Alaska
USA

Beaufort Sea

Prudhoe Bay

Melville
Island

Bathurst
Island

Dev
Isla

Banks
Island

Sommerse
Island

Yukon R.

Fairbanks

Mt. McKinley
6194 ▲

Central

Inuvik

Amundsen
Gulf

Prince
of Wales
Island

ALASKA RANGE

Anchorage

Dawson

Victoria

Island

Boothia
Peninsula

Valdez

Yukon
Territory

6050
▲ Mt. Logan

Great Bear
Lake

Yukon R.

Whitehorse

MACKENZIE MOUNTAINS

Mackenzie R.

Northwest
Territories

Back R.

Nunavut

Gulf

of

Alaska

Haines

Skagway

Watson
Lake

Athabasca R.

Yellowknife

Thelon R.

Great Slave
Lake

Alexander
Archipelago

British
Columbia

Hay River

Fort
Nelson

Fort Smith

C A N A D

Queen
Charlotte
Islands

Hazelton

Alberta

Lake
Athabasca

Saskatchewan

Manitoba

Prince
Rupert

COAST MOUNTAINS

Dawson
Creek

Fort
McMurray

La Loche

Reindeer
Lake

Lynn
Lake

Gilliam

Port Hardy

Grande-
Prairie

La Ronge

ROCKY

Prince
George

Mt. Robson
▲3954

Flin
Flon

Fraser R.

Jasper

Lloydminster

Prince
Albert

Saskatchewan R.

Vancouver

Mt. Columbia
3748

Edmonton

Island

Kamloops

Red
Deer

Lake
Winnipeg

Pickle

Vancouver

Banff

Calgary

Saskatoon

Victoria

Kelowna

Medicine
Hat

Regina

PACIFIC

Lethbridge

Moose
Jaw

Winnipeg

OCEAN

Washington

Seattle

Spokane

Brandon

Portland

Great Falls

Missouri R.

North Dakota

Minnesot

Oregon

Idaho

Billings

Montana

Bismarck

Fargo

Duluth

Snake R.

Boise

South Dakota

Minneapolis

Eureka

4209
Gannett Peak

Wyoming

Rapid
City

California

Reno

Casper

Sioux
Falls

Iowa

Sacramento

Nevada

Salt Lake City

U   S   A

ICELAND

Reykjavik

G r e e n l a n d

B a f f i n

B a y

Arctic Circle

Baffin

Island

D a v i s

S t r a i t

Melville
Peninsula

Foxe

Basin

Iqaluit

L a b r a d o r   S e a

Southampton
Island

Hudson Strait

ATLANTIC

Peninsule
d'Ungava

OCEAN

Hudson Bay

L a b r a d o r

N e w f o u n d l a n d

St. Anthony

P e n i n s u l a

Labrador City

Newfoundland

St. John's

Québec

Havre-
St-Pierre

Albany R.

Anticosti I.

tario

Gaspé

Channel-Port-
aux-Basques

Geraldton

Chibougamau

Chicoutimi

Rimouski

P.E.I.

Sydney

Kapuskasing

Timmins

Val d'Or

Québec City

New
Brunswick

Nova
Scotia

under Bay

Sault
Ste Marie

Sudbury

Trois-Rivières

Maine

Saint
John

Halifax

ke Superior

St. Lawrence R.

Montreal

Sherbrooke

Ottawa

Portland

Kingston

Oshawa

New
York

Vt.

N.H.

L. Ontario

Toronto

Boston

consin

Michigan

Hamilton

Syracuse

Mass.

Providence

waukee

London

L. Erie

Detroit

Pennsylvania

New York

Lake Michigan

Lake Huron

Canada

| 0 | 250 km |
| 0 | 250 miles |

CENTRAL CANADA

Heartland of Canada's colonial history, Ontario and Québec offer a wealth of different experiences for the traveler

Known as the right and left ventricles of Canada's heart (much to the displeasure of the other provinces), Québec and Ontario house not only Canada's most prosperous cities, but also more than half its population. Rich in their cultural traditions, these provinces represent the origins of colonial Canada and contain remnants of the historic tension between their British and French forebears.

They also have the most tourists – 44 percent of all Canada's visitors, who generate 37 percent of the country's tourism revenues. Toronto, with its lakeside setting and bubbling nightlife, is an obvious starting point. The nation's capital, Ottawa, is on the eastern edge of the province of Ontario which extends north and west into the Arctic.

Often overlooked, northern Ontario is a vast but accessible region of pristine lakes and quiet cottage villages. The chapter on the province is designed to give a feel for the area by walking through its cities, towns, rural communities and parks. Ottawa is highlighted, as well as gems such as Stratford, Elora, Midland, Kingston, London and Algonquin Park.

Québec is the other historical center of Canada. Here the emphasis is on Québec's uniquely French nature, its cultural institutions, its festivals and its conflict with British customs and the efforts of the province's inhabitants to retain their heritage. A detailed account of everything Montréal has to offer is followed by a visit to Québec City, and a trip up the St Lawrence River into the countryside, ending at the Gaspé Peninsula in the estuary of the St Lawrence River.

LEFT: Niagara Falls, highlight of any tour to Ontario, comprise the Horseshoe Falls (pictured) on the Canadian side and the American Falls across Goat Island to the northeast. The flow of water varies almost hourly depending on the needs of the power generating stations.

TORONTO:
THE DYNAMIC CITY

*The multicultural city of Toronto has a dazzling assortment of
ethnic neighborhoods, a vibrant waterfront, theaters, concert halls,
clubs, galleries, and some of the best shopping in North America*

Map,
page 138

The largest city in the second largest country in the world is best approached by car and at night. Toronto is cradled within small hills that roll down gently to the calm north shore of Lake Ontario. A sheltered Great Lakes port, it boasts a magnificent downtown skyline when viewed from the highways that hug the lake shore. In the dark, the glowing office buildings and the trademark Canadian National Tower have an alien beauty.

A meeting place

From around 1000 BC natives gathered here to trade, socialize and relax. In fact the name Toronto comes from a Huron Indian word meaning "Place of Meeting". In 1615 an explorer called Etienne Brûlé (who was the first white man to see all the Great Lakes) discovered an Iroquois village here on the Humber River, and later a fur trading post was established by the French in 1720. The British became the ruling power after the defeat of the French on the Plaines d'Abraham in 1759, and in 1787 they purchased the land Toronto now stands on from local Mississauga Indians – who by then had replaced the Iroquois. Gradually a settlement grew around the natural harbor.

In 1793 Toronto, renamed York, became the new capital of Upper Canada (today's southern Ontario). Throughout the War of 1812, York remained loyal to Britain, although in 1813 it was briefly occupied twice by the Americans.

After incorporation in 1834, the city was renamed Toronto. From the early 1800s, waves of British immigrants arrived, and later 40,000 Irish immigrants, as a result of the potato famine in 1847. The first Jewish immigrants arrived from Europe in the 1830s, and another wave came in the 1880s.

Loyal royal subjects

Until the end of the 19th century British immigrants were the largest group by far, and their loyalty to Queen Victoria and to everything the British Empire stood for meant that Toronto life was firmly shackled by a code of rigid moral values, including draconian Lord's Day legislation that prohibited most working, sporting and entertainment activities on the sabbath.

This did not, however, deter immigration. Following World War II, Toronto's population swelled with the arrival of refugees from Europe. In the 1970s, as a result of relaxed federal immigration laws, fresh waves came from Asia, Latin America, Africa and the Caribbean. By the 1990s, Toronto's population of 3.8 million included hundreds of thousands of Caribbeans, Chinese, Italians,

PRECEDING PAGES:
Toronto's gleaming skyline. **LEFT:** banking architecture.
BELOW: Bloor Street.

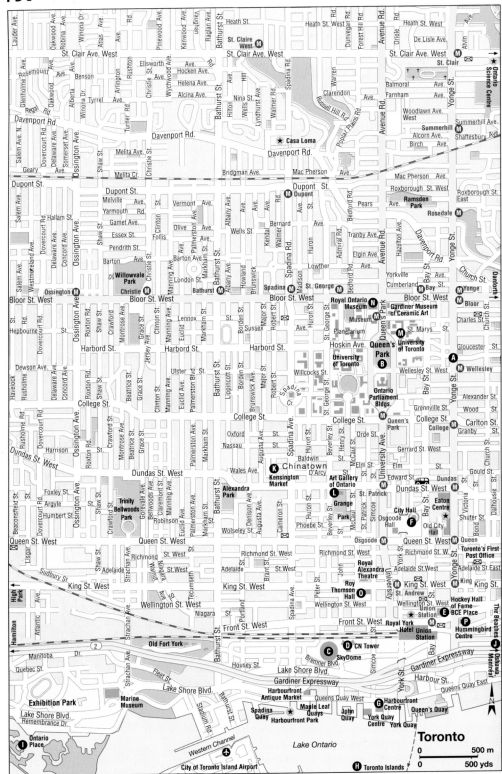

Toronto

0   500 m

0   500 yds

Greeks, and South Asian immigrants and their descendants, along with substantial groupings from most other parts of the world. Today more than 100 languages are spoken by the city's 80 (and counting) different ethnic groups. One result of this vibrant mixture, layered over the solid British underlay, is that Toronto became, *de facto*, the political, cultural and financial juggernaut of Canadian accomplishment.

Map, page 138

Subways, streetcars and buses

Among Toronto's attributes are two subway lines, with all-night buses taking over after the trains stop rolling around 1.30 or 2am. Despite the system's convenience and safety, Torontonians have been switching to automobile use over recent years. Efforts by the Toronto Transit Commission to lure them back to the trains sometimes result in commuters being jolted out of their early morning revery by droll quips from a conductor over the p.a. system.

Electric streetcars are also a distinctive fixture on the downtown streets. The older ones are dilapidated red-and-yellow heaps known as red rockets, with oddly slanted windows and no head room, and they're slowly being phased out. When the latest streetcar line recently opened, along historic Spadina Avenue, some 32,000 enthusiastic riders turned out on opening day, to welcome the 18 clean, smooth-riding electric streetcars that replaced 30 uncomfortable, noisy, fume-belching diesel buses.

Toronto Tram. Transport is a key to the city. From Union Station an "Underground City" has 11 km (7 miles) of passages, with 1,100 shops.

Toronto's longest street

Listed in the *Guinness Book of World Records* as the "longest street in the world", Yonge Street divides the east and west sides of the city. It stretches 8,896 km (1,178 miles) north from the lakeshore in Toronto to Rainy River on the Ontario/Minnesota border. Named after Sir George Yonge, the British Secretary of War in the early 1790s, Yonge Street celebrated its 200th anniversary in 1996. Although the underside of Toronto's thriving economy becomes apparent as you walk along the **Yonge Street Strip Ⓐ**, between King and Bloor Streets, it's worth investigating – not least because Yonge Street has a wonderfully bizarre mix of restaurants and stores that offer some excellent bargains.

BELOW: bustling Yonge Street.

Power play

Usually a peaceful haven in the heart of Toronto, **Queen's Park Ⓑ** is home to the Ontario Legislature Buildings. Built between 1886 and 1892, the imposing sandstone building has a historic Legislative Chamber and an impressive collection of 19th-century and early 20th-century Canadian art. After the landslide victory of the Progressive Conservative party in the 1995 provincial election, and its re-election in 1999, legislation with far-ranging consequences on Ontario's social and municipal infrastructures has been pushed through the Legislature. As a result, protests take place with some regularity on the steps of Queen's Park.

Heart of the matter

What distinguishes Toronto from most North American cities is the vibrancy of its downtown. Running through

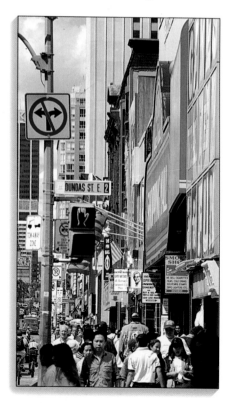

A Blue Jay hero. Baseball is popular in Canada. On 5 September, 1914, the baseball player Babe Ruth hit the first home run of his professional career at Hanlan's Point on Toronto Islands.

its center is **Bay Street**, the main artery of the country's financial capital. Most Canadian head offices and a huge stock exchange are on or close to it, but that is not the entire picture. Minutes away are sizeable clusters of residential housing, from exclusive condominiums to government-financed cooperative housing, the **Theater District** (Toronto claims to have the world's third largest live theater industry, after London and New York) with its attendant restaurants and clubs, and some of the city's most famous attractions.

Toronto's downtown is also grail for thousands of sports fans. The Toronto Blue Jays, the Toronto Argonauts and the Toronto Raptors play baseball, football and basketball respectively, according to the season, at the 56,000-seat **SkyDome** ❺. The world's first retractable domed stadium squats besides another record-breaking building. The **CN Tower** ❻ (open daily; May–Sep till 11pm; Sep–May till 10pm weekdays, 11pm weekends; entrance fee) is, at 553 meters (1,815 ft), the world's tallest freestanding structure, and an ever-present exclamation above the city. There are eateries cheek by jowl in this part of town, from the lofty **360** revolving restaurant at the top of the tower to cheap, cheerful and Italian at **Kit Kat** on King Street West. A few blocks east, in BCE Place, at the corner of Front and Yonge Street, is the **Hockey Hall of Fame** ❼ (open daily; Jun–Jul: Mon–Sat 9.30am–6pm, Sun 10am–6pm; Sep–May: weekdays, 10am–5pm, Sat 9.30am–6pm, Sun 10.30am–5pm; entrance fee). It's a mecca for serious hockey buffs, with its collection dedicated to the history of Canada's national game; grown men have even been seen to weep in front of the hallowed Stanley Cup.

At the intersection of Front East and Jarvis Street is the **St Lawrence Market** (open Tues-Sat), where the tradition of shopping goes back to 1803, although not in the same building. Torontonians still come in droves, every Saturday. The

site was also home to Toronto's first two City Halls. In this historically-preserved neighborhood, where old warehouses have been transformed into offices, studios and restaurants, **Toronto's First Post Office** (open daily; free) on Adelaide Street East is both an active postal station and a museum that shows how a colonial post office functioned in the early 1830s.

Toronto's newest **City Hall** , at the corner of Queen and Bay Streets, which was designed by the Finish architect Viljo Revell in 1965, is striking. Its vast rotunda and two curved towers, which flank the central dome, lord it over Nathan Phillips Square, where visitors can admire the sculptures. Henry Moore's sculpture, *The Artist*, was a controversial addition in the square's early years.

Down on the waterfront

Summers are special on Queen's Quay, at **Harbourfront Centre** (open daily, some events ticketed, many events free). The former warehouse has been converted into specialty stores, restaurants and a theater. Patios overlook the lake, where sail boats, dinner-cruises circling Toronto Islands, and the occasional tall ship grace the waterfront. World class dance companies perform in the Premier Dance Theater, and in nearby York Quay Centre, a dynamic range of cultural ventures take place year round. A short walk west is **Harbourfront Antique Market** (open Tues-Sun), with its immense collection of antiques and collectibles.

Toronto Islands are actually a 5-km (3-mile) strip of sandbar with several names, jutting out into the city's harbor. The island community is a unique aspect of Toronto, with a group of residents intent on preserving their simple way of

Map, page 138

TIP

Peameal bacon, a savory salt-and-sugar cured extra-lean ham, served piping hot on a bun with a cup of strong coffee, is a Torontonian favorite at St Lawrence Market.

BELOW LEFT: ferry to Toronto Islands.
BELOW RIGHT: St Lawrence Market.

Lifeguards on the beach.

life. In summer the choice land swarms with picnickers and, on occasion, youths with ghetto blasters, while the bitter winters bring winds that sweep mercilessly across Lake Ontario. Food and other supplies have to be ferried across or delivered to the tiny light airport at the island's west end. It's not what you'd call easy living, though most islanders wouldn't change it for the world.

For visitors, including mainland Torontonians, it's a lovely haven in summer, and only about 10 minutes away by leisurely ferry. Once there, the 600-acre (243-ha) park offers secluded beaches, meandering bicycle trails, the village community and an amusement park for children. You can transport a bike across or rent one there for some of the nicest riding in the city. The **Rectory Café** is a hidden gem on the southside Boardwalk of Ward's Island, although it's difficult to beat the tranquility of an evening picnic amid the trees bordering the north shoreline, watching the sun set over the city.

Parks and boardwalks

Toronto's waterfront has become increasingly accessible to walkers, cyclists, and in-line skaters, as lakeside trails are extended and widened. They stretch from The Beaches in the east to Humber River in the west. Well worth a detour is **High Park**, the city's largest park and home to a rare stand of black oak savannah and unusual plants such as blazing star and the sassafras tree. More manufactured leisure time can be had at **Ontario Place ❶** (open mid-May–Labor Day; entrance fee), a spacey lake-front attraction that offers prime viewing for the annual Benson & Hedges Symphony of Fireworks Competition.

The Beaches ❿ are a favorite haunt on Toronto's east side. Best time to stroll along the Boardwalk is on weekdays and evenings. Sail boats and seagulls

BELOW: one of Toronto's five Chinatowns.

skim the waves of Lake Ontario on one side, while joggers and strollers enjoy wooded parkland on the other. You can cut up to Queen Street, where an assortment of cafés, restaurants and pubs cater to most palates and budgets. Among them are **Mersini's**, an Italian bakery with a pretty terrace, and the **Remarkable Bean**, which serves limited-edition coffees at chessboard tables.

Exploring Toronto's "villages"

Toronto's neighborhoods reflect the city's vibrant history, from the early Anglo-Saxon, pro-monarchist immigrants to the Afro-Caribbeans, Italians, Greeks, Chinese, Portuguese, Ukrainians, Poles, Indians, and Irish – among many others – who have all poured into the city, each group carving out a neighborhood or two for its own.

You'll find Greeks on the Danforth, Italians and Portuguese on College Street and St Clair Avenue, the Chinese on Dundas Street, East Indians on Gerrard Street, Jamaicans on Bathurst Street, Eastern Europeans on Roncesvalles Avenue or Bloor West Village. It's easy for anyone so inclined to enjoy and cherish the cultural diversity.

Kensington Market , with its old-world boisterousness and scruffy charm, has witnessed much of this, since it began with Jewish immigrants in the 1920s and 1930s, who were later supplanted by Portuguese, Chinese and West Indians. In some ways, it's still the place where these worlds meet on a regular basis.

The main thoroughfares are Augusta and Kensington Avenues, and their connecting streets, Baldwin and Oxford. Here you'll encounter frail, elderly Chinese ladies haggling with the gnarled Portuguese women who sell fruit and do incredible mental arithmetic in lieu of a cash register, leisurely Rastafarian merchants hawking spicy beef patties and sharp ginger beer, black-clad Italian widows carrying home several tonnes of fresh fruit or vegetables on one arm. Drop by **Amadeu's**, a popular Portuguese eatery that specializes in seafood and Portuguese wines at modest prices, at the south end of Augusta.

At Augusta and Dundas Street West, **Chinatown** and Kensington Market meet. With the massive growth of its Chinese population, Toronto now has five Chinatowns. This one is the biggest, and bustles with shoppers and hawkers all day and long into the night. Sprawling along Dundas and north up Spadina are overflowing fruit and vegetable stands, Chinese herbalists, and grocery stores bulging with delicacies like snack packets of dried squid and cuttlefish. Mouth-watering smells wafting through open doors may well prompt you to search out some of the city's best Chinese restaurants – places like **Happy Seven** and **Sang Ho**.

Presiding on the threshold of Chinatown is the **Art Gallery of Ontario** (open Wed–Fri, holiday Mon, noon–9pm; Tues May–Oct, noon–9pm; weekends 10am–5.30pm; entrance fee). The AGO has the world's largest public collection of Henry Moore sculptures, most of them a direct gift from the sculptor. Canadian art, including an impressive collection of Inuit work, comprises over half the permanent collection which ranges from 15th-century European paintings to international contemporary works of art. Another of the

Map, page 138

Toronto has the largest population of gays and lesbians in Canada. XTRA! is the free, biweekly newspaper that outlines events in the city.

BELOW: time for a break downtown in BCE Place.

city's livelier neighborhoods is **The Danforth**. For about 10 blocks, from Broad-view to Coxwell, the Greeks have taken over the main east-west artery of the city. Even the street signs are bilingual, while every other restaurant is a *taverna*. At the long-established **Asteria Souvlaki House** patrons enjoy *bouzoukis* and *souvlakis* on the outside patio in summer, while a highly touted, more recent addition to the scene is **Pan on the Danforth**.

The Italian community is the city's largest non-Anglo ethnic group, number-ing considerably more than 650,000 people. **Via Italia** is one of the earlier com-munities, centered on College Street between Grace and Ossington Streets. Long popular with students and artists, its authenticity is verified by the amount of Italian conversations you're bound to overhear.

A perfect evening begins at **Souz Dahl**, a romantic, candle-lit bar that pours magnificent martinis, continues at **Grappa**, for its cheerful atmosphere and excellent food, and ends at the **Sicilian Ice Cream Company** for Italian gelati and cappuccino.

Close to the **University of Toronto Ⓜ**, The Annex is a well-established stu-dent hangout, stretching along Bloor Street West from Spadina Avenue to Bathurst Street. To the north, gracious buildings on shady streets are either stu-dent fraternity houses or the elegant (and pricey) homes of professionals and artists. Housing south of Bloor is usually of a more modest scale, built to accom-modate the waves of Jewish, Chinese, Italians and Portuguese newcomers as they arrived in Toronto.

BELOW: traditional housing in Mirvish Village.

Inexpensive eateries offering an enticing variety of ethnic cuisines are an inte-gral part of the Annex. Two popular longtime fixtures are **Future Bakery & Café** at the corner of Bloor and Brunswick, and **Pauper's**, a pub housed in a

former bank with a lively piano bar downstairs and a romantic sundown rooftop patio above.

Three remarkable museums border the Annex. The **Bata Shoe Museum** (open Tues–Sat 10am–5pm, Thurs till 8pm and Sun afternoon; entrance fee), at Bloor and St George Street, houses an extraordinarily comprehensive collection of shoes and related artifacts in a dramatic "shoebox" structure designed by renowned architect Raymond Moriyama. Spanning some 4,500 years, its collection of more than 10,000 items explores the extent to which shoes reflect the living habits, culture and customs of the people who wore them.

Within a few minutes' walk away, on University Avenue, is the **Royal Ontario Museum**  (open Mon–Sat 10am–6pm, Sun 11am–5pm; entrance fee, but waived on Tues after 4.30pm). Known locally as ROM, the museum is one of the world's few multi-discipline museums – which means its exhibits range from science to art to archaeology. ROM's East Asian collection is world-renowned, and includes a stunning collection of temple art.

On the other side of University Avenue is the **George R. Gardiner Museum of Ceramic Art** (open Mon–Sat 10am–5pm, Sun 11am–5pm; free admission). It's another one-of-a-kind in North America, with a spectacular collection of pottery and porcelain treasures spanning some 3,000 years.

Abutting the Annex is **Yorkville**, a couple of trendy blocks delineated by Cumberland Street and Yorkville Avenue. The redbrick, Victorian houses were taken over by hippies in the 1960s, but within 20 years developers, retailers and up-market types moved in, and now Yorkville's designer boutiques and trendy art galleries are all the rage. The neighboring streets of Hazelton and Scollard are fertile territory for collectors of North American Native Indian artifacts and Inuit

Map, page 138

Hidden treasures: on the 9th floor of the Hudson's Bay Store, 176 Yonge Street, is the exceptional art collection of the newspaper magnate Kenneth Thomson.

BELOW: the Royal Ontario Museum.

Map, page 138

Canadian hockey superstar, Wayne Gretzky, has opened his own restaurant, Gretzky's, a block north of Sky Dome, complete with hockey memorabilia.

BELOW: Bay Street, the financial heart.
RIGHT: skating outside City Hall.

sculpture and prints. Amid the glitz is **Little Tibet**, a basement level restaurant that dishes up marvelous fare in a thoroughly unpretentious fashion.

The Anglo-Saxon roots of Toronto still hold dominion in one neighborhood, even if they have been squeezed into a few hectares of prime real estate. **Rosedale** is where the reticent, affluent people who run the financial and legal district centered on Bay Street continue to live – frequently with a BMW or two in their garage. One can only imagine their thoughts on the tour buses that detour here from time to time, for a quick, wish-it-were-me-living-here gawk.

When night falls

For decades, it seemed, Torontonians became accustomed to their city being disparagingly referred to as "Toronto the Good" by every other Canadian. Indeed, Toronto night life used to be plagued by a Victorian carry-over, enforcing tight restrictions on the city's bars. Recent legislation permits them to stay open until 2am, so between that and a few all-night dance clubs, night owls have more time to party.

The live-music scene is eclectic and very good, offering jazz, rock, funk, folk or almost anything else you might be into. Toronto has a good underground of amateur bands and it's a habitual stop on most music tours, especially for European bands. Prices and quality vary hugely from place to place so it's best to consult the advertisements in either *Now* or *Eye* magazines, two free entertainment weeklies.

Multiculturalism, naturally, has an imprint on Toronto entertainment. Caravan, an annual summer festival, offers good food and drink and some terrific ethnic music and dancing, even though it may seem a little contrived, while Caribana, the annual Caribbean festival, is an exuberant affair that's one of the city's biggest summertime draws.

On a more erudite note, the Toronto Symphony Orchestra, the Canadian Opera Company and the National Ballet of Canada are all world-class outfits based in Toronto with extensive fall and winter seasons. Those able to meet the pecuniary demands of the **Roy Thomson Hall O** and **Hummingbird Centre P** box offices will undoubtedly be suitably impressed by the performances at both venues.

A cultured city

All of this points to Toronto being well on the way to becoming a first-class city, part of an elevated clique that includes London, Paris, New York, Tokyo, Rome and Rio de Janeiro. On the literary scene alone, with its annual International Authors Festival and year-round Harborfront Reading Series, Toronto in the 1990s has been compared with Paris in the 1920s. Toronto writers and film-makers are recognized as international trend-setters.

And yet Toronto manages to retain, with its varied population, both a small-town aura and healthy dollops of European charm. Well-groomed and safe, like many things Canadian, it is fast discarding its Victorian inhibitions of yesteryear. With enough of whatever it takes to make a great city, it's something of a joy to visit.

ONTARIO:
LAND OF SHINING WATERS

Ontario is one of the world's most urbanized regions with towns standing like high-tech sandcastles by the Great Lakes. Venture north and discover a wilderness of water and forests

Map, page 152

The most American of Canada's provinces, thrust down into the industrial heartland of the United States, Ontario remains profoundly suspicious of the Great Republic and still fairly attached to the British monarchy. It is a highly modernized region, but it is also a wilderness with 90 percent of its area under forest.

But it is a land, a country, a home. Underlying the exotic diversity of Ontario's population is a common love of place, whether that place be a Gothic revival farmhouse at Punkeydoodles Corners or a New Age zucchini plot on Toronto's Markham Street. In 1844 J.R. Godley, a traveler from Great Britain, described Upper Canada as a place where "everybody is a foreigner and home in their mouths invariably means another country." Today Ontario is still a land of many peoples, but its residents have found their home.

PRECEDING PAGES: water-way log-jam. **LEFT:** echoes of the Victorian era in Kleinburg, Ontario. **BELOW:** wheat harvesting on the hills.

The voyageurs' heartlands

Although home to the Canadian Indians for millennia, and corridor for the voyagers' fur trade, the living essence of modern Ontario isn't found in the longhouse or canoe portage, but in the limestone homes of the United Empire Loyalists which stretch along the St Lawrence River.

More than any other region of Ontario, **Eastern Ontario** remains devoted to the Loyalist traditions of "peace, order and good government". The stolid farmhouses, regal courthouses, and towering Anglican spires proclaim that no matter what the "democrats and levelers" in Western Ontario may do, the East will be faithful to the province's motto: "As loyal she began, so shall she ever remain".

There's no more historically resonant place to begin a tour of Ontario than in the counties of **Prescott-Russell** and **Glengarry** wedged between the Ottawa and St Lawrence rivers. The lower Ottawa countryside appears more Québécois than Upper Canadian. Barns boldly decked out in orange and green, silvery "ski-jump" roofs and towns centered on massive parish churches reveal a distinct French-Canadian character.

But this is Ontario, not Québec. Surveyed by British army engineers, all of Southern Ontario is rationally divided into little blocks (lots) within big blocks (townships) dissected by concession roads that irrationally ignore such non-Euclidian features as rocks, boulders, hills, lakes and swamps.

Driving southwest from the Ottawa River the French place names give way to towns named Dunvegan, Lochiel, Maxville and Alexandria, telltale signs that this

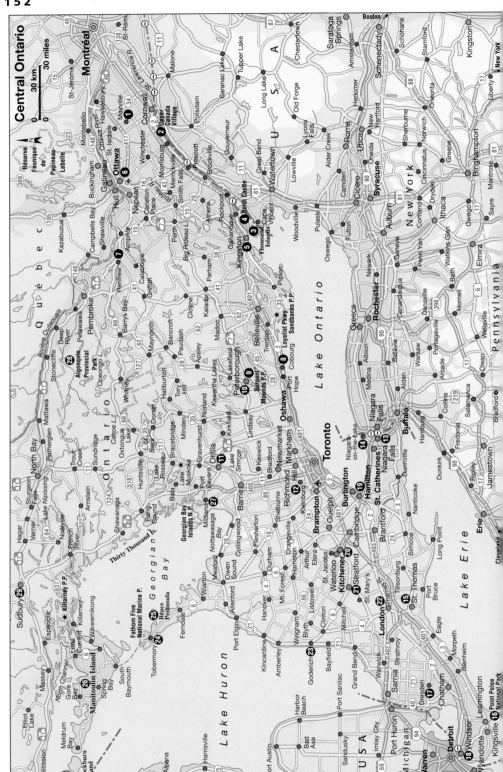

Central Ontario

is now Glengarry County. Glengarry, known throughout the world by the works of novelist Ralph Connor, was the first of the hundreds of Scottish settlements in Ontario.

Beginning with the arrival of the loyalist Royal Highland Emigrant Regiment in 1783, the hill country north of the St Lawrence became the destination of thousands of emigrant Scots. Entire parishes from Glengarry, Scotland, emigrated for the promise of free land and the chance to escape the oppression of their landlords.

In Connor's fictional Glengarry, Presbyterian behemoths like Big Mack Cameron, Black Hugh Macdonald, or the greatest of all, Donald Bhain Macdonald, would piously turn their cheeks to the enemy – once – and then wade into the shantymen brawls crying, "Glengarry forever!" thrashing the Irish Papists to within sight of Judgement Day. The real Glengarry is still as Scottish as its fictional counterpart, though actually more Catholic than Calvinist. Perhaps a case of special pleading? For Ralph Connor was a pen name for the Reverend Charles William Gordon, a minister of the Presbyterian Church.

Each year in early August former residents are drawn back for the Glengarry Highland Games at **Maxville** ❶, 60 km (37 miles) east of Ottawa, to throw a caber or toss back a scotch.

River of empire

At **Cornwall**, Ontario's easternmost city, 30 km (18 miles) south of Maxville, the **Robert Saunders St Lawrence Generating Station** stretches across the river to harness the thrust of the Great Lakes as they are funneled towards the Atlantic. Appropriately, an abstract mural by the artist Harold Town adorns the

Map, page 152

At Dunvegan, near Maxville, one of Glengarry Museum's prize exhibits is a cooking pot used by Bonnie Prince Charlie at Glengarry, Scotland, 1746.

BELOW: friends for life, Upper Canada Village, Morrisburg.

observation tower. For this is a triumph of the modern technological age over
the defiant, age-old barrier of the Long Sault and International Rapids. With the
opening of the **St Lawrence Seaway** in 1959 the interior of the continent was
made accessible to the ocean-going giants and the St Lawrence superseded the
Rhine as the world's foremost river of commerce.

It is a river of empire. The French and English struggled for 150 years to determine control of the Great Lakes waterway, and when they were done the Canadians and Americans took up the cudgels. Indeed, it is a ripe irony typical of
Canada that in order to remain British the American Loyalists emigrated to share
this river with the ancient enemy of the British Empire: *Les Canadiens*.

At **Morrisburg**, upriver from Cornwall, **Upper Canada Village ❷** presents
an historical re-creation of what life was like for these Loyalist immigrants (open
May–Oct: daily 9.30am–5pm; entrance fee). Early log cabins are juxtaposed
with spacious American classical revival houses, illustrating the changing fortunes of the first political refugees to find a Canadian haven.

Iroquois legend tells of two potent spirits, one good the other evil, who battled
for control of the mighty St Lawrence. In their titanic struggle huge boulders
were tossed across the river in a great cannonade, many to fall short into the narrows leading into Lake Ontario. With the triumph of the good spirit, a magical
blessing fell upon the land bringing rich forests of yellow birch, red and white
trillium, silver maple and winged sumac to life upon the countless granite chunks
scattered about the river. Today they are called the **Thousand Islands ❸**.

Brockville, 85 km (53 miles) southwest of Cornwall, a stately Loyalist city
with early architectural treasures along Courthouse Avenue, serves as the eastern gateway to the Islands. Cruises around the numberless islands leave from

BELOW: Boldt Castle
on Heart Island.

nearby **Rockport** and **Gananoque**, a more rambunctious resort town 53 km (33 miles) closer to Kingston.

The Thousand Islands have long been a playground for the very rich who, no matter how bad their taste in architecture, always seem to have an eye for the world's most extraordinary real estate. The most famous of the millionaire "cottages" is an unfinished one named **Boldt Castle** ❹ which broods over Heart Island. Begun in 1898 by George Boldt, king of the Waldorf Astoria, it was never completed due to his grief over his wife's death. Today it stands open to the elements and to the curious. A more lasting monument to Boldt is the Thousand Islands salad dressing that his chef concocted in honor of the region (open mid-May–early-Oct: daily; entrance fee).

The once and future king

Briefly the capital of the United Provinces of Canada (1841–1843), the city of **Kingston** ❺ has never quite recovered from Queen Victoria's folly in naming Ottawa the new capital of the Dominion of Canada in 1857. Kingston certainly meets all the requirements of a capital city: a venerable history stretching back to 1673 and Fort Frontenac; a quiet dignity redolent in the weathered stone houses that line its streets; and a grandiose, neo-Classical **City Hall**, erected in 1843 in expectation of Kingston's greater destiny. The Martello towers strategically placed around the town's harbor and the great limestone bulwark of **Old Fort Henry** are testimony to the enduring fear of invasion that the War of 1812 engendered (open late-May–end Sep; daily; entrance fee).

Apparently, the spirit of 1812 lives on at **Queen's University**, the pride of Kingston, founded as a Presbyterian seminary in 1841. In 1956 the student body

Map, page 152

The Fort Henry Guard, Kingston, in 19th-century dress.

BELOW LEFT: Scottish pipers in Kleinburg. **BELOW RIGHT:** Royal Military College, Kingston.

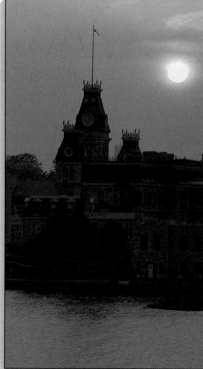

invaded the nearby town of Watertown, New York, under cloak of night, replacing the "Stars and Stripes" flying at public buildings with Union Jacks.

The memory of Sir John A. Macdonald, the first prime minister of Canada, is as permanent a fixture in Kingston as any fort or college. **Bellevue House**, an Italianate villa occupied by Macdonald in the late 1840s, is now a museum filled with memorabilia of the Old Chieftain (open Easter–Oct: daily; entrance fee). More importantly, Macdonald's unofficial political headquarters, the **Grimason House** (now the **Royal Tavern**), is still standing and open for business in the city center.

Just to the east of Kingston, between the harbor and old Fort Henry, lies the southern entrance of the **Rideau Canal.** Built between 1826 and 1832, the canal follows the path of the **Rideau River** route northeast through 47 locks, numerous lakes and excavated channels until it emerges beside **Parliament Hill** on the Ottawa River. Today the canal region is a pleasure-boat captain's delight. Sleek-lined yachts and fat-bottomed cabin cruisers play snakes and ladders with the great stone locks, many of which are as they were over a 150 years ago.

To the thousands of Irish laborers brought to Canada to construct the canal, the route was a foul, mosquito-ridden wilderness and their British Army taskmasters nothing less than Pharaoh's satraps. Rapids were dammed, boulders blasted and huge stone blocks hauled through roadless forests. The cost in human life was terrific. Construction in the 30-km (18-mile) long Cranberry marsh took 1,000 workers through yellow fever.

The purpose of the canal was military, not economic. The British Army wanted a second, more secure route connecting Upper and Lower Canada in the event of an American seizure of the St Lawrence. The military character of the

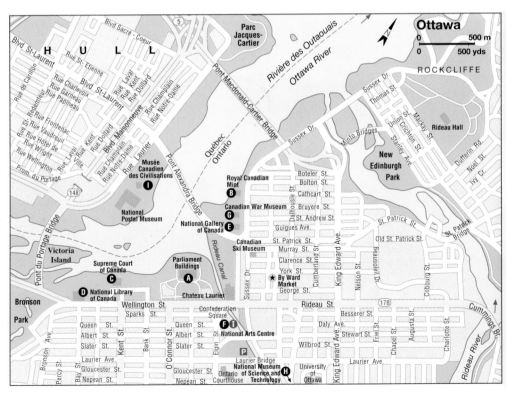

canal is evident at **Merrickville**, 48 km (30 miles) southwest of Ottawa, where the largest of the 22 blockhouses that were built to protect the route still looms over the river.

Many of the canal's laborers settled in the region. A bevy of Scottish master stonemasons, lured across the water to build the locks, stayed on to build the town of **Perth** on the river Tay, 41 km (25 miles) west of Merrickville. Perth today is a feast of exquisite Georgian, Adamesque-Federalist, Regency and Gothic residences – one of the most photogenic towns in Ontario.

Ottawa

Queen Victoria's choice of **Bytown**, then newly renamed **Ottawa** ❻, as her capital in the Canadas was greeted with shock by her trusting subjects. Today's equivalent would be commanding all the capital's stenographers, pollsters and politicos to pack up their bags and begin working in Tuktoyaktuk in the Northwest Territories.

But the indignity wasn't limited to just moving to a backwater, for Bytown in the mid-1800s was also the most notorious work camp in North America. Lumber was king of the region and Bytown was its capital. Rival shantymen gangs the size of regiments set up shack towns here. Worked like machines, ill-fed, isolated and racially divided, the lumbermen spent their recreational hours in drunken bouts of kick fights and eye gouging. It was in these muddy, dangerous streets that the **Parliament Buildings** ❹ were erected between 1859 and 1865, rather like the proverbial pearl in a pig sty (open daily; tours, free).

The contrast between these savage shantymen and their descendants – well-ordered, conformist civil servants – is wonderfully absurd. It is the contrast

Maps: Area 152, City 156

A lighthouse from Nova Scotia, hands-on displays and a vast refracting telescope attract visitors to Ottawa's Museum of Science and Technology.

BELOW: Ottawa's Parliament Hill.

Overlooking the Ottawa River, the National Gallery of Canada shines out like a beacon.

between settlement and wilderness, between convention and epic adventure that runs through Canadian history. The contrast has not quite vanished from Ottawa today. In the **Gatineau Hills** that rise up behind Ottawa to the east, wolf packs still gather to howl. And at the **Royal Canadian Mint ❸**, Canada's money-makers still churn out coins depicting wild birds, moose and beavers (open daily 9am–5pm; small entrance fee for tours).

For Ottawa will never be a capital city in the style of Washington or Brasilia, fashioned around a grandiose design that reorders the world along geometric lines. Initiated in 1937, the Capital Region Plan of designer Jacques Greber emphasizes the area's natural beauty and molds the city around it. Consequently, pleasure craft wend their way through the downtown center's parks in summer, while winter turns the Rideau Canal into an ice-skating promenade. The annual gift of thousands of tulips by the Netherlands, in gratitude for Canada's wartime hospitality to the Dutch Royal Family, makes spring in the city a visual delight.

Because of its national stature, Ottawa has more cultural resources, museums and galleries than a population of 300,000 would normally allow. Besides the Parliament Buildings, the Art Deco **Supreme Court ❸** (guided tours daily; Sep–Apr: closed weekends; free), the **National Library ❹** and the residences of prime ministers, governors-general and foreign ambassadors, Ottawa boasts the **National Gallery of Canada ❺**, the country's foremost gallery, made primarily out of glass (open mid-May–mid-Sep: daily 10am–6pm; mid-Sep–mid-May: Wed–Sun 10am–5pm; free); the **National Arts Center ❻**, comprising opera house, theater and studio and home to the acclaimed National Arts Center Orchestra; the **Canadian War Museum ❼** which traces Canada's wars or involvement in wars from the 17th century (open daily, 9.30am–5pm, Thurs till 8pm; mid-Oct–Apr: closed Mon; entrance fee, free Thurs eve); and the **National Museum of Science and Technology ❽**, containing an impressive display of steam locomotives (open daily 9am–6pm, Fri till 9pm; Sep–Apr: 9am–5pm, closed Mon; entrance fee).

Across the river in Hull, in the province of Québec, stands the outstanding **Musée Canadien des Civilisations ❿**, featuring the history of Canada, the art and traditions of the native cultures and ethnic groups (open daily; mid-Oct–Apr: closed Mon; entrance fee, free Sun 9am–noon).

CULTURAL GEMS

Ottawa's National Gallery of Canada and, across the river, Hull's Musée Canadien des Civilisations, stand out both for their architecture and for their remarkable collections. The glass-turreted National Gallery, by the architect Moshe Safdie, 1988, houses Canadian painting from the18th to the 20th centuries, including the Group of Seven; European and American works from Filippino Lippi to Francis Bacon; and the reconstructed, fan-vaulted, Rideau Street Convent Chapel. Dedicated to the human history of Canada, the Musée Canadien des Civilisations, designed by Douglas Cardinal,1989, features the world's largest collection of totem poles. All aspects of life in Canada, from the earliest native peoples, to the arrival of Norsemen and successive waves of Europeans, are shown in eye-catching displays. Exhibitions of native art make this a museum not to be missed.

The unknown river

Author Hugh MacLennan, in *Seven Rivers of Canada*, describes the Ottawa as the "unknown" or "forgotten" river of Canada. As the St Lawrence superseded it as the principal trade route, the image of the Ottawa was dimmed and it took on the status of a short tributary linking the cities of Ottawa and Montréal. To the *voyageurs* and the lumbermen of early Canada, however, the Ottawa river was *la grande rivière*, the main route to the Upper Great Lakes and the western prairies beyond.

In the **Ottawa Valley**, running north of the capital to **Pembroke** and **Deep River**, the character of the old Ottawa River comes alive. Here at **Champlain Lookout ❼**, high above the town of **Renfrew**, you can see the power of the river's current as it bursts over narrows and understand why the journey either up or down the

Ottawa was dreaded by the *voyageurs*. The Ottawa Valley is full of tall tales of the bigger-than-big lumberjacks like Joe Mufferaw, who waged war on the forest to provide the British Navy with white pine masts. These are best heard in the Valley dialect which is a complex mix of Gaelic, Polish, French and Indian idioms.

Maps: Area 152, City 156

Central Ontario

There are no firm borders separating eastern from western Ontario, let alone the east from the middle. But when classical limestone gives way to red brick Victorian and billboards advertise the pleasures of Toronto Hilton Jacuzzis over free TV and hot water in Cornwall, the nebulous line has been crossed. Firmly within the orbit of Toronto, whose fatted-calf suburbs gobble up rich farmland with alacrity, the hamlets and towns of the region struggle to maintain their own character and traditions.

By the time boaters reach Lake Simcoe from Lake Ontario they will have negotiated 43 locks and ascended 180 meters (598 ft).

The town of **Cobourg** ❽, 96 km (60 miles) east of Toronto, is just far enough away to remain relatively unscarred by bedroom dormitory blight. It, like its neighbors **Port Hope** and **Colborne**, was once a bustling lake port in the age of Great Lake steamers. The harbors are filled with pleasure sails now, but these small lakeside ports are the best places to appreciate the vistas offered by Lake Ontario.

The center of Cobourg is dominated by the neo-Classical **Victoria Hall**. Completed in 1860, it contains a courtroom replica of London's Old Bailey and one of only two acoustically perfect opera houses in North America. In its time it served as a marvelous statement of Canadian pretensions to cultural superiority over the rebel Yankees. Here, the colonial elite had something solid to point to in explaining why they chose to remain impoverished British North Americans while Uncle Sam boomed.

BELOW: on the Trent-Severn Canal.

Finger lakes with bones

To the immediate north of Cobourg the long, thin **Kawartha Lakes** are strung like pegs on a clothesline tied to **Lake Simcoe** on the west. The Kawarthas have a pastoral appeal in contrast to the rugged beauty of the more northerly Canadian Shield lakes. **Rice Lake**, the most southerly of the lakes, is especially beguiling. Framed by gently sloping drumlins bearing Holstein dairy farms on their elongated backs, Rice Lake is dotted with forested islands. Two thousand years ago, a little-known Indian civilization buried their dead by these shores in 96-km (60-mile) long, snake-like ridges. **Serpent Mounds Park** ❾, 20 km (12 miles) southeast of Peterborough, offers a cutaway viewing of the largest mound's bones and burial gifts (open May–early Sep; entrance fee).

The Kawartha Lakes form the basis of the **Trent-Severn Canal System**, which allows houseboats and cabin cruisers to sail uphill from **Trenton** on Lake Ontario to **Port Severn** on Lake Huron's Georgian Bay. **Peterborough** ❿, the center of the Kawarthas region, is the star attraction along the canal. Here the **Peterborough Hydraulic Lift Lock**, the world champion boat lifter since 1904, boosts a boat up with one hand, while sinking a second vessel with the other. Set-

Window of a pioneer church, Hay River.

Peterborough district was reputed in the 1830s to have the "most polished and aristocratic society in Upper Canada". British army officers granted free land and younger sons of the English gentry gave the backwoods of Peterborough and Lakefield a tone uncommon in earlier settlements.

Not that gentility made the hardships of pioneering any more bearable. Susannah Moodie, an early pioneer of Lakefield and of Canadian literature, described in *Roughing It in the Bush* her feelings on being condemned to a life of horror in the New World, from which the only hope of escape was "through the portals of the grave". Today Peterborough seems to have found a middle ground between aristocracy and poverty, for it is a favorite testing ground for the arbiters of middle-class taste – the consumer marketing surveyors.

Sunshine sketches of every town

There isn't much of tourist interest in the town of **Orillia ⑪**, situated on the narrows between Lake Couchiching and Lake Simcoe, 96 km (60 miles) north of Toronto – and that's what makes it so interesting. To be sure, there's a statue of Samuel de Champlain noting the fact that he stopped nearby on his own Great Ontario Tour of 1615, but every town has a monument to someone or other.

No, the appeal of Orillia lies in the very ordinariness of the town: shady maples leaning over spacious side streets; wide front porches for socializing and spying; photographs of local hockey heroes in the barber shop-cum-agora. Stephen Leacock caught the flavor of the place – the flavor, for example, of Mr Golgotha Gingham, town undertaker who "instinctively assumes the professional air of hopeless melancholy" – in his book, *Sunshine Sketches of a Little Town*. A work of irony (one part affection, one part castigation), *Sunshine*

BELOW: spring meadow, Ontario.

Sketches won Leacock praise throughout the world when it was published in 1912. Everywhere, except Orillia. Now, Orillia has adopted the humorist as a favorite son and turned the **Stephen Leacock Memorial Home**, on Brewery Bay, into a literary museum (open daily but check winter hours; entrance fee).

South of Lake Simcoe, 40 km (25 miles) north of downtown Toronto, lies another shrine to Canadian artists: the **McMichael Canadian Art Collection** in the village of **Kleinburg** ⓬. Started as a private gallery, the collection has grown into the finest display of the Group of Seven's canvases in Canada. The McMichael Collection, with more than 30 gallery rooms housed in log and stone buildings, is the perfect place to feast on their labors (open daily; Nov–Apr: closed Mon; entrance fee).

Southern Ontario

The excellent system of roads in Southern Ontario is a sign of its long-accustomed prosperity. The Macdonald-Cartier Freeway, more widely known as the 401, spans the distance between Windsor in the west and the Québec border in the east. But it's on the country roads that travelers begin to encounter Southern Ontario: the rolling fields of corn, wheat, tobacco, or grazing livestock; the majestic elms and maples that line the town streets, and shady farm lanes; the graceful houses, ranging from the earliest log and stone dwellings in "American vernacular" style to stately Victorian and Edwardian homes in red and yellow brick; and the rivers. It's difficult to drive anywhere in Southern Ontario without crossing a creek, stream, or honest-to-God river.

West of Toronto lies some of the richest farmland anywhere. And strung along those smooth roads are towns that sometimes seem to have forgotten how they

Map, page 152

The Group of Seven stood the Canadian art establishment on its head in the 1920s as they sought to portray the Canadian wilderness in all its Nordic harshness.

BELOW: lakeside grain elevators.

got there. But fast food and video rental outlets notwithstanding, the pioneer experience has made a deep impression. Almost every town and village blossoms annually with a fair or festival. Maple syrup festivals. Apple-cider festivals. Bean festivals. And everywhere are people who are determined to remember how they got there, and what it was like before there were roads.

A rich history

Sample the sweet taste of rural Canada: the Maple Syrup Festival is held every April at Elmira, 10 km (6 miles) north of Waterloo.

With the capture of Fort Detroit in 1759, the British finally wrested control of the North American frontier from the French. But the settlement of the vast peninsula, bounded by Lakes Ontario, Erie, and Huron, lagged behind that of the booming colonies south of the Great Lakes. It wasn't until those colonies declared their independence from Britain in 1776 that the wilderness that would one day be Ontario became inviting to settlers. These were the Loyalists, whose impact on Eastern Ontario has already been noted. Their contribution to the western part of the province is even more fundamental. They gave up established homesteads to start all over again in the bush, simply because that bush remained under British law. Yet these people were Americans, and the egalitarian sentiments and pioneering spirit they brought with them helped to shape Ontario.

Southwestern Ontario was sculpted into its present shape by retreating glaciers at the end of the last Ice Age. In the late 18th century this rich soil lay under a different kind of sea: a green, rolling swell of dense forest. The French had not seriously attempted to settle the land. Clearing away the giant trees and draining the swamps would have driven back the beavers whose pelts were so lucrative to the fur traders. For a time the British adopted this attitude as well.

BELOW LEFT: rural retreat at Elora.
BELOW RIGHT: pioneer graves.

The American War of Independence changed all this. Thousands of settlers from the Thirteen Colonies who feared or distrusted the new regime poured across the Niagara River. John Butler, the son of a British army officer, led a group of Loyalists north to Niagara. In 1778 he recruited a band of guerrilla fighters, which became known as Butler's Rangers, and until the end of the war the group harassed the American communities in the area. Butler was stationed at Fort Niagara and charged with keeping the Six Nations Iroquois, whose territory was south of Lake Ontario, friendly to the British. At this he succeeded, even persuading the Seneca and Mohawks to engage in fighting the rebels.

The leader of the Mohawks was Joseph Brant, who had received an English education and was committed to the British tradition. When the former Six Nations lands were ceded to the Americans in the 1783 treaty which ended the war, Brant appealed to the British for redress. He and his followers were given land beside the Grand River to an extent of 10 km (6 miles) on either side. Part of that land took in Elora, where the Grand River has carved a canyon that has become one of the most popular retreats in Ontario. The only land that remains in the hands of Six Nations of the Grand River is at Ohsweken, on the southeast outskirts of Brantford. Today it is one of Canada's largest native settlements.

Famous Falls

The **Niagara Escarpment**, a rolling slope which falls away in a rocky bluff on its eastern face, is another legacy of the last Ice Age. It rises out of New York State near Rochester, follows the shore of Lake Ontario around to Hamilton, snakes overland to the Blue Mountain ridge south of Collingwood, divides Lake Huron from Georgian Bay as the Bruce Peninsula, dips underwater, resurfaces as Manitoulin Island, disappears to emerge again on the western shore of Lake Michigan, and finally peters out in Wisconsin. The first farmers in the Niagara region had no idea of the extent of this formation, but they and their heirs discovered that the soil between the escarpment and the lake was very fertile.

The **Niagara Falls** ⓭, where Lake Erie overflows into Lake Ontario at the rate of 14 million liters of water per minute, have always been the most celebrated feature of the escarpment. Of his pilgrimage, Charles Dickens wrote: "We went everywhere at the falls, and saw them in every aspect… Nothing in Turner's finest watercolor drawings, done in his greatest days, is so ethereal, so imaginative, so gorgeous in color as what I then beheld. I seemed to be lifted from the earth and to be looking into Heaven." Most would agree with Dickens and not with Oscar Wilde, who, noting the popularity of the Falls for honeymooners, remarked that "Niagara Falls must be the second major disappointment of American married life."

The Falls, or rather the crowds that swarm around them, have attracted a host of sideshows over the years. But the greatest carnival draw was Blondin, the French daredevil who first crossed over the cataract on a tightrope in 1859. In 1901, Annie Edson Taylor became the first person to plunge over the Falls in a barrel and live. These and other "daredevils" are remembered in the **Niagara Falls Museum**, 5651 River Road.

Map,
page 152

Niagara Falls have attracted many a daredevil, but none so bold as Blondin, whose high jinks on a tightrope above the cataract included stilt-walking.

BELOW: Blondin, a Frenchman, crosses Niagara Falls on a tightrope, 1859.

The most popular way to approach the Falls is on the *Maid of the Mist*. Wearing hooded raincoats, visitors are boated up to the Table Rock Scenic Tunnels under the Falls for a spectacular, if not intense, encounter with water.

Niagara-on-the-Lake

John Butler and his Rangers founded the town of Newark at the mouth of the Niagara River after the American revolutionary war. In 1792, when John Graves Simcoe arrived, the place was called "Niagara-on-the-Lake". It was the capital of Upper Canada, a province newly created out of the English-speaking portion of Québec. One of the first things Simcoe did was to choose a new capital, for Niagara-on-the-Lake was uncomfortably close to the United States. He selected a site at a fork of the river which he named the Thames. The capital would be called London (naturally). But Dundas Street was no sooner hacked out of the bush than Simcoe moved the capital to Toronto – which he promptly renamed York. The Mohawk Chief Joseph Brant once remarked: "General Simcoe has done a great deal for this province, he has changed the name of every place in it."

Niagara-on-the-Lake ⑭ was blessed by its fall into political obscurity. It is one of the most well-preserved colonial towns in North America. It's also home to the annual **Shaw Festival**, a major theatrical event featuring the plays of George Bernard Shaw as well as works by other writers.

The War of 1812–14

Canadian fears of American aggression were justified in June 1812 when the United States took advantage of Britains's preoccupation with Napoleon to declare war. Many Americans thought Canada would be a pushover. Issac Brock,

TIP

For a somewhat drier encounter with the Falls than aboard a boat, Minolta Tower, 6732 Oakes Drive, and Skylon, 5200 Robinson, both have viewing platforms.

BELOW: Niagara Falls, a natural wonder.

the military commander of Upper Canada, wrote of his predicament: "My situation is most critical, not from the disposition of the people… What a change an additional regiment would make in this part of the province! Most of the people have lost all confidence – I however speak loud and look big." He acted swiftly and decisively. His troops captured Fort Michilimackinac in northern Michigan and repulsed an attack at the Detroit River. These early victories won the native peoples in the area to the British cause and galvanized the settlers.

The Niagara region figured prominently in the war. The Americans attacked **Queenston**, just down river from the Falls, in October 1812. Issac Brock was killed in the Battle of Queenston Heights, though the town was successfully defended. The war dragged on, but without the example of Brock's boldness, the heavily outnumbered colony might not have held out at all.

The War of 1812–14 gave Canada a stronger sense of community identity, though it didn't end the political divisions between Tories and those calling for democratic reform in the province. It also gave a signal to Britain that this colony was still too sparsely settled for its own security.

Southwestern Ontario

Today the highway which hugs the northern shore of Lake Erie is designated **The Talbot Trail** ⓰. **St Thomas**, founded in 1817 between London and Lake Erie, was also named after Colonel Thomas Talbot, who had been granted 19,600 hectares (48,500 acres) to start a settlement in 1803. But Talbot was no saint. He ruled his "principality", as he called it, with stern efficiency. He laid down stringent rules for his settlers. Those who defaulted on the agreed conditions he evicted – a rare procedure on any frontier. And the reason why the Talbot Road was the best in Upper Canada was that farmers were held responsible for maintaining some parts of the road that fronted their properties.

The Talbot Trail rolls through dairy farms and fishing villages, tobacco farms and beaches. West of St Thomas it bends south with the lakeshore into mixed-farming country. This, the westernmost tip of Southern Ontario, is the southernmost part of Canada.

To be precise, **Point Pelee National Park** ⓰, a peninsula jutting south of **Leamington**, 50 km (30 miles) southeast of Windsor, is the southernmost part of mainland Canada. Lying at the same latitude as Rome and northern California, Point Pelee is home to plants and animals that are rarely seen in Canada. A trail through the woods and a boardwalk over the marshlands make it a living museum of natural history (open daily; entrance fee for cars). **Jack Miner's Bird Sanctuary** at **Kingsville**, 10 km (6 miles) west of the park, is one of the earliest, and most famous waterfowl pit-stops in Canada. This haven is free to migrating birds and migrating humans alike. Jack Miner said: "In the name of God, let us have one place on earth where no money changes hands." The sanctuary is run by his family as a public trust (open Mon–Sat).

Southeastern Ontario

The southern border of Ontario played an unusual part in history: as one terminus of the "Underground Rail-

Map, page 152

A legendary figure of the 1812–14 war is Laura Secord, who overheard American soldiers planning an attack and walked through enemy lines to warn the British.

BELOW: Point Pelee National Park.

road". In the early 1800s, runaway slaves from the American South were sheltered by sympathizers along several routes which led to Canada.

Reverend Josiah Henson, a self-educated slave from Maryland, made the trip with his family in 1830. He settled in **Dresden** ⑰, 90 km (56 miles) northeast of Windsor, and subsequently devoted himself to helping other fugitives. Henson was the prototype for "Uncle Tom" in Harriet Beecher Stowe's novel *Uncle Tom's Cabin*. His home in Dresden is part of **Uncle Tom's Cabin Museum** that focuses on his life and works.

Chatham, 80 km (50 miles) east of Windsor, was another terminus of the "railroad". Here the abolitionist John Brown plotted the 1859 raid on the government arsenal at Harper's Ferry, Virginia. He hoped to spark a general uprising of slaves, but he was caught, convicted of treason, and hanged.

The city of **Windsor** ⑱ is the biggest urban center on Canada's border, a kind of half-sister to Detroit. Windsor is also an automobile industry town but, unlike Detroit, has a pleasant downtown with extensive parks and gardens on the riverfront. It is noted for its casino.

The name Ontario comes from the Iroquoian word meaning "shining waters", an apt description for a province dominated by lakes of all sizes.

Lake Ontario

In the 1820s the growing towns and farms positioned along the western curve of Lake Ontario continued to nibble at the wilderness around them. **Ancaster**, **Dundas**, **Stoney Creek** and **Burlington** all eventually lost their bids for supremacy at the lakehead to the town of **Hamilton** ⑲, the "ambitious little city", 70 km (43 miles) south around the lake from downtown Toronto.

The Niagara Escarpment, referred to locally as "the mountain", divides Hamilton into split-levels. The city's steel mills and other heavy industries have given

BELOW: *Queen City,* a legacy of the British in Canada.

Hamilton a grim image in the minds of many. But the somewhat misleadingly named **Royal Botanical Gardens** incorporate a wildlife sanctuary called **Coote's Paradise**, with trails winding through 1,200 acres (485 hectares) of marsh and wooded ravines (Mediterranean Garden open daily, 9am–5pm, outdoor gardens May–Nov: daily; entrance fee).

Hamilton's architectural jewel is **Dundurn Castle**. Sir Allan Napier MacNab – landholder, financier, all-round Tory, and Hamilton's first resident lawyer – had it built in 1835 as a lavish tribute to himself. The finest home west of Montréal at the time and named for MacNab's ancestral homeland in Scotland, it is now restored as a museum to reflect the 1850s when MacNab was premier of pre-Confederation Canada (open daily 10am–4pm, Jun–early Sep; Sep–Jun closed Mon; entrance fee). Every mid-July, Hamilton's northerly neighbor, **Burlington**, hosts the Highland Games – a week of bagpipes, dancing and caber tossing.

Hamilton installed the first telephone exchange in the British Empire in 1878, only four years after Alexander Graham Bell invented the device. It was at his parents' home in **Brantford**, 40 km (25 miles) west of Hamilton, that Bell dreamed up the thing. After preliminary experiments, Bell built a phone on his return to Boston. Some of his other inventions are on display, too, at the **Bell Homestead** (open 9.30am–4pm; winter: Tue–Sun; summer: Wed–Mon; entrance fee). The telephone is not the only great idea to have been conceived in Brantford. The town is visibly proud to be the hometown of hockey great Wayne Gretzky.

The first thing to note about nearby **Kitchener ㉓**, 40 km (25 miles) north of Brantford, and **Waterloo** is how prosperous they are. Kitchener is the fastest-growing municipality in Canada. The second thing to note about the Twin Cities is how German they are. The original settlers in the area were members of the

Map, page 152

"Brantford is justified in calling herself telephone city," said Alexander Graham Bell. "The telephone was invented in Canada. It was made in the United States."

BELOW: Dundurn Castle, Hamilton.

For the Oktoberfest Kitchener and Waterloo sprout 25 "festhalls" where sauerkraut, sausage and beer are enjoyed, to the beat of oompah music.

austere Mennonite sect transplanted from the German communities of Pennsylvania in the 1780s. The Mennonites soon had German neighbors of various creeds and today Kitchener and Waterloo host the biggest **Oktoberfest** (early to mid-October), this side of the Rhine. "Good cheer" is spelled *Gemütlichkeit* in this part of the country.

The Huron road

In the 1820s, the land between Lake Huron and the modern site of Kitchener was a piece of wilderness called the **Huron Tract**. The development of this, and other bits of Crown land, was the target of the Canada Company. The company's success can be attributed to its first superintendent of operations, the Scottish novelist and statesman John Galt, and to his chosen lieutenant, Dr William (Tiger) Dunlop. Galt's first task was founding a city on the edge of the wilderness. **Guelph**, 15 km (9 miles) northeast of Kitchener, was inaugurated in April of 1827 and it is a striking blend of 19th-century architecture. The Roman Catholic Church of **Our Lady of the Immaculate Conception** dominates the skyline with twin Gothic towers.

After surveying the Huron Tract, the exuberant Dunlop had pronounced: "It is impossible to find 200 acres together which will make a bad farm." Galt wanted a road so that settlement could begin in earnest. In 1828, Dunlop directed the construction of that road, through swamps, dense forest and tangled brush. Work was slow and fever plagued the work camps. It was a stupendous achievement that is not diminished by the many improvements the road has seen since. Now Highway 8, the Huron Road became the spine of settlement in the tract.

Eighteen kilometers (11 miles) into the bush, the first Huron Road curved at

BELOW: celebrating the Oktoberfest at Kitchener.

an attractive meadow by a river. Before long the settlement that sprang up there was called **Stratford ㉑**, and the river the **Avon**. The connection to Shakespeare was strengthened in the naming of wards and streets (Romeo, Hamlet, Falstaff) while Stratford boomed in the 1850s by virtue of being the county seat and at an intersection of railway lines.

In the years after World War II, Stratford native Tom Patterson was persistent, and finally successful, in peddling his dream of a Shakespearean theater for the city. On 13 July, 1953, Alec Guinness stepped onto a stage in a riverside tent as Richard III, and the rest, as they say, is history. The tent-like (but permanent) **Festival Theater** was opened in 1957, and its "thrust stage" has influenced a generation of theater-builders. The Stratford Festival now includes two other stages (the **Avon Theater** and the **Third Stage**) and features music as well as plays. Over 500,000 people are attracted to the town annually.

Another road which helped to open up the Huron Tract is the one north from **London ㉒**, 60 km (37 miles) south of Stratford. Or south to London, if you like, because all roads in southwestern Ontario eventually lead to London. Failing to become the capital of Upper Canada, London stayed small till it became the district seat in 1826.

British tradition and the American feeling of wide open spaces are in harmony here. On the street signs of London such names as Oxford and Piccadilly mix with names from Ontario's history, like Simcoe, Talbot and, of course, Dundas Street. Other names, like Wonderland Road and Storybook Gardens, may lead visitors into thinking that they have stumbled into a kind of Neverland. The impression will be reinforced by the squeaky-cleanness, and greenness, of this relentlessly cheerful city. It isn't called "the forest city" for nothing; from any

Map, page 152

Winter transport.

BELOW: Mennonite women in western Ontario.

vantage point above the treetops, London visually disappears under a leafy blanket. The River Thames flows through the campus of the **University of Western Ontario**, a school whose presence is definitely felt in town. London boasts the **Fanshawe Pioneer Village**, a fascinating reconstruction of a pre-railway, 19th-century town, equipped with log cabins, a general store, a weaver's shop and a carriage-maker's quarters (open May–Dec: 10am–4.30pm; entrance fee). Another interesting reconstruction is the **Ska-Nah-Doht Iroquoian Village**, 32 km (20 miles) southwest. The ancestors of this area refused to become involved in the Huron-Iroquois wars and hence became known as the Neutrals. Today, visitors can explore the reconstructed longhouses, the sweat lodge and council chambers (open daily, 9am–4.30pm, July–Aug; Sep–Apr: closed weekends; entrance fee).

Western Ontario and Lake Huron

In Ontario Ministry of Tourism language, the Lake Huron shoreline is called Bluewater Country. What that means is a lakefront with cottages, beaches and a few nice places like **Bayfield**, 75 km (46 miles) north of London. This village, with its intact 19th-century main street, shady beach and fine marina, is a gem.

Twenty-one kilometers (13 miles) farther north is **Goderich ㉓**, Tiger Dunlop's town. Not merely planned, Goderich was designed; the **County Courthouse** sits on an octagonal plot (called The Square) from which streets radiate in all directions. **The Square** is probably the world's most leisurely traffic circle (or octagon). Whether or not Goderich really is "The Prettiest Town in Canada", as the signs proclaim, this spot regularly displays some of the most spectacular sunsets on earth – and that goes for the whole lakeshore, for miles inland.

BELOW: preparing the market stall.

When they saw how quickly the Huron Tract was being gobbled up, the British Government threw open for settlement the Indian territory immediately to the north of it. The Queen's Bush, as it was called, was not as fertile as land farther south, and some of the boom towns soon went bust. The next farming frontier, Western Canada, opened up just in time for the overflow of settlers from the Queen's Bush. Those that remained on the stony soil turned to raising beef cattle. Several railroads snaked into Ontario between 1850 and 1900. Towns along the routes prospered, especially those where lines crossed. But as the rail lines fed city factories, industries in small towns declined and the smallest towns focused solely on the needs of the surrounding farming communities.

In the 1970s there was a swell of interest in the history and architecture of Ontario's small towns. A good illustration of this is the **Blyth Festival**. A community hall was built in 1920 in **Blyth**, 33 km (20 miles) east of Goderich. Upstairs in the hall is a fine auditorium, with a sloping floor and stage, which lay unused from the 1930s until the mid-1970s when it was "discovered" and refurbished as the home for an annual summer festival dedicated to Canadian plays, most of them new, and most of them celebrating small-town and farming experiences. That the Blyth Festival has become the darling of Canada's urban drama critics indicates both its theatrical quality and the potency of its subject-matter, namely the history and people of rural Canada.

About 17 km (11 miles) south of Blyth on the literary map lies **Clinton**, the home of writer Alice Munro. Her beautifully layered stories transcend regional interest and "local color". There is no better introduction than her works to the life of small-town Ontario.

This region has always been sparsely settled; the soil is thin, and navigation on

Map,
page 152

BELOW: sailing on Lake Huron.

the lake hereabouts can be treacherous. But many people make the effort to reach **Tobermory ㉔**, the resort that looks like a fishing village at the tip of the **Bruce Peninsula ㉕**. They might be heading north to **Manitoulin Island ㉖**, the largest freshwater island in the world, on the giant ferry *Chi-cheemaun* (big canoe). Or they might be getting ready to hike the 720 km (450 miles) of the **Bruce Trail** along the Niagara Escarpment, through farmland and wilderness, to the Falls.

South of **Georgian Bay**, on the eastern ridge of the Escarpment, a range of large hills provides the best ski-runs in Ontario. Ontarians call these hills the **Blue Mountains**, but not too loudly in the presence of anyone from the Rockies.

Ste Marie Among the Hurons

To visit the small peninsula poking out into Georgian Bay is to step a little farther back into history than most places in rural Ontario permit. This area is called **Huronia**, where 350 years ago French Jesuit missionaries traveled and preached among the Huron Indians.

When the lonely fortified mission of **Ste Marie Among the Hurons** was established in 1639, it was the only inland settlement of Europeans north of Mexico. It prospered for 10 years; but the Huron nation was eventually destroyed in wars with their enemies, the Iroquois, who also tortured and killed the Jesuits. The movie and novel *The Black Robe* tell this story. Ste Marie was not attacked, but the fort was burned by retreating Jesuits to keep it out of Iroquois hands. After much research, the mission and its everyday life have been re-created on a site 5 km (3 miles) east of **Midland ㉗** (open Apr–Oct: daily; Nov: Mon–Fri; entrance fee). It was in this area that Fathers Jean de Brébeuf and Gabriel Lalament were tortured and then brutally killed by the Iroquois in 1649. Their

BELOW: Georgian Bay coastline.

remains were housed across from the mission in the Martyrs' Shrine, a towering edifice that commands a spectacular vista over the surrounding country. Nearby is **Wye Marsh Wildlife Center** with boardwalks extending over the marshlands. A visitors' center explains the ecology of the area and features guided tours (open daily; entrance fee).

Downtown Midland is a quaint, pretty town with interesting shops, a spooky library, and great doughnuts at **Georgian Bakery**.

The thousands of lakes in Ontario and, particularly, those in the Canadian Shield region, just to the north, provide a cherished escape for city dwellers. The war of extermination against the trees, which was the settlers' rule, has given way to a desire to preserve the woodlands and waters of the near north for recreational purposes.

However, the **Georgian Bay, Muskoka** and **Haliburton** regions can no longer be described as forested wilds, dotted as they are by thousands and thousands of cottages. For Ontario is one of the few places in the world where seemingly everyone, rich and not so rich, has a country estate even if it's only a humble cabin.

A museum in the woods

To the north of Haliburton and the northeast of Muskoka lies the last real expanse of wild land in Southern Ontario – the 7,600-sq-km (2,934-square-mile) **Algonquin Provincial Park** ㉘. Set aside as a provincial park in 1893, Algonquin preserves the primordial, aboriginal and pioneer heritages of Ontario as a kind of natural museum (Visitor Center open end Apr–end Oct: 10am–5pm, daily; Nov–Apr: weekends).

Map, page 152

TIP

Entry to Algonquin Provincial Park is by permit (arrive early or book ahead, tel: 705 633 5538). Avoid peak vacation times if you plan to explore by canoe.

BELOW LEFT: cottage country. **BELOW RIGHT:** Ste Marie Among the Hurons.

Algonquin Provincial Park can only be explored on foot or by canoe. Several day treks, including the Beaver Pond Trail, start from the Highway 60 approach.

BELOW: a thirsty resident of Northern Ontario.

Loons, the oldest known birds, abound in the park's 2,500 or more lakes as they did 10,000 years ago after the last Ice Age. Algonquin Indian "vision pits" can be found in the northwest corner of the park. Here, in these rock-lined holes, a young Algonquin would fast for days waiting for the vision of a spiritual guardian who would draw the rite of passage to a close. And in the park's interior, east of **Opeongo Lake**, lies the last stand of great white pines in Ontario. These few dozen ancient pines are all that are left of the huge forests cut to provide masts for the British Navy.

Algonquin should be seen by canoe. Heading north on **Canoe Lake** away from the access highway, it is only one or two portages before the motorboats and "beer with ghetto-blaster" campers are left behind. In the interior, porcupines, beaver, deer, wolves, bear and moose can all be seen by canoeists. In August, park naturalists will even organize wolf howls, where campers head out *en masse* at night to try and raise the cry of the great canines. The loons, however, need no such encouragement. Their haunting cry, which the Cree believed was the sound of a warrior who had been refused entry to paradise, can be heard on every lake in the park.

Each season brings its own character to Algonquin. Spring is the time of wildflowers, mating calls, white water and blackflies as thick as night. Summer brings brilliant thunder storms, mosquitoes in place of blackflies, acres of blueberries, and water actually warm enough to swim in. In the fall, Algonquin turns into a Group of Seven canvas. The funeral for the forest's leaves is as triumphant and colorful as that of any New Orleans jazz singer. Uniform green gives way to a kaleidoscope of scarlet, auburn, yellow and mauve, while in the winter, the park falls deathly silent as it waits for the resurrection under a mantle of snow.

Algonquin, however, is not without its problems, problems typical of an urban society unable to control its effect upon the natural environment. Not only is most of Algonquin under license to logging interests, whose long-term effect on the ecosystem cannot be gauged, but it is also being scarred by the effects of industrial pollution .

Map, page 152

Northern Ontario

Highway maps of Ontario divide the province in two: one side showing southern Ontario, the other northern. **Sudbury** ㉙, 390 km (242 miles) north of Toronto, is called "the gateway to the north" and it marks the boundary between the two. It is a city of 150,000, known for its copper and nickel mines, and its cultural focus points include **Science North**, an interactive museum for families (open daily; entrance fee), and a lively summer music event, the **Northern Lights Folk Festival**.

Most travelers never give the north of Ontario a look, never turn over the map. Myth has it that northern Ontario is an endless tract of conifers, lakes, bogs, mining camps, moose, and mosquitoes. Like all myths it's true in part, but only in part.

Just north of Algonquin Park is the Near North region of lakes and pristine wilderness areas, such as **Temagami** toward the Québec border. The region's largest center is **North Bay**, a place of middle-class families and Presbyterian values. Here the famous Dionne quintuplets were born in a homestead which is now a museum, complete with the bed where they were delivered. Nearby, at **Temagami Station**, Grey Owl, the Englishman who successfully posed as a native environmentalist writer in the 1930s in the UK and US lived and wrote.

Cars taper off along northern highways and settlements are further apart. Every second vehicle is a logging truck. The gold, copper, and silver mines in such places as **Timmins**, **Cobalt** and **Kirkland Lake** are another vital link to the northern way of life. And every community, it seems, from **Attawapistat** to **Wawa**, has its fishing holes and hunting areas. One of the most popular routes into the wilderness, which Canadians call "bush," is aboard the **Polar Bear Express**. It leaves every day but Friday, late June until Labor Day, from **Cochrane**, a place of fishing poles and down vests, to the Arctic tidewater towns of **Moosonee** and **Moose Factory**. The adventurous bring their own canoes and paddle on to even more isolated James Bay outposts.

Soo, Sault Ste Marie, lying 296 km (184 miles) west of Sudbury, is a cultural and sporting center, whose attractions include the 114-mile (183-km) Agawa Canyon train tour and, for the angler, the largest fish hatchery in Ontario.

Farther west still is the **Lake of the Woods** district and **Kenora**, a pulp and paper center, near the Manitoba border. This land rivals the Muskokas for resorts and bluewater camping. For those whose idea of Canada is a place where you contract a bush pilot and sea plane and fly in to an isolated cabin for a week or two, Lake of the Wood fits. "Fly-in" resorts are extremely popular, with loons, sunsets, a moose or two, and ads that read, "Ask for Don or Lynn". Now that's Northern Ontario.

BELOW: pathway through the snow in Temagami.

MONTRÉAL: WHERE EAST MEETS FRANCE

The second largest French city in the world after Paris, Montréal has extraordinary personality. Worldly but romantic, perhaps a little extravagant, it is earnest in its aim to enjoy life

I n the capital of French Canada, a little patience goes a long way. The Québecois have a proud and sometimes obsessive attitude towards their language and culture and the 6.8 million French speakers of the province are deeply aware of being surrounded by almost 300 million anglophones whose culture seems to impinge upon their own. But there is also a tinge of North American culture with a refreshing and lively approach to both work and play, and a *joie de vivre* is evident on Montréal's rue St-Denis or at the Winter Carnival.

Always ready to celebrate something, Montréal seems to erupt on a fairly regular basis. But there was a day many years ago when this region erupted as it has never done since. The result of this volcanic explosion was the felicitous appearance of **Mont-Royal** Ⓐ and for posterity the park on its crest in the center of the city. And so today, from parking lots on rue Camilien Houde, to the lookout with its splendid view of the city, it's still the ideal place to begin a visit to Montréal.

Surrounded by the waters of the St Lawrence, centering on the mountain and penetrated by a maze of subterranean shopping plazas and passages, Montréal is an unusually three-dimensional city. Everyone refers to Mont-Royal as "the mountain" despite its being only 250 meters (820 ft) high. The surrounding terrain is so flat, however, that the view from the summit is excellent. In the distance lie the other mountains of the Monteregian group. On a clear day, you can see as far as New York state's Adirondacks and the Green Mountains of Vermont.

The city spreads out down the mountainside to the St Lawrence. The view of the downtown core has changed rapidly over the last two decades, but the cruciform tower called **Place-Ville-Marie** on Boulevard Réne-Lévesque and, to the right, the slightly taller **Bank of Commerce** building, still dominate. Between them, staid and austerely Victorian, is the **Sun Life** building, once the tallest building in the British Commonwealth.

French first

French is the language of business as confidently as it is the language of road signs and storefronts, but visitors will still find the city conveniently bilingual. Until the 1980s Montréalers spoke of "two solitudes": a division of labor between English management and French employees and a division of the city between English and (usually less privileged) French quarters. After the election of the separatist Parti Québécois to the provincial government in 1976, many English-speaking Montréalers, or "anglos", left to live in other provinces, though many stayed behind to accept a new relationship with the French language and the Québecois.

PRECEDING PAGES: cold snap, Québec. **LEFT:** summer in the city. **BELOW:** old town, Montréal.

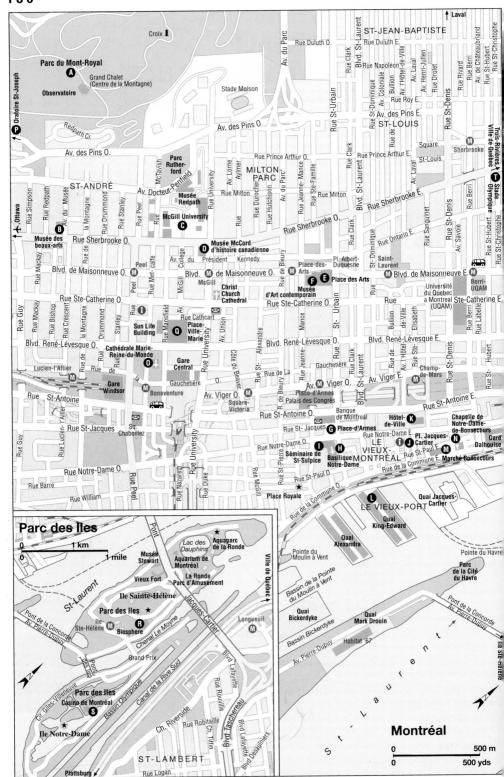

Montréal

Downtown Montréal

Côte des Neiges and rue Guy bring you down into the heart of the downtown shopping district. The finer grade of stores and hotels such as the **Ritz-Carlton** run along this section of rue Sherbrooke, being the lower limit of the "Golden Square Mile", the old domain of the wealthiest anglos. The **Musée des Beaux-Arts de Montréal** ⓑ, known for its recent coups in attracting exclusive exhibitions, is here. It houses an extensive permanent collection of works by both Canadian and European masters (open Tue–Sun 11am–6pm; entrance fee). A few blocks east is **McGill University** ⓒ, former home of Ernest Rutherford, Stephen Leacock and, many insist, Jack the Ripper. Its **Musée d'histoire naturelle Redpath** features fossils, minerals and zoological exhibits (open Mon–Fri 9am–5pm; Sun 1pm–5pm; entrance fee). Opposite the university stands the **Musée McCord d'histoire canadienne** ⓓ with its emphasis on the social history of Canada (open Tue–Fri 10am–6pm; Sat–Sun 10am–5pm; entrance fee).

Rue Ste-Catherine, two blocks south, is livelier. It is lined with boutiques, cafés, department stores, fast-food joints (especially *croissanteries* and smoked-meat delis) and arcades. Intersecting this bustling artery is rue Crescent, one of the concentrations of bistros and restaurants that give Montréal its reputation for nightlife and table-hopping. Here Montréalers indulge their second-favorite sport (ice-hockey is still number one): eating, drinking, seeing and being seen.

Underground travel

Farther east the largest department stores, and a nexus of multi-story shopping centers – **Les Golden Terrasses, 2001 and 2020, Place Montréal Trust, Les Cours Mont-Royal, Centre Eaton** – are joined by underground passages to the Métro, Montréal's advanced subway system. Trains on rubber wheels thread their way between "designer" stations, each having its own bold architecture. Opened in 1966, with its quiet, high-speed trains, it's still the most efficient and pleasant way to get around Montréal.

Kaleidoscope of arts and cultures

Still farther east are the **Complexe Desjardins**, another dramatically conceived shopping center, and the **Place des Arts** ⓔ, comprising the Théâtre Maisonneuve and the Théâtre Port-Royal, housed on top of one another in the step-pyramid style building, and the **Salle Wilfred Pelletier**, with elegant, sweeping curves, the home of Montréal's orchestra and opera.

L'Orchestre Symphonique de Montréal (OSM) has emerged under the leadership of Charles Dutoit as one of the world's great orchestras and is often called "the world's first and finest French orchestra", drawing rave reviews on tours and prizes for many of its recordings. Its home in the Place des Arts also houses Montréal's modern art museum, the **Musée d'art contemporain** ⓕ (open Tue–Sun, 11am–6pm; Wed till 9pm; entrance fee).

Beyond the Place des Arts on Boulevard St-Laurent, there emerges an eclectic jumble of small, ardent businesses representing the ethnic communities who have

Map, page 180

Hockey break

BELOW: browsing on the rue des Artistes.

Montréalers thrive on festivities. The February Snow Festival is followed through the year by fireworks, jazz, comedy, gastronomy, film and dance.

BELOW: on the pitch at McGill University.

made this their neighborhood: Jewish, Italian, Portuguese, Greek. Within this area lies another focus of Montréal's nightlife: **rue Prince Arthur**. Closed to motor traffic, Prince Arthur frequently fills up with hundreds of people lining up to eat at its popular Greek or Vietnamese restaurants. Most of Montréal's Greek restaurants allow patrons to bring their own wine, which makes an excellent dinner easy to afford. (Every *dépanneur,* or corner grocery store sells decent table wine.) The crowds may appear daunting, but the lines move quickly, and street-artists, jugglers and acrobats usually show up to entertain.

Around the corner from the park at the east end of Prince Arthur is rue St-Denis. One stretch of road here was known for many years as the "Latin Quarter" of Montréal: bohemian, a little ramshackle, politicized. Today it surpasses rue Crescent as the hub of Montréal's night-time activity. The annual **International Jazz Festival** and **Just for Laughs Comedy Festival** revolves around St-Denis, and every year on 24 June, the traditional feast day of Québec's patron saint, St-Jean Baptiste, Montréalers flock here to celebrate Québec. But throughout the year, St-Denis has a particularly Québecois vibrancy and charm.

Vieux-Montréal

Although Jacques Cartier discovered an Indian settlement called Hochelaga (near the site of McGill University) when he landed in 1535, Montréal was not permanently settled until a century later. The founders' purpose was to save the pagan "savages": by converting them to Christianity, they would save their souls from eternal damnation. The project began when a secret society of wealthy Frenchmen formed a subgroup, the Société de Notre Dame de Montréal and commissioned Paul de Chomedy, Sieur de Maisonneuve, to establish a settle-

ment in this remote wilderness far from "civilization" – 70 recruits and young Jeanne Mance, a nurse, accompanied him.

The village of Québec in that year, 1642, was having a bad time defending itself against the brutal attacks of the Iroquois and they felt sure Maisonneuve's mission had almost no chance of surviving beyond a few weeks, but Maisonneuve pressed on resolutely. By chance, or perhaps, as Maisonneuve thought, by divine intervention, the Iroquois ignored the new settlement, and when winter came the settlers were able to erect a few huts and a log palisade.

The late 17th-century European vogue for hats made of beaver pelt gave Montréal a secondary purpose, the fur trade, which became its primary object, with greater organization and profits. The accommodation of business and religion as twin forces in Montréal's history is visible everywhere, particularly in Vieux-Montréal.

North up rue St-Pierre and east along rue Notre Dame leads to the hub of Vieux-Montréal, **Place d'Armes** Ⓖ. Banks surround the square on three sides; it was once the heart of the Canadian financial establishment, dominated by anglo-Montréalers. On the south side stands the **Basilique de Notre Dame** Ⓗ, the symbol *par excellence* of Québecois Roman Catholicism. Maisonneuve, standing on his pedestal in the center of the square, seems perhaps caught in a struggle between God and Mammon, between the power and the influence of the "two solitudes". But that is in the past. Today the square is busy with horse-drawn *calèches* and the inevitable tour buses.

The facade of Notre Dame is plain because stone workers were rare in Québec when the church was built around 1829. In stark contrast its interior is a magnificently ornate tribute to the importance of woodworking and decoration in

Map, page 180

For water transport, Quai Jacques Cartier is the departure point for Parc des Îles ferries, jet-boats to Lachine Rapids, water taxis and even a paddle steamer.

BELOW LEFT: Basilique de Notre Dame. **BELOW RIGHT:** Place d'Armes.

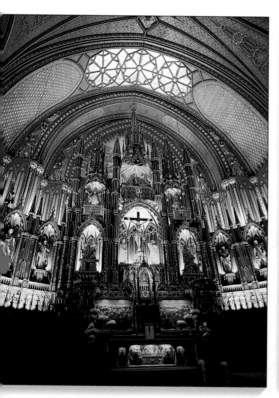

In the 18th century rue St-Jacques vied with New York City's Wall Street for banking supremacy. See mechanical piggy banks at Banque de Montréal's museum.

BELOW: the old city, rue Bonsecours.

Québecois tradition. Everywhere there is paint laced with real gold and the reredos gleams in a vivid blue. Ironically, Montréal's finest church was designed by an Irish American, James O'Donnell, but the interior is the inspiration of a French-Canadian, Victor Bourgeau. Neither ugly nor the epitome of subtle elegance, it is what it was meant to be: simply overwhelming.

Adjacent to the west wall of the basilica stands Montréal's oldest building, the **Seminaire de St-Sulpice ❶**, built in 1685. The Sulpicians became the seigneurs or landlords of all Montréal when they took over missionary responsibilities from the Societé de Notre Dame in 1663. More than 300 years after its construction, the seminary still serves as the residence for the Sulpicians.

Across the square stands the English businessman's retort to Notre Dame's assertion of indomitable French-Canadian values: the serene neo-Classical **Banque de Montréal**, built in 1847. During banking hours, the main hall is open to visitors, as is a tiny interesting museum.

Walking east past the shops and cafés on rue Notre Dame, you encounter on the north side the old Napoleonic-style **Palais de Justice** with its silver dome, and on the south side the less graceful "new" Palais de Justice with its august pillars and heavy doors. The Latin inscription on the cornice, "He who transgresses the law shall seek the help of the law in vain," adds to the severity of the whole effect. Both buildings are government offices today.

Opening off the south side of rue Notre Dame lies **Place Jacques Cartier ❿**, a center of much less serious activity than Place d'Armes. Cobblestoned, floriated, peopled and surrounded by restaurants and terrace cafés in buildings a century and a half old, it preserves the charm, the human scale, of another era. At the top of the square stands **Nelson's Column**, the city's oldest monument. Nation-

alist Québecois have never been entirely happy with the dominance of the square by this hero of the British Empire, the scourge of Napoleon's navy, but Horatio has survived controversy as graciously as erosion. Lest the monument should be thought a rather diminutive replica of the column in Trafalgar Square, know that Montréal's predates London's by 34 years.

Facing Nelson across rue Notre Dame is the **Hôtel de Ville** (city hall), an elegant Second Empire style building with its slender columns and mansard roofs. Opposite, on the south side, stands the **Château de Ramezay** (1705), looking like a sturdy farmhouse, but nevertheless the focal point of more than a century of early Canadian history. Today, the château is a private museum with some impressively equipped 18th-century living quarters and many fascinating artifacts. Look out for North America's first paper money: playing cards authorized as legal tender when a cargo of coins was delayed on its way across the Atlantic (open Jun–Sep, 10am–6pm; Oct–May, 10am–4.30pm, closed Mon; entrance fee).

Yet another site to see here is the **Vieux Port** ●, now an entertainment area that offers summer evenings of music, dancing and beer under the stars with the city skyline as a backdrop. The port also provides the best view of the **Marché Bonsecours** ●, which served as the Lower Canada Parliament during its construction (1849–52), but for almost a century was Montréal's principal marketplace. Its long, classical facade and silver dome greeted thousands of immigrants and travelers in the 19th century. It now houses municipal offices.

Beside the Marché Bonsecours stands the **Chappelle de Notre Dame de Bon-Secours** ●, also known as the **Sailors' Church** as sailors have traditionally come here to give thanks for being saved from a shipwreck.

Rue St-Paul on the west side of Place Jacques Cartier is mostly given over to shops and cafés, where you will find an abundance of Montréal's special brand of *joie de vivre*.

Until the 1960s, religion as much as language set French Canada apart from the rest of North America. In the middle of the anglo business district Monsignor Ignace Bourget built **Cathédrale Marie-Ronde-du-Monde** ●, a one-third scale replica of St Peter's in Rome. But nowhere is the role of religion more obvious than at **Oratoire St-Joseph** ●, the church that rises 152 meters (500 ft) above the street on the western summit of Mont-Royal. It rose up out of a wave of popular devotion to St Joseph, the patron saint of the worker, led by the humble Brother André who became famous for his curative powers during the first half of the 20th century. If the exterior is more remarkable for its size than its beauty (only the dome of St Peter's in the Vatican is larger), the austere simplicity of the modern interior is more lovely. At daily recitals, the organ with its 5,811 pipes thunders through the vast church. Impressive in quite a different way is the crypt with its rows of crutches, donated by the miraculously healed, and banks of devotional candles. Brother André's tiny living quarters still stand in the shadow of the oratory.

St Joseph's represents the Québec of a different era. Ruled between 1936 and 1959 (except for the war years) by Maurice Duplessis, an autocratic premier

TIP

Visit Maison du Sir Georges-Etienne Cartier, 458 Notre Dame Est, for a peek into the life of a 19th-century statesman of Québec (open mid–Apr–mid-Dec: daily).

ORATOIRE ST-JOSEPH

One of the greatest of Montréal's monuments is the immense Oratoire St-Joseph on Mont-Royal. It was the dreamchild of Alfred Bessette, Brother André, who was porter at the nearby Collège Notre Dame when he developed a reputation as "the miracle worker," because of the many cures he performed. The secret of his cure was the application of "oil of St Joseph" to the bodies of the sick. Soon the sick were flocking to him by the thousands.

People were simply asked to donate money or time to its construction and the church began to take shape in 1924. When money ran out during the Depression, the energetic Brother André recommended that a statue of St Joseph be placed in the center of the roofless church. "If he wants a roof over his head, he'll get it," he said. Two months later money was found to continue with the building.

Map, page 180

Île Notre Dame is a haven for picnickers and cyclists and even sports an artificial beach and fresh-water swimming lake.

BELOW: roller-coasting at La Ronde.
RIGHT: picnic on Île Ste-Hélène.

known as *le Chef* or *le Patron*, Québec was conservative and backward. But the 1960s, with the death of Duplessis and an atmosphere of prosperity and change, brought the "quiet revolution", a deep change in the attitudes and ideas of Québecois. The buildings of the 1960s in Montréal are monuments not to the church but to modernity. **Place-Ville-Marie Q**, perhaps the most successful creation of the famous urban architect I.M. Pei (responsible for the pyramid outside the Louvre in Paris), with its cruciform tower and underground plaza, pioneered the concept of the shopping mall in 1962. For Expo 67 Moshe Safdie, a student at McGill University, designed **Habitat**, a sort of cubist representation of the mountain made out of 158 concrete apartment units.

Parc des Îles

The site of **Expo 67**, on two man-made islands in the St Lawrence, is now Parc des Îles de Montréal. **Île Ste-Hélène** and **Île Notre Dame** can be identified by Buckminster Fuller's geodesic dome, built to house the US pavilion. The **Biosphère R**, on Ste-Hélène, is now home to an environmental observation center focusing on the St Lawrence-Great Lakes ecosystem (open July–Aug: 10am–6pm; Sep–June: 10am–5pm, closed Tues; entrance fee). An amusement park, **La Ronde**, is on the island's eastern tip (open weekends only mid–end May, open daily to Labor day; entrance fee). Nearby is the the **Vieux Fort** (1822), with summer re-enactments of maneuvers by the Fraser Highlanders. The **Musée David M. Stewart** provides insight into early European exploration and the settlement of New France. (Fort and museum open early May–mid-Oct: daily 10am–6pm, Thurs till 9pm; mid-Oct–April: 10am–5pm, closed Tues; entrance fee.) By night on the Île Notre Dame, site of the **Canadian Grand Prix**, Montréalers and visitors try their luck at the **Casino de Montréal S** with its fine river and city views (open daily 11am–3am; free).

The Big O

Perhaps the most impressive of Montréal's modern monuments is the **Parc Olympique**, one of the world's most ambitious sports complexes, located on rue Sherbrooke Est. The **Stade Olympique T** is the pride and despair of Montréalers. Known variously as the *Big O* and the *Big Owe*, it cost taxpayers more than $700 million and was not fully completed until 11 years after the Olympic Games it was built to serve. The controversial stadium, with its suspended retractable roof and the highest inclined tower in the world, is a magnificent piece of architecture. It has one of the best views in the city (tours in English twice daily, 12.40pm and 3.40pm; closed mid-Jan–mid-Feb; entrance fee). Its main occupants today are professional baseball's Montréal Expos.

Next to the stadium is the **Biodôme de Montréal**, featuring flora and fauna from four different ecosystems (open daily: 9am–5pm, summer till 7pm; entrance fee).

Opposite the Parc Olympique are the **Botanical Gardens**, the world's third largest after London and Berlin, with 73 hectares (180 acres) of flora (the **Arid Regions** greenhouse is the best place to escape from a Montréal snowstorm). More than 250,000 species are housed in the **Insectarium** (open daily 9am–5pm in winter, till 7pm in summer; entrance free).

GETTING A KICK OUT OF THE GREAT OUTDOORS

The country's huge land and water masses and varied climate provide countless opportunities for outdoor pursuits and sports – not just ice hockey.

Canadians are avid tourists in their own country. Some families spend entire summer vacations in their favorite national and provincial parks in pursuit of outdoor activity. Others have vacation homes, known as "cottages," regardless of their size. Boaters head for the waters, tenters to the back-roads. Bird-watchers, fishermen and canoeists, too, find plenty of space for these gentle pursuits. If all that sounds too tame, there is plenty of scope for whitewater rafting, heli-hiking, even heli-fishing. Parks have campgrounds, supervised beaches, hiking and cycling trails.

Even city-dwellers can enjoy walking and cycling trails cut through municipal parks, well endowed with wooded areas, rivers and lakes.

PARTICIPANT SPORTS

In the realm of participant sports, golf and tennis are summer's favorites. Cricket and soccer have their adherents. Lacrosse, which originated as a rough native tribal contest, has been tamed to a seven-a-side game.

In winter, ice and snow are welcomed by many. That's when city walking and cycling paths are transformed into cross-country ski and snow-shoeing trails; fishermen cut holes in the ice, dog-team enthusiasts have race meets, amateurs enjoy sleigh rides,while alpine skiers head for the mountain slopes.

△ **WHITEWATER RAFTING**
The South Nahanni River, which flows through Nahanni National Park in the Northwest Territories, offers some of the most thrilling whitewater in the country.

▷ **HORSE RIDING**
Stables and outfitters operate throughout Canada. You can join up with prairie cowboys or ride long ocean beaches, but best of all is trail-riding in the Rockies' national parks.

▷ **ICE HOCKEY**
An important ice hockey match will bring the country to a halt. Top teams include the Montréal Canadiens and the Toronto Maple Leafs.

△ HIKING

Parks have well marked trails, graded for most abilities. Also there is a growing network of long-distance footpaths, such as the Rideau Trail in Ontario, or the West Coast Trail in BC.

▽ RIVER EXPEDITIONS

Canada's magnificent scenery and wildlife are often best observed from the water. Canoes can be rented and outfitters offer guided river expeditions through otherwise inaccessible areas.

ON THE SLOPES

The mountains of Québec, Alberta and British Columbia are the most popular skiing areas. For added excitement, helicopters drop skiers on remote mountain tops.

FISHING

Canada's lakes, rivers and coastlines provide a haven for fishing enthusiasts with salmon, Arctic char, lake trout and grayling among the catches. Permits are required.

SPORTS WORTH WATCHING OUT FOR

Baseball, ice hockey and Canadian football all have amateur and professional teams and hordes of enthusiastic supporters. In summer youngsters play "little league" baseball. A treat for the kids around Toronto is to visit the Sky Dome to watch the Toronto Blue Jays play American opponents.

In winter little-leaguers trade baseball mits for hockey skates and take to community ice rinks. While the origins of ice hockey (known in Canada simply as "hockey") are murky, there is no doubt it is Canada's sporting gift to the world. This is a major spectator sport, with teams competing from all over North America. If the Edmonton Oilers, Montréal Canadiens, or Toronto Maple Leaves arrive at the annual Stanley Cup game in late spring, then the country comes to a halt to watch.

Canadian football, which has its origins in 19th-century English rugby, is played by high school and university teams as well as commercial league teams. Football's high point is the Gray Cup in late November or early December. Parades and post-game festivities bring Gray Cup fever to a high pitch; the game itself often has well fortified fans cheering their teams on.

QUÉBEC:
HEART OF FRENCH CANADA

Fiercely proud of its French-speaking traditions, the province of
Québec, from the frozen north to the fertile land
along the St Lawrence, has developed its own distinct culture

Map,
pages
192/193

A t 1,504,687 sq km (594,860 sq miles), Québec is the largest eastern province, lying between Ontario and New Brunswick, Hudson Bay and the Gulf of St Lawrence. Montréal, Québec City and the other main population centers are along the St Lawrence River and on the east coast. The 6.8 million Québecois are deeply aware of being surrounded by almost 300 million anglophones whose culture seems to impinge on their own. Don't be surprised if you sometimes encounter a protective and proud attitude towards language and culture, two great local preoccupations.

The Eastern Townships

For hundreds of years, the Eastern Townships have been a place of refuge and of peace. Once predominantly English, the region is now 90 percent French (though the majority can speak both languages) and is now known as *Cantons-de-l'Est*. During the American War of Independence, many who preferred to stay loyal to the British crown settled in these parts and it has retained an English and American flavor throughout its history. It also drew benefit from the American Civil War, when southerners who felt uncomfortable in the northern states would spend holidays in one of the Townships' many fine old hotels. But no friction between the Townships and New Englanders survives and today they are the closest of neighbors. The international border runs right down the main street of **Beebe Plain** and in one town straight across the counter of the general store – a problem that the owner solves by putting one cash register at each end of the counter.

Highway 10 from Montréal will get you into the Townships in about one hour. **Granby**, just north of the highway, 84 km (52 miles) east from Montréal, is known for its zoo and collection of fountains.

Head on for another 45 km (37 miles) towards **Mont Orford ❶** (a ski resort with a chairlift to the summit year-round) and **Magog** for the most beautiful country. The gentle hills and valleys are an extension of the ancient Appalachian mountain range, and with its intricate network of lakes and streams, its country villages, dairy cattle, sheep and strawberry fields, this part of Québec has a bucolic charm that is unusual in the often rugged terrain of the province. Indeed, **North Hatley** (on Route 108 at the north end of Lake Massawippi) rests in a shielded valley, warmed by sunlight reflected from the lake, giving it a "microclimate" that prolongs summer and softens winter enough to make it the home of hummingbirds and flora normally found far to the south. Equally unusual in Québec is the English-language

LEFT: ice sculptures at Québec's winter carnival.
BELOW: the thrill of hot-dog skiing.

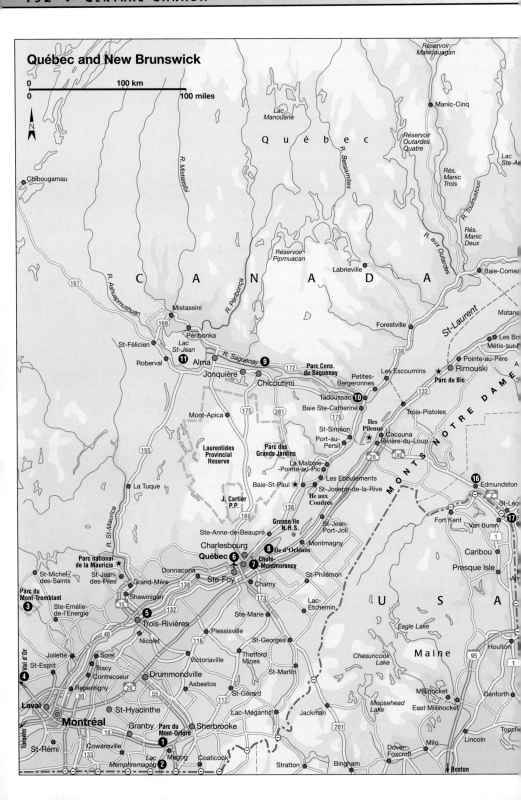

Québec and New Brunswick

0 ____ 100 km
0 ____ 100 miles

N

Chibougamau

Q u é b e c

Lac Manouane

Réservoir Mahidouagan

Manic-Cinq

Réservoir Outardes Quatre

Rés. Manic Trois

Lac Ste-A

R. Mistassibi

R. Péribonca

R. Betsiarnites

R. aux Outardes

R. Toulnustouc

Rés. Manic Deux

C A N A D A

167

R. Ashuapmushuan

Labrieville

Baie-Comea

Mistassini

169

St-Félicien

Péribonka

Lac St-Jean

Forestville

St-Laurent

Matane

Les Bo
Métis-sur-l

Roberval

11

Alma

R. Saguenay

Jonquière

9

Chicoutimi

172

Parc Cons. du Saguenay

Petites-Bergeronnes

Les Escoumins

138

Pointe-au-Père

Rimouski

Parc du Bic

132

Mont-Apica

175

381

Tadoussac

10

Baie Ste-Catherine

Trois-Pistoles

St-Siméon

170

Iles Pilenus

M O N T S   N O T R E   D A M E

155

Laurentides Provincial Reserve

Parc des Grands Jardins

Port-au-Persil

Cacouna

Rivière-du-Loup

La Malbaie -Pointe-au-Pic

20

185

La Tuque

J. Cartier P.P.

169

Baie-St-Paul

Ile aux Coudres

Les Eboulements

St-Joseph-de-la-Rive

16

Edmundston

St-Léo

138

Grosse Ile N.H.S.

St-Jean-Port-Joli

Fort Kent

Van Buren

17

Parc national de la Mauricie

St-Michel-des-Saints

St-Jean-des-Piles

Grand-Mère

Donnaconna

Ste-Anne-de-Beaupré

Charlesbourg

Québec

6

Chute-Montmorency

7

8

Ile d'Orléans

Montmagny

St-Philémon

1

Caribou

Presque Isle

Parc du Mont-Tremblant

3

Ste-Emélie-de-l'Energie

Shawinigan

15

5

Trois-Rivières

132

138

Ste-Foy

Charny

173

St-Joseph-de-la-Rive

Lac-Etchemin

Eagle Lake

U   S   A

Nicolet

116

Ste-Marie

Plessisville

St-Georges

Chesuncook Lake

Maine

95

Houlton

1

Val d'Or

Joliette

40

Sorel

Tracy

Victoriaville

Thetford Mines

St-Martin

Moosehead Lake

St-Esprit

4

Contrecoeur

Drummondville

Asbestos

30

20

Repentigny

112

St-Gérard

Millinocket

Danforth

Laval

St-Hyacinthe

Lac-Mégantic

Jackman

East Millinocket

Montréal

Granby

Parc du Mont-Orford

1

Sherbrooke

201

Dover-Foxcroft

Milo

Lincoln

Topsfie

Toronto

10

St-Rémi

Cowansville

Magog

Coaticook

Stratton

Bingham

Boston

133

Lac Memphremagog

2

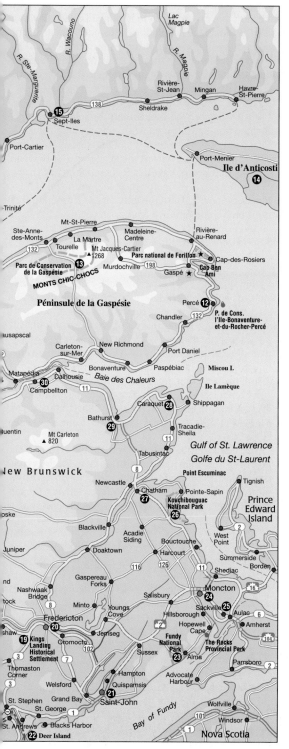

summer theater performed at **The Piggery**.

Long, slender **Lake Memphrémagog**
❷ is the largest in the area; boat cruises
and a variety of water sports are available
at the town of Magog on its northern tip.
On its west shore, the beautiful hillside
Benedictine monastery of **St-Benoît-du-
Lac** manufactures cheese and chocolate
(open Mon–Sat: 9–10.45am, 2–4.30pm).

The Laurentians

Spring, which in Québec lasts about a day
and a half, is the only season in which
Montréalers avoid the Laurentians. It is
the playground just beyond the backyard
of the metropolis; though its wooded
lakes and hills are still lovely, the difficulty is often where to get away from it all
when everyone has come to do just that.

Winter is ski season; almost everyone
in Montréal skis either cross-country or
downhill. In summer, families pack up the
car and head to the cottage for swimming,
sailing, windsurfing and waterskiing. In
fall, the leaves turn those deep shades of
red and orange that draw hikers parading
over the hills and valleys.

Not all the Laurentian towns are equally
picturesque. Prettiness tends to be in proportion to size, though **St-Sauveur-des-
Monts** and **Ste-Adèle**, 60 km (37 miles)
northwest of Montréal), are worth visiting for their restaurants and character.

The best bet, however, is to take
Autoroute 15, or the more scenic and slow
Rte 117 to **Parc du Mont-Tremblant** ❸.
About 140 km (87 miles) from Montréal,
Mont Tremblant offers all the attractions
and beauty of the other areas and seclu-
sion to boot.

The Laurentians are among the oldest
mountain ranges in the world, so for the
most part erosion has softened peaks into
gently rounded hills perhaps 300 meters
(1,000 ft) high. Mont Tremblant is the
region's highest mountain at 975 meters
(3,200 ft); chairlifts operate all-year round
to transport visitors up to the summit.
There are more than 380 lakes scattered
over the park, and facilities are available
for windsurfing, canoeing, white-water
rafting on the Rivière du Diable, fishing
and swimming.

For an introduction to the dominant pulp and paper industry of the region, visit the Centre d'Exposition sur l'industrie des pâtes et papiers in Trois-Rivières.

Val d'Or ➍ means Valley of Gold and it lies at the eastern extreme of the Cadillac Break, a gold-rich fault that extends west to Kirkland Lake in Ontario. Though the mines here have sustained the population ever since Stanley Siscoe struck the glittering metal in 1914, it takes about five tons of ore to yield an ounce of gold. Still, high gold prices have kept the miners working and recently the town has found another source of prosperity: its strategic location on the road north from Montréal to the vast James Bay hydroelectric project.

Val d'Or got its start when the Lamaque mine opened during the Depression and the mining company built a village called **Bourlamaque** exclusively for its employees. This meant that the hundreds of men who came looking for work had to pitch tents nearby, and it was this makeshift community that evolved into Val d'Or. Bourlamaque today is a well-preserved historic quarter of 75 pinewood houses and a small museum. As for Greater Val d'Or, its population has grown to 35,000, yet it seems to retain that slightly impermanent look common to mining towns. A cheerful and entrepreneurial spirit prevails. Each October it hosts the **Moose Festival**, during which some fortunate Valdorian beauty is crowned Moose Queen. The festival sponsors a week of events such as parades and canoe races and ends with a moose-calling competition.

Paper town

Ten percent of the world's newsprint, 2,500 tons a day, once came from **Trois-Rivières ➎**, 142 km (88 miles) northeast of Montréal. Though still important commercially, today it struggles to overcome its image as a lackluster industrial town. It prospered since 1610, but the fires that regularly swept through all Québec's communities have left little to show from the town's first two centuries. In Rue des Ursulines, the **Manoir de Tonnancour**, housing temporary art exhibitions (open: Tues–Fri 10am–noon, 1–5pm; free), the **Maison-de-la-Fresnière** (now a wine store) and the **Musée-des-Ursulines** survive, at least in part, from the early 18th century (open Mar–Apr: Wed–Sun; May–Sep: Tue–Sun; Nov–Feb: closed; free).

The town's attractions are modern: the **Grand Prix** races through the city streets in August, the **International Poetry Festival** takes place in October, the **Laviolette Bridge** spans the St Lawrence. The revitalized area for entertainment and recreation at the port is also well worth a visit.

Thirteen kilometers (8 miles) east of the city, just off the Boulevard des Forges, Parks Canada opened **Les Forges du Saint Maurice**, a re-creation of the old ironworks here (open mid-May–mid-Oct: 9am–5pm; free). Like other national historic parks in Canada, the forge is a hybrid between park and museum, full of user-friendly displays that invite you to learn through participation.

Nowhere in the vicinity draws as many visitors as the shrine, 10 km (6 miles) north of Trois-Rivières, called **Notre-Dame-du-Cap**, in the small town of Cap-de-la-Madeleine. The little church of Notre-Dame-du-Rosaire was built in 1714 and drew a moderate number of pilgrims until the day in 1883 that Father Frederic Jansoone and two others saw the statue of the Virgin open her eyes. Trois-Rivières stands at the confluence of

BELOW: old Québec mill house on Rivière du Loup.

the St-Maurice and the St Lawrence rivers, begging the question: where is the third river? In fact, there isn't one. If you travel up the St Lawrence by boat, as Jacques Cartier and Samuel de Champlain did, the two delta islands at the mouth of St Maurice give the impression that *trois rivières* end here. The name survives from then.

Maps, page 192, city 196

Ville de Québec

"The impression made upon the visitor by this Gibraltar of North America: its giddy heights; its citadel suspended, as it were, in the air, its picturesque streets and frowning gateways; and the splendid views which burst upon the eye at every turn: is at once unique and everlasting."

Remarkably, Charles Dickens's comment on the **Ville de Québec ❻** is still appropriate more than a century after his visit. It retains its 18th-century ambience with narrow, winding streets and horse-drawn carriages and fine French cooking behind charming facades. The only dramatic change in the old town is the construction at the turn of the century of a castle-like hotel that perches on its promontory overlooking the St Lawrence River: the **Château Frontenac Ⓐ**.

The province's cryptic motto, *Je me souviens* (I remember), insists upon the defense of Québecois tradition, language and culture. Here in the provincial capital, reminders are everywhere that this was once performed by soldiers with guns from turrets and bastions. Today, the politicians and civil servants of Québec City have taken over the job, using the milder instruments of democracy, but are hardly less ardent in their purpose.

Québec City still stands sentinel over the St Lawrence, the only walled city on the continent north of Mexico. The views are as lovely as ever: from the

BELOW: Château Frontenac, a Québec City hotel.

City vantage point:
a perch on the
Terrasse Dufferin.

Terrasse Dufferin Ⓑ in front of the Château Frontenac, one looks out at the blue Laurentian hills and Mont St-Anne, the rolling countryside and the boats passing on the shimmering St Lawrence 60 meters (200 ft) below.

Diagonally opposite **Place d'Armes** Ⓒ, the former drill and parade ground, rue du Trésor runs down to rue Buade. This lane, named after the building where colonists used to pay their dues to the Royal Treasury, is today the artists' row: hung with quite decent watercolors, etchings, silkscreens. Rue Buade winds downhill to **Parc Montmorency** (usually tranquil however busy the rest of the old town becomes), opposite the grand **Ancien Bureau de Poste** with its rather pompous monument to Bishop François-Xavier de Laval-Montmorency, first bishop of Québec and founder of its largest university.

Côte de la Montagne drops steeply down to the left, winding down into the Lower Town, following the ravine that Québec's first settlers used to climb from the Lower Town to the Upper. Just beyond the **Porte Prescott**, a recent reconstruction of the original erected here in 1797, is **L'Escalier Casse-Cou**, the "Breakneck Stairway". This staircase, not quite as daunting as it sounds, leads to the narrow Petit-Champlain, which is lined with crafts shops.

From the foot of L'Escalier Casse-Cou, **Place Royale** is just around the corner. Thus one tumbles from the Château Frontenac into the cradle of French civilization in North America.

Place Royale, where the first settlement in America stood, was the business center of Québec City until about 1832. Its name derives from the bust of Louis XIV, the great Sun King of Versailles, that was erected here in 1686. Today, it is the scene of constant play and concert performances, usually re-creating the culture of the 17th and 18th centuries. **Eglise Notre-Dame-des-Victoires** Ⓓ, dom-

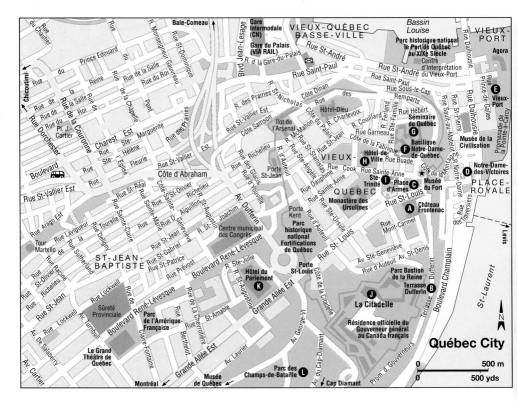

Québec City

inating the square, was built in 1688 and reconstructed after Wolfe's devastation of the lower town in 1759 . The church is named for two early victories against the Anglo-Americans – or rather, one great victory and one lucky accident. A Bostonian, Sir William Phips (knighted for discovering 32 tons of shipwrecked bullion), sailed to Québec with 34 boats and 2,000 men in October 1690, and demanded its surrender.

Governor Frontenac promised to reply with his cannon, and during six days of fighting his guns hammered the fleet. By land, snipers, fighting Indian-style against Phips's troops drawn up in formal battle-order, killed 150 men with only one loss to their own party. Phips withdrew on the sixth day, unaware that the French had just run out of ammunition. The lucky accident – or to the French, Our Lady's victory – was the storm in the Gulf of St Lawrence that destroyed the enormous British fleet of Sir Hovendon Walker in 1711, saving Québec from almost certain defeat. Both these events are depicted in little scenes above the odd, turretted altar.

Crossing the road that runs along the waterfront, rue Dalhousie, you leave the 18th century behind and encounter the more modern world of the port. On the right is the entrance to the government-operated ferry services to **Lévis** on the other side of the river, while straight ahead the *M.V. Louis-Jolliet*, a colorful and popular cruise boat, docks.

Walking north beside the river leads to the new commercial and community complex, called **Le Vieux Port ➎** despite its thoroughly contemporary design: overhead walkways of red and silver tubing and plexiglass walls connect spacious, functional pavilions. The complex surrounds the **Agora**, a 6,000-seat amphitheater set among flowerbeds, waterfalls and fountains and used for cul-

Map, page 196

A monument to Sieur de Maisonneuve, founder of Montréal, stands in Québec's Place d'Armes. Legend has it that he killed an Indian chief here in battle in 1644.

BELOW: café life in Québec City.

The Musée de la Civilisation, designed by the contemporary Canadian architect Moshe Safdie, incorporates Maison Estèbe, a merchant's house, circa 1752.

tural events, particularly evening concerts throughout the summer. The award-winning modern **Musée de la Civilisation** on rue Dalhousie, in the center of Le Vieux Port, presents thematic exhibitions on such subjects as language, thought, the body and society (open mid-Jun–early Sep: daily 10am–7pm; early-Sep–mid-June: closed Mon; entrance fee; Sep–Jun: free on Tue).

The easiest way to get back to the Upper Town is by taking the little funicular at the head of rue Sous-le-Fort, which is worth the small charge to save wear and tear on the feet in this city-made-for-walking. It shinnies up the cliff from the house of Louis-Jolliet (the explorer of the Mississippi River) to the Terrasse Dufferin (daily 7am–midnight).

At the intersection of rue Buade and Côte de la Fabrique is the Baroque cathedral of Québec City, **Basilique Notre-Dame-de-Québec** ❻ (open daily 7.30am–4.30pm). The city's main church has been here since 1633 when Samuel de Champlain built Notre-Dame-de-la-Recouvrance in gratitude for the recovery of New France from the British. As with the later victories, the French settlers considered this rescue from Protestant infidels an act of God. Next door stands the **Séminaire de Québec** ❼ and the **Université Laval**. The Jesuits established a college here in 1635, a year before Harvard opened, but the Seminary was officially founded only in 1663 by Bishop Laval (guided tours in summer; entrance fee).

The university still exists, though its modern campus is now in the suburb of **Ste-Foy**, and these buildings serve their original purpose as a seminary and high school. The seminary's museum is probably the city's finest general museum, with splendid modern facilities for the displays of Baroque and Renaissance art and some of the finest of 19th-century Canadian art. There is also a gruesome unwrapped mummy from the time of Tutankhamen, an oriental collection, and

BELOW: rue du Trésor, Québec City.

some intriguing old scientific contraptions (open Jun–early Sep: daily 10am–5pm; Sep–June: closed Mon; entrance fee). Across the street from the cathedral is the monument to **Cardinal Taschereau**, looking formidable, as if ready to carry out his threat to excommunicate any worker who joined a union. Behind is the gray, ample **Hôtel-de-Ville** ⓗ.

Around the corner stands the only rival to the Château Frontenac on the city's skyline, the **Price Building**. With 17 stories, it just about qualifies as the old town's only skyscraper. One is enough, and fortunately the 1937 Art-Deco style is not out of keeping with the neighborhood. Straight on, however, stands the **Cathédrale Ste-Trinté** ⓘ, the first Anglican cathedral built outside the British Isles and thoroughly English from its design (on the model of St Martin-in-the-Fields in Trafalgar Square) to its pews made of oak imported from the Royal Windsor Forest. There is also a throne in the apse called the King's Bench, but rather ironically, though it has been graced in its 200 years by queens, princes, princesses and governors-general, it has not, so far, been the seat of a king.

Lively **rue St-Louis**, with its snug little restaurants and *pensions*, slopes up from the end of rue Desjardins to the Porte St-Louis, rebuilt in a grand neo-Gothic (complete with turret and crenellated gun-ports) to replace the 17th-century original. Just in front of the gate is the lane that leads to the **La Citadelle** ⓙ, the star-shaped bastion on the summit of **Cap-Diamant**, 100 meters (400 ft) over the St Lawrence (tours Apr–Oct: daily; entrance fee).

The Citadel, with its Changing of the Guard ceremony (mid-Jun–Labor Day: 10am daily) and Beating of the Retreat (Jul, Aug: Wed–Sat 6pm), appeals to childhood notions of soldierly glory and adventure. But however colorful, it continues to play a military role as the headquarters of Canada's French-only

Map, page 196

BELOW: getting around Québec City.

Québec City thrives on festivals: early February is Carnival, with parades and canoe racing on the frozen St Lawrence. In July its streets are alive with music.

BELOW: bitter winds on the St Lawrence.

Royal 22e Régiment, known as the "Vandoos" (a rather crude rendering of *les vingt-deuxième*). Built by the British in the early 1800s according to plans approved by the Duke of Wellington, with double granite walls and a magnificent position above a sheer cliff, it was considered one of the most impregnable strongholds in the Empire.

Beyond the wall's confines, the city becomes suddenly roomy, opening out onto the **Grande-Allée** and the lawns of the **Hôtel du Parlement ⓚ**, the seat of the National Assembly, Québec's provincial government. Though not old by the city's standards (building began in 1881), the elaborate French Renaissance design by Eugène-E. Taché does seem to embody Québec's distant roots in the court of Louis XIII. Its symbols, however, are purely Québecois; the important figures of her history are all there, each trying to outdo the other's elegant pose in his alcove on the façade: Frontenac, Wolfe, Montcalm, Lévis, Talon… Below, Louis-Philippe Hébert's bronze works include dignified groups of Indians, the "noble savages" of the white man's imagination.

Outside, the terraces of the Georgian houses that border the Grande-Allée west from the National Assembly are cluttered with tables where visitors and civil servants enjoy the cuisine, the wines and the serenading violins of Québec's liveliest restaurants. A block south, there is gentle peace. **Parc des Champs-de-Bataille ⓛ**, or the **Plains of Abraham**, runs parallel to the Grande-Allée with spectacular views across the St Lawrence to the Appalachian foothills. Its rolling lawns and broad shade trees have known far more romance than fighting, many more wine-and-cheese picnics than violent deaths, but however incongruously, it commemorates a vicious 15-minute battle in which Louis-Joseph, Marquis de Montcalm, lost half of North America to the British. It wasn't quite

that simple, but the fact remains that the Indian fighting style of the Canadians had won them success after success against the British until the Marquis de Montcalm, a traditionalist and a defeatist, became head of the land troops. Always ready to retreat even after a victory, and rarely pressing an advantage, Montcalm steadily reduced the territory that he had to defend.

General Wolfe, who sailed down the St Lawrence with half as many troops as Montcalm held in the fortress of Québec City, never really hoped to succeed in taking it and so he destroyed 80 percent of the town with cannon fire.

Montcalm would not emerge to fight a pitched battle and, in a last-ditch, desperate attempt, Wolfe took 4,400 men up the cliff in silence by cover of night to the heights where there was no hope of turning back. Montcalm had been expecting Wolfe at Beauport, north of the city, and he rushed back to fight on the Plains. Throwing away every advantage, time, the possession of the city stronghold, and the sniping skills of his men, Montcalm fought the kind of European-style set battle that his troops were improperly trained for. Wolfe was killed, Montcalm mortally wounded and, though the British held only the Plains at the battle's conclusion, the French surrendered the city.

Two robust little **Martello** towers within the park were built as out-posts of the British defense system between 1804 and 1823. Their walls on the side facing the enemy are 4 meters (13 ft) thick, narrowing to a mere 2 meters (7 ft) on the side facing the town (open early Jun–early Sep: daily; free).

At the far end of Parc des champs-de-Bataille, just beyond the now vacant jail called the **Petit Bastille**, stands the **Musée de Québec**, the imposing neo-Classical home of a large proportion of the best Québec art. Painters such as Alfred Pellan, Marc-Aurèle Fortin and Jean-Paul Riopelle are not quite household

Map, page 196

BELOW: winter activities on the icy river.

The best observation points for spotting whales in the St Lawrence are in the area of the Parc du Saguenay at Pointe-Noir Promontory and Cap-de-Bon-Désir.

BELOW: rich farmland on the Île d'Orleans.

hold names throughout the world, but the work of these modern artists has a wide range from expressionistic landscapes to frenetic abstracts (open early June–early Sep: daily 10am–5.45pm, Wed till 9.45pm; early Sep–late-May: closed Mon; entrance fee).

Pack your bathing suit when you head east for 10 km (6 miles) either by the upper Route 360 or the lower road, Route 138, to **Parc de la Chûte-Montmorency** ❼ (open daily; free). These falls at 83 meters (272 ft) are considerably higher than Niagara Falls, though less dramatic because they are so much narrower. Here, however, instead of looking at the falls from the top down, you approach the base, which means that the closer you get, the wetter you get from the spray. The province has thoughtfully built a large granite platform at the base of the falls so that visitors can actually stand inside the chilly cloud of spray. In winter, the spray forms a solid block which grows up from the bottom into a "sugarloaf" of ice and snow, providing a splendid slope for tobogganing.

Fertile island

Just a mile south of the falls, the bridge over the **Île d'Orléans** ❽ turns off the autoroute. In 1970, the provincial government declared the island a historic district to prevent the encroachment of the city and the tourist trade from destroying the milieu of one of Québec's most picturesque and historic regions. The exceptionally fertile soil brought prosperity early to the island. In the 1600s there were as many inhabitants here as in Montréal or Québec, and farming is still the vocation of most of the families here, many working plots that have been passed down since Québec's earliest days.

Few visitors can resist indulging themselves at the roadside stands that offer

fat strawberries swimming in lakes of thick, fresh cream topped off with maple sugar. **Ste-Anne-de-Beaupré**, a nearby town on the St Lawrence's North Shore, houses a cathedral which millions of Catholics have visited. The fountain of St Anne, in front of the church, is said to have healing powers.

Map, pages 192/193

The Saguenay and Lac St-Jean

Among all Québec's uncountable lakes and waterways, perhaps none can match the splendor of the **Saguenay 9**, its ragged cliffs looming hundreds of feet over the broad, blue river. Vikings and Basque fishermen came and went long before Jacques Cartier named it "the Kingdom of the Saguenay" when he came seeking the Orient in 1535. Its spectacular beauty survives today, and the whales never fail to gather in the deep estuary each July, staying until December, when they swim away to unknown destinations. The cruise boats that leave from the wharf at **Baie-Ste-Catherine**, 71 km (44 miles) north of Québec on Route 138, can virtually guarantee whale sightings.

A ferry takes passengers and cars across the river to **Tadoussac 10**, where North America's oldest wooden church, **Petite Chapelle de Tadoussac**, has stood since 1647 (open late-Jun–early-Aug: daily; entrance fee), and New France's first fort, built in 1600, has been reconstructed. If the **Tadoussac Hotel** looks familiar, it may be because the movie *Hotel New Hampshire* was filmed here.

Farther inland, the terrain levels out onto the fertile plain of the **Lac St-Jean 11** region. Fur-trading companies held a monopoly on the area until the mid-19th century and it was barely settled until railroads brought pulp and paper developments after 1883 followed by large hydroelectric and aluminum smelting plants which brought prosperity to Lac St-Jean.

BELOW: higher than Niagara Falls, Chûte Montmorency.

For visitors, however, the industry is relatively insignificant except in the commercial centers of Chicoutimi, Jonquière and Alma. The rich soil produces 4.5 million kgs (10 million pounds) of blueberries a year and, coupled with award-winning local cheeses, these provide the materials for an endless supply of mouth-watering, heart-stopping blueberry cheesecakes. Less decadent regional specialties include various *tourtières* (spiced meat pies) and a dried-bean soup called *soupe à la gourgane*. Local fish – trout, pike, doré, and plentiful freshwater salmon – complete the menu.

Beyond the commercial centers several beautiful small towns cluster around Lac St-Jean, such as **Péribonka**, the setting of Louis Hémon's novel *Maria Chapdelaine*, and **Mistassini**, the blueberry capital. **Val-Jalbert**, a ghost-town for some 35 years, has recently re-opened, preserving its original character and buildings. The old mill stands against the 72-meter (236-ft) **Ouiatchouan Falls**.

Péninsule de la Gaspésie

Route 132 begins and ends at **Ste-Flavie**, looping around the **Péninsule de la Gaspésie** in a 560-km (348-mile) circle that strings together the sleepy fishing villages of the eastern coast. The Micmacs called it *Gespeg*, "the end of the earth". Though the Gaspé has been settled since Shakespeare's time, it has suffered almost no industrial development. Even the roads and trains that came with the later part of the 19th century

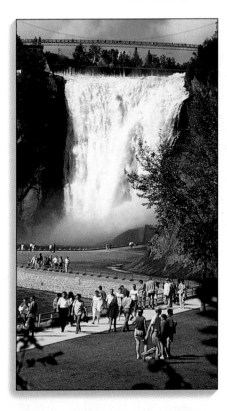

left its rural tranquility and Acadian culture largely the same as ever.

From Ste-Flavie, the road cuts southeast down the Matapédia Valley, following the "river of 222 rapids", which cascades through a deep gorge at the edge of the Chic-Choc mountains. At the village of **Matapédia**, 150 km (93 miles) south, the road turns northeast and follows the Baie des Chaleurs. Once known as the "Canadian Riviera", the bay is thankfully too wild and unspoiled to merit the name today. Herons and terns gather on the sandbars and the long, sandy beaches are often virtually deserted. The road weaves among coves and villages, some with English names such as New Carlisle, New Richmond and Douglastown, given to them by Loyalists who settled here to escape the American War of Independence. Eventually the coast wends northward and meets the red, rocky cliffs where the Chic-Chocs veer down to the sea. Rounding a curve, suddenly the **Percé Rock ⓬** appears, a 400-million-ton block of limestone jutting improbably out of the sea. Roughly oblong in shape, there were once as many as four arches driven by the tides through this treeless crag, which also goes by the name "pierced rock". Nearby, the bird sanctuary on **Île Bonaventure** is home to 50,000 gannets.

The north coast of the Gaspé is more rugged: the road winds along the bluffs at the edge of the highest mountains in eastern Canada. **Mont Jacques-Cartier** rises 1,268 meters (4,160 ft) a few miles inland at the edge of the **Parc de la Gaspésie ⓭**. This stretch along the south St Lawrence shore provides perhaps the most dramatic scenery on the Gaspé: the road hugs the steep cliffs that the sea washes below. At **Mont-St-Pierre,** near Ste-Anne-des-Monts, a hang-gliding festival is held each July, its competitors jumping like Icarus over the St Lawrence.

An aura of danger seems to linger on this coast from the days when ships were swept against the rocks to ruin. A number of families who live along the shore

The mountains, meadows, limestone cliffs and sandy beaches of Gaspésie's Parc National de Forillon are home to a wealth of flora and fauna (open daily).

BELOW: Péninsule de la Gaspésie.

Map, pages192/193

are descended from Irish immigrants whose boats were destroyed on the coast. Some remember the day in 1914 when the *Empress of Ireland* collided with another boat and sank in 15 minutes, with the loss of 1,014 lives. A gentler civilization reappears at **Les Jardins de Métis** near Métis-sur-Mer where Lord George Stephen built **Reford House** in the last century with its beautiful English garden displaying 2,500 floral varieties (open Jun–mid-Oct: daily; entrance fee).

The round trip from Québec City covers 1,600 km (1,000 miles) – not exactly a Sunday afternoon drive, but worthwhile if you can afford a couple of Sundays, and the week between.

Anticosti Island

Looking like something coughed up out of the mouth of the St Lawrence, the 8,000 sq-km (3,000-sq-mile) **Île d'Anticosti** ⑭ may seem a little remote. It is. Populated by 300 people and 100,000 adorable white-tailed Virginia deer, the island became a park when the provincial government purchased it from a pulp and paper firm in 1974.

Since the early 1980s, the island has been divided between four outfitters (SEPAQ Anticosti, Safari Anticosti, Pourvoirie Cerf-Sau and Pourvoirie du Lac Geneviève), with the exception of the village of **Port-Menier**. Reservations with an outfitter are definitely recommended for hunting and fishing (mainly sea trout, salmon and speckled trout), and permits are required for fishing and hunting anywhere in Québec. Access is convenient: daily flights leave from **Havre-Saint-Pierre**, and a ferry boat, the *Relais Nordik*, takes passengers from Rimouski or **Sept-Îles** ⑮ to Port Menier.

Surrounded by steep cliffs and treacherous reefs, Anticosti was known in the days before sophisticated navigational systems as "the graveyard of the gulf". About 400 shipwrecks scatter the coast, some of them quite recent. Despite both hazards and isolation, the island has served various private interests since the day, in 1680, when Frontenac awarded it to Louis Jolliet, the Mississippi explorer.

A few farmers settled there and later English entrepreneurs tried to colonize the island, but in 1895 a wealthy French chocolatier named Henri Menier bought it for his sporting pleasure. It was he who imported the first deer, which have proliferated so impressively; the charred remains of his villa are still visible near the eponymous Port-Menier, having been burned by pulp and paper firms that bought the island from Henri's son.

Anticosti suddenly became a concern to Canadians when Nazi Germany almost bought the island in 1937, ostensibly for its timber, but eventually backed out after much negative public attention.

There are three hotels in Port-Menier, **Auberge Port-Menier**, **Auberge Place de l'Île** and **Gîte au Vieux Menier**, and another, **Auberge de Pointe Ouest**, at Pointe Ouest, approximately 20 minutes from Port-Menier. There are also eight campgrounds offering a total of around 100 campsites. Though a vast area is untouched by humans, centuries of occasional habitation have left their marks: ghost-towns, overgrown cemeteries, an old railroad and the 4,000-year-old remains of its earliest inhabitants.

BELOW: feathered traveler at anchor.

THE EAST

Canada's four Atlantic provinces are bound by seafaring traditions, yet each has its own rich cultural identity

The host to Canada's first European visitors, and with the freshness of air laden with sea spray, the east coast is perhaps one of the most startlingly beautiful regions of Canada. Here are the achingly lonely beaches of Nova Scotia, the peculiar but charming friendliness of the people of Newfoundland, the quaint, unembarrassed potato obsession of the Prince Edward Island farmers, and the graceful elegance of New Brunswick's towns.

The four provinces that constitute Canada's eastern region are bound together by their proximity to the Atlantic Ocean, yet each possesses its own singular charm. New Brunswick's rugged coastline begins the section and reveals the province's unusual blend of eastern reserve and wanton wildness in its towns and landscape. Nova Scotia, "New Scotland", is explored by following its circuitous coastline and stopping to examine some of its unusual cities and delightful towns.

Newfoundland is perhaps the most quirky of all the provinces and its rugged beauty and remoteness serve as a background to a portrait of the area's friendly inhabitants. The east section ends at Prince Edward Island, Canada's tiniest province. Surrounded by singing ocean and covered with potato fields, it offers some of the area's most beautiful beaches.

PRECEDING PAGES: winding through a carpet of burnished colors in the fall.
LEFT: King's Landing Historic Settlement, a reconstructed Loyalist village.

NEW BRUNSWICK:
GATEWAY TO THE ATLANTIC

New Brunswick serves as a perfect beginning to experiencing the east coast lifestyle. Settled by French-Acadians and Anglo-Loyalists, it is a province rich in traditions

Map, pages 192/193

H ere in New Brunswick the pace is slow and the friendly people take the time to talk. Magnificent wild forests cover 85 percent of the land, supporting a substantial pulp and paper industry. Under these lie lead, copper and zinc, providing a healthy mining industry. And then there is the mining of the sea, fishing.

The Acadians and Loyalists

The first people to settle in this region after the Micmac and Maliseet Indians were the French in 1604. They arrived with Samuel de Champlain and called the land they worked Acadie; it covered the Atlantic provinces and Maine. The Acadians were constantly fighting battles with the British during the Anglo-French wars of the 17th century. French rule ended in 1713 and mainland Nova Scotia was controlled by the British. In 1755 the British Governor Charles Lawrence delivered an ultimatum to the Acadians – take an oath of allegiance to the British crown, or face deportation. The Acadians did not want to take the oath for fear of being forced to fight fellow Frenchmen on behalf of Britain. The infamous Deportation Order forced 14,600 Acadians into exile. Many settled in Louisiana where the Cajuns survive to this day. When peace was declared between England and France in 1763 most of the Acadians returned to Nova Scotia, only to find their land had been occupied by new English colonists. Once again they moved on and settled in what is now New Brunswick. Today almost 33 percent of the province's population is French-speaking.

The deportation may have had catastrophic results for the Acadians, but for descendants from the British Isles it was a windfall that started a trend. Many New Englanders moved, and during the American Revolution even more crossed the border. They were known as the Loyalists. With them they brought the maritime traditions of the seafaring colonies.

Saint John River Valley

The Saint John River is New Brunswick's lifeblood. It was the route traveled by Maliseet and Micmac, Acadians and Loyalists, Scots and Danes. In the northwestern region of the province it creates a border with Maine and from there the waterway can be traced along its winding course to Saint John. Samuel de Champlain arrived at this point and named it the greatest of the province's estuaries.

New Brunswick's westernmost outcrop, a thumb-like parcel of land bordered by Québec, Maine and the Saint

LEFT: Acadian days.
BELOW: kayaks sail into Hopewell Cape.

Fredericton Rail Museum exhibit: a fine example of engineering from the great age of steam.

BELOW: living history at King's Landing.

John River, is popularly known as the Republic of Madawaska. The region's inhabitants created this mythical realm in the 1800s because they were fed up with being pawns in border negotiations between Canada and the United States. With their own leader (the Mayor of Edmundston) and their own flag, the Madawaskans (mostly francophones) are both proud and exuberant. At no time is their spirit more in evidence than during the festival called *Foire Brayonne* (the French in this region are known as Brayons, after a tool used in processing flax). The midsummer event features both folk dancing and lumberjack competitions. The first town along the Trans-Canada Highway in Madawaska is Saint-Jacques. This is the home of Les Jardins de la République, a campground that includes nature trails, an amphitheater and a children's adventure playground.

Edmundston ⓰, an important pulp and paper center and the capital of Madawaska, is situated where the Saint John and Madawaska rivers converge. Of particular interest is the Church of Our Lady of Sorrows, containing woodcarvings (The Stations of the Cross) by New Brunswick artist Claude Roussel.

To the south, the beautiful and productive Saint John River Valley has always been a major thoroughfare. The northern segment of the valley, from Saint-Léonard to Woodstock, is known as the "potato belt". This tuber is a major regional crop, celebrated each year at the Potato Festival in Grand Falls ⓱, during which flower-strewn boats are sometimes launched over the town's waterfalls. This custom harks back to the legend of Malabeam, which laments the death of a young Indian maiden who led her captors over the falls to their death. The gorge into which the water plunges is one of the largest cataracts east of Niagara Falls. Eighty kilometers (50 miles) downstream is the small agricultural town of Hartland ⓲, known for its majestic covered bridge, which spans the Saint John River. This is not just any covered bridge, but the world's longest with seven spans, traversing 391 meters (1,282 ft).

Just south is Woodstock, whose residents pride themselves on their tradition of hospitality. A landmark here is the restored Old Courthouse, which over the years has served not only as the seat of justice, but as a social hall, a coach stop and a political meeting house. It's only fitting that such a busy little town be the birthplace of Canada's first dial telephone system in 1900.

For a look at Loyalist life in the Valley from 1820 to 1890, visit King's Landing Historical Settlement ⓳, 37 km (23 miles) west of Fredericton (open end May–mid-Oct: daily 10am–5pm; entrance fee). This reconstructed village, built on the banks of the Saint John River, depicts daily life among the Loyalists of that era.

In 1783 Loyalists exploring the valley came upon the area and, realizing its natural advantages, settled here the same year. They endured the hardship of a very severe first winter and with the onset of spring proceeded to build a town whose spirit exists to this day – Fredericton ⓴, "The City of Stately Elms." It is an appellation that befits this provincial capital.

Fredericton is the cultural center of the province, thanks in large part to the generosity and high profile of the publisher and statesman, Lord Beaverbrook, who never forgot his boyhood home. The Beaverbrook Art

Gallery, Queen Street (open June–Sep: daily; Oct–May: Tues–Sun daily, closed Sun am; entrance fee), houses his personal collection, representing the work of Dali, Gainsborough and the Group of Seven, among others. The Legislative Building (open Jun–Aug: daily; Sep–May: Mon–Fri; free) displays portraits by Joshua Reynolds as well as a rare copy of the *Domesday Book*. Fredericton is often referred to as the pewter capital of Canada due to the widely acclaimed pewtersmiths who have congregated here. The city's most elegant structure is Christ Church Cathedral. Completed in 1853, it is considered one of North America's best examples of decorated Gothic architecture.

What's left of the Old Military Compound now incorporates the York-Sunbury Historical Society Museum (open Apr–May: Tues–Sat; Jun–Dec: Mon–Sat; entrance fee), which chronicles Fredericton's military and domestic past. Traces from that period can be found at the Military Compound where reenactments of the changing of the guard are staged (open Jul–Aug: daily 10am–8pm). Real military life exists by following the Saint John River south-east from Fredericton to Oromocto, home of Canada's largest military training base and a military museum.

Quiet, riverbank communities from Jemseg south have become havens for craftspeople. Roadside stands offer fresh fruits and vegetables in season, and car ferries criss-cross the Saint John River at several points, enhancing the opportunity for exploration and discovery.

First city

Weathered Saint John ㉑, Canada's oldest city, sits along the Bay of Fundy at the mouth of the Saint John River. Samuel de Champlain landed here in 1604,

Map, pages 192/193

Mactaquac, near King's Landing, is the site of a provincial park. People flock to this area for what is reputed to be the best bass fishing in

BELOW: moored in Saint John.

bestowing the location with its name, but its true birth came in 1783 with the arrival of 3,000 Loyalists from New England and particularly New York. "The Loyalist City", as it is known, celebrates its heritage each July during **Loyalist Days**. The week-long festivities include a reenactment of the Loyalists' landing at Market Slip, as well as the Great Bay of Fundy Whaler Race.

Determined, energetic and ambitious, the Loyalist citizenry catapulted their new home into the forefront of wooden shipbuilding. The thriving port city declined following a disastrous fire in 1877 along with the eventual obsolescence of wooden ocean-going vessels. Recent waterfront development and urban renewal have provided Saint John with a much needed transfusion. It claims the first police force in North America, the first newspaper and bank in Canada.

To catch up with the city's past there are three walking tours: Prince William's Walk, a Victorian Stroll and the Loyalist Trail. One attraction the tours are sure to include is **Barbours General Store** (open mid-May–mid-Oct: daily), a restored and fully stocked 19th-century store. The building was originally located upstream and laboriously shipped down the Saint John River to this site. Thousands of artifacts, including 300 "cure-all or kill-alls," bring the past to life.

Saint John's Loyalist roots are nowhere more evident than at **King Square** (opposite the Loyalist Burial Ground), landscaped in the form of the Union Jack; and at **Loyalist House** (open June and Sep: Mon–Fri; July–Aug: Mon–Sat; closed Sun am; rest of year by appointment; entrance fee), a Georgian mansion completed in 1807. Occupied for about a century and a half by Loyalist David Daniel Merritt and his descendants, it is the oldest structurally unaltered edifice in the city; indeed one of the few buildings to survive the Great Fire of 1877.

New Brunswickers are very particular about never abbreviating Saint John, perhaps to avoid confusion with St John's across the sea in Newfoundland.

BELOW: Saint John's City Market.

With most of its original furnishings still intact, Loyalist House is a tribute to the fine craftsmanship of 19th-century Saint John.

Saint John's City Market is another survivor of the Great Fire. This institution has provided unflagging service since 1876, making it Canada's oldest market. Then as now, the market clerk rings a bell to close commercial proceedings. The building , filled with New Brunswick produce, is a pleasure to the eye, with its ship's hull roof, its big game trophies and its ornate iron gate.

The gem of Saint John's revitalized downtown waterfront district was officially christened Market Square in 1983. Its success has brought business, tourism, employment and pride back to the city. An early 19th-century brick facade serves as an invitation to a warm and lively center for shopping and dining. There is a boardwalk by the sea, a grand Food Hall and a regional library with a fine collection of early Canadian printed work. A beacon-like clock stands at the entrance to Market Square, serving more as a conversation piece than a timepiece. It is a clock without hands, using a serpent's tail to indicate the hour, and making room for three realistic, seated figures at its base.

Every August Saint John stages a national performing arts festival, Festival By The Sea. It features up to 500 performers from across Canada, and is presented at various sites around the city. For a panoramic view of the city and its waterfront visit Fort Howe and the Carleton Martello Tower.

Lily Lake, in Rockwood Park, is the pride of local swimmers, fishers and skaters – the latter only when "deemed safe by the Saint John Horticulture Association". The country's oldest museum, the New Brunswick Museum (open daily; closed Sun am; entrance fee) has treasures from around the world, and particularly artifacts pertaining to the history of New Brunswick, from a 13,000-

Map, pages 192/193

TIP

Saint John's City Market is the place to sample dulse, a dried, deep-purple seaweed from the Bay of Fundy; and fiddle-head greens,which are like asparagus.

BELOW: covered bridge at Hartland.

At Reversing Falls Rapids, the twice-daily high tides of the Bay of Fundy meet the Saint John River and spectacularly force the river to flow back upstream.

BELOW: a New Brunswick farmer.

year-old mastodon tooth to a gold-plated cornet, bestowed upon a member of the Saint John City Cornet Band.

The Fundy coast

West of Saint John, the idiosyncratic Fundy coast is characterized by picture-perfect fishing villages. This is where United Empire Loyalists settled *en masse* after the American Revolution.

Carved out of the Bay of Fundy, between Maine and New Brunswick, is **Passamaquoddy Bay**. At its eastern edge sits **Blacks Harbor**, famed for possessing the Commonwealth's largest sardine factory; it hosts the North American Sardine Packing Championship each year. Nearby **Lake Utopia** could be called the Loch Ness of New Brunswick, for there are those who believe it to be the domicile of a sea monster.

Rounding the bay takes you through **St George**, where visitors can meander about one of the oldest Protestant graveyards in Canada, while nearby **Oak Bay** is the site of a beachfront Provincial Park.

Probably the best known community on the bay is **St Andrews**, a fishing village, resort and marine biological research center, studded with 18th- and 19th-century mansions. Founded by Loyalists following the American Revolution, some families floated their homes here (one piece at a time) when the border with Maine was determined in 1842 – hence the New England atmosphere. St Andrews is home of the **Algonquin Hotel**, one of Canada's oldest resort hotels; but its most distinctive landmark is **Greenock Church**. This pristine structure, encircled by a white picket fence, is embellished with a carved oak tree design, a clock and a weathervane. The village also houses the **Huntsman Marine Laboratory and Aquarium** (open mid-May–mid-Oct: daily; entrance fee), which gives visitors a chance to see just what swims around the Bay of Fundy.

St Stephen, New Brunswick, stands face to face with Calais, Maine. These border towns have traditionally been the best of friends – even during the War of 1812 when St Stephen loaned Calais gunpowder for its Fourth of July celebration. Today, the towns hold joint festivities each summer. The world's first chocolate bar is thought to have been invented here at the Ganong factory in 1910.

Roosevelt's paradise

A paradise for birdwatchers, whale-watchers, fishermen and other outdoor types exists on the **Fundy Islands** where Passamaquoddy Bay widens into the Bay of Fundy. The rustic beauty and natural riches of the islands have attracted nature lovers, from James J. Audubon to Franklin Delano Roosevelt.

Grand Manan Island is the largest and farthest from the coast. It is a particular favorite of ornithologists, with about 230 species of birds, including the puffin, which has become somewhat of a symbol here. For the artist there are lighthouses and seascapes to paint or photograph. Grand Manan is also famous for the edible seaweed known as dulse.

Campobello, the "beloved island" of F.D. Roosevelt, is accessible by bridge (from Lubec, Maine). It brings you to the Roosevelt-Campobello International Park (open end May–mid-Oct: daily 10am–6pm), a natural preserve in the southern portion of the island. Visitors can see round Roosevelt's 34-room "cottage", built in the Dutch Colonial style, from where he viewed so many sunrises.

Located smack on the 45th parallel (and proud of it), Deer Island ㉒ is a mere 12 km (7.5 miles) long. It compensates for its size by having the world's largest lobster pond and, offshore, the world's second largest whirlpool, "Old Sow" named because of the auditory experience it provides.

The southeast

The southeast region of New Brunswick, from Saint John to Moncton, reveals the cultural texture of the province; towns and villages gradually reflect a transition from areas settled by Loyalists to those settled by Acadians.

Beyond the seacoast village of St. Martins is Fundy National Park ㉓, 80 km (50 miles) east of Saint John, a showcase for the spectacularly dramatic Fundy tides and coastal terrain. It once reverberated with the clamor of a thriving lumber industry which, along with intense trapping in the area, nearly destroyed its natural gifts. By 1930 the population of Alma, on the eastern edge of the park, once a roaring lumber town, was reduced to two struggling families. Thanks to Parks Canada, the region is now being returned to a wilderness state, with protection of its forests and reintroduction of its wildlife and fish stocks, particularly salmon.

Hopewell Cape , 40 km (25 miles) east of Alma is perhaps better known than the national park, and it is also better known as home of the "Flowerpot Rocks", which is what these peculiar formations look like at low tide, when you can

Map, pages 192/193

Fundy National Park, Alma, covers an area of rugged shoreline, forests and gorges. Trails provide views of the Bay of Fundy and the chance to see rare birds.

BELOW: low tide at Alma, now a protected region.

Of interest to nature lovers, the dunes at Bouctouche, north of Shediac, support rare plants and fragile marshes, and are home to endangered piping plover.

explore the tidal pools surrounding them. Beyond the Fundy coast is the city of **Moncton** ❷, an old railroad town, called the "hub of the Maritimes". It was first settled by Middle Europeans, but following the era of deportation and the influx of Acadians into what is now New Brunswick, it became known as the unofficial capital of Acadia. The **Université de Moncton** is the only French college in New Brunswick. Moncton is also a good place to observe the phenomemon of the Fundy tides.

Near Moncton, between Hillsborough and the tiny hamlet of Salem, is the **Salem and Hillsborough Railroad**. An antique steam locomotive, complete with open-air gondolas, snakes along the banks of the Petitcodiac River. This romantic excursion into the past traverses the salt water marshes, where the early Acadian settlers first harvested hay – with difficulty. The **Hiram Trestle**, an intricate bridge made of timber, is the trip's most outstanding feature.

Sackville ❷ is a tiny town which resembles an English village. It is the home of **Sackville Harness Limited**, which has the distinction of being the only place on the continent where horse collars are still made by hand. Sackville is also a university town. The first degree given to a woman in the British Empire was handed out by the town's **Mount Allison University** in 1875.

Nearby **Fort Beauséjour** is where the French and English last battled in this region. Today, there is little echo of its past, but a rather magnificent panoramic view of the surrounding area.

The Acadian coast

The coastal region of New Brunswick, north of Moncton, is known as the "Acadian Coast". Washed by the warm tides of the Northumberland Strait, it is pri-

BELOW: Hopewell Cape, Bay of Fundy.

marily to this region that the Acadians returned following the deportation. They say that Shediac has the warmest water on the coast. It is also reknowned as the lobster capital of the world.

Tiny Acadian fishing villages are strung along the coast, Bouctouche is particularly well-known for its oysters. The Kouchibouguac National Park ㉖, 100 km (62 miles)north of Moncton, has preserved miles of deserted but fine sand beaches. It is a pleasant drive out to Point Escuminac, a place that has never forgotten its distinction as the site of the province's worst fishing disaster. A powerful monument to the men who lost their lives here in 1959, carved by New Brunswick artist Claude Roussel, stands with its back to the sea, as a constant reminder of this tragedy.

Farther north along the coast are Chatham ㉗ and Newcastle, early lumber towns that have preserved some British culture. This area is famous for its ballads and folklore, as well as for its illustrious native sons. Chatham's once busy shipyards have now been replaced by port facilities for exporting local wood products. Newcastle was the boyhood home of Lord Beaverbrook, who was exceedingly generous in his bequests to this town.

Acadian flags, a French tricolor with a yellow star in the upper part of the blue stripe, become increasingly visible as you continue northward. Shippagan is a typical fishing village, home of an exceptionally fine Marine Center (open May–Sep: daily; entrance fee) devoted to the world of fishing in the Gulf of St Lawrence. (Everyone's favorite exhibit is an unusual royal blue-tinged lobster.) A ferry will transport you to the delightfully deserted beaches of Miscou Island.

Caraquet ㉘, 20 km (12 miles) west of Shippagan, is the most prosperous town on the Acadian coast and a cultural center for the region. The Acadian Festival each August draws celebrants from up and down the coast and includes the traditional blessing of the fleet. The town also has one of the largest commercial fishing fleets in New Brunswick and the only provincial fisheries school. There are boat builders and fish markets on the wharf. Caraquet's Village Historique Acadian (open Jun–Sep: daily; entrance fee) has recreated an Acadian settlement reflecting the century from 1780 to 1880, a time of re-establishment here following the deportation. It is nestled near the marshland *levées* constructed by early Acadian settlers.

Bathurst ㉙, 60 km (37 miles) west of Caraquet, represents a successful blending of French and English cultures. Off the coast are the waters of the Baie de Chaleurs, literally "Bay of Warmth". Named by Cartier in 1534, the bay is notorious for a phantom ship, which has been sighted along the coast from Bathurst to Campbellton. Some people believe it to be the ghost of a French ship lost in battle while others suggest there must be a more scientific explanation.

Dalhousie and Campbellton ㉚, at the western end of the Bay of Chaleur, were settled by Scots, Irish and Acadians and a fine-tuned ear is needed to place the accents. Campbellton rests at the foot of Sugarloaf Mountain; it is a center for salmon fishing and winter sports, and a gateway to Québec.

Beyond, to the north, lie the Atlantic Provinces, Nova Scotia, Newfoundland and Prince Edward Island.

Map, pages 192/193

Early July is the time of the lobster festival in Shediac, when lobster suppers, a lobster-eating contest and a parade feature on the itinerary.

BELOW: wood carver makes his mark.

NOVA SCOTIA: LOOKING OUT TO SEA

This Maritime province, where French, Loyalist and Scottish cultures predominate, has a rich seafaring past. Its rugged coast and sheltered inlets were home to pirates and shipbuilders alike

Map, page 222

The name of Nova Scotia brings to mind a vision of craggy highlands, echoing with the sound of bagpipes. But before Highlanders fled to "New Scotland", there were Micmacs, French, British and Loyalists from the American colonies. All have left a stamp on this province. Today 77 percent of Nova Scotians are of British descent and 10 percent of French (Acadian) extraction. Nova Scotia also has the largest indigenous black population in Canada.

Nova Scotians are as close to the sea as they are to the past – inextricably bound to it by their nature, by economics and by geography. Part of the province, Cape Breton, is an island; and the mainland is attached to Canada by the Isthmus of Chignecto. Appropriately, the shape of the province resembles a lobster, with no point more than 56 km (35 miles) from the sea. People are drawn to Nova Scotia for its overwhelming friendliness, exemplified by the traditional Gaelic greeting *Ciad mile failte* – 100,000 welcomes.

Out of the past

The original inhabitants of Nova Scotia, the Micmacs, still walk this land and fish these waters, though their numbers are greatly reduced. It is thought possible that Norsemen visited here around AD 1000. Some evidence of this has been substantiated. Centuries later, John Cabot, exploring under the English flag, touched upon northern Cape Breton Island. And French and Portuguese fishermen caught and cured fish here in the 16th century.

The French called this land Acadie. It encompassed what is now Nova Scotia, New Brunswick, Prince Edward Island and Maine. They settled along the Bay of Fundy and on the marshy land surrounding the Annapolis River, developing what is still the most fertile land in Nova Scotia.

A sense of Maritime pride and tradition still runs strong in Nova Scotia, but great prosperity largely abandoned the province with the advent of the 20th century. Often central Canada looks upon the area as a liability because of the financial aid it receives from the federal government. But many Maritimers claim central Canada was desperate to include the Maritime provinces in the Confederation because it had no winter ports. Maritimers believe their leaders were seduced into accepting Confederation in 1867. But history books tell another story, saying Canada permitted Nova Scotia and New Brunswick to join her.

Long before the St Lawrence became the foremost river of commerce, with the creation of the St Lawrence Seaway in 1959, the area's importance as a transporta-

LEFT: a seafaring inhabitant. **BELOW:** a lonely beacon at Peggy's Cove.

Skilled sea raiders, the Micmac were the province's first masters of wooden boats. Their canoes were adapted for use by the early explorers and fur traders.

tion channel had been greatly diminished. Steam-powered, steel-hulled vessels rendered the wooden sailing ships obsolete, and killed off an all-important industry and economic base. Coal mining later supplanted shipbuilding economically, only to falter after World War II.

But the province also has other natural endowments to fall back on: forestry is the number two jobs provider; there's abundant freshwater and saltwater fishing grounds, and the rich productive land of the Annapolis Valley, once so highly prized by the Acadians. And then there is tourism, which is a long-standing tradition here and a major contributor to the economy of the region.

Twin cities

The first and second largest Nova Scotian cities respectively, **Halifax**, the provincial capital, and **Dartmouth** ❶ sit on opposite sides of one of the world's great harbors, connected by two suspension bridges. Magnificent **Halifax Harbor** is the world's second largest natural harbor, as well as being free of ice year round. The Micmacs called it *chebucto,* meaning "big harbor". It has long been a bustling international port and naval base.

As the commercial and educational center of Atlantic Canada, Halifax is unquestionably the more dominant and favored of the twins, yet Dartmouth is not without its charms. Though known for its industry, they call it the "City of Lakes" for its 25 sparkling bodies of water.

This allows Dartmouthians to enjoy freshwater fishing and canoeing all through the summer without leaving the city and lake-top skating parties in the winter. **Dartmouth** was founded in 1750 (a year after Halifax), when British troops from across the harbor came on woodcutting expeditions. It was to

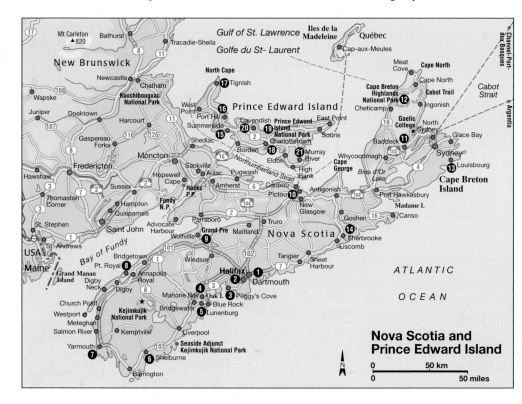

Nova Scotia and Prince Edward Island

0   50 km

0   50 miles

develop largely in response to Halifax's needs, and as early as 1752 it began operating a ferry between the two settlements. The boats continue to ply the harbor, in what is the oldest saltwater ferry service in North America.

Quakers from Nantucket Island settled here between 1785 and 1792 following the American Revolution. They made Dartmouth the headquarters of a whaling company whose operations were centered at what is now the **Dartmouth Shipyards**. They also left behind a number of homes, many of which still stand. These simple structures, with their front doors placed off-center, were built to endure; a stroll down Ochterloney Street shows several, including the historic **Quaker House**, probably the oldest house in Dartmouth (open June–Labor Day: guided tours daily; contribution).

In recent years Dartmouth has expanded and developed to meet existing and potential industrial needs. With the addition of the second suspension harbor bridge in 1970, the **Dartmouth Industrial Park** experienced phenomenal growth; there are now more than 750 businesses located in the area.

The twin waterfronts of Halifax and Dartmouth have been undergoing a significant transformation as have waterfronts across Canada. **Halifax's** restoration and redevelopment has been the most dramatic.

In the mid-1960s the people of **Halifax ❷** took it upon themselves to transform their city's gray image. The waterfront area now known as **Historic Properties** was saved from demolition and is now Canada's oldest surviving group of waterfront warehouses. Tourists can shop, dine and explore in this cobblestoned area, which externally appears as it did in the 19th century when privateers used it to cache their goods. Nearby, off Lower Water Street, are the more recently restored **Brewery Market** and the Maritime Museum of the Atlantic. Alexander

Map, page 222

In Dartmouth, the Evergreen Historic House on Newcastle Street was the home of the folklorist and author, Dr Helen Creighton, author of "Bluenose Ghosts".

BELOW: a boat for every household.

Keith, the one-time mayor of Nova Scotia, built his brewery in 1820 and its courtyards and arched tunnels are filled once again with spirit. Amid the variety of enterprises is the Halifax **City Farmers' Market** (open: Sat, 9am–1pm), which operates year round.

The **Maritime Museum of the Atlantic** (open daily; Nov–May: closed Mon; entrance fee) not only features a magnificent view of the harbor, but a huge hydrographic ship, the *CSS Acadia*. Now moored behind the museum, the *Acadia* once plied the frigid waters of the Arctic and North Atlantic while charting northern coastlines.

Just to the west of the waterfront is Halifax's business district. Amid the office towers and hotels is the new **World Trade and Convention Centre**. Easily spotted by its huge weathervane depicting the schooner *Bluenose*, it plays host to trade shows, conventions and live concerts. North on Prince Street beside the Old Montreal Trust Building is where 14 newspapers used to be published. The eight pre-Confederation buildings, where the likes of Charles Dickens, Oscar Wilde, and Victor Hugo's rebellious daughter are all said to have stayed, have been incorporated into an attractive complex called **Founders Square**.

Halifax was founded in 1749 not only because of its great harbor, but as a fortress to counter the French installation at Louisbourg. On a hill overlooking downtown Halifax is the **Citadel** (open daily; Sep–mid-June: free; mid-Jun–Aug: entrance fee). The current star-shaped 19th-century structure is the fourth to occupy this pedestal. It no longer serves as a military installation, but as a National Historic Park, housing the expansive collection of the **Army Museum** (open: daily; entrance fee), while affording a spectacular view of downtown and the waterfront. This is the best vantage point from which to see

BELOW LEFT: Halifax harborfront.
BELOW RIGHT: City Farmers' Market.

the **Town Clock**. With its four clockfaces and belfry to ring the hours, Haligo-
nians (residents of Halifax) need not wear wristwatches. Its construction was
ordered by Prince Edward, Duke of Kent, a stickler for punctuality.

Two churches not to be missed are **St Mary's Basilica**, topped by the world's
tallest polished granite spire, and **St Paul's Church** (1750) on Grand Parade,
the oldest Protestant church in Canada (open Jul–Aug: Mon–Sat; Sep–Jun: Mon-
Fri; free). The Grand Parade also serves as an open-air venue for Maritime
artists. Nearby on Hollis Street is **Province House** (open Jul–Aug: daily;
Sep–Jun: Mon-Fri; free)), Canada's oldest standing legislative building. Charles
Dickens referred to it as "a gem of Georgian architecture".

At the foot of the Citadel are the resplendent **Public Gardens**. Established
in 1867, these are the oldest Victorian formal gardens in North America. Near the
gardens on Summer Street is the **Museum of Natural History** (open Jun–mid-
Oct: daily; mid-Oct–May: closed Mon; entrance fee), headquarters of a
province-wide system incorporating 24 sites. The collection here is devoted to
the natural and social history of Nova Scotia, particularly Micmac artifacts.

Going back to the waterfront, at the southern tip of the peninsula that Halifax occupies, is **Point Pleasant Park**. The federal government rents this piece of
greenery to the city for one shilling a year under the terms of a 999-year lease.
The Prince of Wales' Martello Tower (open July–Labor Day: daily; free) was
raised here in 1796 and still stands, the first in a series of these circular stone
sentinels to be constructed along the coastal regions of North America and the
British Isles. The park, a favorite with joggers, hikers, swimmers, picnickers
and ship-watchers, is said to be the only place on the continent where Scottish
heather grows wild (from seeds shaken from the mattresses of British soldiers).

Map, page 222

BELOW: "New England blue" found in Nova Scotia.

Flowers bloom on the Atlantic South Shore.

At the other end of Halifax stands another park, **Fort Needham**, in memory of the **Halifax Explosion** in 1917 (see below).

The South Shore

The rugged and idiosyncratic Atlantic coastline, southwest from Halifax, is known as the **South Shore** and promoted by the tourist bureau as the "Lighthouse Route". It is an accurate appellation, yet despite these sentinels of the night, this beautiful, mysterious and punishing coastline is no stranger to shipwrecks. Nor are its people strangers to the wrath and bounty of the sea.

The circuitous South Shore with all its bays, coves, inlets and islands, was a favorite of pirates and privateers. Just west of Halifax is **Shad Bay**, where **Weeping Widows Island** is the subject of a morbid legend connected with the notorious 17th-century pirate, Captain Kidd. The Captain decided to bury a portion of his treasure here and engaged the services of 43 men to dig two pits. Unfortunately he interred the men along with the treasure, thereby transforming their wives into weeping widows. Today a deep shaft on the island is evidence of the numerous treasure hunts that have taken place here.

Nearby at **Indian Harbor** and **Peggy's Cove ❸**, 45 km (28 miles) from Halifax, fishing villages nestling among and atop the granite outcroppings are treasures of a different sort. The latter has become a semi-official showcase for the province and is said to be the most photographed fishing village in the world. Yet it has not been robbed of its simplicity and authenticity. There is some quandary over the name Peggy's Cove. Some believe it to be a diminutive of St Margaret's Bay, while others believe it was named after the sole survivor of a shipwreck, who subsequently married one of the local men.

BELOW: pumpkin stall, Mahone Bay.

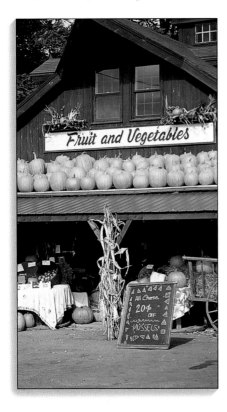

THE HALIFAX EXPLOSION

On December 6, 1917, a catastrophic explosion shook Halifax, causing enormous loss of life. A French munitions ship, the *Mont Blanc*, loaded with a cargo of ammunition and explosives, including TNT, collided with a Belgian relief ship, the *Imo*, in Halifax harbor. As the ships burst into flames, people came rushing down to the waterfront to watch.

Suddenly the *Mont Blanc* exploded. Two thousand men, women and children lost their lives in an instant, many thousands more were injured, and a large area of northern Halifax was destroyed. Windows were shattered as far away as Truro, 100 km (60 miles) from the city. It is said to have been the largest man-made blast prior to the bombing of Hiroshima in 1945.

Halifax picked up the pieces and symbolically placed a sculpture containing remnants of metal from the *Mont Blanc* – some discovered several kilometers away – in front of the Halifax North Memorial library as a monument to those who lost their lives.

The event features beside the Titanic in an exhibition of Nova Scotia's seafaring past at the Maritime Museum of the Atlantic, Water and Prince Streets (open daily; Nov–May: closed Mon; entrance fee).

The late William E. de Garthe (1907–83), a marine artist who resided here, apparently sided with the latter theory. Taking a decade to complete, he carved the images of 32 local fishermen, their wives and children, in a 30-meter (100-ft) face of granite rock located behind his house, which became known as the "Fisherman's Monument". De Garthe also included the image of the young woman of the shipwreck legend. The **Lighthouse**, combined with post office, is a landmark that draws many to Peggy's Cove. Sadly, the tragedy of a Swissair jetliner that plunged into the ocean off Peggy's Cove in the summer of 1998, with 229 people on board, is a memory that the locals – who played an heroic role in the rescue and salvage operations – will be living with for years to come.

St Margaret's Bay, named by Samuel de Champlain in 1631, is known for its fine sand beaches and summer cottages. It is followed by the notorious **Mahone Bay ❹**, with its 365 islands. This was once the realm of pirates and its name was probably derived from the French *mahonne,* a low-lying craft used by these sea raiders. Other names echo that era, such as **Sacrifice Island** and **Murderer's Point**, but **Oak Island** is the most intriguing. Long the site of treasure hunts, it is said that Captain Kidd buried another part of his treasure here. The island was once densely covered by large oaks and according to local legend the mystery of the buried treasure will not be solved until all the oaks have died and seven lives have been lost. (Six persons have so far lost their lives and only a few trees remain standing.)

Home of the Bluenose

"A Snug Harbor since 1753". That's what they say about **Lunenburg ❺**, one of Canada's most important fishing ports. Nowhere in Canada are the traditions

Map, page 222

BELOW: the sun sets over the shipyards of Lunenburg.

Lobster catch

BELOW: William de Garthe's "Fisherman's Monument" at Peggy's Cove.

of the sea more palpable – carried on by sailors, fishermen and shipbuilders. The renowned schooner *Bluenose,* the "Queen of the North Atlantic", winner of four international schooner races, was built here in 1921.

A symbol of pride for the people of Lunenburg (her image is even on the Canadian dime), she was ultimately lost off the coast of Haiti in 1946. The shipyards of this city later made the ship used in the film *Mutiny on the Bounty;* it was sailed to Tahiti by a Nova Scotian crew. This inspired the creation of *Bluenose II,* a replica of the original, built by the same shipwrights, which is open to visitors when in port. In Lunenburg each August is the Nova Scotia Fisheries Exhibition.

Inland on the bank of the LaHave River is **Bridgewater**, "The Hub" of the South Shore, an industrial pocket that plays host each July to the **South Shore Exhibition**. "The Big Ex", as it is known, features the International Ox Pull Championships, in which the owners of these beasts of burden cajole them towards victory.

Caribbean trading port

Back to the coast, south of Bridgewater, is **Port Medway**. Quiet now, it was a major port in the late 19th century, engaged in a brisk Caribbean trade: fish and lumber in return for rum and molasses. Things are still bustling in **Liverpool**, 142 km (88 miles) west of Halifax, which is built on the banks of the Mersey River like its English counterpart. Privateering figures prominently in the city's history, and this heritage is celebrated each July during "Privateer Days". Of particular interest here is the **Perkins House Museum** (open Jun–mid-Oct: daily; free) built in 1767. Perkins kept a diary which chronicled life in colonial Liverpool and his home is a showcase for the same.

West along the coast is **Port Mouton**, a pleasant fishing village named by Sieur de Monts and his party in 1604 when one of their sheep was lost overboard here. Tiny **Port Joli** is a bird sanctuary, a favorite spot of Canadian geese in autumn and winter.

Shelburne ❻ lies 67 km (41 miles) west of Liverpool. A treasure trove of 18th-century history, it's referred to as "The Loyalist Town", for it was settled by 16,000 United Empire Loyalists from America between 1783 and 1785. It became an instant boom town – not only bigger than Halifax, but also Montréal. The population dropped abruptly after 1787 with the termination of government support and by the 1820s fewer than 300 people called this home. Shelburne's **Ross Thomson House** (open Jun–mid-Oct: daily; entrance fee), built in 1784, is a Loyalist home and store – thought to be the only surviving 18th-century store in Nova Scotia. It now functions as a provincial museum, fully stocked and decorated to reflect the 1780s.

Another group of people tried to settle in Shelburne more recently. In 1987 a boat arrived from Holland carrying 174 Sikhs. Over the past few years Canada has become a desirable destination for people claiming refugee status. When the Sikhs landed illegally they were met by true east coast hospitality – a local woman brought them peanut butter and jelly sandwiches.

The only surviving New England style meeting house in Nova Scotia (*circa* 1765) is in nearby **Barrington**, with a 19th-century woolen mill. The town was settled by the French and called *Le Passage* until it was destroyed by New Englanders, and its people deported to Boston. In 1760 colonists from Cape Cod and Nantucket came here, making it one of the oldest outposts of settlers from New England.

Edging north toward the **Bay of Fundy** brings you to **Yarmouth** ❼. As terminus of ferry services from the States, this is the start of many a Canadian journey. During the golden age of sail this was one of the world's great ports.

The French Shore

The **French Shore**, home of Nova Scotia's largest Acadian population, is synonymous with the municipality of **Clare**, midway between Yarmouth and Digby, which locals are fond of saying rivals Toronto's Yonge Street as the largest main street in the world, for it consists of 27 villages, more than half of which sit along the main thoroughfare. Many Acadians returned to this area following the deportation to start anew, some on foot through the wilderness.

In **Meteghan**, 40 km (25 miles) north of Yarmouth, a short footpath takes hikers down to a secluded beach with a natural cave, purported to have been a cache for contraband rum during the days of Prohibition in the United States. Here, traditional skills are alive and well, as evidenced by Atlantic Canada's largest wooden boat-building facility in Meteghan.

Most Acadian villages are dominated by their church and in **Church Point** (*Pointe d'Eglise*) this is particularly true. **St Mary's Church**, built early in the 20th century, is the tallest and largest wooden church in North America. Its 56-meter (185-ft) spire, swayed by

Map, page 222

At Port Joli in 1750 an American crew captured by natives were given the option of standing barefoot in a fire or jumping into the sea; they jumped and drowned.

BELOW: the end of a hard day.

For unsurpassed views of St Mary's Bay on the northwest coast, a hiking trail heads out along the cliff-tops between Cape St Mary and Bear Cove.

bay breezes, is stabilized by 36 tonnes (40 tons) of ballast. This landmark sits on the campus of the **Université Sainte-Anne**, the only French university in the province. As a center for Acadian culture, the institution hosts the **Festival Acadian de Clare** every July.

East of St Mary's Bay, at the southern tip of the Annapolis Basin and over-looking Digby Gut, is **Digby**. The town has a long maritime history and was named for the commander of a ship which carried Loyalists here from New England in 1783 (among them, the great-grandfather of inventor Thomas Edison). This is home of the renowned **Digby Scallop Fleet** (the world's largest). The town has fish-processing plants and is famous for its smoked herring called Digby Chicks. Anglers come en masse each May for the Digby to Windsor Fisherman's Regatta.

The Annapolis Valley

Champlain wrote of the Annapolis Basin: "We entered one of the most beautiful ports which I had seen on these coasts." His compatriot Marc Lescarbot considered it "a thing so marvelous to see I wonder how so fair a place did remain desert." Orchards and other farmlands have replaced the primeval forest along the Annapolis Basin and River, and this region, although completely transformed, is still beautiful to behold.

Built in the 1780s, **Old St Edward's Loyalist Church** in **Clementsport** is situated high on a hill within an ancient cemetery. It was one of the province's earliest museums, showing off not only its own architectural integrity, but a fine collection of Loyalist artifacts. Its elevated setting also provides one of the best vantage points from which to appreciate the Annapolis Basin.

BELOW: apple blossom in the Annapolis Valley.

On the other side of the basin is **Port Royal** ❽, 10 km (6 miles) from Annapolis Royal, with its reconstructed **Habitation** (open mid-May–mid-Oct: daily; free), the settlement built by Sieur de Monts and Samuel de Champlain in 1605. It is a place that witnessed many firsts: the first permanent North American settlement north of Florida; the first Roman Catholic mass celebrated in Canada; the first Canadian social club (Champlain introduced the Order of Good Cheer as an antidote to the prospect of another dismal winter); and the first Canadian dramatic production (*The Theater of Neptune* orchestrated by lawyer and writer Marc Lescarbot in 1606). Burned by the English in 1613, its reconstruction in 1939, after years of research, was one of the first great successes of Canada's historic preservation movement.

The Annapolis Valley, sheltered by the North and South Mountains and extensively dyked by Acadian settlers, is an agriculturally and scenically gifted area, known particularly for its apples. In spring the scent of apple blossoms lingers in the air, and the **Apple Blossom Festival** is celebrated.

Though settled primarily by Planters and Loyalists following the deportation, the valley pays homage to Acadians – nowhere more poignantly than in **Grand Pré** ❾, the village immortalized by Longfellow in *Evangeline*. Grand Pré was the most important Acadian settlement in Nova Scotia before the deportation. Longfellow's *Evangeline – A Tale of Acadie* (1847) describes the separation of a young couple during the deportation and the subsequent search by the woman for her lover. At **Grand Pré National Historic Park** (open all year; guided tours, mid-May–mid-Oct; free), a simple stone church contains many artifacts relating to Acadian culture. Outside the church stands a statue of Longfellow's tragic heroine.

Map, page 222

BELOW: Longfellow's heroine, Evangeline, at Grand Pré.

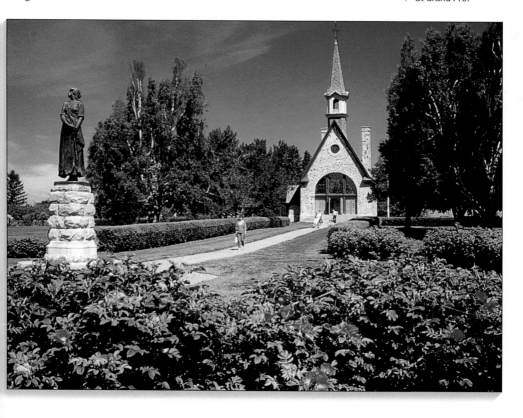

Southeast of Grand Pré, where the Avon and St Croix rivers converge, is the town of **Windsor**. Anyone fond of expressions such as, "raining cats and dogs", "quick as a wink", and "an ounce of prevention is worth a pound of cure", should visit Windsor's **Haliburton House** (*circa* 1839). Now a museum, it was once the home of judge, humorist and author Thomas Chandler Haliburton who created *Sam Slick*, the fictional Yankee peddler who spouted his witticisms on his travels through Nova Scotia (open Jun–mid-Oct daily; contribution).

Chignecto Isthmus

The northern aspect of mainland Nova Scotia is washed by the Bay of Fundy, with the highest tides in the world; and on the other side of the Chignecto Isthmus, by the Northumberland Strait. Whereas some bizarre natural phenomena occur only once in a lifetime, the Fundy tides put on their show twice daily, with a repertoire that varies according to the location. **Burntcoat Head**, on the **Minas Basin**, is the point at which the world's highest tides have been recorded – a difference of 17 meters (54 ft) between low and high.

Perhaps this atmosphere of extremity inspired William D. Lawrence to construct Canada's largest wooden ship in nearby **Maitland**, 20 km (12 miles) west of Truro. His namesake, a fully rigged sailing vessel, was launched in 1874 and was a technical and financial success. Lawrence's stately home is now a museum containing artifacts and memorabilia relating to ships and shipbuilding, including a model of the record-breaking *William D. Lawrence*.

Truro was originally settled by Acadians (they called it Cobequid), and later by people from Northern Ireland and New Hampshire. It is a good place to observe the tidal bore, or "wall of water", in which the incoming Fundy tide

TIP

Wine lovers should visit the Grand Pré Estate Vineyard, one of the most renowned wineries in eastern Canada. (Tours and tastings: Mon–Fri, three times a day).

BELOW: lobster traps at Trout River.

rushes into the Salmon River at the rate of 0.3 meters (1 ft) a minute. East across the isthmus is a region washed by the Northumberland Strait, strung with beaches and often echoing with the sound of bagpipes. It is said that more clans are represented in Nova Scotia than in Scotland and a good number of them can be found right here. **Pictou ❿**, 76 km (47 miles) east of Truro, is the "Birthplace of New Scotland", where the first Scottish Highlanders arrived aboard the *Hector* in 1773. This fine harbor saw many subsequent waves of Scottish immigration. Today it is a center for shipbuilding and fishing. Each July brings the **Pictou Lobster Carnival**.

Like Pictou, **Antigonish**, 74 km (46 miles) southeast, took its name from the Micmacs, and later became characterized by the culture of Highland Scots. The annual **Highland Games** draw competitors from far and wide every July, in what is the oldest such spectacle in North America. With Scottish music, dance and sports, it also features the ancient caber toss.

Cape Breton Island

Alexander Graham Bell once wrote: "I have traveled around the globe. I have seen the Canadian and American Rockies, the Andes and the Alps and the highlands of Scotland; but for simple beauty, Cape Breton outrivals them all." Bell's words have not gone unheeded; **Cape Breton Island** is the most popular tourist destination in Nova Scotia. Ironically, the island is also the most economically depressed region in a province less affluent than much of the rest of Canada, due in some part to the decline in coal mining.

Cape Breton has always been a place apart – occupied by the French longer than the rest of Nova Scotia (they called it *Ile Royale*) and a separate province

Map, page 222

Pugwash, 30 miles (50 km) east of Amherst, is a Scottish center. It hosts the annual Gathering of the Clans every July, and the town's street signs are in Gaelic.

BELOW LEFT: Bay St Lawrence fisherman.
BELOW RIGHT: bust of John Cabot.

At Chéticamp the
Acadian Museum
tells the story of the
first settlers to arrive
in the region in
the 1780s, following
the deportation
(open daily; free).

until 1820. The **Canso Causeway**, an umbilical cord to the "Mainland", was not constructed until 1955.

The Cabot Trail, which is named after the explorer John Cabot, is a 301-km (187-mile) loop which rollercoasts around the northern part of Cape Breton. It is a region greatly reminiscent of the Scottish Highlands, to the eye and to the ear. This road is popularly thought of as one of the most spectacular drives to be found in North America, winding through lush river valleys, past (and often clinging to bluffs high above) a rugged and dramatically beautiful coastline, through dense forest lands, and over mountains.

It was once a series of death-defying footpaths and later, equally treacherous trails. Northern communities were especially isolated, with **Cape Smoky** on the east coast presenting the greatest barrier. By 1891, a narrow wagon trail forged its way circuitously over Old Smoky, featuring a sheer rock cliff off one side and a 366-meter (1,200-ft) plunge to the sea off the other. Automobiles began taking their chances here in 1908; one of these early motorists' tricks was to tie a spruce tree behind the car to prevent it running away downhill. The trail still has its hair-raising stretches and most people drive it in a clockwise direction, clinging to the inside of the road.

Alexander Graham Bell, himself born in Scotland, built a summer house in **Baddeck ⓫**, the official beginning and terminus of the Cabot Trail, and spent his last 35 years here. As a teacher of the deaf, he directed Helen Keller's education and undertook research which led to the invention of the telephone. **The Alexander Graham Bell National Historic Park** (open daily; entrance fee), through photographs and exhibits, is a monument to Bell – the teacher, inventor and humanitarian. The Cabot Trail, traveling clockwise beyond Baddeck, traces

BELOW LEFT: Cape
Breton Ceilidh.
BELOW RIGHT:
traditional Scottish
dancing.

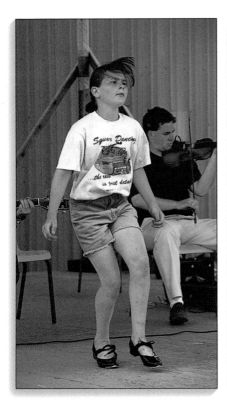

the **Margaree River**, renowned for its beauty and an abundance of trout and salmon. The stretch of Gulf of St Lawrence coastline from the Margaree to the Cape Breton Highlands National Park is dotted with Acadian fishing villages, inhabited by descendants of the mainland French who came here at the time of the deportation.

Map, page 222

Just as the Acadian language has retained its 17th-century flavor, the culture of the people here has remained relatively undiluted. Acadian flags fly in the sea breeze, and a church steeple signifies the next community. Such is the case with **Chéticamp**, the biggest town in these parts. **Cape Breton Highlands National Park** ⓬ begins a few miles north of Chéticamp, extending from the Gulf to the Atlantic and bordered on three sides by the Cabot Trail. This magnificent wilderness preserve is a paradise for hikers, swimmers, campers, golfers and other lovers of the great outdoors.

The Cape Breton National Park covers an exceptional landscape of mountains and coastline with 27 hiking trails. Enquire locally about whale-watching excursions.

The trail reaches its northernmost point at **Cape North** and from here another road heads farther north to the fishing village of **Bay St Lawrence**. En route, at the base of **Sugar Loaf Mountain**, is the site where Cabot is believed to have landed in 1497. This event is re-enacted each June 24.

At the eastern exit from the Park are the **Ingonishs**, a group of communities which have long been a great attraction for visitors. Just beyond Ingonish Harbor is Cape Smoky, its head in the clouds, rising 366 meters (1,200 ft) above the sea. Tourists can ski its slopes in winter while looking out upon the Atlantic. In summer, a ride on the chairlift to the top of Cape Smoky provides a breathtaking view (weather permitting) of this rugged, misty isle.

The stretch from Cape Smoky to Baddeck is known as the **Gaelic Coast**. Skirting the coast of St Ann's Bay will take travelers to **Gaelic College**. As the only institution of its type in North America, it serves as a vibrant memorial to the Highland Scottish who settled here and has been nurtured by their descendants. The sound of bagpipes, the weaving of tartans, and the whirl of tartan-clad dancers can all be experienced in summer. In early August the clans are well represented as they gather for the annual **Gaelic Mod**, a seven-day festival of Celtic culture. While on campus, visit the **Great Hall of the Clans** (open Jul–mid-Oct: daily; late Oct–mid-Dec and mid-May–Jun: Mon–Fri; entrance fee). It displays memorabilia of Angus McAskill, a 19th-century Cape Bretoner, nearly 2.4-meters (8-ft) tall who once worked with the midget Tom Thumb.

BELOW: Scottish heritage, a lone piper in Halifax.

Coal and steel country

Jumping off the Cabot Trail into what is called **Industrial Cape Breton** became an introduction to a world of smokestacks and steel mills. Coal was once king in this area. Today the Nova Scotia government still uses coal for the majority of its electrically generated stations.

Cape Breton Miners' Museum in **Glace Bay** has developed into one of Nova Scotia's finest museums (open Jun–Labor Day: daily; Labor Day–May: Mon–Fri; entrance fee). Artifacts and photographs chronicle the history of coal mining in this town and commemorate the men who risked their lives working in the depths; but the highlight of any visit here is the

Period costume in Fortress Louisbourg. It was built as a massive fortification by the French in the early 18th century, attacked twice, and finally destroyed by the British in 1758.

BELOW: a French guard at Fortress Louisbourg.

mine tour. Salty, veteran miners bring visitors down into the **Ocean Deeps Mine** (carved from under the ocean floor), and tell stories of pain, death, pride, hard work, low wages and camaraderie.

Coal has been mined in the vicinity of Glace Bay since the 18th century when soldiers from nearby Louisbourg were assigned this duty.

The last French stronghold

Passing by the sentries into **Fortress Louisbourg ⑬** is like stepping back in time to the summer of 1744. Fortress Louisbourg was the last great military, commercial and governmental stronghold of the French in the region that was once Acadia, but by 1758 it was in ruins. The site remained untouched until two centuries later when reconstruction began, in what has been termed the most ambitious project of its kind ever undertaken in Canada. Fifty buildings have now been fully reconstructed. From the costumed staff, trained in 18th-century deportment, to the authenticity of the structures and their furnishings, Louisbourg never fails to impress (open May–Oct: daily; entrance fee).

A center for scuba diving is **Louisbourg Harbor**, and the waters off the southern coast of Cape Breton are known as fertile ground for "wreck-hunting" – the legacy of centuries of maritime activity.

Off the south shore, just before reaching mainland Nova Scotia, is **Isle Madame**, reached by a small bridge across the Lennox Passage. A scenic loop meanders through Acadian fishing villages. Of particular note is **Le Noir Forge Museum** in Arichat (open May–Sep; contribution), a restored stone blacksmith shop with working forge, in what is the oldest building on the island (1793). At Little Anse, a trail leads to **Cap Rouge** at land's end. From here you can look out upon **Green Island** with its lighthouse, one of the last remaining manned beacons in the province.

The Eastern shore

The eastern shore of Nova Scotia, between Cape Breton and the Twin Cities, is characterized by its unspoiled beauty, an abundance and variety of fishing opportunities, and its traditional personality. Locals maintain that things have changed little over the years. In certain communities salt cod lying on flakes in the open air can still be seen, drying just as it was done back in the 19th century.

Closer than all other mainland communities to the great Atlantic fishing banks, **Canso** has developed into a center for fishing and fish processing. Its harbor has witnessed the history of this region, from the early European fishermen and traders, to the British fleet that made its rendezvous here before the final assault on Louisbourg.

Along the banks of St Mary's River is the village of **Sherbrooke ⑭**, 80 km (50 miles) west of Canso. It was a French fur-trading post in the 17th century, but the first permanent settlers came here in 1800 attracted by the tall timber and the river, then as now, filled with salmon. Sixty-one years later something happened to change the face of this town for all time – they discovered gold. The boom, referred to as "Sherbrooke's Golden Age", lasted only 20 years.

Sherbrooke became quiet again, left alone except for seasonal visits by salmon fishermen, until the 1970s when a restoration project was established. The heart of town is now almost entirely restored to the 1860–1880 period, and certain streets have been closed to traffic to create **Sherbrooke Village**. It's inhabited by people in costume going about their daily business, so visitors can walk through 21st-century Sherbrooke and happen upon a town steeped in another era.

In use since the 1870s, **The Blacksmith Shop** produces items used in the restoration and sold in the Emporium, as does **Sherbrooke Village Pottery**. Most fascinating of all is the jail, built in 1862 and used for 100 years. Not a jail really, but an ordinary 19th-century home inhabited by a jailor, his family and the offenders.

In earlier days, the distance between Sherbrooke and Halifax was described as "60 miles of horrible roads". Today, while the roads are excellent, there are scenes along the way reminiscent of a bygone era. On the edge of town is, the reconstructed **McDonald Brothers Mill**, where the sights, smells and sounds of a 19th-century sawmill are re-created.

Continuing for 85 km (52 miles) west along the coastal road brings visitors to **Tangier**, home of an enterprise known to gourmets and gourmands the world over – J. Willy Krauch and Sons. Krauch, now joined by his sons, has spent the better part of his life smoking Atlantic salmon, mackerel and eel, using the Danish system of wood-smoking.

A farther 30 km (18 miles) west at **Jeddore Oyster Pond** is the **Fisherman's Life Museum** (open Jun–mid-Oct: daily; free). The museum is the modest homestead of James Myers (1834–1915), restored to reflect the period after the turn of the 20th century.

Map, page 222

BELOW:
Louisbourg's
arched gateway .

WHALE-WATCHING IN COASTAL WATERS

For the Inuit whaling meant survival, for the Europeans it was big business. Today whales live under the watchful eyes of scientists and tourists.

While Christopher Columbus and Jacques Cartier were still recounting their New World discoveries, Basque whalers were quietly making fortunes on the Canadian coast. Their Red Bay, Labrador, whaling station employed 1,000 men and refined up to two million liters of valuable oil each season. At the same time, unknown to the Basques, Inuit were catching whales in the Arctic Ocean far to the west, and the Nootka people were hunting off Canada's west coast.

Other European and later American whalers joined the Basques, expanding their hunts to the edges of the known world on each of Canada's three coasts. They would pursue the whale in a small boat, thrust their harpoon into the mammal, and let out a line. The frenzied whale would take the boat on what became known as a "Nantucket sleigh ride" until, exhausted, it would fall victim to its hunters. Then its carcass would be towed ashore for stripping.

When the 19th century brought efficient steam-ships, and harpoon guns to shoot a missile which exploded inside the animal, whale stocks went into decline.

WHALING GIVES WAY TO WHALE-WATCHING

By the onset of World War 1, profitable whaling had ceased in the Canadian Arctic, but it continued along the British Columbian and Newfoundland coasts with the introduction of factory ships for processing. The International Whaling Commission began controlling catches in the late 1940s, but stocks off Canada's coasts diminished at a dramatic rate. Commercial whaling was ended by the government in 1972. Today only the Inuit are allowed to take whales, for their own consumption.

A new tourism-based industry now employs part-time fishermen in the business of whale-watching. Sometimes viewing is done from cruisers carrying from 20 to 200 passengers. Often small dinghies are lowered from the mother-ship, taking two or three passengers at a time to within a meter or so of the massive creatures.

▷ WHO LIVES WHERE
Canada's coastal waters provide a habitat for various species of whales: bowhead and white whales are found around Baffin Bay, while the legendary narwhal with its long, twisted horn lived even further north. Humpback, sperm, minke, fin and right whales inhabit the east coast; orcas and gray whales can be seen off British Columbia.

▽ IN FOR THE KILL
Inuit were the most skilled at finding a use for almost every part of the whale. They ate the skin, blubber and flesh, used the bones for weapons, tools and building, and the oil for light and heat. The Europeans were more wasteful, often extracting only the oil to make soap, cosmetics, candles, margarine and paint.

WHERE TO SPOT A WHALE

NEWFOUNDLAND'S north-coast ports, including those in Trinity and Bonavista Bays, date back to the heyday of whaling. Today operators combine whale-watching with sighting bald eagles and other rare bird species. A bonus here is a close-up look at spectacular icebergs as they drift south.

Further to the south, the BAY OF FUNDY has krill-rich waters stirred by enormous tides. These attract families of huge right whales, so called by whalers who found them valuable and easy to catch. Most popular spot for viewing is New Brunswick's GRAND MANAN ISLAND, where expeditions are run by marine biologists.

At the confluence of QUÉBEC's Saguenay and St Lawrence Rivers whales are readily seen from the shore and on guided expeditions. Several species here include a permanent colony of small white beluga whales, the only such group found outside the Arctic.

Churchill, on MANITOBA'S Arctic Coast, also includes belugas among its whale species. In addition to the traditional excursions, visitors here can go scuba diving among the whales.

On BRITISH COLUMBIA'S coast, excursions leave from Vancouver and Victoria and many smaller ports. Gray whales, which migrate each spring down the west coast of Vancouver Island, are best seen between mid-March and early April.

▷ WHALE POWER

Whaling was a dangerous occupation. Here a sperm whale destroys a boat. In Canadian waters the most prized whale was the bowhead, found in Baffin and Hudson Bays. Its baleen (whalebone) was used to make corset stays, skirt hoops, buggy whips, umbrellas and fishing rods.

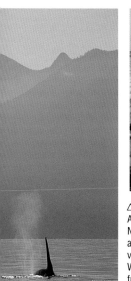

△ CLOSE ENCOUNTER

Around Grand Manan Island, New Brunswick, passengers are taken in small boats to view the mammals close up. Whales may also be seen from the ferry to the island.

PRINCE EDWARD ISLAND: 'CRADLED ON THE WAVES'

The birthplace of the Canadian Confederation and the setting for L.M. Montgomery's novel "Anne of Green Gables", Prince Edward Island is the tiniest province in a land of vast horizons

Map, page 222

P rince Edward Island (P.E.I.) rests in the Gulf of St Lawrence, cut off from the mainland by the Northumberland Strait. Less rugged than its fellow Atlantic Provinces, P.E.I.'s quaintness seems untouched by the modern world. Agriculturally, the land is well groomed and cultivated. Some go so far as to describe the island as two beaches divided by potato fields. The importance of potatoes cannot be overestimated; they are the pre-eminent crop. Tourism is second in economic importance. There are 130,000 inhabitants on the island, most of them the descendants of early French, Scottish, English and Irish settlers.

P.E.I. is an island begging to be explored. Since 1997 it has been joined to the mainland by the Confederation Bridge, an imposing 13-km (8-mile) structure between Borden and Cape Tormentine, New Brunswick. There is also a ferry service between Wood Islands and Caribou, Nova Scotia.

Abegweit

According to Micmac legend, the Great Spirit molded brick-red clay into "the most beautiful place on earth" and gently placed it in the Gulf of St Lawrence. He presented it to his people and they came here in summer to camp and to fish nearly 2,000 years ago. They called it *Abegweit*, "land cradled on the waves". Today the Micmacs account for less than one percent of the population of the island.

The first European to covet the island was Jacques Cartier, who claimed it for France in 1534. He considered it "the fairest land 'tis possible to see…!"; yet **Île-St-Jean**, as the French affectionately named it, had no permanent settlement until 1719 at **Port La Joye**. It became the breadbasket for the French stronghold at Louisbourg and the island still serves a similar function for the region as the "Garden of the Gulf".

The west: Lady Slipper Drive

P.E.I. is geographically separated into three parts: traveling from west to east – **Prince**, **Queens** and **Kings**. The westernmost region is less developed than the other two in terms of tourism, but it is no less attractive.

Lady Slipper Drive (named for the delicate, pink orchid which is the provincial flower) meanders around a deeply indented coastline; past sandstone cliffs and sun-bleached dunes; and through tiny villages, many of them ringing with the sounds of Acadian French. (Close to five percent of P.E.I.'s population is French-speaking.)

The route begins and ends in **Summerside ⓑ**, the biggest town in this province with the exception of only one city, Charlottetown. Located on **Bedeque Bay**, the

LEFT: weathered resident of Prince Edward Island.
BELOW: catch of the day – lobsters are a P.E.I. specialty.

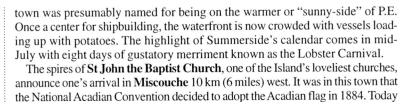

*Covehead Harbor
Light at Brackley
Beach*

town was presumably named for being on the warmer or "sunny-side" of P.E. Once a center for shipbuilding, the waterfront is now crowded with vessels loading up with potatoes. The highlight of Summerside's calendar comes in mid-July with eight days of gustatory merriment known as the Lobster Carnival.

The spires of **St John the Baptist Church**, one of the Island's loveliest churches, announce one's arrival in **Miscouche** 10 km (6 miles) west. It was in this town that the National Acadian Convention decided to adopt the Acadian flag in 1884. Today this banner can be seen throughout French-speaking regions of Atlantic Canada. Miscouche is also home of **Le Musée Acadien** (open July–Aug: daily 9.30am–7pm; Sep–Jun: Mon–Fri 9.30am–5pm; Sun 1–4pm; entrance fee) whose collection of antique tools, household items, religious artifacts, photographs and documents aims to preserve the culture of these early settlers.

Oyster center

Five kilometers (3 miles) north of Miscouche is **Malpeque Bay**, where the world-renowned Malpeque oysters were first discovered. The Tyne Valley Oyster Festival celebrates these bivalves annually in August. Malpeque Bay is also known for its fine sand beaches and for having been a great center for shipbuilding in the 19th century, a part of the island heritage commemorated at **Green Park Provincial Park** in **Port Hill** ⓰ to the west of the bay. Green Park is the former estate of shipbuilding magnate James Yeo, Jr., which today includes his restored home, Yeo House (*circa* 1865), a shipbuilding museum and a re-created 19th-century shipyard (open Jul–Labor Day: daily; rest of year: closed; entrance fee). The yard is home of a partially completed brigantine schooner.

BELOW: sanctuary in the woods.

Beyond Port Hill is a causeway leading to **Lennox Island**, a reservation inhabited by 50 Micmac families. Lennox Island's Indian Arts and Crafts specializes in the sale of beaded and silver jewelry, clay pottery, wood carvings, woven baskets and ceremonial headdresses made by Indians from many different nations.

The **Cape Kildare** area, 45 km (28 miles) north of Port Hill, is where Jacques Cartier dropped anchor in 1534, thereby "discovering" the island. A provincial park honors the explorer, stretching along the dune-lined coast for 5 km (3 miles). Inland 12 km (7 miles) to the north is **Tignish** ⓱, a community founded in 1799 by a group of Acadians who were later joined by two Irishmen. Both cultures are still well represented and, typically, the church is the focal point of the community. The **Church of St Simon and St Jude** has a fine pipe organ, which is played at recitals every Wednesday during July and August (times advertised locally).

The northernmost tip of P.E.I., **North Cape**, is a continually eroding point, so much so that the lighthouse and the road that encircles it have been moved inland several times. Its strategic location prompted development of the **Atlantic Wind Test Site**, a national facility for the testing and evaluation of wind generators, where visitors are welcome.

South from North Cape, along the Northumberland shore, tourists are likely to see Irish moss drying by the road or perhaps, following a storm, being gathered and hauled by horse-drawn carriages and pickup trucks along the beach. The area around Miminegash is particularly known for the harvesting of this commercially viable seaweed. Sightings of a "ghost ship", full-rigged and aflame, are frequently reported between **Campbellton** and **Burton** on this shore. Legends abound here, from the Micmac explanation for the red-stained rocks at **Cape Wolfe** – the god Thunder, betrayed in love by a young maiden, wrathfully threw her to earth – to tales of Captain Kidd's buried treasure at **West Point**.

Inland from West Point is **O'Leary**, in the center of one of P.E.I.'s richest and largest potato-producing areas, home of the **Potato Museum** (part of the **O'Leary Museum**) and host to the annual Potato Blossom Festival (July).

Tracing **Egmont Bay**, approaching the Summerside area, is the Région Acadienne – punctuated by the villages **Abram-Village**, **Cap-Egmont** and **Mont-Carmel**. There are some excellent opportunities to experience Acadian culture and *joie de vivre* during the summer season, from the Cap-Egmont Cover Festival in mid-July to the National Acadian Celebrations in late July, and *l'exposition agricole et le festival acadien* over the Labor Day weekend. The latter both include agricultural competitions, step-dancing, fiddling, lobster suppers, the Blessing of the Fleet and more. Abram-Village is also a center for crafts (particularly quilts and rugs), which are demonstrated and sold at the local Handicrafts Co-operative. And as for the lively arts, tradition is very much alive and stepping at Club 50's Saturday night square dances.

The seaside community of Cap-Egmont has a rather unusual attraction – **The Bottle Houses**. A recycling project (undertaken in retirement) of the first magnitude, Edouard T. Arsenault built his glass houses and chapel from bottles (the first called for 12,000 of them). After a "long winter cleaning bottles", the for-

Map, page 222

When the British Deportation Order of 1758 forced Acadians into exile, about 30 families remained in hiding on P.E.I. – the ancestors of many local Acadians.

BELOW: bottle house at Cap-Egmont.

P.E.I. events include the Charlottetown Festival of music and theater (Jun–Oct); Jazz and Blues Festival (July); Lucy Maud Montgomery Festival (August).

mer fisherman and carpenter began work in 1980, lovingly laboring over the project until his death four years later. Arsenault's typically Acadian spirit, a mixture of creative energy and humor, shines through the walls.

The island's city

Not the least of **Charlottetown**'s ⑱ considerable charms is that it is still predominantly wooden (structurally, but decidedly not in demeanor). It is the center of all things for P.E.I. – government, commerce and culture; and it is the province's only city, though it seems more like an elegant small town, complete with a town crier and gaslights. Historically, Charlottetown is best known for being the "Cradle of the Confederation". The 1864 meeting, which led to the formation of the Dominion of Canada three years later, was held in **Province House**, the province's first public building (open June–mid-Oct: daily; mid-Oct–end May: Sat, Sun only; free). Ironically, P.E.I. was at first hesitant to join Canada, and it did not enter the Confederation until 1873. This neo-classical stone structure is now a National Historic Site and the chamber where the Fathers of Confederation met has been restored, though it still houses the legislature.

Next door is the **Confederation Center of the Arts**, established to commemorate the centennial of the main event (open Jun–mid–Oct: daily; Oct–May: Sat, Sun only). Each province contributed 15 cents for each of its citizens to help to finance construction. It includes gallery and theater spaces and is host each summer to the **Charlottetown Festival**. Running from mid-June until the middle of October, it is Canada's best-known music and theater festival. One of the loveliest parts of town is **Rockford Square**, shaded by 110 trees, the legacy of Arbor Day 1884. Adjacent to the square is **St Peter's Anglican**

BELOW LEFT: a precious plateful.
BELOW RIGHT: potato farming.

Church (1869) with a notable attachment, **All Souls' Chapel**, created in 1888 as a memorial to one of the cathedral's first clergymen. It was a labor of love for William Harris, who designed it, and for his brother Robert, who created luminous wall paintings. Harris specified that Island materials be used, from the rich, red sandstone exterior to the wood and stone used for interior carvings. This High Victorian Gothic-style shrine is a testament to the spirit of both brothers, and to the skill of Island craftspeople.

Map, page 222

The center: Blue Heron Drive

The central region of Prince Edward Island is traced by the route known as **Blue Heron Drive**, which comes full circle at Charlottetown. It is distinguished by fine beaches – white sand along the Gulf shore and red sand along the Northumberland shore – colorful fishing villages, *Anne of Green Gables*-related attractions (an Island sub-industry) and community lobster suppers. Every summer night throughout P.E.I.'s small towns and districts, amazing feasts are organized and prepared by local women. Held either in churches or big halls, as many as 400 to 500 people are fed. For a reasonable price travelers can experience some of the best homemade food and lobster dishes they've had.

Most of **Queens County**'s gulf coast belongs to **P.E.I. National Park ⓳**, 24 km (15 miles) northwest of Charlottetown), with some of the finest beaches in eastern Canada (open all year; entrance fee Jun–Sep). The Victorian mansion of Dalvay-by-the-Sea, now a hotel, near the eastern entrance to the park, was built in 1896 by the oil magnate, Alexander Macdonald.

Rustico Island, part of the National Park, is the summer home of a protected colony of great blue herons, the possessors of 2-meter (6-ft) wing spans, while

BELOW: relic of colonialism.

"Anne of Green Gables" is big business on P.E.I.

North Rustico is a traditional fishing village. You can purchase seafood practically off the boats here, pass the time talking with locals or go out on a tuna charter.

Green Gables House

Still within P.E.I. National Park, 10km (6 miles) west of the Rusticos, is **Cavendish ⑳**, the center of *Anne of Green Gables* country. Visitors come from far and wide to see the settings described by Lucy Maud Montgomery in her book about an orphan girl, published in 1908, and other works of fiction, as well as to explore landmarks in the author's life. The lovely **Green Gables House** itself, on Highway 6, has undergone restoration following a fire in 1997. The **L.M. Montgomery Birthplace** can be found in **New London** 15 km (9 miles) southwest. A brochure sets the stage by stating: "As you walk through the rooms of the Birthplace, you will thrill to the realization, that it was in this house that Lucy Maud first saw the light of day."

    Victoria (its residents like to call it Victoria by-the-Sea), 30 km (18 miles) southwest of Charlottetown facing the Northumberland Strait, is an English-flavored town, which is is both an active fishing port and a center for antiques and fine crafts. From late June to Labor Day theater performances take place at the restored **Victoria Playhouse**. The Provincial Park, which is edged by red sand, is a good place to have a picnic.

The east: Kings Byway

BELOW: watching the day go by, Cavendish.

The easternmost piece of P.E.I., most of it corresponding to Kings County, is encircled by the **Kings Byway**. This is the longest of the three routes. In the **Orwell Corner Rural Life Museum**, 30 km (19 miles) east of Charlottetown,

the atmosphere of a late-19th century rural crossroads community has been recreated (open mid-May–mid-June: Mon–Fri; June–Labor Day: daily; Sep–mid-Oct: Tues–Sun; mid-Oct to 22 Oct: Mon–Fri). Most of the early settlers here were Scottish and in summer the sounds of the Highlands can be enjoyed at weekly *ceilidh* (pronounced kay-lee).

In 1803 a Scotsman by the name of Lord Selkirk financed the immigration of three shiploads of Highlanders to P.E.I. The "Selkirk Pioneers" settled in **Eldon**, 13 km (8 miles) south of Orwell, and today a restoration and reconstruction, the **Lord Selkirk Pioneer Settlement**, provides insight into their existence. It is one of the largest collections of authentic log buildings in Canada. The clans gather in Eldon every year in early August for the Highland Games.

Map, page 222

Sculptors and seals

Farther east in the community of **Flat River**, 13 km (8 miles) from Eldon, you'll find **Flat River Craftsmen**, featuring the pottery of Robert Wilby and the batik of his sister Roslynn. A life-size nude sculpture beckons visitors to come in and browse. The artists welcome spectators to watch their works in progress. Eighteen kilometers (11 miles) beyond **Woods Island** (a boarding point for the Nova Scotia ferry) is **Murray River ㉑**. This lovely town was once an activity center for shipbuilding, but today wood is worked on a much smaller scale. **Murray Bay** is the home of a large natural seal colony. These sleek creatures can be best observed from the **Seal Cove Campground** in **Murray Harbor North**, cavorting in the sun on their offshore sandbar.

Approaching the easternmost tip of P.E.I. is the **Bay Fortune Area**, washed by a string of legends. There is talk of the early 19th-century murder by a tenant of landlord Edward Abell at **Abell's Cape**, of buried treasures along the sandstone cliffs, and of actor Charles Flockton, who in the late 19th century bought the cape and spent each summer here with his comedy company. American playwright Elmer Harris was inspired to feature nearby **Souris** as the setting for his book *Johnny Belinda* (based on the local legend of a young deaf and dumb girl). Today Souris is an embarkation point for passengers heading for the nearby Îles de la Madeleine.

Basin Head, 12 km (7 miles) east of Souris, is home of the **Fisheries Museum** (open mid-Jun–Sep: daily; entrance fee). August brings the **Harvest of the Sea Festival** where time-tested Island recipes can be sampled. The museum is located beside a particularly beautiful stretch of dunes, where the sand "sings" as you walk. Rounding **East Point** (called *Kespe-menagek*, "the end of the Island", by the Micmacs), brings one to **North Lake**, the "Tuna Fishing Capital of the World". Tourists flock here in pursuit of the giant bluefin tuna – regarded as the ultimate in sportfishing.

Heading back to Charlottetown one realizes that in 2,000 years little has changed. The Micmacs were right in calling P.E.I. *Abegweit*. The island is indeed a land cradled by waves. The Gulf Coast provides endless water activities for travelers, from fishing and boating to swimming and digging a clam dinner out of the brick-red sand beaches. Inland the flat, quaint terrain provides a perfect route for adventurous trekkers and cyclists.

BELOW: touring the island by bicycle.

NEWFOUNDLAND: THE ROCKY OUTPOST

Map, page 251

While settlements are sparse and many areas are only accessible by boat or light plane, Newfoundland's craggy coastline, mountains, lakes, and rich history appeal to visitors worldwide

Newfoundland's mountains are not as high as the Rockies and are much less accessible. There are no theme parks or world-class art galleries. Tourist facilities, while adequate, are rarely luxurious. Yet Newfoundland's remoteness has cultivated the most individualistic part of North America. Imagine a land mass three times the area of New Brunswick, Nova Scotia and Prince Edward Island combined, then remember that the rugged terrain is home to less than four people per square mile. A fifth of the total population live in the area of St. John's on the east coast, while the rest live mainly in fishing villages known as "outports". English is the most common language spoken (99 percent) and 96 percent of the people who live in Newfoundland were born here. Jokes about Newfies can be heard across the country, but Newfoundlanders have their own brand of humor, calling Newfoundland simply "The Rock".

The first explorers

To understand Newfoundland, one must understand some of its history. The **Grand Banks**, Newfoundland's greatest asset, are the fishing grounds southeast of Newfoundland that have been worked by European fishermen since the 15th century. Giovanni Caboto from Italy (also known as John Cabot) sighted this coast in 1497 and claimed the land for the English king, Henry VII, who had financed his voyage. Henry, who had hoped the expedition would find gold, gave him £10 and had to be content with fish. Cabot reported that the cod were so numerous that "they would fill a basket lowered over the side". The Spanish, Portuguese and French who also fished in the area, salted their catch to preserve it for the trip home. But the English, who lacked a source of cheap salt, had to dry their cod, and to do this the fleets needed to go ashore.

Britain originally did not want a colony and actively discouraged settlement. In fact it was illegal for anyone to winter in Newfoundland. The "Masterless Men" were the first European settlers after the Vikings to come to Canada. They were sailors who jumped ship, preferring life in one of the many natural harbors along Newfoundland's coast to life aboard. Their independence and spirit of survival are still very much a part of Newfoundlanders' character today.

The Viking settlements ("Markland") of the 10th century did not survive, perhaps because of a change in the climate or a vitamin deficiency causing a weakening of the bones. Stories of Markland have indicated that the first child born in the Americas of European origin was Snorri Torfinnsson. When Christopher Columbus vis-

LEFT: a sailor from the east coast.
BELOW: lobster with a dash of lemon.

ited Iceland in 1487, five years before his "discovery" of the New World, he probably would have heard the stories of the Newfoundland voyages of the Vikings. The site of Markland is at L'Anse aux Meadows at the northern tip of the Great Northern Peninsula.

Oral tradition

If you remember that St John's is closer to Ireland than to Toronto, you won't be surprised by the language. It is a unique blend of dialects from England's West Country and southwest Ireland, brought over by the original settlers and left largely unchanged by the passing centuries. It is the closest dialect in the modern world to Shakespearean English and the only place where many words and expressions which were common in the 17th century still survive.

A tradition preserved in Newfoundland is storytelling. The oral form of handing down stories from generation to generation is still alive. Times are changing but not all Newfoundlanders will change with them. Guglielmo Marconi was dubbed an "irrepressible dandy" when he came to Newfoundland to receive the first transatlantic wireless message in 1901. The "old days" are described as the times when "most people could neither read nor write, but my, how they could talk!" Modern times differ only in that people can now read and write as well.

In fact, Newfoundland is Canada's most recent province. Confederation (union) with Canada was and sometimes still is one of the liveliest topics for discussion in Newfoundland. It did not take place until 1949 and was a hard-won victory for the federalists. An old Newfoundland song sings of the island:

> *Her face to Britain, her back to the Gulf,*
> *Come near at your peril Canadian wolf.*

BELOW: fisherman satisfied with the day's catch.

Life in the 20th century

Until well into the 20th century the majority of Newfoundlanders lived along the coasts making a difficult living from the sea. Cod, which was the foundation of Newfoundland's economy, has virtually disappeared from the waters off Canada's east coast now and governments have placed an embargo on its fishery. Migrating salmon are caught at sea, and in the larger rivers along the south coast crab and lobster are trapped.

As long as there has been human habitation on the island there has been a seal hunt off Newfoundland in the spring. In 1983 animal rights groups from outside the province persuaded foreign governments to ban the import of seal pelts on humanitarian grounds. This polarized Newfoundland fishermen who were proud of their humane killing methods and adherence to quotas. Today many argue that there is an overpopulation of seal herds.

In the last 50 years mining and forest industries have taken a larger place in Newfoundland economics. Although the fishing industries are still the largest employers, the province no longer depends upon them exclusively for its livelihood. In recent years gas and oil reserves to rival those in the North Sea have been discovered off the coast. Tourism is a relatively recent phenomenon in Newfoundland. The prevailing attitude is still that the visitors should "take us as they find us". In the "Hospitality Home Program" tourists can sleep and eat in Newfoundland homes. This is a good way for visitors to meet the locals and a source of entertainment for both.

Screech, found in many households and taverns, is the drink for which Newfoundland is famous. Originally it was the washings and dregs from casks of rum. It's now bottled under government supervision and, although safer than in earlier days, it is still like the Newfoundland character – more interesting than it is refined. For the seafood lover Newfoundland homes are the ideal venue. Fish is served as often and in as much variety as one could wish: halibut, crab, Atlantic salmon, lobster and much more. You can still find cod on the menu, but now it is one of the most expensive items, imported from Russia or farther afield.

Exploring the province

The independent traveler will need a car. There are bus services to virtually all locations but the farther off the beaten path, that is to say the more interesting your destination, the more infrequent the service. There are still many locations that are best reached or only accessible by boat. The main road in Newfoundland is the **Trans-Canada Highway** which runs through Newfoundland on an indirect path between **Channel-Port-aux-Basques ❶** in the west, terminus for the ferry from North Sydney, Nova Scotia, to St John's in the east. It's 905 km (576 miles) long and is the lifeline of the province.

The National Parks are a source of pride for the Newfoundlanders and a source of delight to the visitor. On the west coast is mountainous **Gros Morne National Park ❷**. Its fjords are best seen by boat from **Western Brook**; here you have the chance of seeing whales, seals, caribou and moose. It is even rumored that there are polar bears which have swum ashore from passing icebergs. **Terra Nova**

Map, page 251

Gros Morne means "great bluff". Here you can wade along sandy beaches or set off on a four-day hike into the wilderness across the glacier-carved landscape.

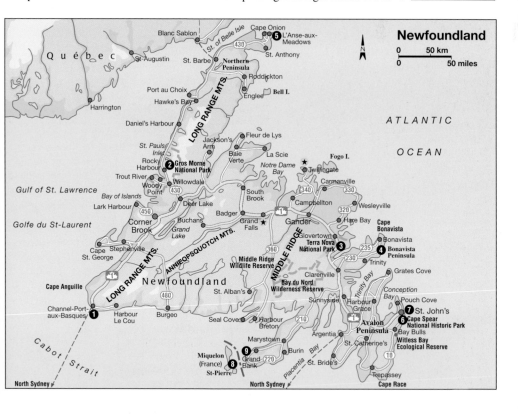

Whales can often be seen in the waters off Cape Spear in spring and summer – ask a park ranger where to look. This is also a good place to see icebergs.

BELOW: a solitary church.

National Park ❸ on the east is a piece of typical Newfoundland fishing coast. Here there is boating, fishing and moonlight cruises on beautiful **Clode Sound**. Inland in the park there is good camping and hiking, and the water in the lakes is warm enough to swim.

East of the park lies the **Bonavista Peninsula ❹**. This region attracted world-wide attention in 1997 when, in a re-enactment of Cabot's voyage 500 years earlier, a replica of his boat, the *Matthew,* sailed from Bristol, England, and landed amid great ceremony at Cape Bonavista. Visitors can get a feel for life on this isolated cape at the **Lighthouse**, restored to the 1870s period (open mid-Jun–mid-Oct: daily), and the **Ryan Premises National Historic Site** (open mid-Jun–mid–Oct: daily 10am–6pm; entrance fee).

The park at the 10th century site of the Viking settlement at **L'Anse aux Meadows ❺** at the most northerly tip of the island is well worth a visit. Dwellings have been reconstructed and at the Visitor Centre (open Jun, Jul, Aug: daily). Norse artifacts found on site are displayed.

Cape Spear National Historic Park ❻ is the most easterly point of both Newfoundland and the continent. Take a boat tour to see and listen to the school of whales. On even the shortest boat ride off Newfoundland's coast you will be reminded of the power of the sea. One of the world's most infamous sinkings happened just off this coast on April 15, 1912. The luxury liner *Titanic* sank after hitting an iceberg, taking the lives of 1,513 people. Locals tend to paint their houses in bright colors to ensure they can be spotted by fishermen.

Sport fishing opportunities are as many and as varied as the Newfoundland coast and all the rivers and lakes inland. Fishing lakes are known as "ponds". Salmon, arctic char, northern pike and giant bluefin tuna are the favored catches.

St John's

The capital of Newfoundland and Labrador, **St John's 7**, sited on the northeast of the Avalon peninsula, is one of the oldest cities in North America. Its streets were originally cowpaths wandering up from the harbor. The statue of Peter Pan in a downtown park is polished only by the bodies of the children who climb over it. **Government House** was built with a moat to keep out snakes, although there are none in the province.

Signal Hill Park must be seen: more events of historical importance have taken place on this site than in most other provinces. It was here that the first transatlantic wireless message was received by Marconi. Signal Hill was the site in 1762 of one of the final battles of the Seven Years' War. Visitors to this site can still see fortifications ranging from the Napoleonic Wars to World War II. Despite its historic significance, Signal Hill got its name originally from the practice of putting up flags to let people know of ships in the harbor.

The best way to get a sense of St John's is to walk the main street. It is called Water Street, the oldest street on the continent. When Newfoundland joined Canada in 1949 most of the province lived in poverty, but Newfoundland had more millionaires (they were known as "Water Street Men") per capita than elsewhere in North America. Of special note is the **Rothwell House** on Circular Drive. Two sisters, who insisted upon being different from one another, lived here. As a result, each half of the house is designed in a different period.

The **Newfoundland Museum** on Duckworth Street is devoted to the province's history with notable displays of the Beothuk Indians and Labrador Inuit (open: daily). Five fires devastated St John's in the 19th century. One of the few buildings to escape was the clapboard **Commissariat House**, King's

Map, page 251

BELOW: a bay near St. John's.

Map, page 251

Quidi Vidi Lake is the site of the annual Royal St. John's Regatta. Held since 1826, it is the oldest continuing sporting event in North America.

BELOW: Ashuanipi River, Labrador.
RIGHT: remote spot, Newfoundland.

Bridge Road, now restored to reflect the 1830s. **Quidi Vidi Village**, 3 km (2 miles) north of Signal Hill, has the typical "pocket" harbor of an outport.

Outpost of France

Not only is Newfoundland closer to Ireland than Toronto but it is also closer to France than to Nova Scotia. At least it's closer to a part of France. Just off the end of the Burin Peninsula on Newfoundland's southern coast are the islands of **St Pierre and Miquelon ❽**. They are the remnants of France's once great empire in North America. The islands can be reached by ferry from **Grand Bank ❾** or by air and a passport is usually required. It truly is a taste of Europe with narrow streets and European cars. With a population of 6,000, St Pierre and Miquelon send a *député* to the French Parliament and a member to the Senate.

Journey to Labrador

For the truly adventurous, Labrador beckons, just 17 km (10 miles) across the Strait of Belle Isle from northern Newfoundland. Subject to the weather, ferries make the short crossing from **St Barbe** to **Blanc Sablon** on the Labrador-Québec border. From here the 80-km (50-mile) paved Route 510 connects a string of coastal settlements, including the fishing village of **L'Anse-au-Clair**, founded by the French in the early 18th century, **L'Anse-Amour**, where Aboriginals are known to have lived 9,000 years ago, to **Red Bay**, site of a Basque whaling station, *circa* 1550.

Tall stories

Newfoundland's first day as a Canadian province was April 1, 1949. The First of April is traditionally April Fool's Day, the day when practical jokes, especially ones involving tall stories, may be played with impunity. Humor is such a part of the Newfoundland way of speech and life that it is often hard to know when a joke is being played. It is not true, for example, that those icebergs you may see off St John's in the winter are styrofoam structures towed out for decoration by the Chamber of Commerce – although if your informant recognizes you as a mainlander he or she may manage to assure you to that effect.

The time to see Newfoundland is now. In the last 30 years the changes have been profound and show no sign of slowing. The consolidation of the outports, a program for moving inhabitants of isolated outports into major centers, has been compared to the clearances of the Scottish Highlands. The importance of the fishing industries is diminishing and will have even less prominence if the Hibernia Oil Fields (a multi-billion dollar project taking place just off the east coast of St. John's) live up to their expected potential. These rich offshore oil reserves could bring with them the single thing most likely to cause an irreparable change to the fabric of Newfoundland society – that of industrial prosperity.

In many ways Newfoundland is the most unusual Canadian province, in many other ways it is the most typical. It is a land of beauty and of hardships, a place of hospitality and isolation. It is a place where even the short-term visitor may gain memories to last a lifetime.

THE WEST

*From Manitoba to the Pacific coast, western Canada offers a
rich diversity of landscapes and cultures*

Smoldering from the off-handed treatment it has historically
received from Ontario and Québec, the West has recently
emerged as a powerful presence in Canada. Rich in minerals,
oil and natural gas, Manitoba, Saskatchewan and Alberta have
become forces to be reckoned with.

Sometimes referred to as Canada's "Garden of Eden", British
Columbia, the most westerly region that flanks the Pacific, is the
West's warmest province. It encompasses not only the splendid and
irascible Rocky Mountains, but also a gentle coastline.

The West section opens with an exploration of Vancouver and
British Columbia, beginning with a description of Indian life and the
arrival of European explorers. Modern B.C. is encountered first in
Victoria, the province's capital city. After a stroll through its streets,
readers are taken along the coastline and into the area's awesome
wilderness.

Then follow chapters on Canada's Prairie provinces: Alberta,
Saskatchewan and Manitoba. These three provinces constitute the
remainder of Canada's "official" west. Alberta begins the search for
the "prairie existence" and demonstrates the unexpected diversity of
the region by journeying up into Canada's vast playground: the
Rocky Mountains. Banff's isolated beauty contrasts with the exciting
city-life of Edmonton and Calgary. Saskatchewan is explored
through its rich history and its proud and prolific cultural features.
Manitoba, concluding the section, provides an experience of the
prairie itself: wide open spaces, no longer shaded by forests, rolling
on to a distant horizon.

PRECEDING PAGES: looking westward – the lakes, forests and mountains of British
Columbia. **LEFT:** laying in stocks of winter fuel.

VANCOUVER: SHINING STAR OF THE WEST

Sited between the Pacific Ocean and the Rocky Mountains, this green and vibrant city combines a diverse heritage with a thriving arts, cultural, entertainments and sports scene

Map, page 264

Victoria, on the southern end of Vancouver Island, is the capital of British Columbia, but the mainland town of **Vancouver** is the West Coast's shining star. Set with its back firmly against the continent, it looks to its future out across the Pacific, attracting big investors from Hong Kong and growing at a rate that has impressed its usual blasé neighbors in the US over the border to the south who have been dropping by to see just how a city should grow into the 21st century.

First among Canada's major cities, Vancouver seems forever building, whether it's a flashy mansion for an incoming Chinese millionaire or an office tower for the finance, investment or real estate trade. Pan-Pacificism, the orientation to regard Sydney and Seoul, not Toronto and Truro, as future economic partners has shown some pay-off.

As the travel writer Jan Morris put it, Vancouver could become "a teeming metropolis of banks, investment houses, and cosmopolitan speculators… shirt-sleeved money manipulators keyed in to Tokyo and Hong Kong, power breakfasts with Japanese brokers at the Vancouver Club."

Evidence of prosperity can be seen in the swish quality of its luxury hotels downtown, most notably the Canadian Pacific Waterfront Center Hotel and the Pan-Pacific Hotel Vancouver, at $100 million the most expensive ever built in Canada, which adjoins **Canada Place Ⓐ**. Built as the Canada pavilion for the Expo '86 world's fair which marked Vancouver's centennial, Canada Place is meant to approximate a clipper ship leaving port like the Sydney Opera House and Rockefeller Center. The scalloped domes have come to symbolize the place and its people.

If Canada Place is the first sight, one of the most magnificent urban parks, **Stanley Park Ⓑ**, is the first stop for the rest of the senses. This 405-hectare (1,000-acre) thumb of forest jutting into the Burrard Inlet and almost surrounded by water, is home to Douglas fir, cedar and hemlock. It was dedicated in 1889 in the name of a govenor general, Lord Stanley, the same Stanley whose name stands for supremacy in professional hockey: the Stanley Cup.

Docked across Coal Harbor to the east of the park is the *MV Britannia* cruise ship. From here the double-decked ferry follows the coast north through Howe Sound to Squamish, B.C. Only the seas in the Middle East teem with more life than Howe Sound. The sheer rocky walls, topped by towering firs, are reminiscent of Scandinavian fiords. The 65-km (40-mile) return trips from Squamish are usually made aboard the restored

PRECEDING PAGES: enjoying a picnic in Stanley Park. **LEFT:** Vancouver's Lion's Gate Bridge. **BELOW:** a young girl in Chinatown.

For some of the best views of the harbor, city and mountains, take a 13-minute ride on one of the seabuses plying between Downtown and North Vancouver.

Royal Hudson Steam Train, the last operating public service steam train to be found in Canada.

Stanley Park has a 10-km (6-mile) perimeter paved pathway around the sea wall that offers a panoramic view of the water, as well as the thousands of recreational boats and more than 200 cruise vessels that are docked regularly in the harbors. Vancouver is not only Canada's premier port, but it's also perhaps the most important port on the North American west coast. It is here that grain from the prairies, and lumber, coal and sulphur from the interior of B.C. are shipped to Japan and elsewhere in the Pacific.

One of the highlights of the park is the **Aquarium**, the third largest in north America, located in the southeast corner of the park. This is more than a place to see a killer whale kiss a pretty volunteer on the nose; it is a serious center for the study of the sea (open daily; entrance fee). One of its most popular programs is a 12-hour overnight stay, bedding down beside the whales.

Watching the otters and seals play and cavort is glorious, whether seen in an aquarium or in nature, but seeing, a moment later, a great white shark devouring a huge piece of meat in the blink of an eye, gives an excellent idea of the power and variety of the water life (the Aquarium holds more than 8,000 creatures) that covers three-quarters of this planet.

In addition to the flesh and blood attractions of the Aquarium, Vancouver is filled with museums of history and fine art. Leading these on the campus of the University of British Columbia is the **Museum of Anthropology ⓒ**, which contains the greatest collection of Indian wood carvings in the world, including examples of totem poles created before the arrival of Europeans to the region, as well as contemporary work by living Indian sculptors (open mid-May–early

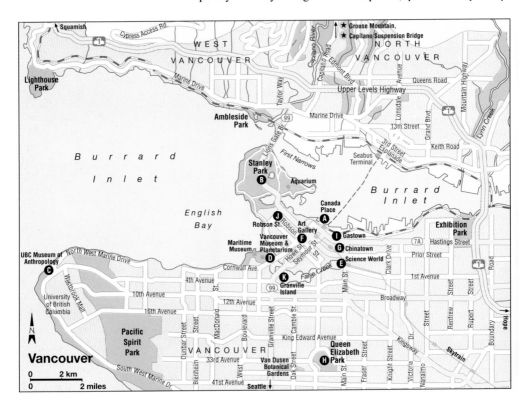

Sep: daily; entrance fee; Sep–Apr: closed Mon). In a similar vein is the **Vancouver Museum** ... in Chestnut Street, Canada's largest civic collection, which traces back the history of the native peoples to the Stone Age, and includes exhibits on the history of white settlers and the modern history of the province (open Jul–Aug: daily; Sep–Jun: closed Mon; entrance fee).

Also here in the grounds of the museum, the site of the first known inhabitants, the Coast Salish people, are the **Gordon Southam Observatory**, the only public observatory in Western Canada, and the **H.R. MacMillan Planetarium**, one of North America's most up to date. Surround-sound laser shows with such rockers as U2 and Led Zeppelin are a specialty (open Jul–Aug: daily; Sep–Jun, closed Mon; entrance fee).

Another place hugely popular with kids is **Science World B.C.** at the waterfront Expo '86 site. The ultimate hands-on experience, the dome has everything from exploding zucchinis (charged with 80,000 volts), to the interior of a beaver lodge (open daily; entrance fee). There is also an **Omnimax Theater**, with the largest screen of its kind in the world.

On the corner of Robson and Howe streets is the **Vancouver Art Gallery**, which has an impressive collection of the works of the Canadian artist, Emily Carr (open daily; entrance fee).

The theater season runs from September to June and offers every kind of performance. The most famous theater in Vancouver is the **Orpheum** on Smithe Street, home of the Vancouver Symphony Orchestra. Traditional theater can be found at the **Queen Elizabeth Theatre** on Cambie Street, which houses two stages and several restaurants. The two universities in the area feature modern theater by members of their drama departments. Avant-garde theater is performed

Map, page 264

BELOW: China Gate in the heart of downtown.

Map,
page 264

Capilano Suspension Bridge in North Vancouver is a sight not to be missed. This 140-meter (450-ft) undulating steel cable bridge crosses a dramatic canyon.

BELOW: Gastown steam clock.
RIGHT: Stanley Park.

at the **Arts Club** on Granville Island, and outdoor theater is shown in Stanley Park's **Malkin Bowl** in summer. With as much annual rainfall (145 cm/57 inches) as any large city in North America, indoor attractions are also popular. But the rain and mild climate create the best in parks and gardens in Canada. The **Dr Sun Yat-Sen Classical Chinese Garden** in **Chinatown** **G** (see below) opened for Expo '86. It is the first such garden to be built outside China, and includes boulders, pavilions, and covered walkways, most of which were imported from China (open daily). More conventional, with its rose garden, conservatory, tennis courts and miniature golf circuit is **Queen Elizabeth Park** **H**, south of here.

Neighborhood life

The real strength of the city, like any great city, is in its neighborhoods. These are the places where people and buildings are not just anonymous cogs in some swirling commercial mass, but where they take on a character of their own, and live out a culture unique to their block or avenue. Vancouver has several distinctive neighborhoods that give it this kind of life.

One of the most famous of these is **Gastown** **I**, named after "Gassy" Jack Deighton, the area's premier barkeeper. The area, which sprang up around a sawmill, and had little to do with gas but much to do with poverty, has now undergone a transformation similar to that of Cabbagetown in Toronto, or SoHo in New York. The neighborhood gets its flavor more from craft and antique dealers than skid-row bars, and is a haven for all types of creativity: pottery, leatherwork, linens, a variety of crafts, and working artists.

The area around **Robson Street** **J** is another tale of a neighborhood's transformation. The flavor was supplied by German immigrants who settled along Robson Street in the 1950s, but it took a more high-rise direction, as the West End of the city became a center of boutiques, restaurants and specialty stores. Visitors interested in old-world cooking, or in purchasing items from around the world, will find this is the place to go and browse on a warm afternoon.

Diners will not want to miss the **Granville Island Public Market** **K**, where food is the main ingredient in the restoration of an abandoned warehouse section (open: daily 9am–6pm). Aside from restaurants there are art galleries, boutiques, theaters and hotels.

The king of neighborhoods is **Chinatown**, home for many of the 370,000 Asians in Vancouver, at the heart of downtown. It's the second largest Chinatown in North America, falling just behind San Francisco. While it offers a diversity of shopping for everything from cooking supplies to artworks, the main attraction is the food. In most of the restaurants the food is served *dim sum* style, which involves waiters and waitresses taking around trays of small dainty dishes, from which one can select. The bill for the meal is based on the number of dishes on a table when diners call for the check.

The Asian community has more than earned its position here: Chinese immigrants helped to keep the gold rush going when white frontiersmen had lost interest and left for home, and their contribution to the construction of the Canadian-Pacific Railway is something of which they can be justly proud.

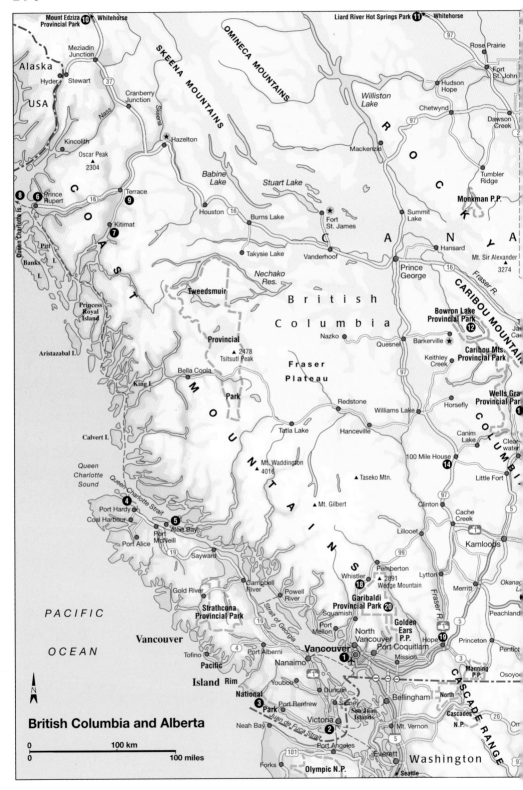

Mount Edziza Provincial Park · Whitehorse
Liard River Hot Springs Park · Whitehorse

Meziadin Junction

SKEENA MOUNTAINS

OMINECA MOUNTAINS

Rose Prairie

97

Hyder · Stewart
Alaska
USA
37
Cranberry Junction
Kincolith
Nass
Skeena

Oscar Peak
2304

★ Hazelton

Fort St. John

Williston Lake

Hudson Hope

Chetwynd

Dawson Creek

2

Mackenzie

Tumbler Ridge

R O C K Y

Monkman P.P.

Babine Lake
Stuart Lake

Terrace

8 · 6 Prince Rupert
Queen Charlotte Is.

16

9

7 Kitimat

Pitt
Banks I.
Princess Royal Island

C O A S T

Houston 16 Burns Lake

★ Fort St. James

Summit Lake

C A N Y A

Hansard

Mt. Sir Alexander
3274

Takysie Lake

Vanderhoof

Prince George

16

Fraser R.

CARIBOU MOUNTAIN

Nechako Res.

Aristazabal I.

Tweedsmuir

B r i t i s h

C o l u m b i a

Nazko

Quesnel

Barkerville ★

Bowron Lake Provincial Park

12

Keithley Creek

Caribou Mts. Provincial Park

Ja Ca

King I.

Provincial

▲ 2478 Tsitsutl Peak

Fraser

Plateau

C O L U M B I

Calvert I.

Bella Coola

Park

Redstone

Williams Lake

Horsefly

Wells Gra Provincial Par

1

M O U N T A I N S

Tatla Lake

Hanceville

Canim Lake

Clear-water

Queen Charlotte Sound

Queen Charlotte Strait

4 Port Hardy
Coal Harbour

5 Alert Bay
Port McNeill

Port Alice

Sayward

19

Gold River

Campbell River

Strathcona Provincial Park

19

▲ Mt. Waddington
4016

▲ Taseko Mtn.

▲ Mt. Gilbert

100 Mile House

14

Little Fort

Clinton

97

Cache Creek

5

1

Kamloops

Lillooet

99

Pemberton

Whistler

18 ▲ 2891 Wedge Mountain

Garibaldi Provincial Park

20

Lytton

Merritt

Okanag L.

Peachland

PACIFIC

OCEAN

Vancouver

Powell River

Squamish

North Vancouver

Golden Ears P.P.

Port Coquitlam

Fraser R.

5

Princeton

Pentict

Pacific

Rim

Tofino · Port Alberni

Nanaimo

Port Mellon

4

Vancouver

1

Mission

Hope

19

3

Manning P.P.

Osoyoo

Island

National

Youbou

Duncan

Bellingham

North

CASCADE RANGE

3 Port Renfrew
Neah Bay

Park

Sidney
San Juan Islands

Victoria

2

Mt. Vernon

North Cascades N.P.

20

Om

Juan de Fuca Strait

Port Angeles

5

Everett

101

Forks

Washington

Seattle

9

N

British Columbia and Alberta

0 — 100 km
0 — 100 miles

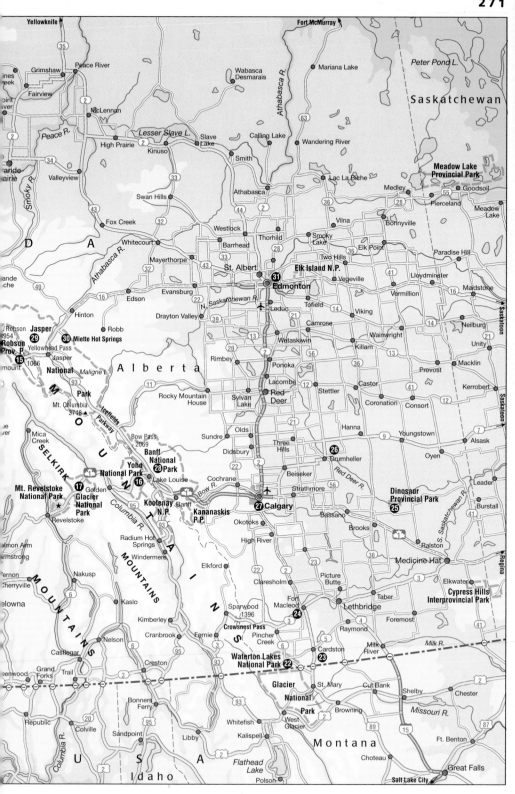

BRITISH COLUMBIA: THE GOOD LIFE

People are drawn to the overwhelming natural beauty of British Columbia – its rocky coastline and thick forests, teeming mountains, mild temperatures – and to its relaxed lifestyle

Map, pages 270/271

Almost half the people who live in British Columbia (B.C.) were born somewhere else. The area has attracted health enthusiasts, die-hard hippies and vegetarians, monarchists and trade unionists and profit-oriented business people. With its diverse interests and great beauty, the 3.3 million residents can't be wrong about B.C.'s attractiveness. Nor can the millions of visitors who come to explore **Vancouver** ❶ and the surrounding province each year.

It is the natural beauty of the land that attracted the Haida people to this far coast of Canada. The Indians have always lived quietly and harmoniously here, even after they were "discovered" by Captain Cook in 1778. A Scotsman, Simon Fraser (1776–1862), adopted Canada as his home, and dedicated his life to exploring and developing the richness of British Columbia. He established the Fraser River as an important fur-trading route.

Fur trading in the 19th century was big business, and the competition for control of this new market marks the early history of British Columbia. The North West Company was chartered by the British Government specifically to develop the resources of the northwest. The company had to fight for trade routes and profits with the Hudson's Bay Company, an older "eastern" company that already had a monopoly on Canadian trade with Europe.

The Nor'west, as the company became called, established an inland trading post, Fort George, which is now the city of Prince George. The Hudson's Bay Company, being the larger of the two enterprises and seeing the value of the fur trade as well as the future of lumber and mining, bought out Nor'west in 1821 and maintained virtual monopoly control over the area until 1858.

The 49th Parallel

In the 19th century, the fur trade along the Columbia River was carried out largely by Americans and the American population grew faster than the British . The desire of the southerners to control the river trade became increasingly clear. The American battle cry "Fifty-Four-Forty or Fight!" (referring to the latitude that marked the northern boundary of the territory) prompted the British to build Fort Victoria in 1843.

The territory was finally divided in two at the 49th parallel. This handed most of the Columbia River, and the best fur-trading territory, over to the United States.

The British Loyalists needed to find an "all British route" inland to the fur trapping territory. In 1856 James Douglas, a bear-like man with political skill, called for Vancouver Island's 774 whites (half of whom were under the age of 20) to elect their first legislature. Two

PRECEDING PAGES: Rocky Mountain skier. **LEFT:** B.C. hideaway. **BELOW:** ski slope fashion.

*Victoria, garden city
and capital of British
Columbia, was
founded in 1843 as
a trading post on
Vancouver Island by
the Hudson's Bay
Company.*

BELOW: dining out
at Whistler.

years later Queen Victoria named the region British Columbia and made Douglas
the first governor.

Gold and its aftermath

In April 1856 a group of Indians had discovered gold in the North Thompson
River, just above Kamloops. A survey team subsequently reported that there
was gold in B.C. and the rush, in often perilous conditions, was on.

As the mainland developed, the city of Victoria suffered from an economic
hangover. Its glory days were over, and the bust that followed the gold rush
made Vancouver Island an economic parasite living off the bright future of the
rest of the colony. New industry was needed to diversify the island's economy
and to provide jobs for those who didn't make their fortunes in the Cariboo (the
Indian name for the upper Fraser River), where the best goldfields were found.

Remember, gold was not the first wealth offered by the rich land, it had simply replaced furs. The whites of Vancouver Island looked at the vast forests and
saw the future in lumber. The Alberni Sawmill, the first sawmill west of the
Rockies in Canada, was built on the west coast of Vancouver Island, on land
stolen from Indians. This not only created tensions between whites and Indians,
but the sawmill created a hierarchy of labor as whites were paid 25 cents an hour
to log and work the mill, while Asians and Indians were paid a mere 15 cents.

This was not the glorious future imagined by the gold-rushers of 1858. The
river beds had been panned out, and working in a sawmill or a gold mine was
similar to the factory work back east: low-wage labor and difficult to get.

The independent spirit of the colony had to face the economic reality of its
need for the outside world. A final attempt to get the colony to defect to the

United States was defeated by the offer to build a Canadian-Pacific Railway, which would link the young city of Vancouver with the rest of Canada. British Columbia became a Canadian province in 1871. Today it continues to survive by exploiting its natural resources. It produces approximately a quarter of the marketable timber in North America (it provides the world with chopsticks), making forestry the province's number one industry. Mining is still important, as is fishing.

Maps:
Area 270,
City 276

Victoria

Just as the history of British Columbia begins in **Victoria ❷**, the capital is still the "first" city in the province for many. Victoria is equidistant between Vancouver and Seattle: 183 km (114 miles) by ferry to either. Although this proximity to its southern US neighbor should imply shared characteristics, Victoria is not only thoroughly Canadian, but more British than Vancouver.

The Parliament Buildings 🅐 make an excellent place to begin a tour of this province (open late-May–Labor Day: daily; Sep–early-May: Mon–Fri; free). The province's political parties use the forum of the Legislative Assembly to haggle with the premier over public policy. With intense debating going on within these walls, instant relief can be found by joining people who still celebrate the British monarchy in style at **The Empress Hotel 🅑**.

Named after Queen Victoria, Empress of India, the hotel was designed by English-born Francis Mawson Rattenbury. It was renovated in 1987 at a cost of $45 million. Two decades earlier a similar overhaul had replaced heating and electrical systems, laid 6 km (4 miles) of new carpeting, booked special looms for the creation of hundreds of bedspreads and checked for period authenticity

Not only gold, but timber attracted the Europeans. George Vancouver described the land in the 1860s, "Well covered with trees of large growth principally...pine."

BELOW: Victoria's Empress Hotel.

Experience the world of gracious living by taking tea in the Palm Court of the Empress Hotel, (served 12.30–5pm; reservations advised; no jeans or shorts).

BELOW RIGHT: the Parliament Building, Victoria.

the thousands of new (that is, old) pieces of furniture for the additional rooms, which now total 481. The new pastry chef arrived with references from Buckingham Palace. The entire operation took place under the demure name of "Operation Teacup". Afternoon tea at the Empress has achieved "mythic proportions", according to one writer who reports that the hotel constantly receives enquiries from around the world about how to brew and serve tea correctly. Guests reserve a table ahead in order to find out.

Another introduction to the various sides of **Vancouver Island** can be had by visiting the city's museums. The **Royal British Columbia Museum Ⓒ** covers the history of the province (open daily; entrance fee). Its Main Street Exhibit, for example, shows what life was like in 19th-century Victoria. There are also many interesting displays covering the natural history of the coast, the culture of its native inhabitants, and an excellent introduction to the explorers who brought Europe to this remote wilderness.

The city has several fine art collections – notably The **Art Gallery of Greater Victoria Ⓓ**, on Moss Street (open daily; entrance fee), and the **Maltwood Art Museum** on the campus of the **University of Victoria**. Both have collections of modern paintings and sculpture, as well as an important collection of oriental art: Tang and Ming Dynasty rugs at the Maltwood, and Japanese prints at the Art Gallery of Greater Victoria.

Even though the sun only shines about half the year in this part of the world, tourists would miss the greatest of the islands' offerings if too much time were spent indoors. To begin with, the whole province is a vast fisherman's paradise – saltwater and freshwater, game fishing and just plain good eating. Salmon reigns supreme. There are also trout and steelhead in the freshwater, while the

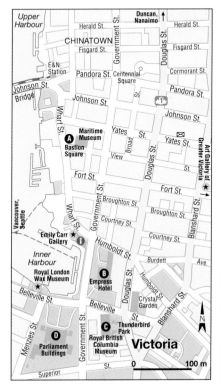

saltwater offers tuna and cod, as well as crabs, clams, oysters and shrimp. It is essential for everyone planning on fishing to get the proper licenses and to follow all the regulations. The Canadian authorities are quite serious about wildlife preservation, and enforce the regulations thoroughly.

A trip to **Barkley Sound** on the west coast offers topnotch fishing, and the scenery of the **Pacific Rim National Park ❸**. Here is an excellent view of the Pacific Coast in all its glory: rocky islands, sea lions playing in the crashing surf, harbor seals hiding in the coves, and sea birds hovering above.

Hitting the trail

The area also holds a wealth of backpacking opportunities. The **Broken Group Islands**, off the southwest coast of Vancouver Island, are accessible by boat, and Long Beach has hiking trails and sunsets into the endless Pacific.

There's much to see on the **Gulf Islands**, situated between Vancouver Island and Vancouver. The islands share the same climate as Victoria and artists and writers tend to make the area their home. Hardier backpackers have the opportunity to hike the "Life-Saving" Trail, from **Bamfield** to **Thrasher Cove**. The 80-km (50-mile) trail got its nickname when it was built to help shipwrecked victims find their way back to civilization through the densely forested shoreline. The trail offers views of gray whales, sea lions, seals, rock formations, two lighthouses, and good spots for surf-casting. This trail is a serious backpacker's dream – full of steep hills, narrow muddy paths, nearly impenetrable forests, and stretches along the beach that can only be traversed at low tide.

More civilized backpacking is available in any of British Columbia's Provincial Parks. They offer excellent views and invigorating exercise, as well as a

Maps:
Area 270,
City 276

BELOW: cruising
Victoria's coastline.

TIP

The best time to sail north from Port Hardy to Prince Rupert along the Inside Passage is in summer, when the ferry makes the 15-hour trip in daylight.

BELOW LEFT: Indian house posts.
BELOW RIGHT: Liard River Hot Springs Provincial Park.

closeness to nature that can make every tree seem like a unique experience in color.

The best way to see the coast in all its glory is to take the trip on the **Prince Rupert Ferry**. Once the only way to get from Victoria to Prince Rupert or Alaska, it still makes the journey, leaving from **Port Hardy ❹**, at the northern tip of Vancouver Island (reservations advised). On the way to Port Hardy stop at **Port McNeill**, 350 km (217 miles) north of Victoria, and take the short ferry to **Alert Bay ❺** for an education in what is the most important art form in the northwest: Indian wooden carvings, or totem poles. Alert Bay is a Kwakiutl village, and the best place to see traditional carvings is at **U'mista Cultural Centre** (open Sep–Jun: Mon–Fri; Jul–Aug: Mon–Sat; entrance fee).

The carvings are statements of family identity, serving a purpose roughly similar to family crests in European culture. There is a great deal of status associated with the number of animals depicted. Poles 9-meters (30-ft) tall, blend from one animal to another, in shapes and characterizations that remind one of modern art. These animals have influenced Picasso and others.

It is rare to find pre-20th-century sculptures still in native ownership, but that is what one will see here, as well as recent sculptures in the new styles developed in the revival of carving that has taken place since the 1950s.

From **Prince Rupert ❻** it is possible to visit a number of other sites where carving is practised: more Kwakiutl sculpture at **Bella Bella** and **Kitimat ❼**, 150 km (93 miles) southeast of Prince Rupert, Nishga work at **Kincolith**, north of Prince Rupert, and Tsimshian carvings in the area around **Kitwancool Lake**, northeast of Prince Rupert. Another ferry to the **Queen Charlotte Islands ❽** (6 hours 30 minutes) will take travelers to see the highly-regarded work of the

Haida at **Skidegate** and the beaches at **Sandspit**, where Indian legend says the raven *Ne-kil-stlas* landed and began the propagation of the race.

Map, pages 270/271

Northern lake country

Heading inland from Prince Rupert the amount of open land becomes overwhelming. The choice of direction is limited by the shortage of roads. Aside from the main East/West Highway (16), most are unpaved and only one-and-a-half lanes wide (they were designed for logging rather than for tourism).

One of the longest and most beautiful roads north is from **Terrace ❾** to the Alaska Highway near **Watson Lake**, Yukon, and offers side trips to **Mount Edziza Provincial Park ❿** and the town of **Stewart**. From Stewart one can cross over to **Hyder**, Alaska. The road to Stewart passes through the Cambria snowfield and offers spectacular views of **Bear Glacier**.

There are literally thousands of lakes in central B.C., and countless rivers and streams connecting them. Everything from moose and caribou to the bald eagle and the white Kermode bear can be seen here. The fishing offers both quantity and variety. The lakes to the south have rainbow, lake- and brook-trout, and the delicious Dolly Varden – a large salmon-like fish not as heavy as salmon, but meatier than trout. Farther north in the **Peace River Area** the fishing action turns to the arctic grayling and the northern pike.

One wonderful stop in the northeast corner of the Province is the **Liard River Hot Springs Park ⓫** at Mile 493 of the Highway. The springs are naturally heated, slightly sulfurous pools of water, surrounded by orchids and tropical vines as thick as the northern forests just a few yards away. The water is over 43°C (110°F) and is so relaxing it is literally difficult to get up the steps out of

BELOW: bird's-eye view of the Rocky Mountains.

Popular with climbers and hikers, Glacier National Park on the Trans-Canada Highway features 422 glaciers, best seen by taking a mapped trail.

BELOW: Hudson's Bay trading post at Fort Langley.

the water. The pools are a favorite with the truckers who travel the Highway, and they recommend that taking a nap before driving again: the heat of the water can often make a motorist sleepy enough to drive off the road.

Gold Rush route

South of the Alaska Highway, around **Quesnel** travelers will find the history of the Cariboo Gold Rush. The streams and lakes along the Fraser River had been either played out or claimed by 1860, and the miners had trekked farther north to Quesnel, discovering even richer finds within a few years. With the completion of the Cariboo Wagon Road in 1865, the rugged interior was made relatively accessible for wagons carrying supplies and new miners.

The **Cariboo Highway** now follows roughly the same route as the old Cariboo Wagon Road. Ironically the completion of the road, as well as the exhaustion of easily panned gold, helped to end the frontier phase of the gold rush and made way for more organized shaft-mining operations. While gold continued to be mined in quantity until the 1870s, the romance was gone. Canadian and American miners were replaced by immigrant Chinese, and this accounts for the Oriental flavor found along much of the coast of Canada.

The fact that the rush is over should not discourage tourists from trying their hand at panning for wealth at **Bowron Lake Provincial Park ⓬**. Two days' panning should enable you to collect enough "dust" to buy a newspaper back in Vancouver. Visitors may prefer to hike along the streams that have beds of raw jade stone, although the green stone might not be as impressive as the gold.

Organized camping is possible in the many provincial parks in this area. One of the largest is the **Wells Gray Provincial Park ⓭**. It has all the beauty that the

THE GOLD RUSH TRAIL

The forested plateau of the Cariboo, lying north of Lillooet, between the Coast Mountains and the Cariboo Mountains, may not be the most scenically spectacular region of British Columbia, but what it lacks in high peak drama it makes up for in its rich history.

Gold was discovered in the area in the late 1850s by prospectors travelling north from California. But it was here at Williams Creek in 1862 that Billy Barker, a Cornish sailor, struck the vast quantities that sparked the Cariboo Gold Rush. Boom towns such as Barkerville appeared within months and a 640-km (400-mile) supply road was constructed in a remarkable feat of engineering along the inhospitable Fraser River canyon from Yale in the south. But within 10 years the gold deposits were exhausted.

Today Highway 97 and Highway 26 follow the route of the original Cariboo Highway to Barkerville, which has been restored as a living museum with all the atmosphere of a gold rush town. Among the original buildings there are stores, saloons and hotels; during summer (except Fridays) shows are staged at the Theatre Royal and courtroom dramas re-enacted at Richfield Courthouse. (Open May–Labor Day: daily 8am–8pm; Oct–Apr: dawn to dusk; entrance fee.)

rest of B.C. has shown, but is also a place where one can search for old home-steads abandoned by families that did not survive the 19th-century frontier days, or extinct volcanoes that are considerably older.

This is also British Columbia's cowboy country, where most of the region's cattle industry is located. Here travelers are able to see modern-day cowboys, in addition to helping the area to celebrate the old glories with rodeos and horse-back riding. The hub of much of this summer activity is **100 Mile House** ⓮.

Continuing south and west, all roads begin to lead to Vancouver, but there is still plenty to see in the areas that border the US. For example, while Banff and Jasper in Alberta are more famous, there is no denying the beauty of the **British Columbia Rockies**, and the parks that preserve it are well worth visiting: **Mount Robson Provincial Park** ⓯ contains the highest point in the Canadian Rock-ies, while **Yoho** ⓰ and **Glacier National Parks** ⓱ have camping, skiing and views of snowfields. Another favorite spot for skiing is **Whistler Mountain** ⓲. Canadians flock here to race down its sides. Whistler was the site of the Winter Olympics in 1960, and since has become the area's premier ski resort. In summer there is mountain-biking and walking, as well as cultural events: the Vancouver Symphony Orchestra performs annually on top of Whistler Mountain.

North of Whistler 32 km (20 miles), a pleasant half-hour walk along the Green River leads to **Nairn Falls**. Although not particularly high, its powerful tumble is loud and very impressive. Highway 1 north from **Hope** ⓳ to **Cache Creek** travels along the Fraser and Thompson rivers. Built by the Royal Engineers in the 1860s, the old Cariboo Wagon Road is now a modern highway, but it still goes through the **Fraser Canyon** and gives some idea of the challenges facing the miners, as well as those that still pit their wits against the salmon.

Map, pages 270/271

In July Williams Lake, 15 km (9 miles) northwest of 100 Mile House, stages one of the biggest rodeos in Canada – second only to the Calgary Stampede.

BELOW: Whistler Village, the Rockies' top resort.

Map,
pages
270/271

More adventurous types, traveling in the summer, can try what was then a short cut: a route that bypassed the treacherous Fraser Canyon. The **Lillooet Shortcut** takes one around **Garibaldi Provincial Park ⑳**, along a logging road to Lillooet. Since no canoe could be counted on to survive the current of the Fraser River, this was the best way to get to the interior in the days before the existence of the Cariboo Road.

South of Vancouver

An episode of the experience of Asians in Canada can be seen in the Japanese fishing village of **Steveston**, a little way south of Vancouver. In 1887 a single Japanese fisherman came to this tiny town for the salmon season. Just forty years later there were 3,000 Japanese here, mostly fishermen. However, the Canadian government feared this new community would displace the white fishing industry, and placed quotas on the number of fishing permits allowed to Japanese immigrants.

This subculture was dealt its most severe blow when the government began forcibly evacuating Japanese families from coastal areas during World War II. Virtually the entire village of Steveston was evacuated, and all their boats and fishing equipment was confiscated. Many people were moved to Northern Ontario. Freed after the war, they returned to Steveston.

Today Steveston is a great place to browse in the shops and wander down to the wharves where the day's catch of salmon, rock cod, snapper, prawns, crab, shrimp, sole, and herring is sold right off the boat.

The **George C. Reifel Waterfowl Refuge** on **Westham Island** at the mouth of the Fraser River supports the largest wintering population of waterfowl in Canada. The 340-hectare (850-acre) carefully controlled habitat and estuarine marsh serves as a sanctuary to more than 240 species of birds. In November, vast flocks of migrating snow geese stop here on their route from their breeding grounds in the Arctic to the Sacramento River Valley in California.

Continuing southeast from Vancouver, the geography begins to change slightly. The rainfall is less frequent, there are arid hills and even sagebrush. This is Canada's best known fruit belt – the Okanagan Valley. Water from **Lake Okanagan ㉑** is used for irrigation and, combined with huge amounts of sunshine, creates a lush garden. Apples, peaches, plums, grapes, cherries, apricots and pears are all grown here in abundance.

The area is also known for its wine-making, sandy beaches and lakes. Some favorite spots for travelers are **Penticton** between Lake Okanagan and Lake Skaha, and **Kelowna**. Kelowna is the marketing center for the Okanagan fruit belt and is famous for its **International Regatta** held in August.

Many towns in British Columbia, notably **Nelson** in the southeast corner of the province, grew up as supply routes to the gold miners. Nelson still has a number of original buildings, which is probably one reason why the town has served as a backdrop to several feature films. There are beautiful routes just to drive along. Highway 3, the "Crow's Nest Road", offers views of the Rockies and a few surviving gold mines.

Four hours by car south from Vancouver is the Okanagan, famous for fruit and wine. Here you can windsurf or waterski on the warm waters of Lake Osoyoos.

BELOW: suspended above the foaming Fraser river.
RIGHT: native dress.

hell's gate
1

FLORA AND FAUNA OF THE UNTAMED WEST

Stretching from the 49th parallel to the North Pole, western Canada provides diverse habitats for a rich array of plants and wildlife.

Western Canada is blessed with a multitude of different environments. The north has tundra and some of the continent's loftiest mountains, while the south includes prairie grasslands, thousands of lakes and mountain ranges. It even has the northern tip of the central American desert, and yet a few hundred kilometers away you can find lush temperate rainforest. Given this huge assembly of habitats, western Canada's flora ranges from lichens clinging to permanently frozen rocks through varieties of cacti and lush ferns to such exotica as wild rhododendrons, azaleas and wild orchids. Perhaps most striking are the fir trees and aspens which make up forests stretching to the horizon.

TRADITIONAL EMBLEMS

In spring Canada bursts into color with a host of wildflowers. An indication of the variety is seen in the floral emblems of the territories and provinces. Yukon is depicted by the brilliant pink fireweed, while the Northwest Territories has pretty mountain avens. The western dogwood is British Columbia's floral representative, Alberta has the wild rose, Saskatchewan the Prairie lily and Manitoba the Prairie crocus. Among its fauna, beavers are traditionally recognized as Canada's emblem because their valuable pelts were a major stimulus to early exploration. They are often seen in ponds and lakes; the dams and intricate lodges they build are even more evident.

◁ **GONE FISHING**
The grizzly bear can be found in the remoter areas of the Rocky Mountains, where it lives on fish, vegetation and berries. It can be identified by its shoulder hump.

▽ **MIGHTY TREES**
Douglas Firs, the forest giants of the West Coast, can grow as tall as 90 meters (295 ft) high. Some 1,000-year-old specimens still exist, but they are under threat from loggers.

▽ **BISON COUNTRY**
The bison (buffalo) is North America's largest mammal. Hunting and disease have depleted the herds, and those that remain in Canada can be found in the grasslands, and in particular at Wood Buffalo Mountain Park, Alberta.

◁ **KING OF THE EAGLES**
The bald eagle, symbol of the United States, is more common along Canada's Pacific coastline than south of the 49th parallel. It is a highly successful predator; hunters were once rewarded for each bird they destroyed; today the eagle is a protected species.

RUNNING WILD IN CANADA'S PARKS

◁ **ROCK GARDEN**
Alpine fireweed, Banff National Park: even above the timber-line in the Rockies, and across Arctic Canada, a wide variety of plants survive freezing winters to burst into bloom in the summer months.

△ **POLAR BEARS**
Inuits lead safaris across the Arctic in search of polar bears, but in October you only have to go to Churchill, Manitoba, "polar bear capital of the world," to see the bears wandering about town.

◁ **CARIBOU COUNTRY**
Caribou are a relative of the deer family. They are known as *tuktu*, or *tuktuk*, by the Inuit who depended on them for food, clothing, tools and weapons. The age of a caribou can be determined by its antlers, the most magnificent belonging to older animals.

▽ **FIREWEED**
Floral emblem of Yukon: summer might be short, but flowers still flourish.

The national and provincial parks of Canada provide natural habitats for many species. For spectacular beauty, rich in wildlife, few areas in the world can match the Yukon's Kluane National Park, with its herds of caribou, Dall sheep, wild goats and the rare blue bear.

While black bears are found all over Canada, grizzlies are confined to the forests and wetlands of the west. Many are regular campground visitors, so it's wise to heed the rangers' warnings – even baby bears should be considered dangerous, since they are bound to have a very big Mom lurking nearby.

White-tailed deer, with Bambi-like spotted fawns, are common place in the parks. So are the huge, prehistoric-looking moose, readily spotted in the swamp-lands. In the Rocky Mountains' parks there are elk, wild goats and mountain sheep, coyotes and wolf.

The largest population of bison is in Wood Buffalo National Park on the Northwest Territories/ Alberta border. Some 6,000 buffalo live here, as do white pelicans, rare whooping cranes, eagles and wolves but, since this park is the size of Switzerland, you will need a guide to help locate them for you.

ALBERTA:
THE BEST OF THE WEST

*From the soaring peaks of the Rockies to the wide open prairies,
snow-capped national parks to arid dinosaur trails, modern cities
to small towns, Alberta is a province of dramatic contrasts*

Map,
pages
270/271

I f a province could walk, Alberta would swagger just a bit, chest out, chin up,
eyes fixed firmly on the future. And why not? It has the best of the West: fertile farmland; oil, gas and coal in abundance; exciting cities like Calgary and
Edmonton; and the incomparable blue Canadian Rockies for a playground.
Albertans exuberantly inform the rest of the country about the virtues of their
province, and their pride sounds to some like flat-out American bragging. The
petroleum industry, which fueled Alberta's tremendous economic growth in the
1970s, was founded mostly by Americans. Their can-do spirit, essential in a
business that rewards risktakers, seems to have rubbed off on everyone else.

Oil-rich Alberta

Rancher John Lineham didn't risk much when he sank a well in 1920 among
the oil seepage pools along **Cameron Creek** in the southwest corner of the
province. Kutenai Indians had been using the oil for centuries as a balm to heal
wounds. Lineham's well, the first in Western Canada, produced 300 barrels a
day until the flow ebbed after four years. The site of **Discovery Well** is marked
with a cairn in **Waterton Lakes National Park ㉒**, 250
km (155 miles) south of Calgary.

PRECEDING PAGES:
the Rockies loom
above Lake Louise.
LEFT: prairie farmer.
BELOW: tranquil
Waterton Lakes.

The park's landscape changes abruptly from rolling
grasslands to snowcapped peaks chiseled by Ice Age
glaciers. Boat tours on the lakes pass outstanding glacier-carved formations, including hanging valleys high
up mountain walls. A hiking trail winds through **Red
Rock Canyon**, streaked with the red, purple, green, and
yellow of mineral deposits; another path leads to
Cameron Lake, a blue gem set in a bowl-shaped valley.

Canada's only Mormon temple, a pristine white marble edifice built in 1913, gleams in the prairie sun at
Cardston ㉓, 45 km (28 miles) east of the park. It was
founded by Charles Ora Card, a son-in-law of Brigham
Young. Visitors can tour the grounds and Card's 1887
cabin. The Mormons emigrated from Utah in 1887.
They developed Canada's first major irrigation project
soon after their arrival, digging 96 km (60 miles) of
canals out from the St Mary River, and growing bumper
crops of vegetables.

Less desirable American immigrants were the traders
who came up from Montana in the 1870s to swap furs
and buffalo hides with the Indians for a shot of rot-gut
whiskey. **Fort Macleod ㉔**, 60 km (37 miles) north of
Cardston, was built in 1874 and manned with North
West Mounted Police who halted the trade. The fort
museum tells about daily life around the post; interpre-

*The rich fossil beds of
Dinosaur Provincial
Park conceal the
remains of 35 species
of dinosaurs from
75 million years ago.
Visit the Field
Station (open daily).*

on horseback (open May–mid-Oct: daily; mid-Oct–Christmas and Mar–Apr: Mon–Fri; entrance fee).

The first and most notorious of the whiskey forts the Mounties put out of business was **Fort Whoop-up** (open May–Sep 1: daily; Sep–Apr: closed Mon, Sat; entrance fee). A reconstruction stands in **Indian Battle Park** at **Lethbridge**, 75 km (46 miles) northeast of Cardston. Locals claim Lethbridge gets 4,000 hours of sunshine a year, more than any other Canadian city. The town's role in a dark chapter of the country's history is brightened by the **Nikka Yuko Japanese Garden**, a serene oasis of water, rocks and willows (open May–Oct: daily; entrance fee). The garden was built by the city in 1967 in remembrance of the 6,000 Japanese-Canadians who were interned here during World War II.

Prehistoric finds

The **Alberta Badlands**, once part of a subtropical swamp that sheltered a vast array of prehistoric life, contain one of the world's finest repositories of dinosaur fossils. The most spectacular badlands are preserved along the Red Deer River in **Dinosaur Provincial Park ㉕**, 175 km (108 miles) east of Calgary, selected as one of UNESCO's World Heritage Sites. From a lookout near the park entrance, visitors can survey 7,000 hectares (18,000 acres) of this gnarled sandstone landscape with its weirdly eroded formations. A circular 5-km (3-mile) drive with sidetrips on foot leads to dinosaur bones preserved where they were found. Other areas of the park are accessible on organized bus tours and hikes (May–Oct; reservations tel 403 378 4342).

The town of **Drumheller ㉖**, 138 km (86 miles) northeast of Calgary, lies deep within the badlands, which drop abruptly here below the lip of the prairie.

BELOW: Dinosaur Provincial Park.

The sheer unexpectedness of the scene shocks the eye and delights the imagination. A 48-km (30-mile) circular drive called the **Dinosaur Trail** takes motorists from the impressive **Royal Tyrrell Museum of Paleontology**, 6 km (4 miles) northwest of Drumheller), containing one of the best collections of dinosaur fossils in the world (open Victoria Day–Thanksgiving: daily; mid-Oct–May: closed Mon; entrance fee), up to the rim of the mile-wide valley. Highlights of the trip are the lookout at **Horsethief Canyon** and the **Bleriot Ferry**, one of the last cable ferries in the province.

Calgary

In the late 1970s, Pierre Trudeau reputedly remarked that **Calgary** ㉗ looked as if it had been unpacked just before you arrived. The former prime minister's comment still applies to this young prairie metropolis, the most dynamic city in the newly rich Canadian West.

Suburbs sprawl in all directions, and the city keeps boosting civic pride with public structures such as the $75-million performing arts center, home of the Calgary Philharmonic, and the 17,000-seat **Saddledome**, where the hockey and skating competitions of the 1988 Winter Olympics took place, now the home-base for the Calgary Flames Hockey Team. Part of the price for this rapid growth is downtown congestion. Fortunately the city created a three-block pedestrian mall along Stephen Avenue, a civilized thoroughfare of two-story buildings and street-level shops, with benches to sit on and wandering musicians to provide entertainment.

Elevated promenades further ease foot traffic. Nearly half the downtown core is connected by "Plus 15s" – skyways 5 meters (15 ft) over the traffic that link

Map, pages 270/271

BELOW: Calgary's Saddledome.

The town of Banff is named after Banffshire in Scotland, the birthplace of two of the financiers of the Canadian-Pacific Railway.

new high-rises, shopping complexes and hotels. At an elevated indoor park called **Devonian Gardens**, office workers on their lunch break brown-bag it on benches scattered amid waterfalls, ponds and greenery.

Rodeo days

The slicker the city gets, the more it seems to revel in the down-home fun of the Calgary Stampede, the world's largest rodeo, with $500,000 in prize money. For 10 days in early July residents of Canada's number-one cowtown don stetsons and cowboy boots and let loose at free flapjack breakfasts, square dancing and parades. The most thrilling and popular event on the **Exhibition Grounds** is chuck-wagon racing.

Pioneer days are also relived at **Heritage Park**, on Heritage Drive, a first-rate collection of reconstructed buildings and authentic structures gathered from all over the province (open May–Labor Day: daily; Sep–mid-Oct: weekends and holidays; entrance fee). A vintage steam train tours the site, and a replica paddlewheeler plies the **Glenmore Reservoir**.

Delve further into the past at the **Glenbow Museum**, which displays perhaps the best collections of First Nations peoples' artifacts in the world (open: daily; entrance fee).

If Calgary's hectic pace becomes overwhelming, escape to **St George's Island** in the Bow River, where picnickers and nature lovers share the woods with life-size reproductions of dinosaurs.

Travelers heading for the mountains can get a taste of the Alpine adventure to come by ascending the 190-meter (626-ft) high **Calgary Tower** (open daily, entrance fee). Below is the city, all 420 sq km (162 sq miles) of it, and to the

west, the serrated ridge of the **Rockies**, much of which is protected by national and provincial parks. One such area is **Kananaskis Provincial Park**, a 45-minute drive southwest of Calgary, containing foothills, mountains, ice caps and sparkling lakes. Dirt-bike trails thread its forests, fishermen try their luck in dozens of prime trout streams, and downhill skiers challenge the slopes at **Fortress Mountain**, site of skiing events for the 1988 Winter Olympics. One of the best ways to enjoy the Kananaskis is to stay at a guest ranch, where greenhorns work up mountain-size appetites on trail rides or hiking trips and then satisfy themselves with filling home-cooked fare.

Jewel of the Rockies

Crown jewel of the Rockies, **Banff National Park** ㉘ has some of the continent's finest mountain scenery within its confines along the eastern flank of the Continental Divide. The park was founded more than a century ago as Canada's first national preserve to protect hot springs just outside the present-day town of **Banff** to the southeast. The springs were first noted during the construction of the transcontinental railroad in the 1880s.

The restored **Cave and Basin Hot Springs Centennial Centre** on Cave Avenue, Banff, features a natural cave pool fed by a hot spring. The center's museum traces the history of the Canadian parks and geology of the area (open daily; entrance fee). Visitors can take a dip in the sulphurous waters at **Upper Hot Springs**, Mountain Avenue, where the average temperature of the mineral water feeding the outdoor public pool is 40°C (108°F). The bath-house has been restored to its early-1930s glory, and even offers 1920s-style swimsuits and towels for hire (open daily; entrance fee).

A gondola ride up **Sulphur Mountain**, 3 km (2 miles) from Banff (open daily; entrance fee), ends at a summit tea-house where mountain sheep are often seen snuffling for snacks. Here a boardwalk trail leads to the restored 1903 weather observatory. A ski tow up **Mount Norquay**, 8 km (5 miles) out of town, also affords panoramas of encircling peaks.

Jutting above the trees are the granite spires of the **Banff Springs Hotel**, a 600-room Scottish baronial castle built in 1888, complete with kilted pipers and a ninth-floor ghost. Sunday brunch here has long been a popular outing.

Banff has all the flavor of an Alpine town. In summer its sidewalks are crowded. Strollers browse in the dozens of gift shops or munch on delights from the **House of Banff Chocolate** in the Cascade Plaza. In winter après-ski life abounds. Stores stay open late and there is a wide variety of restaurants.

To escape the crowds, wander the grounds of the **Banff Center**, St Julien Road, an advanced conservatory of fine arts, music and drama. In this Salzburg of the Rockies the summerlong Banff Arts Festival showcases opera, dance, cabaret, musical theater and jazz.

Glacier country

Lake Louise, 90 km (56 miles) north of Banff, a jade gem set against the backdrop of Victoria Glacier, is one of the Rockies' most famous beauty spots. A Scottish

Map, pages 270/271

A visit to the Banff Information Centre, 224 Banff Avenue, is a must for up-to-date park information, walking and touring brochures and permits (open daily).

BELOW: Peyto Lake, Banff National Park.

TIP

Take a rubber-tired SnoCoach along the Athabasca Glacier, 105km (65 miles) south of Jasper (May–Oct, 9am–5pm, buses depart every 15 minutes).

piper wanders among the flowers and pines in the grounds of **Château Lake Louise;** the echo of his skirling resounds from surrounding peaks. Romantics rent canoes and sigh as they stroke about the lake. Athletic types hike the 3-km (2-mile) trail to **Lake Agnes** to a tea house perched near the top of a waterfall.

The junction of Highways 93 and 11, 76 km (47 miles) north of Lake Louise, is the starting point of the **Icefields Parkway**, one of the world's great mountain drives. The beauty of Lake Louise is challenged within 40 km (25 miles) by **Peyto Lake**, set in the **Mistaya River Valley**. A platform at the end of a half-mile trail off the parking lot affords unobstructed views of the lake, 240 meters (800 ft) below.

The Parkway continues north in the valley of the Mistaya (Cree for "grizzly"), then follows the braided channels of the North Saskatchewan River to the Rockies' apex: the **Columbia Icefield**, at 326 sq km (126 sq miles) the biggest ice cap in the range. This "mother of rivers" feeds three systems, the Columbia, the Athabasca and the Saskatchewan. **Athabasca Glacier**, one of dozens that flow from Columbia's bowl of ice, extends almost to the parkway.

Here, the Parkway enters **Jasper National Park ㉙**, largest and most northerly in the Rockies. Take the scenic alternate route, 93A, along the west bank of the Athabasca River to Athabasca Falls, which thunder over a 30-meter (100-ft) high ledge and hurtle through a narrow canyon. A self-guiding trail along the gorge provides close-ups of the violent beauty of the powerful cataract.

Nearby **Mount Edith Cavell**, a snow-covered dome of rock rising sheer from **Angel Glacier**, absolutely has to be seen. Fur traders in the early 1800s called this the "mountain of the great crossing"; in World War I it was renamed after a heroic British nurse. A hiking trail climbs into alpine meadows spangled with

BELOW LEFT: take to the inside at West Edmonton Mall.
BELOW RIGHT: city skyline, Edmonton.

colorful wildflowers; another path wanders across the boulder-strewn out-wash of the glacier.

The town of **Jasper**, smaller and quieter than Banff, is the starting point for dozens of scenic hiking trails, bicycle routes and driving tours. The Jasper Tramway, 4 km (2 1/2 miles) south of the town, whisks sightseers to the stony summit of **The Whistlers**, a 2,464-meter (8,084-ft) peak. From its summit looking 77 km (48 miles) northwest into British Columbia, you can glimpse on a clear day the solitary tip of the highest peak in the Rockies, Mount Robson (3,954 meters/12,972 ft). (Tramway operates: end May–end Oct.)

Jasper's answer to the Banff Springs Hotel is the more rustic **Jasper Park Lodge**, a cluster of 50 chalets along **Lac Beauvert**. Room service comes on a bicycle, bears have been known to commandeer the lawns, and a moose once took over a pond on the golf course. And, yes, there is a piper. He performs at a sunset flag-lowering ceremony.

The **Maligne Valley Drive** offers spectacular views of **Maligne Canyon**, 11 km (7 miles) east of Jasper, where the river plunges into a steep-walled limestone gorge; **Medicine Lake**, 16 km (10 miles) southeast, drained by a vast underground river system; and **Maligne Lake**, a further 10 km (6 miles) on, which can be explored by boat in summer and is a cross-country ski center in winter. En route to Edmonton, take a side-trip to the **Miette Hotsprings** ❸⓿, 60 km (37 miles) north of Jasper, the hottest in the Rockies. The waters are cooled to 39°C (102° F) before being fed into a huge swimming pool (open: mid-May–mid-Oct; swimsuits, towels, lockers available for rent). Guest ranches scattered through this region include the renowned **Black Cat Guest Ranch** off Highway 40.

Travelers reluctantly leave the Rockies behind as they head east through the parklands and forests of northern Alberta. Hearty fare like Russian borscht and Ukrainian cabbage rolls from the Homesteader's Kitchen at the **Stony Plain Multicultural Centre** may take the edge off the disappointment, 20 km (12 miles) west of Edmonton (open daily, donations). On Saturdays, don't miss the farmers' market for a sample of other regional food.

Edmonton

Provincial capital and Canada's most northerly metropolis, **Edmonton** ❸❶ is a world-class city. The **West Edmonton Mall** is the largest in North America, with an astounding 800 stores, restaurants, fast-food outlets, and the world's largest indoor amusement park; the **Citadel Theatre** is Canada's largest; the **Space and Science Centre** (open daily; Sep–Jun: closed Mon; entrance fee) houses Canada's largest planetarium and the western world's largest Zeiss-Jenastar projector.

Oil deals are made at the head offices in Calgary; the actual work of turning black gold into commodities such as gasoline and diesel occurs in Edmonton. The city flexes its industrial muscle along **Refinery Row**, a glittering galaxy of tubes, giant storage tanks and gas flares that light up the night sky like a scene from a science fiction movie. The Row produces 10 percent of the nation's petrochemical products.

But Edmonton is no blue-collar town. In fact, it seems more sophisticated in some ways than its southern rival,

Yellowhead Highway 16, heading northeast from Jasper, follows the route of the fur traders. Viewpoints offer dramatic glimpses of the terrain they endured.

Map, pages 270/271

BELOW: saloon hustler at Alberta's Heritage Park.

Map,
pages
270/271

where the backyard mountains attract lots of outdoors types more interested in backpacking than Bach. Seat of provincial government and home of the **University of Alberta**, Edmonton has opera and classical ballet companies, a symphony orchestra and several professional theater groups. Why, crystal chandeliers even adorn a couple of subway stations.

Klondike days

All this refinement completely disappears for 10 days during the month of July beneath sourdough stubble, battered hats and checked shirts as the city gets grizzled during Klondike Days, a 10-day revival of the tempestuous 1890s Klondike Gold Rush.

False storefronts sprout in the city center, roulette tables spin at the Silver Slipper Saloon on the Exhibition Grounds, a flotilla of bathtubs, barrels and home-made houseboats float downstream on the North Saskatchewan River during the Sourdough Raft race. Downtown streets become pedestrian malls so Edmontonians can stroll about in their Klondike finery during the Sunday Promenade. Contests ranging from rock lifting to log chopping are held to determine the King of the Klondike. (It is followed by Heritage Days in August – an ethnic festival.)

An outdoor museum beside the river, **Fort Edmonton Park** is perhaps a clearer window on the past (open May–Sep: daily; entrance fee). Thirty-five buildings along three small-town streets recapture the flavor of three separate eras: 1846, 1885 and 1920. Old Strathcona, the city's original commercial district, preserves along its narrow streets early structures such as the **Old Firehall**, **Strathcona Hotel** and **Klondike Cinema**. The **Old Strathcona Foundation** distributes free walking-tour maps of the area, which is also the site of the Fringe Theater Event in August. This nine-day festival attracts performers from all over North America and Europe. The streets echo with mime music, puppet shows and plays.

Canada's largest urban greenbelt preserves 16 km (10 miles) of riverbank along the North Saskatchewan River, where you can hike, cycle, picnic and ride horseback. Guides at a nature center near Fort Edmonton conduct walks in all seasons. Four glass pyramids nestled in the valley house the **Muttart Conservatory**, a showcase of plants from the tropics to the deserts of the world (open daily; entrance fee).

The valley is also the site of a man-made wonder that expresses Alberta's exuberant spirit. As his contribution to the province's 75th anniversary celebrations in 1980, artist Peter Lewis installed a series of water pipes along the top of the **High Level Bridge**. Now, on civic holidays in summer, a tap is turned somewhere and the bridge becomes a waterfall.

Relations with the east

Alberta and the prairies once seemed like a land apart, cut off from the Pacific Coast by the mountains of British Columbia, isolated from the industrial heartland of Ontario and Québec by the Canadian Shield. But the region has well and truly come into its own economically and politically in the last 20 years.

A typical 1890s Eastern European settlement has been recreated at the Ukrainian Cultural Heritage Village, 50 km (30 miles) to the east of Edmonton.

BELOW: Klondike country.

Rodeos:
an Alberta passion

Almost any summer or autumn weekend you'll find a rodeo somewhere in Alberta's cattle country. Big or small, it will give you a day of excitement and fun along with a generous slice of western Canadian culture. In fairgrounds across the province, locals urge neighbors on as they compete at bronco-busting, steer-wrestling and calf-roping, while big city stadiums attract professional rodeo riders from all over North America competing for valuable purses.

Originating in 16th-century Mexico, rodeos continue to demonstrate cowboy skills. For example, that bronco-buster riding the wild horse must adapt to its bucking gait, while keeping his spurs above the animal's shoulders and without touching it with his hands.

The niceties of bullriding may be lost on the average tenderfoot tourist, but still it is one of the most exciting rodeo events. With only one hand on the single halter, a contestant has to ride the back of a huge Bramah bull for eight seconds. Then after the inevitable fall, he escapes the enraged animal's flailing horns and hooves in his race for safety. The rider's sole protection is a team of fleet-footed rodeo clowns who run interference across the bull's path. To the crowd's delight they must sometimes take refuge in barrels strategically placed around the arena.

Tension gives way to hilarity in the wild cow milking contest, in which participants are required to get at least some milk into their pails. Calf-roping calls for yet a different set of skills, including excellent horsemanship. Speed is everything here as the rider lassoes his sturdy calf, then dismounts and ties its legs. All the while the horse keeps the lasso rope taut, positioning the calf for branding.

These are just some traditional features of Alberta's rodeos. For pure drama, the larger events add chuck-wagon races. They hark back to an era when cowboys slept in bedrolls under a prairie sky and depended on these primitive mobile kitchens for meals.

On Saturday afternoons they would race their wagons home, and the last driver to reach home bought the first round in the town saloon. Now, with prizes of $50,000, modern races are held in heats of four competing wagons, each drawn by four horses with its own team of outriders. Each outfit must race around a figure of eight course, then dash to the finish line, where the iron stove is unloaded and a wood fire coaxed into flame. In view of the number of horses involved on a tricky course, accidents are commonplace.

Billed as "The Greatest Show on Earth" the annual Calgary Exhibition and Stampede in early July dates from 1912. It involves the whole city. Street parades, fireworks and pancake breakfasts cooked and served on city sidewalks, agricultural exhibitions and fun fairs are all part of the big show. During stampede week most locals and visitors go about their business dressed in western clothes. If that seems a bit ambitious, you should at least buy a ten-gallon hat. It's part of the rodeo tradition.

See Travel Tips for the Calgary Exhibition and Stampede.

RIGHT: bronco-buster tames his steed.

SASKATCHEWAN: NATURE'S GREAT SECRET

*Canada's Old Northwest lies at the very heart of Saskatchewan,
a province of highlands, plains, deserts
and lakes, once home to gangsters, gun runners and fur traders*

Map, page 300

A hush falls over the crowd as the solemn jurors return to the courtroom with their verdict. They pass the dock where the defendant Louis Riel kneels in prayer. Riel has been charged with high treason for leading the Métis people in rebellion against the Crown. Dressed in black, Riel rises to meet his fate. The clerk of the court asks the foreman if the jury members are agreed upon their verdict. "How say you: Is the prisoner guilty or not guilty?"

"Guilty."

The foreman asks the judge for leniency, but the judge passes his sentence: Riel will hang. This scene from *The Trial of Louis Riel*, a play by John Coulter, is re-enacted every summer at the Shumiatscher Theater at the MacKenzie Art Gallery, Regina. Each time the jury finds Riel guilty beyond a shadow of doubt.

Traitor to some, hero to others, Riel twice tried to defend the rights of his people, the mixed-blood offspring of Indian mothers and French fur-trading fathers. In 1869 he established a provisional Métis government in Manitoba, an ill-fated experiment in self-determination that ended when the Canadian militia put down the insurrection. Riel fled to Montana where he lived quietly as a school teacher.

LEFT: Cypress Hills cowboy. **BELOW:** The Mounties come to Regina to train.

Métis uprising

In 1884 federal agents began surveying Métis lands in the Saskatchewan River Valley in preparation for the coming of white settlers. Métis leaders again called on Riel, who returned to Canada to lead a ragtag army against the Canadian militia. The Métis' brief uprising ended in defeat at Batoche on 15 May, 1885. Riel was tried in Regina, and was hanged later that year.

Saskatchewan has a hard time with heroes, especially with Riel, a fiery, French-speaking Catholic who once called himself "Prophet, Infallible Pontiff and Priest King". That sort of talk delayed his acceptance as an authentic folk hero for about 80 years; this province demands humility, even from its hockey stars.

Saskatchewan's indifference to Riel has been due in part to another tragedy that looms larger in prairie hearts and minds: 10 lost years called the Depression, when the forces of nature combined with the vagaries of the economy to reduce the region to destitution, and nurtured a cautious people skeptical about the pronouncements of politicians.

The 1930s will color provincial perceptions as long as anyone who lived through the era is alive. But the experience also produced sturdy self-reliance. Take Regina, for example, provincial capital and Queen City of the Plains. Its less-than-regal setting prompted Sir John A. Macdonald, Canada's first prime minister, to

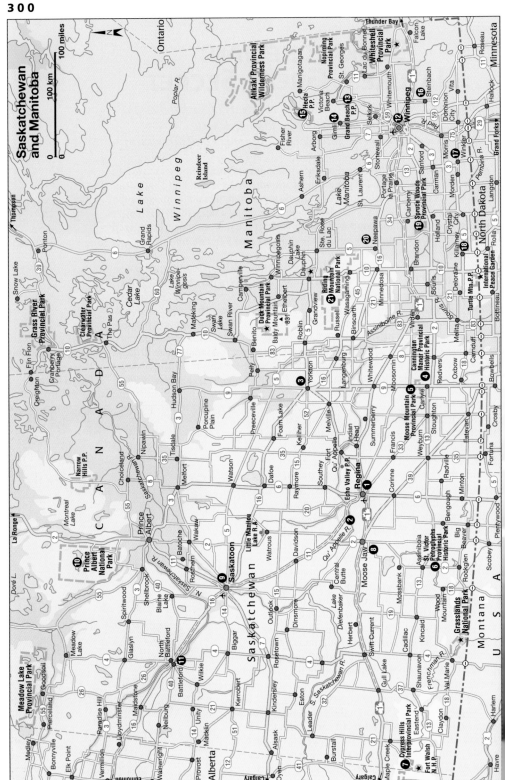

Saskatchewan and Manitoba

remark in 1886: "If you had a little more wood, and a little more water, I think the prospect would be improved."

Map, page 300

The making of Regina

When **Regina ❶** was named capital of the newly formed province of Saskatchewan in 1905, city leaders took Macdonald's suggestion of "more wood" to heart. They dammed muddy Wascana Creek to create a small lake, erected the Legislative Building, planted trees, laid out formal gardens, and splashed it all with fountains, including one from London's Trafalgar Square.

The result was **Wascana Center**, still an oasis of woods and water (open May–Oct; free). A ride through the 930-hectare (2,300-acre) park on a double-decker bus is a fine way to see the sights. Cyclists and joggers circle the lake, picnickers take a ferry out to shady **Willow Island** (mid-May–Labor Day: noon–4pm; charge), and bird-lovers feed the Canada geese at the waterfowl sanctuary. You can also admire the Egyptian sculpture in the **University of Regina's** art gallery, or visit the **Saskatchewan Science Centre**, featuring the human body, astronomy and geology (open daily). The **Royal Saskatchewan Museum**, one of the finest natural history museums in Canada, offers an excellent introduction to the province's flora and fauna. Its First Nations Gallery traces 10,000 years of aboriginal culture (open daily; free).

Regina's 40-float Buffalo Days Parade in late July heralds a week of horse racing, rodeo riding, agricultural and livestock shows and free entertainment.

Wide and open prairies

To the north-west of Regina the **Qu'Appelle River Valley ❷** is a welcome change from the Queen City in topography and tempo. Carved by glacial melt-waters, this verdant furrow in the brown prairie divides the flat and open plains

BELOW: Legislative Building, Regina.

THE MOUNTIES

Once headquarters for the North West Mounted Police (1882–1920), Regina is home to Canada's training academy for the Royal Canadian Mounted Police. The history of the Mounties is central to Saskatchewan. In 1874 a detachment of North West Mounted Police was sent from Manitoba to establish law and order in the North West where the illegal trade in whiskey, guns and fur was growing apace. Today the inter-provincial highway has been named the Red Coat Trail after their epic 800-mile trek west on horseback. They set up posts across the province, many of which have been restored and are open to visitors, including Fort Walsh in the Cypress Hills and Fort Battleford to the north.

Displays in the RCMP Centennial Museum in Regina recount such legendary Mountie exploits as the Lost Patrol, and tell the stories of notorious villains such as the Mad Trapper of Rat River. Prized artifacts include the handcuffs worn by the rebel, Louis Riel, and the crucifix he carried to his execution on a site just outside the museum (open daily; free, donations welcomed). Visitors can watch cadets parading and the colorful Sunset Retreat Ceremony (tel: 306 780 5900 for dates and times; free).

to the south and rolling parkland to the north. The valley is best appreciated from Highway 56 where it flanks the **Fishing Lakes** – four broadenings in the Qu'Appelle River. **Echo Valley** and **Katepwa** provincial parks offer camping, fishing, swimming and nature trails that wind through wooded ravines.

Eastern spires crown many churches northeast of the Qu'Appelle, testifying to the predominance of Ukrainian settlers. In **Yorkton ❸**, a stroll through the **Western Development Museum** reveals household scenes of early settlers. A colorful Ukrainian pioneer kitchen, brightened with ceramic tiles and embroideries, contrasts with an austere English parlor. In the summer the museum sponsors the Threshermen's Show, with wagon rides, threshing competitions and square dancing (open May–mid-Sep: daily; entrance fee).

British eccentricity

Eccentricity is an old Saskatchewan tradition, and few were more flamboyant than the English aristocrats who tried to re-create a corner of their sceptered isle on the bald-headed prairie at **Cannington Manor ❹**, now an historic park 200 km (125 miles) southeast of Regina. Here, in 1882, Captain Edward Pierce established a manorial village, where blue bloods bred racehorses, played rugby and cricket, and hired immigrants to do the farming. When the railroad bypassed Cannington, the settlement became a ghost town. Still standing are the **Maltby** and **Hewlett** houses, a carpenter's shop, and **All Saints Church**. Beside the log church is the grave of Captain Pierce, far from his beloved England (open mid-May–early Sep: daily; voluntary entrance fee).

Moose Mountain Provincial Park ❺, 27 km (17 miles) northwest, is a favorite with bird-watchers who scan the skies for turkey vultures, teal, ducks

Little Manitou Lake, 120 km (70 miles) to the southeast of Saskatoon, was known by the Indians as "place of healing waters." It is now a well-established spa.

BELOW LEFT: Farewell's Trading Post. **Right:** the Mountie barracks at Fort Walsh.

and dozens of other species. There's also horseback riding, fishing and camping.

The Badlands

At the turn of the century the **Big Muddy Badlands** south of Regina sheltered a community every bit as strange as Cannington Manor. Outlaws such as Bloody Knife and the Pigeon Toed Kid hid out in caves between cattle rustling raids on Montana ranches.In July, guided auto tours start in **Big Beaver**, 176 km (109 miles) south of Regina, and go through the badlands, past the outlaw hideouts.

After a while, the pancake-flat prairie produces a yearning for anything higher than just a gopher mound. **St Victor Petroglyphs Provincial Historic Park ❻**, 150 km (93 miles) southwest of Regina, satisfies that need with a weirdly eroded sandstone outcrop, where prehistoric Indians carved dozens of designs in the soft rock. The outcrop also affords a panorama of chessboard crops, alkali lakes, escarpments and brightly painted grain elevators, those "cathedrals of the plains" which give prairie towns their distinctive (and only) skylines. South-central Saskatchewan is the province's predominantly French-speaking region.

Wood Mountain, 50 km (30 miles) southwest of St Victor, briefly became a refuge to Sitting Bull and his band of Sioux after the Battle of Little Big Horn in 1876. The barracks and mess hall of a Mountie post established to watch over the Sioux have been re-created in the **Wood Mountain Post Historic Park** (open June–mid-Aug: daily;voluntary entrance fee).

Cypress Hills Provincial Park ❼ on the southwest border with Alberta, is situated in one of the few parts of Western Canada left uncovered by Ice Age glaciers. The hills rise like a long, green wedge near **Eastend** and extend west into Alberta. This oasis of coniferous forests, cool valleys and rounded buttes

Map, page 300

Grasslands National Park, on the border with the US, is a good site to view prairie wildlife, including black-tailed prairie dogs and endangered burrowing owls.

BELOW: the wide open landscape of the Prairies.

has long been a refuge for travelers on the hot and dusty plains. Campgrounds, cabins, tennis, golf and skiing are all available at **Loch Leven**.

There is history here, too, at **Fort Walsh**, built by the North West Mounted Police in 1875 to eradicate the illicit whiskey trade to Plains Indians, who swapped buffalo hides for swigs of a vile concoction that was one part alcohol and three parts water, colored with tobacco juice and spiced with Jamaica ginger. The re-created fort shelters the officers' quarters, commissioner's residence and other buildings (open May–Labor Day: daily; entrance fee). A few miles away, **Farewell's Trading Post** is staffed with guides in 1870s dress, and stocked with whiskey kegs and patent medicine (open May–Labor Day).

Fifty km (30 miles) north of Cypress Hills the "Old Cow Town" of **Maple Creek** drowses beneath its canopy of cottonwoods. Capital of bone-dry ranchland, Maple Creek is about as Old West as Saskatchewan gets.

Sheltered in a broad valley 312 km (194 miles) east on Highway 1, **Moose Jaw ❽** is a quiet city with a past. In the 1920s bootleggers and brothels flourished along **River Street**, and Chicago gangsters cooled their heels here. Most of the excitement today comes in May when the Kinsmen Band Competition attracts 5,000 musicians, and in June when the Canadian Forces host an air show. Moose Jaw's **Western Development Museum** emphasizes early transportation with biplanes, antique autos and a steam locomotive (open daily; entrance fee).

Saskatoon's temperance days

Bootleggers never darkened the streets of **Saskatoon ❾**, founded in 1884 as a temperance colony, a legacy that endures only in the sign for **Temperance Avenue**. The city's best feature is the **North Saskatchewan River**, which flows

The province's oldest museum, The Old Timer's Museum at Maple Creek, features Indian artifacts (Jun–Sep: daily; Oct, Apr, May: Mon–Fri; entrance fee).

BELOW: fortress on the plains.

between high, wooded banks protected from development by parks. The summer cruise boat *Northcote* passes riverside landmarks such as the turreted **Bessborough Hotel**, the **Mendel Art Gallery and Conservatory** and the graystone buildings of the **University of Saskatchewan**.

The university gives Saskatoon a cultural and cosmopolitan cachet. Five theater groups and a symphony orchestra perform here, and restaurants can be found that border on the bohemian by Saskatchewan standards.

The city commemorates Louis Riel in a relay race, in which teams canoe, run and ride horseback. The contest initiates the city's July **Saskatoon Exhibition**, a week of rodeo events, tractor pulls, even a demolition derby with combines. Fair-goers can ride to the nearby **Western Development Museum** in a covered wagon. The museum's centerpiece is a prairie community with 22 buildings and staff in pioneer costume (open daily; Jan–Mar: closed Mon; entrance fee).

Historic sites

On the northern edge of Saskatoon the **Wanuskewin Heritage Park** (pronounced Wah-nus-kay-win, Cree for "peace of mind") portrays 6,000 years of Northern Plains Indian culture. Here, with the help of native elders, visitors can see what life was like in a Plains Indian encampment (open daily; entrance fee).

Continuing north towards Prince Albert a high bluff commands a mighty bend of the South Saskatchewan River where the Métis made their last stand during the Northwest Rebellion of 1885. The only remains of the Métis "capital" at **Batoche** are a simple white church, which served as Louis Riel's headquarters, and a bullet-scarred rectory. A few miles west stands palisaded **Fort Carlton**, once the most important fur-trade depot between the Red River and the Rockies (open mid-May–Labor Day; entrance fee).

Eighty km (50 miles) northeast of this battle-scarred valley is **Prince Albert**, gateway to the province's northlands, famous among fishermen for both its pristine lakes and its record-size trout. Prince Albert is also home to **Lund Wildlife Exhibit**, where hundreds of Canadian animals and birds are stuffed and mounted in re-creations of their natural habitats (open Jun–Oct: daily; entrance fee).

Straddling a transition zone between parkland and boreal forest is **Prince Albert National Park** ⑩. Pines scent the air of **Waskesiu Lake**, park headquarters, attractive year-round resort town and home port of the popular paddlewheeler *Neo-Watin*. Sailboats and fishing boats are available at the townsite.

About 160 km (100 miles) southwest of the park, **Battleford** ⑪, the former capital of the Northwest Territories, occupies a wooded setting far superior to that of its successor, Regina. The **Fort Battleford National Historic Park**, a Mountie post where Canada's last public execution took place in 1885, contains officers' quarters and residences, and other carefully restored buildings. The fort's most poignant artifact recalls Louis Riel. For there stands the Gatling gun used in the Battle of Batoche. The weapon's brass is as shiny as a century ago, when the dreams of the Métis died on a bluff above the North Saskatchewan River (open mid-May–mid-Oct: daily; entrance fee).

Map, page 300

TIP

In Prince Albert National Park, little-visited lakes, including Ajawaan, former home of the British naturalist, Grey Owl, can be seen at their best by canoe.

BELOW: Maple Creek grain elevators.

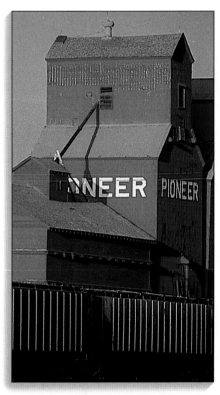

MANITOBA: PRAIRIE SURPRISE

A traveler coming from the east through the forests of Ontario will find Manitoba bursting upon the senses with space, light and color, with towns and cities as varied as the settlers themselves

Map, page 300

Ah, thinks the traveler, approaching Manitoba along northern Ontario's corridor of ragged trees, the prairie at last. Suddenly the land rolls on and on to a distant horizon. The sky, once confined to a gray strip above the highway, expands into a dome of deep blue.

Well, yes and no. The boreal forest is close by, blanketing the northern two-thirds of Manitoba with a lake-dotted wilderness that remains virtually unpopulated. And the sunny south refutes the old equation of prairie equals flat. West of Whiteshell Provincial Park, the land rises in stone and gravel ridges, flattens around Winnipeg, turns marshy south of Lake Manitoba, dips into the valleys of the Pembina and Assiniboine rivers, then rises again in the western uplands.

The towns and cities are as varied as the land, and herein lies Manitoba's special appeal. Settlers from Europe and Eastern Canada established towns with character, not just supply centers for farmers, and proudly added their ethnic flavor: French-Canadians at Ste Anne, Icelanders at Gimli, Russians at Tolstoi. The vigor of these communities is remarkable considering the overwhelming presence of **Winnipeg ⑫**, provincial capital and home to 700,000 people, more than half of Manitoba's population.

LEFT: taking part in a Ukrainian festival.
BELOW: Legislative Building, Manitoba.

Provincial capital

Winnipeg looks similar to other Western Canadian cities, although there's no mistaking the junction of Portage and Main, reputedly the widest, windiest, coldest street corner in Canada. But downtown avenues curve with the Assiniboine and Red rivers, giving some buildings delightfully quirky angles and avoiding the West's usual rigid street grid. Leafy residential areas, originally separate towns, are more distinctive than the tract-housing communities of the suburban West.

They also contain outstanding green swathes such as **Assiniboine Park**, with its excellent **Zoo** (open daily; entrance fee), tropical conservatory and cricket grounds, and **Kildonan Park**, designed by Frederick Law Olmsted, architect of New York's Central Park. Kildonan is home to the 2,300-seat **Rainbow Stage**, where outdoor musical events and plays are presented.

Winnipeg is also an old city in a young land. The first Europeans to build on this site were French fur traders who constructed Fort Rouge in 1738 near the flood-prone confluence of the Red and Assiniboine rivers, silt-laden waterways which eventually gave the city its Cree name of *Win-nipi* (muddy water). After the French came those fierce fur-trade rivals, the London-based Hudson's Bay Company and the North West Company of Montréal. During the late 18th and early 19th centuries, the

*The Byzantine domes
of Holy Trinity
Ukrainian Orthodox
Cathedral, Winnipeg.
Ukrainians form the
second-largest ethnic
group in Manitoba.*

two companies built a series of palisaded forts within shooting distance near the Assiniboine and Red rivers.

In 1812 Scottish crofters who had been turned out of their homes by the Highland Clearances arrived on the scene with a few farming implements and a bull and a cow named Adam and Eve. The trip, tools and livestock were courtesy of the Scottish humanitarian, Lord Selkirk, who established farming colonies throughout North America for homeless Highlanders. But like cattle ranchers and sheep farmers, fur traders and settlers did not mix. Conflict erupted on June 19, 1816, when Métis employees of the North West Company slaughtered 20 settlers in what became known as the Seven Oaks Incident.

Lord Selkirk heard the bad news in Montréal, and promptly marched west with a private army. He arrested the fur traders and their Métis employees, then re-established his settlement, which eventually prospered. There are several reminders of the fur-trade era in Winnipeg. **Grant's Old Mill** is a working replica of the settlement's first gristmill, built in 1829 by Cuthbert Grant, leader of the Métis at the massacre (open May–Labor Day; entrance fee).

The **Seven Oaks House** (open late-May–Labor Day: daily; entrance fee) and the **Ross House** (open Jun–Aug: Wed–Sun; free), both built in the 1850s by fur traders, are museums worth visiting, as is the **Manitoba Museum of Man and Nature**. Its most impressive fur-trade display is a full-size replica of the *Nonsuch*, a Hudson's Bay Company vessel that in 1669 brought the first cargo of furs from Canada to England (open mid-May–Labor Day: daily; Sep–May: closed Mon; entrance fee).

The most evocative relic of this exciting era is the lone remaining gate of **Upper Fort Garry**, built by the Hudson's Bay Company in 1836, and now pre-

BELOW: mischievous
trio from Anishabe
Days, Winnipeg.

served in a quiet park in the shadow of the turreted **Hotel Fort Garry**. This was once the center of the settlement's social life. Dr John Blum wrote in the 1840s, "To describe the balls would be a task beyond the weakness of human nature. There were cards for the infirm and lazy, brandy for the thirsty, and unremitting hospitality. All became hiccups and happiness."

Multi-cultural influences

The city's economic good times arrived with the completion of the Canadian-Pacific Railway in 1885 and the hundreds of thousands of immigrants who followed the ribbon of steel: Europeans fleeing persecution, British city dwellers hungry for land, Americans who saw their own West filling up. Almost all came through Winnipeg, and enough stayed on to swell the city's population.

Each year for two weeks in August, Winnipeg remembers its rich ethnic mosaic with **Folklorama**, a festival held in some 40 informal pavilions scattered throughout the city. In the evening church basements and school auditoriums are filled with the aromas of Polish sausage and Ukrainian cabbage rolls and the strains of German polkas and Greek *sirtakis*, as each group celebrates its heritage with food, song and dance.

Ukrainian-Canadians are particularly prominent in Winnipeg. The pear-shaped domes of half a dozen major churches grace the skyline, and the **Ukrainian Cultural and Educational Centre** contains a museum displaying such treasures as 17th-century church vestments, as well as a series of rooms decorated with the hand-carved furniture and hand-painted ceramics typically found in village homes (open Tue–Sun; entrance fee). The **Ukrainian Museum of Canada, Manitoba Branch** displays folk arts like tapestries (*kylymy*) and Easter

Map, page 300

The Manitoba Museum of Man and Nature offers the best introduction to the history of the province, with excellent displays and reconstructions.

BELOW: weekend entertainment – dog sled races.

eggs (*pysanky*) (open Jun–Aug: Mon–Sat; free). East across the Red River is **St Boniface**, bastion of French culture, where streets are *rues*, and domes yield to the belfries of **St Boniface Basilica**, built in 1908 and partially destroyed by fire in 1968. Here once rang the bells of St Boniface, celebrated by John Greenleaf Whittier in the *Red River Voyageur:*

The voyageur smiles as he listens
To the sound that grows apace:
Well he knows the vesper ringing
Of the bells of St Boniface.

Winnipeg still offers the greatest cultural diversity in the prairies. Vacationers between September and May can enjoy the Manitoba Opera Company, the Winnipeg Symphony Orchestra, mainstream plays at the Manitoba Theater Center and experimental works at the MTC Warehouse Theater. And if you're really lucky, the celebrated Royal Winnipeg Ballet will be in town during your visit.

Once considered something of a dowager by the younger, upstart prairie communities such as Calgary and Edmonton, Winnipeg is turning its age into an asset with a flurry of sandblasting, wood stripping and brass polishing. This fling with the past is centered on the historic **Exchange District**, a 15-block area which is bounded by Main and Princess streets and William and Notre Dame avenues. Here, the largest concentration of commercial early 20th-century architecture in the West has been given a new lease of life.

Visitors who want more tranquil pursuits can board the *Paddlewheel Princess* or the *Paddlewheel Queen*, and cruise north on the Red River to **Lower Fort Garry National Historic Park**, North America's last intact stone fur-trade fort and the most impressive historic site on the prairies, restored to the 1850s' era.

Step back to the 19th century at Riel House, the family home of Louis Riel, leader of the Métis, 330 River Road, St Vital, (open daily, mid-May–Labor Day).

BELOW: prairie fields of plenty.

The landscaped grounds and the riverside setting are complemented by costumed attendants demonstrating how old-timers made candles and pressed beaver pelts into 41-kg (90-pound) bales (grounds open daily; buildings open: mid-May–Labor Day daily; entrance fee).

Lakeside retreats

Larger than Lake Ontario, vast **Lake Winnipeg** stretches north into the wilderness. Cottage communities ring its southern end: **Grand Beach ⑬**, 87 km (54miles) north of the provincial capital, **Winnipeg Beach**, **Victoria Beach**, all slightly commercialized and crowded but blessed with long stretches of white sand where it's still possible to find seclusion.

Seventy-six kilometers (47 miles) north on the western shore, the Icelandic community of **Gimli ⑭** remembers its past with a statue of a Viking and the **Gimli Historical Museum**, which explains the fishing economy established on Lake Winnipeg by the town's forebears (open Jul–Aug: daily; voluntary entrance fee). **Hecla Island ⑮**, 50 km (30 miles) north, once a self-governing Icelandic republic, is now part of a provincial park. Sunrise bird-watching safaris, hiking and ski trails, tennis courts, and a fine golf course are among the attractions.

The good earth

South of Winnipeg stretches flat farmland with rich black gumbo soil of silt and clay. This land was described by the 18th-century fur trader, Alexander Henry, as "a kind of mortar that adheres to the foot like tar." In the middle stands **Steinbach ⑯**, whose tidy streets and freshly painted houses reflect the enduring values of the town's industrious Mennonite founders. The **Mennonite Village**

Winnipeg's site at the confluence of the Red and Assiniboine rivers is marked by The Forks, a "meeting place" with river walks, historic port and amphitheater.

BELOW: children enjoy a corn husking contest in Morden.

Map, page 300

Manitoba's Hutterite communities have little contact with the outside world. They originated in Moravia and began settling on the prairies in 1918.

Museum recalls the old ways with reconstructed thatched-roof cabins, a blacksmith's shop and a wind-driven gristmill. Excellent borscht and spicy sausages are served at the museum restaurant (open May–Sep: daily; entrance fee).

West of the Red River and south to the American border lies the **Pembina Triangle**. Sheltered by the gentle Pembina Hills, the region has Manitoba's longest growing season and the only apple orchards between the Niagara Peninsula and the Okanagan Valley.

Seemingly every town in the region advertises the local agricultural specialty with theme fairs. Fields of sunflowers nodding in hot prairie breezes around the Mennonite community of **Altona**, 98 km (61 miles) south of Winnipeg, inspired the Manitoba Sunflower Festival, held in July. Nearby **Winkler** ⑰, 24 km (15 miles) west, settled by Anabaptist Hutterites, holds the Winkler Harvest Festival each August with barbecues, pancake breakfasts and old-time sidewalk sales.

The **Pembina Valley** is steep enough at **La Rivière**, 61 km (38 miles) west of Winkler, for a downhill ski run. The valley was carved by the willow-fringed Pembina River, which broadens into a chain of sparkling canoeing and fishing lakes – **Pelican**, **Lorne**, **Louise** and **Rock**.

About 64 km (40 miles) west, the attractive town of **Killarney** ⑱ has a small lake at its feet and a hill wooded with maple and oak at its back. This setting, said to be reminiscent of Kerry, Ireland, has produced Killarney's Celtic touches: a green fire engine, and Erin Park with its replica of the Blarney Stone.

The **International Peace Garden**, 32 km (20 miles) southwest of Killarney, straddles the North Dakota-Manitoba border, near the geographical center of the continent. Dr Henry Moore, an ardent gardener from Toronto, tabled a modest proposal for a joint peace park in 1929 at a meeting of the Gardeners Asso-

BELOW: mist over Portage la Prairie.

ciation of North America. Three years later, his dream became a reality.

If all this cultivation creates a craving for wilderness, visit the **Carberry Sand Hills** in **Spruce Woods Provincial Park** 145 km (90 miles) west of Winnipeg: grassy plains and barren sand dunes along the sinuous Assiniboine River. The sandhills were formed about 12,000 years ago when a mile-wide glacial river deposited a vast delta of sand, silt and gravel.

Ernest Thompson Seton, a naturalist-author who homesteaded near Carberry in the 1880s, made them the setting for his book, *The Trail of the Sandhill Stag.* He spent every spare moment in what came to be known as "Seton's Kingdom" observing grouse, deer and wolves. Be sure to try the self-guiding **Spirit Hills Trail**, which winds through barren dunes inhabited by rarities like hognose snakes, spadefoot toads and northern prairie skinks. Fifty kilometers (30 miles) west lies **Brandon**, Manitoba's second city, noted for handsome public buildings and gracious private homes dating from the early 1900s.

Highway 10 leads north past fields of wheat and rye interspersed with pothole lakes that attract millions of ducks and geese during spring and fall migrations. A short detour takes you to **Neepawa** ⓴, 75 km (47 miles) northeast of Brandon, where you can visit the childhood home of the acclaimed Canadian author Margaret Laurence (open May–mid-Sep: daily; entrance fee), before continuing north into the forests of **Riding Mountain National Park** ㉑.

Approaching the park from this direction, the usual reaction is: *Where's the mountain?* Patience will be rewarded on reaching the edge of the park, where the "mountain" rises abruptly, 450 meters (1,500 ft), above a patchwork of crops: yellow rapeseed, brown squares of oats and barley, and rolling green and gold wheatfields. Ah, thinks the traveler, once again the endless prairie.

Map, page 300

TIP

Explore Brandon on foot and discover its most notable historic buildings with the help of a walking tour brochure distributed by the Chamber of Commerce.

BELOW: prairie flower power.

THE NORTH

*The long sunny days of summer lend themselves to exploring
what is perhaps Canada's last uncharted frontier*

The North is the nation's most sparsely populated region. Here it genuinely *is* bitterly cold in winter, here some people *do* live in snow huts, and here dog-sled racing across the frozen tundra *is* a popular form of entertainment.

Despite its formidable geography, the North is the natural habitat of the "first Canadians", the Inuit, who have survived here for thousands of years and who, in 1999, finally acquired their own territory of Nunavut.

While Canada's northern hinterland may not be the vacation spot for everyone, for those intrigued by unusual habitats, landscapes and wildlife the North presents an exciting adventure. The Yukon, the Northwest Territories and Nunavut are regions of delicately balanced ecosystems and glacial beauty unparalleled anywhere in the world.

The Yukon is the first of Canada's three northern regions to be explored in the following pages. Here, the reader can discover the significance of the gold rush for Canada's neglected North and is provided with a description of the Yukon's geography, climate and spectacular vistas. The section also provides information about the province's sights and the kinds of vacations that are suitable to the area.

The Northwest Territories are treated in much the same fashion, although with greater emphasis on geological formations and wildlife. As Nunavut is a newly created territory, its political evolution is touched upon, along with the diverse range of activities awaiting its visitors. The three chapters together present a comprehensive picture of the radically different world looming over Canada's other 10 provinces.

PRECEDING PAGES: heading north, the rugged peaks and steep valleys of Jasper National Park invite exploration. **LEFT:** vestiges in the snow.

THE YUKON: STRIKING GOLD

Today tourists trace the footsteps of the gold prospectors who once made their fortunes in this northerly outpost. Glaciers, wide plateaus and magnificent mountains characterize the Yukon

Map, page 320

Before 1896 the northwest corner of Canada was a mountainous wilderness where few outsiders, besides the occasional whaler and fur-trader, ventured. Other than the Dene Indians who had lived here for perhaps 60,000 years, it was unknown to most. But in 1896 this forgotten land was suddenly overrun by man and beast. Gold, and lots of it, had been discovered in the Klondike.

The young Dominion of Canada, like any new heir, soon had the headaches that accompany sudden wealth. If the government could not bring order (or at least a civilizing influence) to the North, it might lose millions in gold tax revenues. Therefore the Queen's ministers, in recognition of the sudden prominence of a land most knew little about, decided to redraw the map of Canada. They roped off the northwest corner of the Northwest Territories and created the Yukon Territory. What the federal officials lassoed in their haste to reassert Canadian sovereignty is a territory larger than the New England States, double the land mass of the British Isles, and two and a half times the size of Texas.

This is a land whose wild beauty could easily outstrip the pecuniary ambitions of its new "citizens". Collectively the Yukon region is known as part of the Western Highlands. Along the eastern border of the territory there lie the **Mackenzie Mountains** that pass over into the NWT and gently roll up to the mouth of the **Mackenzie River**. Within this range there are rivers carved into the rock by ancient glaciers. One such river, the **Nahanni**, contains Virginia Falls. However, unlike Ontario's great Niagara, no one has ever attempted to go over these falls in a barrel.

LEFT: an inquisitive sled dog.
BELOW: from the Alaska Highway, Yukon's main artery.

Mountain country

Mountains are an omnipresent sight in the Yukon. The **Selwyn Mountains** lie to the west of the Mackenzie mountain range and to the north are the very ancient **Ogilvie Mountains**.

The best known peaks are **St Elias** and **Mount Logan** on the province's southwest border with Alaska. Standing at 5,959 meters (19,550 ft), Mount Logan is second only to Mount McKinley in Alaska as the highest mountain in North America.

Many peaks in the St Elias Range must push through glaciers, glaciers that are in part sustained by the "chill factor" associated with great heights. The St Elias Range, besides offering some of the most spectacular sights in the world, also acts to block much of the moisture coming off the Pacific Ocean. It is because of this that most of the interior of the Yukon receives little

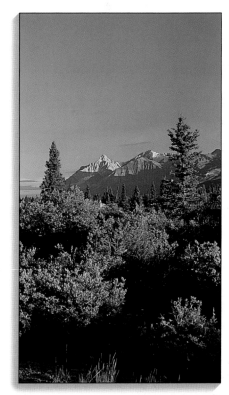

Walking trails through Kluane National Park give access to the woods, meadows, mountains and icefields that are home to eagles and Dall sheep.

precipitation. The average in **Whitehorse** ❶, capital of the Yukon, is 26 cm (10 inches) a year. In the High Arctic there is less precipitation than farther south. Yet the Yukon does receive more precipitation than the NWT and, because of the relatively cold temperatures and high altitudes, whatever snow falls in winter will not evaporate until spring. This snow helps provide excellent cross-country trails.

Plateau land

Between the mountain ranges are plateaus, the **Pelly**, the **Porcupine** and the **Yukon**. Each plateau is named after the river that flows through it. The Yukon Plateau is the largest of the three. Although glaciers remain in Yukon Territory, much of the Yukon Plateau was untouched by the last glacial era and for this reason it is unique among geological areas in North America. Thus the Yukon River, unlike the other northern rivers that felt the effects of glaciation, flows gently through the plateau and is devoid of rapids, falls and other such unpleasantness that can make canoe trips an unholy excursion. Ice-free millennia have allowed the Yukon River to find its own path.

Within the plateau one finds mountains that have dome-like summits rising to heights of 1,800 meters (6,000 ft). These domes were formed by a million years of sediment accumulating on top of the mountains. Unlike the neighboring ranges, such as the Mackenzie or St Elias that have been scoured by glaciers and left with whittled down pencil-shaped peaks, the mountains of Yukon Plateau have few rocky outcroppings.

This plateau is a relic of another age, one that stands apart from the geological violence of the last Ice Age. For that reason ancient mastodon and mammoth species survived far longer here. Likewise, the plateau offered shelter for Asians

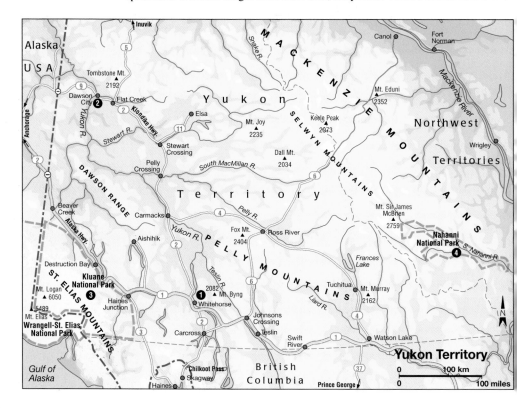

who entered North America across the Bering Strait thousands of years ago.

The rich soil deposits in the Yukon allow for a tremendous variety of flora and fauna. Except for its barren northern tip much of the Yukon is covered in forest and heavy underbrush that can support a sizeable local logging industry. Owing to the plenitude of vegetation there is an excellent food supply to support the many species of animals, including moose, caribou, Dall sheep, mountain goats, cougars, grizzly and black bears. Within the rivers of the Yukon there are usually large runs of salmon that have traveled thousands of miles from the Pacific.

Golden days

There was a time when not only thousands of salmon swam through the Yukon River, but thousands of men waded into her. Unlike the salmon, these men came to seek out the placer gold that laid buried deep in the sediment of river beds.

In contrast to the manner in which it is extracted, placer gold is created by the eternally slow process of erosion. Gradually the river flows over a rock face wearing down the quartz bearing gold until it breaks off into pieces varying anywhere in size from that of a tennis ball to a microscopic speck.

This iridescent mineral lay complacently in Yukon river beds for thousands of years, quite unaware of the lust men held for it. Finally on 17 August, 1896, a day that is now a territorial holiday, three men, Skookum Jim, Tagish Charley (two Yukon Indians), and George Washington Carmack (an American) became the founding fathers of the gold rush. They struck gold at **Rabbit Creek** (renamed **Bonanza**) and the love affair with the **Klondike** began. Eventually, close to 80,000 men would scurry northward to seek their fortune, with the gold stories that were published in William Randolph Hearst's hyperbolic newspapers

Map, page 320

To the east of Yukon, Nahanni National Park features gorges deeper than the Grand Canyon. Visit Fort Simpson to arrange tours, flights and canoe rentals.

BELOW: Chilkoot Pass, "deathly trail" of the gold seekers.

Whitehorse comes alive in February for the Sourdough Rendezvous, when people dress in 1898 costumes and dogs race on the frozen Yukon River.

rattling in their heads. The routes which some miners chose to take were rather bizarre. A group of Edmonton businessmen, for instance, advertised a trail through the rugged interior of Alberta and British Columbia. Little did those who took this passage know that Dawson City, the center of the goldrush, lay a few thousand miles away and that this "trail" was a hoax. Of the thousands who attempted this route many lost their lives and only a handful managed to straggle on into the Yukon.

Soapy Smith and Sam Steele

A more conventional route was to travel by steamer to Skagway, Alaska, and then onwards through either the White Pass or Chilfort Pass into Yukon. Although these trails were better than the Edmonton trail, they posed many dangers: not the least of which was your fellow miner. In Skagway a ne'er-do-well named "Soapy" Smith managed to gather around him a rather unscrupulous flock who fleeced many a would-be prospector of his stake long before he got to Dawson. The Wild West made quite a revival in northern Skagway. Soapy's downfall came when a group of armed townsfolk drew him and his boys out. The gang quickly scattered; Soapy held his ground and was shot dead, but not until he had managed to mortally wound the vigilante who shot him.

The Canadian authorities looked upon both the outlaw activity and the vigilantism with disdain. The Canadian cabinet ordered that 300 North West Mounted Police be sent to the Yukon.

They were headed by a man whose name almost stereotypically symbolized not only his own character but that of his police force – Sam Steele. Steele was charged with several tasks, the first of which was to enforce and impress upon the prospectors Canadian sovereignty. More than 90 percent of those entering the Yukon were Americans. Another of Steele's responsibilities was to ensure that every man and woman entering the Yukon had enough supplies to last an entire year. Steele stationed Mounties at all mountain passes and ordered that all would-be Yukoners with less than 453 kg (1,000 lbs) of equipment and food be turned back. This was a sensible order: you could hope for, but not depend on, charity in the Yukon.

Carrying the requisite equipment through mountain passes 1,160 meters (3,800 ft) or more in height was a Herculean task. In April of 1898, with spring well on its way, 63 people were smothered to death in an avalanche at Chilkoot Pass. Within a day the pass was reopened and people continued their grim ascent.

Boom to bust

During the early years of the gold-rush in **Dawson City** ❷ inflation was an endemic problem: an orange sold for 50 cents a piece and a pint of champagne cost $40. Gold poured out of the Yukon. In 1896, $300,000 worth of gold was produced; the following year $2.5 million worth was mined; in 1898, $10 million in gold was extracted; and by 1900, the peak year, more than $22 million worth of gold was taken from the Yukon. Yet every boom has a bust and the Yukon's halcyon days began to abate in 1902. There was simply less gold to

BELOW: autumn gold borders the Klondike Highway.

be had. In addition, large companies began filing claims on many "used" claims and then reworking them. In this way corporations consolidated the gold industry and displaced the traditional small-time operators.

With the exodus of the original "sourdoughs" there followed the closing of the dance-halls, gambling parlors and drinking establishments. The freewheeling and freespirited days were over. At the height of the gold rush the Klondike region had a population of 30,000, some 16,000 of whom were in Dawson City. By 1910 there were only 1,000 inhabitants. Today about 900 people live there, and few are prospectors.

There has been speculation that both the Yukon and Canada missed a great opportunity to develop what would have become an indigenous industry. If the small-time operator had been encouraged to stay, perhaps a tertiary industry could have sustained the remarkable culture. Interestingly, there remain roughly 200 one- or two-man placer gold outfits who are still working the rivers of the Yukon, long after the large gold companies have left.

Mining has always been the backbone of the Yukon's economy. When the gold production began to slow, large zinc, lead and silver deposits were discovered and mined in the Yukon. However, with the world mineral markets in a state of depression there has been a corresponding depression in the Yukon.

Map, page 320

Gold rush glamor: the Palace Grand Theater, Dawson City, built in 1899.

The Yukon today

With the mining industry in a slump, one part of the Yukon's Gross National Product (GNP) that is growing is tourism. Naturally Klondike nostalgia is used as a major theme. So even if the gold boom broke 80 years ago, today its legacy is still paying a modest dividend. In Dawson City, the former capital of the Yukon and hub of the goldrush, there stands Canada's first legalized casino. In the summer months this little gambling establishment, along with a Klondike-style dance revue, is a reminder that the Yukon was founded by hustlers, gold diggers and dreamers, not fishermen or farmers. There are tours that will take travelers down the same rivers that paddlewheelers once traveled and prospectors worked.

Along the riverbanks and hiking trials are the remains of the prospectors' old camps and abandoned towns; tourists to the Territory can relive the "golden days" of the Yukon's Klondike. Ironically, many in the tourist industry now wish to restrict or eliminate the activities of the modern placer-gold prospectors. Placer-gold extraction has done and can do tremendous environmental damage to riverbeds.

There is more to the Yukon than a land of faded "glory days". It is interesting that if you ask people who are vaguely familiar with Canada for a sketch of the country they will invariably mention Mounties, mountains, snow and ice. What they are describing is the Yukon. The portrait they often describe is a little like saying that the *Mona Lisa* is a sketch of a smiling lady. This wilderness with its rivers, meadows, mountains, plateaus, wildlife and glaciers existed long before fortune hunters from the south made their way noisily into the interior. The Yukon remains a silent beauty long after those men have left.

THE YUKON'S BIG CITIES

Whitehorse, capital of the Yukon since 1953 with two-thirds of the province's population, began as a Yukon River shanty town in the late 1890s. North-bound prospectors constructed a tramway here to bypass White Horse rapids. The city rose and declined with the gold rush and was finally established with the building of the Alaska Highway in 1942. Visit the steamboat *SS Klondike* that once plied the river to Dawson City (open May–Sep; entrance fee), and Miles Canyon, 9 km (6 miles) south.

Dawson City, site of the gold rush, and the largest city in western Canada at the end of the 19th century, retains its frontier-town atmosphere. Theaters, restaurants, bars and brothels lined its streets, some of which remain. Start at the Visitor Reception Center in Front Street, then capture the essence of the Klondike at the city museum (both open mid-May–mid-Sep: daily; museum entrance fee).

LIVING IN A WHITE WORLD OF SNOW

In a country where great numbers of people exist under a snowy white blanket for many months of the year, how do they cope with everyday life?

Snow angels practically define a Canadian childhood. You plonk yourself down on your back, flap your legs and arms up and down over the snow's soft surface, then leap up to inspect the enchanting result. This instinctive communing with nature frequently launches a lifelong affair with snow. Every winter, lakes, rivers, even back yards, are converted into ice rinks, where youngsters play hockey and oldsters simply skate. Countless Canadians are addicted to outdoors activities from skiing to snow-shoeing, snowmobiling, dog-sledding, ice fishing, and horse-drawn sleigh rides.

INDOOR PURSUITS

Not all Canadians welcome snow with such enthusiasm. Fortunately winter also heralds a plethora of cultural activities, from experimental theater to symphony concerts and operatic galas, literary fests and eye-popping art exhibits. Sports fans' weekends revolve around *Hockey Night in Canada*, a long-standing Saturday night TV fixture. January and February's gloom is often brightened by extravagant culinary and wine tastings, and by March stores are awash with sparkling springtime fashions and Easter bunnies.

In urban centers, snow is more easily avoided. From Vancouver to St. John's, Canadians take refuge in networks of underground passageways where shops, restaurants, theaters, even ice rinks, offer diversions galore from the harsh reality of winter.

▷ SNOW HOME

Igloo building began in the fall, when snow was compacted into blocks. Warmed only by an oil lamp, the inhabitants depended on animal skins for warmth and further snow for insulaton.

◁ A DOG'S LIFE

In January Inuvik residents celebrate the return of the sun after a month of darkness. Bonspiels, dogsled races and other celebrations take place in March, April and May to mark the return of spring. The annual Yukon Quest 1000 Mile International Dog Sled Race is run from Whitehorse to Alaska in February along the gold rush routes.

▽ WORD PLAY

Snow is a way of life for the inhabitants of northern Canada. It is often said that the Inuit have several hundred words for "snow." In fact, they use just one word "*aput.*"

◁ NORTHERN TRAVEL

Travel to the north is not without excitement: visitors can "mush" a dog team, experience the Northern Lights, watch caribou migrating across frozen lakes, snowmobile on the tundra, ice fish, camp in an igloo, or stay in a trapper's cabin.

◁ MODERN TRANSPORT

Snowmobiles have largely replaced the dogsled teams as a means of transport across the snow. The huskies' diet of Arctic char, caribou and seal meat enabled them to work for days on end without food when supplies were low. Today fuel supplies are flown in to remote areas.

▽ CHANGING SEASONS

Nearly one out of every six tourists visiting the Northwest Territories arrives in winter. A popular NWT T-shirt depicts the four seasons of the year as "June," "July," "August," and "Winter."

◁ SNOW BLANKET

In the Yukon much of the land lies under a snowy blanket from October to April, providing opportunities for all kinds of outdoor pursuits and excuses for festivities such as the Sourdough Rendezvous.

SURVIVAL IN THE FAR NORTH

Hunting and trapping have been the lifeline of Arctic communities for several thousands of years. Huskies (or *qimmiit*) were the workhorses of the Arctic, pulling wooden sleds (*qamutiit*) carrying Inuit hunters and their provisions for hundreds of miles during the fall, when extensive caribou hunts were necessary to provide sufficient food for the family. *Inukshuks*, which were slabs of rock piled high, were built to guide startled caribou into a blind where hunters waited with bows and arrows. Once the meat was removed, the skins were turned into clothing and blankets.

Winter was spent largely within their igloos, which were heated by *qulliqs* – soapstone oil lamps fueled by seal blubber. To break the monotony, storytelling, wrestling contests, throat singing and drum dances took place in a *qaggiq*, which was a large snowhouse.

In the longer days of March, the huskies helped to locate seal breathing holes in the ice, and the hunters then waited patiently with their harpoons for seals to emerge. Spring and summer saw the return of Arctic char, birds, and an abundance of Arctic berries. Inuit survival depended on the riches of both land and sea.

THE NORTHWEST TERRITORIES

Map, page 328

Far away from the pressures of urban life, the Northwest Territories conceal a sparkling landscape of mountains, rivers and canyons. Here visitors can climb, canoe, fish and watch wildlife

Many would picture the Northwest Territories, usually referred to as the NWT, as a flat and perennially icy slab stretching from the 60th parallel toward the North Pole with the occasional polar bear or Inuit igloo to give some relief to this monotonous landscape. However, if you look further than a stereotypical picture, you find not one land but a multitude of lands – lands that are foreign to most people, and yet so mystical that each person who visits there is not so much a tourist as an explorer. This wilderness can stir something undiscovered within oneself.

The Northwest Territories cover an immense area of 1.2 million sq. km (0.5 million sq. miles). Their southern border commences at the 60th parallel and stretches 3,400 km (2,110 miles) up to the North Pole and runs 4,260 km (2,645 miles) from east to west. This means that the total landmass of the NWT is close to half that of the contiguous United States, yet the area has a population of a mere 39,000.

LEFT: transformed by contact, a modern-day Inuit.

Scars of the Ice Age

If the NWT seems short on cultural history, it is certainly long on geophysical history. It was only 10,000 years ago that the last Ice Age finally retreated from much of the area. That Ice Age, the Pleistocene, began somewhere around 1.8 million years ago and left behind moraines, dry gravel beds and drumlins.

Venturing north above the tree line into the tundra where it is too cold for lush vegetation and forests to survive, the scars of thousands of centuries of geological history stand before the eyes.

One legacy of this recent Ice Age are the thousands upon thousands of rivers and lakes that cover more than half of the NWT's landmass. Many of these lakes and rivers, particularly those in the Mackenzie Delta, were formed by glaciers creating indentations in the earth and leaving behind melted glacial ice.

However, much of the territory is classified by geographers as desert. The stereotypical picture of the Canadian North being smothered in snow is surprisingly inaccurate. In fact, the mean annual precipitation for both the eastern and western Arctic is only 30 cm (12 inches), which is the equivalent of just a single Montréal snowstorm.

During the long Arctic winters, however, the sun may only appear for a few brief hours if at all, so whatever snow does fall will not melt until spring. The Territories would be completely devoid of fresh water if it wasn't for the frigid temperatures that prevent evapo-

A RIVER RUNNER'S DREAM

The idyllic rivers of Canada's Northwest Territories are untamed, unpolluted and flow through hundreds of miles of unmatched wilderness, offering some of the most wonderful paddling experiences in the world. In Boreal forest rivers including the Nahanni, the Natla-Keele, the Mountain or the Slave, deep canyons, rapids and spectacular plunging waterfalls prove great challenges to the paddler and the photographer alike.

Arctic rivers also have incredible appeal, powerfully meandering their way through the expansive open tundra, where the majority of plants grow no taller than a foot (approximately 30cm) high, where the view is infinite, and where great wildlife spectacles may include the mid-summer migrations of the barren-ground caribou or grizzly bears and tundra wolves.

ration. Temperatures in the region are legendary. In the Mackenzie Delta the average winter temperature is a perishing –26°C (–15°F), while in summer it averages 19°C (66°F). In the Arctic region of the NWT the average daily temperature of the warmest month of the year never exceeds 10°C (50°F). Generally the farther one moves north and toward the center of the Arctic Ocean, the cooler it becomes.

Yet a traveler should not be misled. When summer arrives and there is sunlight for 20 hours a day, and the temperatures rise in the Mackenzie Delta to 16 to 24°C (the high 60s and mid-70s°F), conditions are ideal for hiking or camping. In fact, the summer in this region is remarkably similar to that in the rest of Canada, except of course that there is more sunshine in the north.

Breeding grounds

While the NWT receives relatively few human visitors, it is estimated that 12 percent of North America's bird population breeds here during the spring and summer months. Almost all of the estimated 80 species of birds in the NWT are migratory. Biologists claim that these birds are attracted to the North primarily because of the lack of natural predators. Many species of birds live below the tree line in the taiga, where there are coniferous trees, dense brush and an abundant source of food. Birds such as chickadees, jays, woodpeckers and crossbills are just a few of the species found here.

Below the tree line, where the weather is less harsh and the trees offer protection from the elements, there are moose, beaver, marten, muskrat, red fox, timber wolf and black bear, as well as huge herds of caribou and bison. Above the tree line are arctic wolves with white coats, as well as arctic fox, lemmings

TIP

To view the tundra and mountains north of the Arctic Circle, take the 730-km (450-mile) Dempster Highway from Dawson City, Yukon, to Inuvik, NWT.

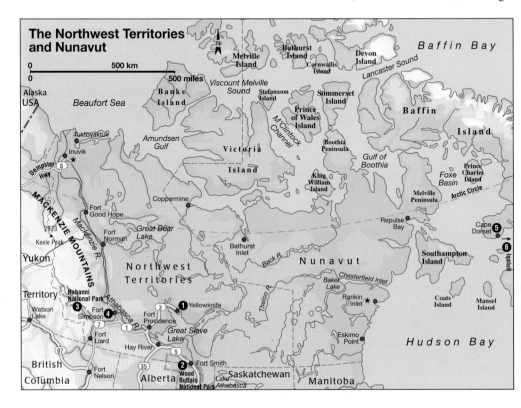

The Northwest Territories and Nunavut

in the east, and, in the summer and fall, caribou. Along the coastline and on the islands polar bears, seals and walrus can be seen. **Melville Island** in the far north is inhabited by the exotic hirsute musk ox.

Map, page 328

Life in the tundra

Perhaps one of the most remarkable facts about survival on the tundra is the dependency of all life on soil frozen to a depth of between 30 and 300 meters (100 to 1,000 ft). This ground is appropriately called permafrost. During the summer, the sun's rays are able to melt topsoil here to a depth of 24 meters (80 ft). It is within this layer of soil that small organisms including lichen grow. Lichen and low-lying vegetation are a main source of food for the mammals of the tundra.

In summer seasons that are too short in length for plant life to grow, all species lose members from their population. Although over many seasons, decimated species eventually recover and the natural order is maintained, this order becomes a precarious one and any external force can disrupt the fragile ecosystem. It is for this reason that the intrusion of southern development is seen as a dangerous threat.

Catch sight of the Aurora Borealis, or Northern Lights, from late-August through winter, when the night sky comes alive with a dazzling display of colors.

Early explorations

For southern intruders (or outsiders), the North has always held a sense of mystery. Many believed there were untold fortunes to be made there.

The first recorded European exploration of the Arctic was undertaken by the Elizabethan, Martin Frobisher, who searched for gold and the elusive Northwest Passage in 1576. Frobisher found neither gold nor the Passage on his first

BELOW: a black bear races across the highway.

Yellowknife owes its existence to the discovery of gold here in 1934. Named after the copper knives of the local Indians, the city became capital of NWT in 1967.

or many subsequent journeys. However, he did manage to bring back to England seven hundred tons of fool's gold from Baffin Island (now part of the new territory of Nunavut).

Henry Hudson was another intrepid English explorer who set out to try his luck and find the Passage. Hudson traveled extensively in the North for several years. Not only did he fail to find the Northwest Passage but his long-suffering crew mutinied, causing havoc. Hudson, his son and seven other explorers were set adrift in a barque in the bay that now carries Hudson's name. The nine men were never seen again. Owing to the discouraging results of expeditions undertaken by Frobisher, Hudson and others of the era, the British Crown and other financial backers became disenchanted and abandoned the search for a northerly route to the Orient and India.

Within Canada, fur traders were searching for routes to markets in Europe. One such entrepreneur was Alexander Mackenzie, who in 1789 followed the Mackenzie River for its entire length (4,240 km/2,630 miles) in the hope that it would eventually lead to the Pacific Ocean. It led instead to the Arctic Ocean. Little did Mackenzie realize in the 18th century that he had reached an opening to a sea that covered vast and lucrative oil deposits.

Even though this area had proven to have little commercial value in the 17th and 18th centuries, there were those in England during the 19th century who looked towards the Arctic region with a mixture of wide-eyed romanticism and genuine scientific curiosity. This era in Arctic exploration was similar to the period of space exploration of the 1960s and 1970s. Prizes were put up by the British Parliament for any person who could find the Northwest Passage and/or discover the North Pole.

BELOW: after the snow, a display of Alpine flowers.

Other daring explorers include William Parry, who managed to collect a purse of £5,000 for his excursion to the far Western Arctic islands (1819–21), and John Franklin, who, in characteristic, bloody-minded British bulldog manner, risked his life a great number of times on his journeys mapping the Arctic coastline.

On his final journey in 1845, Franklin departed from England with a crew of 129 men aboard two ships; their lofty objective was to find the Northwest Passage. Unfortunately the ships were locked in the ice for two years at Victoria Strait. In 1848 search parties were sent out, and eventually over the next eight years articles of clothing, logbooks and mementos were found strewn across the chilly coastline. Of the 129 men on the Franklin expedition not one survivor was found.

Traveling today

Today however, travel for "outsiders" to the Arctic is thankfully a great deal less hazardous than it was in Franklin's day. After the Franklin debacle, "outsiders" began to pay attention to the ways of the Inuit, a people who had lived in the North for so long, learning from them how best to survive such extreme and difficult conditions.

At the same time technology improved, particularly communications, and with the arrival of the airplane in the early 1920s the NWT became far more accessible to the outside world. Air travel is now both routine and safe in the Territories. To reach many communities, air routes have become the "real" highways for the North. The NWT is served by several airlines from major cities in Canada to all large communities in the Territories. Once in the NWT, there are approximately 40 scheduled and chartered services between cities and remote camps.

The NWT has conventional highways too, which connect the majority of the large communities, including **Yellowknife ❶**, **Hay River**, **Fort Smith**, **Inuvik** and **Tuktoyaktuk**, with the outside world. These highways are all hardpacked gravel, rather than paved, so some adjustment to your driving style may consequently be necessary.

Owing to a distinct lack of vehicular traffic, travel in the territories can indeed be a relaxing experience and a great relief to those more accustomed to aggressive city driving. Drivers are more likely to have their trip interrupted by wildlife, such as moose or caribou wandering out across the road, than by meeting another vehicle. In fact, the **Dempster Highway** does place restrictions on travel during fall and spring while vast herds of caribou numbering in the thousands make their annual migration.

As far as accommodations go, there are relatively modern hotels in most major centers such as Inuvik or Yellowknife. In general, though, the North does not often provide ordinary luxuries; its camps and hotels provide the opportunity to view the last genuine wilderness in the world.

The Western Arctic

In all the territory west of **Great Slave** and **Great Bear Lake** up towards Inuvik – the Western Arctic – there

Map, page 328

The 40-km (25-mile) Ingraham Trail winds east from Yellowknife along a string of canoeing and fishing lakes. Spot bald eagles, ospreys and green jays en route.

BELOW: an Arctic treat, the glorious midnight sun.

Map, page 328

TIP

Yellowknife has one of the NWT's few golf courses. However, the only course with grass greens rather than sand is at Hay River.

BELOW: Inuit sculpture, Yellowknife.
RIGHT: Inuit in caribou fur with bear-skin trousers.

are numerous equipment stores in the major communities. Below the tree line, canoe trips take place from late May to mid-September. In the tundra area most trips take place from mid-June to mid-August. In recent years, cross-country skiing trips have been set up during the spring so that tourists can witness the spectacular migration of caribou herds in style. Participants are flown into a base camp, and from there they glide onto frozen lakes and rivers to observe the caribou migration.

Domain of the bison

In the southern region of NWT there are two spectacular national parks. **Wood Buffalo National Park ❷** is located on either side of the Alberta–NWT border and was established in 1922 to preserve the bison. This objective has been a success and one can now attend a "Bison Creep" to view these creatures. The National Park covers a remarkable landscape of forests, meadows, sinkholes and an unusual salt plain.

The second national park, further to the west, is located on the Yukon border. **Nahanni National Park ❸**, which is a UNESCO World Heritage Site, is in the Deh Cho Region, also known as the Nahanni-Ram, in the vast and remote southwest corner of the Northwest Territories. The region was once home to a mysterious band of natives called Nahaa or Nahannis. Legends of wild mountain men, a white queen, evil spirits, lost maps, lost gold and headless men are myths that prevail to this day.

Bird enthusiasts are one group that hasn't been deterred from venturing into the Deh Cho. Approximately 280 species of birds have been recorded here, including the white pelican, peregrine falcon, sandhill crane and the threatened trumpeter swan. Visitors can also see impressive river gorges, underground caves and bubbling hot springs. Those who enjoy water travel can journey down the meandering South Nahanni River until they arrive at **Virginia Falls**, which plunge 90 meters (300 ft), almost twice that of Niagara Falls. Access to the park by road or air is from **Fort Simpson ❹**.

Culture in Yellowknife

If traveling to Yellowknife, a stop at the newly established **Yellowknife Cultural Center,** where drama and music are regularly performed, is recommended. Also in Yellowknife, overlooking Frame Lake, is the **Prince of Wales Northern Heritage Center** (open Jun–Aug: daily; Sep–May: closed Mon; free), which houses excellent histories and artifacts of the Inuit, Dene and Métis Indian tribes.

A unique experience

The Northwest Territories is a land different from anywhere else on the globe because so much of it is completely untouched by civilization. Here, the traveler cannot but realise how minuscule a role humankind has played in the history of this region. The impressive mountains, the barren grounds, the stunted forests, the over-arching skies, the thousands of freshwater lakes and rivers of this vast land combine to create a unique and humbling experience.

Map, page 328

NUNAVUT: THE NEWEST TERRITORY

Nunavut – Canada's most recently established territory and home to large Inuit communities – is a vast terrain of barren ground, plateaus and mountains, and a hauntingly beautiful retreat

The Eastern Arctic, including much of the Archipelago and the terrain east of Great Slave Lake, remained a hidden world until the age of the airplane. It became the new territory of Nunavut – which means "our land" in Inuktitut – on April 1 1999, when the Northwest Territories were split into two. Approximately 85 percent of Nunavut's population is Inuit and it had been vying for independence since 1973, fueled by the desire for a self-governed territory with firm control over its own future. The Nunavut Land Claim Settlement, proclaimed in July 1993, is now regarded as a global benchmark in aboriginal matters and includes title to nearly 356,000 sq. km (138,000 sq. miles), mineral rights, a share of federal royalties on oil, gas and mineral development on Crown lands, and the right of first refusal on sport and commercial development of Nunavut's renewal resources.

The Great Outdoors

Canada's newest territory is also its largest, occupying about 20 percent of the country's land mass, almost entirely above the treeline and spread across three time zones. Nunavut extends from the eastern shores of Baffin and Ellesmere Islands, west to the plateaus and cliffs of the Arctic Coast on the Coronation Gulf, and north to the High Arctic Islands and the North Pole. It is home to various outpost settlements and 26 communities, the largest of which is the capital, Iqaluit, with a population of around 4,500 citizens.

BELOW: mask, Cape Dorset culture.

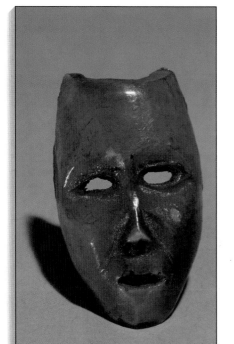

Although neither cheap nor easily accessible, the delights of Nunavut's great outdoors still draw those who can afford the time and money to visit. As there are virtually no roads in Nunavut, other than a 21-km (13-mile) stretch between Arctic Bay and Nanisivik, travel by air, snowmobile or dog sled are the only options. The challenging weather conditions also mean frequent delays and changed itineraries. That said, the rewards are infinite.

Most tourists come during the two-to-three-month summer, with its 24 hours of sunshine, when temperatures average 12°C (54°F). Nonetheless, some seasoned adventurers brave the lows of the Arctic winter, when the mercury plummets to –46°C (–51°F), to accompany a traditional Inuit seal hunt or view the spectacular Northern Lights under winter's dark skies.

Irrefutably, Nunavut's main draw is the outdoors. Outfitters arrange packages from building igloos to polar-bear watching, dogsledding and encounters with narwhals (one-tusked whales at one time believed to be cousins to the mythical unicorn). The skin and blubber form an Inuit delicacy called *maqtaak* – traditionally eaten raw and best when still warm from the whale. Early English explorers were encouraged to eat it, as this unappetizing source of essential vitamins helped to keep scurvy at bay.

Baffin Island

Baffin Island is home to roughly a quarter of Canada's Inuit population and some of the oldest northern communities in the world. **Cape Dorset ❺**, on the southwest coast, is the home of modern Inuit art, the understated simplicity of which expresses the harmonic Inuit vision of Arctic life. Inuit art has been attracting international attention since it was first developed commercially in the 1950s, and it continues to do so today. Examples are on display and for sale at the **West Baffin Eskimo Co-op** (tel: 867/897-8997). For action-lovers, Cape Dorset also offers hiking and cross-country skiing tours. **Iqaluit ❻** (formerly known as Frobisher Bay), on the southeast coast, is the capital of Nunavut and another Baffin Island community rich in Inuit heritage. Here, the Inuit have created extensive walking trails that pass by ancient cairns, built ages ago to act as landmarks. Some trails overlook cliffs from which ocean and harp seals and even the occasional whale can be seen.

The glaciers on Baffin Island are another source of inspiration. The **Penney Ice Cap** is 5,700 sq. km (2,200 sq. miles) of ice and snow. To view this glacier high up in the mountains of **Auyuittuq National Park Reserve** is to revisit the Ice Age. Sections of Baffin Island's east coast, where there are fjords and spectacular cliffs that rise to a height of 2,100m (7,000 ft), higher than the walls of the Grand Canyon, also offer a taste of the Ice Age. Tours by snowmobile or dog sled to the floe-edge – where landfast ice meets the open sea and plankton attract huge schools of shrimp and fish, followed by the seals and whales that feed on them – offer a fabulous way to experience Baffin Island's wildlife, especially during the spring migration.

Summer is spectacular on the Arctic coast, when drifts of minute tundra flowers carpet the ground. Visitors come to photograph musk oxen or caribou, fish for arctic char or paddle a canoe in the mystical light of a summer evening. The lure of abundant wildlife and an historic Inuit settlement make Bathurst Inlet a magnet for naturalists, birdwatchers, photographers and botanists alike.

Baker Lake

Situated on the shores of **Baker Lake** (its Inuit name – *Qamani'tuaq* – means "huge widening of the river") is the small community of Baker Lake, which lies at the heart of the Keewatin barrenlands and is the geographical center of Canada. This is another popular base for delving into Arctic history and Inuit culture. Baker Lake is known for its soapstone carvings, fabric wall-hangings and exquisite prints. Northeast of here is the Thelon River, first explored by Europeans in 1893, when two brothers, James and Joseph Tyrell, descended the Thelon on behalf of the Geological Survey of Canada. The area has long been occupied by Inuit, whose art and heritage is well documented in the **Inuit Heritage Centre** (Tel: 867/793-2598) in Baker Lane.

BELOW: glaciers on Baffin Island.
OVERLEAF: Canada goose

Travel Tips

New Insight Maps

Maps in Insight Guides are tailored to complement the text. But when you're on the road you sometimes need the big picture that only a large-scale map can provide. This new range of durable Insight Fleximaps has been designed to meet just that need.

Detailed, clear cartography
makes the comprehensive route and city maps easy to follow, highlights all the major tourist sites and provides valuable motoring information plus a full index.

Informative and easy to use
with additional text and photographs covering a destination's top 10 essential sites, plus useful addresses, facts about the destination and handy tips on getting around.

Laminated finish
allows you to mark your route on the map using a non-permanent marker pen, and wipe it off. It makes the maps more durable and easier to fold than traditional maps.

The first titles
cover many popular destinations. They include Algarve, Amsterdam, Bangkok, California, Cyprus, Dominican Republic, Florence, Hong Kong, Ireland, London, Mallorca, Paris, Prague, Rome, San Francisco, Sydney, Thailand, Tuscany, USA Southwest, Venice, and Vienna.

☀ INSIGHT GUIDES
The world's largest collection of visual travel guides

CONTENTS

Getting Acquainted

The Place

Area 9,970,600 sq. km (3,850,000 sq. miles).
Population 30,330,000. (1997, currently increasing by just over 1 percent annually).
Capital Ottawa
Largest City Toronto (population 4,100,000 – Greater Toronto Area)
Language (self-reported mother tongue): English (61 percent), French (24 percent), Aboriginal languages 1 percent, Other 14 percent.
Religion Roman Catholic (46 percent), Protestant (35 percent).
Weights & Measures Officially metric, but former imperial system is often used informally.
Currency Canadian dollar (approximately $US1.5; £1=Can$2.5).
International Dialing Code 1. (Ottawa + 613, Toronto + 416, Montréal + 514, Vancouver + 604.) For further practical information *see* page 337–339.

Climate

It is difficult to generalize about the Canadian climate. Most visitors come during the summer, when temperatures average around 24°C (75°F). During July and August, however, the mercury can climb into the 90s on the prairies and in southern Ontario. In northern Canada, summer temperatures stay at 15°C (65°F) during the day, but can drop close to freezing at night. Don't forget to pack some protection against mosquitoes and other biting insects, especially if you are traveling in the early summer.

Time Zones

Canada straddles six time zones. Daylight savings last from the final Sunday in April to the final Sunday in October but are not observed in Saskatchewan.

● **Pacific Standard Time**
(8 hours behind GMT) the Yukon, BC. (Alaska Time is one hour behind the Yukon).
● **Mountain Standard Time**
(7 hours behind GMT) Alberta, western NWT.
● **Central Standard Time**
(6 hours behind GMT)
Saskatchewan, Manitoba, central NWT, western Nunavut.
● **Eastern Standard Time**
(5 hours behind GMT) Ontario, Québec, eastern NWT, eastern Nunavut.
● **Atlantic Standard Time**
(4 hours behind GMT) New Brunswick, PEI, Nova Scotia, most of Labrador.
● **Newfoundland Standard Time**
3½ hours behind GMT (half an hour ahead of Atlantic Standard Time); Newfoundland (including part of Labrador).

Canadian winters have been slightly exaggerated in popular lore. Winter temperatures average between –5°C and 10°C (10°F and 25°F) from the Maritimes through southern Ontario. It gets colder and windier from northern Québec through the Rockies, with temperatures ranging from –18°C to –5°C (0°F to 10°F). In the Yukon, Northwest Territories and Nunavut the mercury can drop to as low as –40°C (–40°F). On the balmy southern coast of British Columbia (BC), however, warm Pacific currents generally keep the temperature above freezing during the winter.

The snowfall is consistently heavy throughout Canada, with the exception of parts of southern BC. Skiers take to the slopes and trails by late November, and the snow lasts generally until April or even May in the mountains.

Economy

Traditionally, Canada's economic strength lies in its natural resources. Forestry accounts for about 1 percent of Canadian employment, newsprint and lumber being the premier products. Minerals and energy are important exports, as Canada is a leading producer of uranium, potash, asbestos, nickel, silver and gold, coal, oil and gas, and hydro-electricity. Farming, which remains important throughout Canada, is a way of life on the eastern prairies. While commercial fishing has suffered a prolonged slump, it continues to exert a profound influence on the coasts.

The manufacturing base, though less renowned, is just as important. Transportation equipment is the largest industry, followed by food processing. Next come the paper and allied products industries, and the chemical and chemical products industries. Electronic and computer companies now also have a particularly strong presence.

Banking, insurance, and real estate are thriving business sectors and they have already made significant inroads into US markets. Tourism makes up more than 5 percent of the GNP, and employs one Canadian in 10.

With regard to visitors and taxation, the 7 percent "goods and services tax" (GST), or a portion of the 15 percent harmonized sales tax (HST) in NS, NF and NB is refundable on accommodation and items purchased for export. Although you can only start the reclaim process once you are back in your home country, you should obtain forms from Canada Customs before leaving the country. With the exception of Alberta and the Territories, those provinces which do not participate in the HST levy their own sales taxes at rates ranging from 7 to 12 percent.

Government

As a constitutional monarchy, the Queen of England is the titular head of government, acting through her appointed Governor General in Canada. However, both the Queen and Governor General are figureheads, as actual power rests with the Prime Minister in Ottawa, Canada's capital.

The Canadian Parliament is a bicameral legislature, with a 301-member elected House of Commons, and a 104-member appointed Senate. The Senate has hardly any power, beyond delay, and has very little more than a counseling function.

The national elections of 1997 retained the Liberal Party with Jean Chrétien as Prime Minister. The election gave the Liberals a small overall majority, with the opposition provided by the Reform Party led by Preston Manning, with smaller representation by the Bloc Québecois, the New Democratic Party and the Progressive Conservative Parties.

Canada is a federal state, with shared powers between the national and provincial governments. The federal government in Ottawa oversees national defense, trade and foreign affairs, banking, commerce, criminal law, fisheries, etc. The national and provincial governments concurrently assume responsibility for unemployment insurance and agriculture.

Provincial governments are also parliamentary, although their legislatures have no upper house. With jurisdiction over health, education, natural resources and highways, the provinces enjoy considerable power – certainly more power than a US state. As a result, laws in the country differ greatly from province to province – witness the various sales tax rates. Canada is a diverse country in which provincial governments have emerged as the principal defenders of regional interests.

The Yukon and Northwest Territories with their vast areas and comparatively small populations enjoy somewhat less autonomy than the provinces. On April 1, 1999, Northwest Territories were divided and the eastern portion became a new territory – and the largest one in Canada – known as Nunavut.

The Provinces

- **ALBERTA:** (*abbreviated* Alta)
  Capital: Edmonton
  Size: 661,190 sq. km
  (255,310 sq. miles)
  Area Code: Calgary and Southern Alberta 403; Edmonton and Northern Alberta 780
  Postal Address: AB
- **BRITISH COLUMBIA:** (BC)
  Capital: Victoria
  Size: 947,800 sq. km
  (365,980 sq. miles)
  Area Code: 604 for Vancouver and southwestern section/250 for remainder, including Vancouver Island.
- **MANITOBA:** (Man)
  Capital: Winnipeg
  Size: 649,950 sq. km
  (250,970 sq. miles)
  Area Code: 204 unless otherwise stated
  Postal Address: MB
- **NEW BRUNSWICK:** (NB)
  Capital: Fredericton
  Size: 73,440 sq. km
  (28,360 sq. miles)
  Area Code: 506 unless otherwise stated

- **NEWFOUNDLAND AND LABRADOR:** (Nfld)
  Capital: St. John's
  Size: 405,720 sq. km
  (156,600 sq. miles)
  Area Code: 709 unless otherwise stated
  Postal Address: NF
- **NORTHWEST TERRITORIES:** (NT)
  Capital: Yellowknife
  Size: 1,526,320 sq. km
  (589,410 sq. miles)
- **NUNAVUT:**
  Capital: Iqaluit
  Size: 1,900,000 sq. km
  (733,600 sq. miles)
  Area Code: 867
  Postal Address: NT
- **NOVA SCOTIA:** (NS)
  Capital: Halifax
  Size: 55,490 sq. km
  (21,430 sq. miles)
  Area Code: 902 unless otherwise stated
- **ONTARIO:** (Ont)
  Capital: Ottawa
  Size: 1,068,580 sq. km
  (412,610 sq. miles)
  Area Code: Toronto 416; Ottawa 613
  Postal Address: ON

- **PRINCE EDWARD ISLAND:** (PEI)
  Capital: Charlottetown
  Size: 5,660 sq. km
  (2,190 sq. miles)
  Area Code: 902 with Nova Scotia
  Postal Address: PE
- **QUÉBEC:** (PQ)
  Capital: Québec City
  Size: 1,540,680 sq. km
  (594,900 sq. miles)
  Area Code: Montréal 514; Québec City and Eastern; Québec 418; Southern Québec 450; Rest of Québec 819
  Postal Address: PQ
- **SASKATCHEWAN:** (Sask)
  Capital: Regina
  Size: 652,330 sq. km
  (251,880 sq. miles)
  Area Code: 306
  Postal Address: SK
- **THE YUKON:**
  Capital: Whitehorse
  Size: 483,450 sq. km
  (186,680 sq. miles)
  Area Code: 867 with the Northwest Territories and Nunavut
  Postal Address: YK

Planning the Trip

What to Wear

Visitors to urban and resort areas from Europe or the US should be perfectly comfortable in the clothes they wear at home under similar circumstances. Visitors planning a canoeing or hiking trip should bring suitable layers of clothing, including warm and waterproof garments, as weather conditions change rapidly.

In winter, wind chill can reduce ambient temperatures, leading to frostbite. Tourists planning to ski, hike, or take part in any other outdoor activity, should wear very warm clothing and be prepared to cover exposed skin. Canadians wear both synthetic and non-synthetic clothing in layers to retain heat.

Visas and Passports

Crossing the Canada–US border is relatively simple. American citizens or permanent residents do not need passports or visas, but may be asked for identification. Citizens of other countries need a valid passport; no visas are required of the citizens of most British Commonwealth or European Union countries. Prospective visitors who are in any doubt about which documents they will need, should check with their travel agent or the nearest Canadian consulate. Visitors may be asked to produce return tickets and possibly evidence that they have the funds to support themselves while in Canada.

Non-Canadian visitors going from Canada to the US, however briefly, will require a visa or a simpler "visa waiver." Check this with a travel

Public Holidays

Each province has holidays in addition to the following national holidays:

- **January 1** New Year's Day
- **Movable Feasts:**
  Good Friday
  Monday preceding May 25
  (Victoria Day, the Queen's birthday)
- **July 1** Canada Day
- **First Monday in September** Labor Day
- **Second Monday in October** Thanksgiving Day
- **December 25** Christmas Day
- **December 26** Boxing Day (except Québec)

agent or the nearest US consulate before leaving home.

Customs

Canada's customs requirements for vacation visitors are fairly simple. Personal effects for use during the stay may be brought into the country. There is no problem with bringing rented cars from the US, but drivers should carry the contract in the car (this is also important if stopped by police for any reason).

You may bring in a hunting rifle or shotgun (with 200 rounds of ammunition), but handguns or automatic weapons are prohibited. Limits on duty-free tobacco, alcohol and personal gifts are like those in other countries. For more details on customs regulations and what you can bring to Canada, write to:
Revenue Canada,
Customs and Excise,
191 Laurier Avenue West,
Ottawa, ON K1A OL5.
Tel: 613/954-7129.

Pets require a veterinary's certificate of good health and vaccinations, etc. Plant imports should be accompanied by a certificate acceptable to Agriculture Canada. For further information, contact Agriculture Canada, Ottawa ON KIA OC6. Tel 613/995-7900.

Money Matters

The Canadian and US dollars have a different rate of exchange. All dollar prices quoted in this book are in Canadian dollars.

There is no limit to the amount of money visitors may bring to, or exchange in, Canada. To get the best rate, exchange your money before leaving home. Canadian banks and foreign exchange bureaux will convert funds for a fee. US funds are readily accepted by many department stores and hotels, etc., but may not offer the most advantageous rate.

CREDIT CARDS AND TRAVELER'S CHECKS

Major credit cards are widely accepted in Canada. Interac, Cirrus, Plus and similar international bank cards are useful because banks use wholesale exchange rates and so reduce costs. Car rental companies prefer credit cards to cash.

Traveler's checks offer a safe way to carry funds. Just countersign, show proper identification and they will be accepted as cash. Buying checks denominated in Canadian funds saves the expense of exchanging upon arrival. American Express, Thomas Cook and Visa traveler's checks are widely accepted.

Getting There

BY AIR

Many people choose to fly into Canada, then continue their trip by bus, train, rented car or plane. Most major cities have direct air connections with US cities. Many international airlines connect Toronto, Montréal and Vancouver with all parts of North and South America, Europe and Asia. There are more limited services between Europe and Edmonton, Calgary, Halifax and St John's Newfoundland. Air Canada and Canadian Airlines International connect with extensive feeder routes operated by

Airline Companies

- **Air Canada**
UK: London. Tel: 0990-247226
US: toll free 1-800/361-6340
- **Canadian Airlines International**
UK: London. Tel: 020 8577 7722
Other areas. Tel: 0345-616767
US: toll free 1-800/665-1177

subsidiaries and associated companies within the country.

Pilots of private planes are required to file a trans-border flight plan prior to departure and to land at a Customs port of entry. Full aircraft and personal documentation is required.

BY SEA

There are car ferry services between Maine and Nova Scotia, and between Washington State and British Columbia. A number of cruise lines sailing from the US call at ports on the Atlantic and Pacific coasts and there are also a few cruises in Arctic waters. Many US yachtsmen sail to favorite Canadian cruising grounds on the Pacific and Atlantic coasts and within the Great Lakes, but in summer dock space can be tight. US and other foreign yachts are required to clear Canadian Customs at a designated port of entry.

BY ROAD

From the US, visiting Canada by car is simply a matter of driving to the border, then passing through customs and immigration.

The major bus company with routes into Western and Central Canada is Greyhound (US) and its associated companies. Some routes end at a city just over the border, where you can subsequently transfer to a Canadian carrier, but there are also special packages from certain US cities (including Boston, New York, Chicago and San Francisco) to Vancouver, Winnipeg, Toronto, Montréal, and other destinations in Canada. Greyhound offers a 7-day, 15-day, 30-day and 60-day International Canada Travel Pass, which can be used the country. Greyhound Lines of Canada have packages for use solely in Canada. Voyageur Colonial Lines, which runs buses in Ontario and Québec, also offers package discounts. These options are often honored by regional and provincial bus lines. For further details, contact Greyhound Canada on 1-800/661-8787 or Voyageur on 416/393-7911.

BY RAIL

Amtrak offers two direct passenger train routes into Canada: Seattle to Vancouver, Washington, and New York to Montréal. VIA Rail has similar services from New York to Toronto via Niagara Falls and from Chicago to Sarnia, London and Toronto. VIA Rail offers group, family, and senior citizen's discounts, as well as flat-rate "Canrail" passes. Both first class and coach accommodations are available, each with dining cars.

For further information, telephone the nearest train station or contact:
VIA Rail,
2 Place Ville Marie,
Montréal,
PQ H3C 3N3,
Tel: 1-800-835-3037.
Or you can call the following toll-free numbers:
Ontario 1-800/361-1235;
Quebec 1-800/361-5390;
Western Canada 1-800/561-8630.
To call **Amtrak** in the US dial 1-800/903-8350; in Canada dial 1-800/872-7245; or visit their website: www.amtrack.com

UK Tour Operators

There are many Canadian tour packages offered by UK tour operators, but here is a sample. For further details, look in *Canadian Travel Planner*, which can be obtained by calling the Visit Canada Centre at 0891-715000 (calls cost 50 pence at all times).

For tours to **Canada's North**:
Arctic Experience/Discover the World
29 Nork Way,
Banstead,
Surrey SM7 1PB.
Tel: 01737-218800
www.arctic-discover.co.uk
For tours to **BC and Alberta** for 18 to 30 year olds:
Contiki Holidays,
Wells House,
15 Elmfield Road,
Bromley,
Kent BR1 1LS.
Tel: 020 8290 6422
www.contiki-tours.com
Ski trips to Quebec, Ontario, Manitoba, Alberta, British Columbia and the Yukon are the focus of:
Frontier Ski/Frontier Adventures,
6 Sydenham Avenue,
London SE26 6UH.
Tel: 020 87768709
www.frontier-ski.co.uk
Travelpack
Clarendon House,
Clarendon Road,
Eccles, Manchester M30 9TR.
Tel: 0990-747101
Offers escorted tours, coach tours, rail tours, self-drive itineraries, adventure packages and city packages across the country.
Eco-tours to Newfoundland, New Brunswick Quebec, Manitoba, British Columbia, the Yukon, Northwest Territories and Nova Scotia are offered by:
Animal Watch
Granville House,
London Road,
Sevenoaks,
Kent TN13 1DL.
Tel: 01732-741612
www.animalwatch.co.uk
Committed **anglers** may consider **Anglers World Holidays**,
46 Knifesmithgate,
Chesterfield,
Derbyshire S40 1RQ.
Tel: 01246-221717
Their website at: www.anglers-world.co.uk gives further information.

Practical Tips

Emergencies

Visitors are urged to obtain **health insurance** before leaving their own country. Anyone using prescription medicine should bring an adequate supply with them, as well as a copy of the prescription in case it needs to be renewed. Travelers requiring medical attention needn't worry – Canadian hospitals are known for their high medical standards.

In an emergency requiring the **police**, an **ambulance** or **firemen,** immediate action can be had in Canada's major cities by dialing **911.** Emergency telephone numbers are listed in the front of all local telephone directories. If caught in a legal bind, foreign visitors can contact their consulates, a partial listing of which is shown in the Consulates and Embassies section (see page 343).

Business Hours

Standard business hours for stores are 10am–6pm, or 9pm in many large cities. Stores in many parts of the country are open for more limited hours on Sunday. Drug and convenience stores generally close at 11pm but may nevertheless still operate for 24 hours. Banking hours vary greatly. The majority of banks now open long hours, which may include Saturdays, and, in some instances, Sundays.

Banks, schools, government offices, beer and liquor stores all close on national holidays. Hotels, restaurants and most retail outlets stay open. See the section on Festivals (see pages 382–385) for further information on and listings of provincial holidays and festivals.

Media

NEWSPAPERS AND MAGAZINES

The recently launched *National Post* (an expanded version of the former *Financial Post)* and the national edition of *The Globe and Mail* are distributed throughout Canada. *La Presse* is the ranking Québec daily. Newsstands sell major American, British and French newspapers.

Canada's largest circulation news magazine, *Maclean's,* is published weekly. The monthly *Saturday Night* is popular among pro-Canada intellectuals. Such international magazines as *The Economist, Time* and *Newsweek* are widely available.

RADIO AND TELEVISION

The Canadian Broadcasting Company (CBC), a Crown Corporation, operates two nationwide networks (French and English), while CTV broadcasts a third. Other regional and provincial networks, along with independents and US broadcasting, account for the remainder.

Most of Canada has access to US network telecasts, and this number has been growing yearly with the advent of cable. Cable networks enable viewers to see programs produced in all parts of Canada and the US, along with a sampling of programs from Great Britain, Australia, France and other countries. The majority of large cities originate at least one multilingual, or ethnic, channel.

Canadian-based broadcasts feature excellent news coverage and top-notch sports programs, documentaries and performing arts. Many entertainment viewers prefer American fare.

CBC operates the sole national radio network, both AM and FM, in English and French. There are hundreds of private stations that fill the airwaves with news and music, from classical, jazz and nostalgic to pop and funk.

Telecoms

The telephone system in Canada is similar to that in the US. Pay phones cost 25 cents. For collect or other operator-assisted calls, dial "0" then the number you wish to reach. Dial "1" for long-distance calls charged to the originating phone. Any exchanges beginning 800 or 888 indicate toll-free numbers; to get out of the local exchange, you simply dial a "1" first.

The first pages in public phone books explain everything you need to know, including emergency numbers, North American area codes and long-distance country codes. Canada is in the lead in use of e-mail and the Internet in both official languages.

Postal Services

Stamps may be purchased at post offices (open daily during business hours) or from many convenience and drug stores.

Canada Post and a number of international courier companies provide express services across the country and to foreign destinations. Canada Post, along with private establishments, can also send faxes from coast-to-coast or overseas.

Tourist Offices

One of the smartest things you can do upon arrival in Canada is to go to the nearest tourist information center. Each city has at least one staffed with knowledgeable, friendly personnel. Aside from being able to answer questions, they distribute travel brochures and maps on areas of interest to you. Each province and territory also has a toll-free number for tourism information (see the following list). For general information on traveling in Canada, you can contact:

Canadian Tourism Commission, by visiting their website at www.canadatourism.com

Tel: 613/946-1000. Canadian consulates in foreign countries also provide some travel information. *See* the Consulates and Embassies section (pages 343) for further details. Some provinces maintain tourism offices in foreign cities.

ALBERTA

The Alberta Tourism distributes *Accommodation and Visitors' Guide* in Alberta, updated annually, which lists approved hotels, motels, campgrounds and resorts. For this, and more specific information, contact:
Travel Alberta, Box 2400, Edmonton, AB T5J 2Z4. Tel 403/4321 or 1-800-/661-8888 toll-free in North America.
Calgary Convention and Visitor Bureau, 237-8th Avenue SE, Calgary, AB T2G 0K8. Tel: 403/263-8510 or 1-800/661-1678 toll free in North America. For comprehensive information about the provincial capital, contact:
Edmonton Tourism, 9797 Jasper Avenue, Suite 104, Edmonton, AB T5J 1N9. Tel: 780/426-4715 or call the toll-free number 1-800/463-4667 in North America.

BRITISH COLUMBIA

For complete information about traveling in British Columbia, call or write to:
Tourism British Columbia, Box 9830, Station Provincial Government, 3rd Floor, 1117 Wharf Street, Victoria, BC V8W 9W5. Tel: 250/387-1642 or toll-free 1-800/663-6000 in North America (website: www.travel.bc.ca).
   Most communities operate Travel InfoCenters at least during the tourism season. In the major cities they are:
Tourism Vancouver, Plaza Level, 200 Burrard Street, Vancouver BC V6L 3L6. Tel: 604/683-2000 or 1-800/926-8815 toll-free in North America.

Victoria Convention and Visitors Bureau, 812 Wharf Street, Victoria, BC V8W 1T3. Tel: 250/382-2127.

MANITOBA

The provincial government distributes the free *Manitoba Vacation Planner*, which will direct you to accommodation and campgrounds, and contains a fishing and hunting guide. The planners are available from any provincial information center, or from:
Travel Manitoba, 155 Carlton Street, Winnipeg, MB R3C 3H8. Tel 204/945-3777 or toll-free 1-800/665-0040 in North America. www.gov.mb.ca/Travel-Manitoba

NEW BRUNSWICK

For road maps, assistance in choosing accommodations, and suggestions for itineraries in New Brunswick, contact:
Tourism New Brunswick, Box 12345, Woodstock, NB, E7M 5C3. Tel: 506/452-9500 or 1-800/561-0123 toll-free in North America. www.tourismnbcanada.com

NEWFOUNDLAND AND LABRADOR

For complete information about traveling in Newfoundland, write to:
Newfoundland and Labrador Tourism Marketing, Box 8730, St. John's, NF, A1B 4K2. Tel: 709/729-2830 or toll-free 1-800/563-6353 in North America. www.gov.nf.ca/tourism

NORTHWEST TERRITORIES

This territory distributes its yearly *Explorers' Guide*, a listing of hotels, lodges, restaurants and activities. This, and more information, is available from:

NWT Arctic Tourism, Box 610, Yellowknife, NT X1A 2N5. Tel: 867/873-7200 or toll-free 1-800/661-0788.

NOVA SCOTIA

For information about Nova Scotia contact the
Department of Tourism, Box 130, Halifax, NS, B3J 2M7. Tel: 902/425-5781 or toll-free within North America: 1-800-565-0000. www.explore.gov.ns.ca

NUNAVUT

Canada's newest territory produces its own *Arctic Traveler* and further information is available from:
Nunavut Tourism, Box 1450, Iqaluit, NT X0A 0H0. Tel: 867/979-6551 or toll-free 1-800/491-7910. www.nunatour.nt.ca

ONTARIO

It takes a comprehensive travel bureau to describe and explain all that the province has to offer, but **Travel Ontario** fits the bill. It distributes booklets and brochures which explain nearly every facet of traveling the province. Among these are:
● The road map.
● The *Ontario Discovery Guide*, which covers the 12 travel regions of Ontario, with information on what to do and see, including a section on adventure for outdoors enthusiasts, and where to stay, from roofed accommodation to camping.
● *Auto Tours* – scenic routes for optimal viewing of Ontario's fall colors.
● *Ontario Snow Country*, a guide to all the winter activities and community celebrations.
● Seasonal *Events* calendars, which list the what, where and when of special events around the province.
   To contact Travel Ontario, call toll-free from Canada or the continental

US 1-800/668-2746; and in Toronto 416/314-0944 (English) or 314-0956 (French). Write to Travel Ontario, Queen's Park, Toronto, ON M7A 2R9. Travel Ontario also operates a number of Travel Information Centres, open all the year round. Most have currency exchanges. The five listed are all at border points. There are others at St Catharines, Fort Erie, Fort Frances, Sarnia and Barrie.
● Cornwall, 903 Brookdale Ave, at the Seaway International Bridge.
● Niagara Falls, 5355 Stanley Ave, Hwy 420, west from Rainbow Bridge.
● Sault Ste Marie, 261 Queen St W. At the International Bridge.
● Windsor, 1235 Huron Church Rd, east of the Ambassador Bridge.
● 110 Park St. East at the Windsor/Detroit Tunnel.
Algoma Kinniwabi Travel Association, 485 Queen St E, Ste 204, Sault Ste Marie, ON P6A 1Z9. Tel: 705/254-4293 or toll-free 1-800/263-2546.
Almaguin Nipissing Travel Association, 1375 Seymour St, Box 351, North Bay, ON P1B 8H5. Tel: 705/474-6634 or toll-free 1-800/387-0516.
Cochrane Témiskaming Travel Association, PO Box 920, 76 McIntyre Rd, Schumacher, ON P0N 1G0. Tel: 705/360-1989 or toll-free 1-800/461-3766.
Festival Country Travel Associations, 180 Greenwich St, Brantford, ON N3S 2X6 or toll-free 1-800/267-3399.
Georgian Triangle Tourist Association, 601 First St, Collingwood, ON L9Y 4L2. Tel: 705/445-7722 or toll-free 1-800/461-1300.
Muskoka Tourism Association, Hwy 11, Kilworthy ON P0P 1G0. Tel: 1-800/267-9700.
Niagara Resorts and Tourist Association, 5433 Victoria Avenue, Niagara Falls, ON L2G 3L1. Tel: 800/563-2557.
Niagara Parks Commission, Queen Victoria Parkway, Box 150, Niagara Falls, ON L2E 6T2. Tel: 905/356-2241.

North of Superior Tourism Association, 1119 Victoria Ave E., Thunder Bay, ON P7C 1B7. Tel: 807/626-9420 or toll-free 800/265-3951.
Ontario East Travel Association, RR1, Reynold Rd & 1000 Islands Parkway, Lansdowne, ON K0E 1L0. Tel: 613/659-4300 or toll-free 1-800/567-3278.
Ontario's Sunset Country Travel Association, 102 Main St, 2nd Floor, Box 647T, Kenora, ON P9N 3X6. Tel: 807/468-5853, or toll-free 1-800/665-7567.
Ottawa Tourism and Convention Authority, 130 Albert St, Ste 1800, Ottawa, ON K1P 5G4. Tel: 800/363-4464.
Rainbow Country Travel Association, 2726 Whippoorwill Avenue, Sudbury, ON P3G 1E9. Tel: 705/522-0104 or toll-free 1-800/465-6655.
Southwestern Ontario Travel Association, 4023 Meadowbrook Dr, London, ON N6L 1E7. Tel: 519/652-1391 or toll-free 1-800/661-6804.
Kingston Tourist Information Office, 209 Ontario St, Kingston, ON K7L 2Z1. Tel: 613/548-4415 or toll-free 1-888/855-4555.
Kitchener and Waterloo Kitchener and Waterloo Visitor & Convention Bureau, 2848 King St E, Kitchener, ON N2A 1A5. Tel: 519/748-0800 or toll-free 1-800/265-6959.
Ottawa Tourism and Convention Authority, 130 Albert St, Ste 1800, Ottawa, ON K1P 5G4. Tel: 613/237-5150 or toll-free 1-800/363-4465.
Toronto Tourism, 207 Queen's Quay, Suite 590, Box 126, Toronto, ON M5J 1A7. Tel: 203-2500 or toll-free 1-800/363-1990 from anywhere in North America.
The Metropolitan Toronto Reference Library, aside from standing as a architectural masterpiece, is an impressive storehouse of information on Toronto and Ontario history. It can be found at 789 Yonge St, just north of Bloor.

Windsor Convention and Visitors Bureau, 333 Riverside Dr. W, Suite 103, Windsor, ON N9A 5K4. Tel: 519/255-6530 or toll-free 1-800/265-3633.

PRINCE EDWARD ISLAND

The Visitor Information Centres at Confederation Bridge and Wood Islands ferry terminal are extremely helpful. For advance information on what's on offer on the island, you can write to:
Tourism PEI, Box 940, Charlottetown, PE C1A 7M5. Tel: 902/629-2380 or toll-free 1-800/463-4734 in North America. www.peiplay.com

QUÉBEC

Québec is divided into 19 regional Tourist Associations, each of which is eager to offer information and tours to visitors to the region. Contact:
Tourisme Québec, Box 979, Montréal, Québec, H3C 2W3. Tel: 514/873-2015 or toll-free 1-800/363-7777. Tourisme Québec also maintains offices in both Montréal and Québec City:
Infotouriste Centre, 1001 rue du Square-Dorchester, Montréal. Tel: 514/873-2015 or 1-800/363-7777.
Greater Québec Area Tourism and Convention Bureau, 835 Avenue Wilfrid-Laurier, Québec City, QC G1R 2L3. Tel: 418/649-2608. www.tourisme.gouv.qc.ca

SASKATCHEWAN

The Saskatchewan Vacation and Accommodation Guides list and rate accommodations and provide additional information concerning campgrounds, parks, resorts and outfitters. For further details, contact:
Tourism Saskatchewan, 500-1900 Albert Street, Regina, Saskatchewan, S4P 4L9.

Embassies Abroad

Travelers who want to plan ahead can do so by writing to the Canadian embassy or consulate in their own country for information. Listed below are the addresses and telephone numbers of a selection of Canadian tourist information centers:

- **France** Canadian Embassy, First Secretary for Tourism, 37 avenue Montaigne, 75008 Paris. Tel: +33 1 44 43 29 00
- **United Kingdom** Canadian High Commission, 1 Grosvenor Square, London W1X OAB. Tel: 020 7258 6600.

- **US** Canadian Embassy, 501 Pennsylvania Ave NW, Washington, DC 20001. Tel: 202/682-1740

There are Canadian consulates in every major American city, including:

- 1251 Avenue of the Americas, New York. Tel: 212/596-1600.
- 2 Prudential Plaza, Suite 240, 180 North Stetson Avenue, Chicago, IL. Tel: 313/616-1860.
- Plaza 600, Suite 412, Sixth Avenue and Stewart Street, Seattle, WA. Tel: 206/443-1777

Tel: 306/787-2300 or toll-free 1-800/667-7191 in North America.

THE YUKON

Tourism Yukon provides a wealth of information for visitors to the territory. Its useful publication *Yukon Vacation Guide* lists lodgings, restaurants, service stations and campsites. Road maps and other brochures can be obtained by contacting Tourism Yukon, Box 2703, Whitehorse, Yukon, Y1A 2C6. Tel: 867/667-5340. www.touryukon.com

Consulates and Embassies

While foreign visitors are traveling in and across Canada, they may need to contact their own country in case of an emergency. Consulates can be most helpful for example if a passport is stolen or if a message needs to be relayed quickly back home. The following list gives details of all the consulates located in the major Canadian cities.

BRITISH COLUMBIA

Australia 888 Dunsmuir Street, Suite 1225, Vancouver. Tel: 604/684-1177.

France 1130 West Pender Street, Suite 1100, Vancouver. Tel: 604/681-4345.
UK 1111 Melville Street, Suite 800, Vancouver. Tel: 604/683-4421.
US 1095 West Pender Street, 21st Floor, Vancouver. Tel: 604/685-4311.

NOVA SCOTIA

US 2000 Barrington Street, Suite 910. Tel: 902/425-2480.

ONTARIO

Australia 175 Bloor St E, Suite 314, Toronto. Tel: 416/323-1155.
France 130 Bloor St W, Suite 400. Tel: 416/925-8041.
UK College Park, 777 Bay St, Suite 2800, Toronto. Tel: 416/593-1267.
US 360 University Ave. Tel: 416/595-1700.

QUÉBEC

France 1 Place Ville Marie, Suite 2601, Montréal. Tel: 514/878-4385
UK 1000 de la Gauchetière Ouest, Suite 4200, Montréal. Tel: 514/866-5863.
US PO Box 65, Postal Station Des-jardins, Montréal. Tel: 514/398-9695.

Getting Around

Domestic Travel

For travelers who know where they want to go to in Canada, there are a number of different transportation options available.

Domestic air services are preferable both for traveling long distances and for accessing any particularly remote areas.

Buses are inexpensive and are especially good for shorter distances or for getting to small towns not serviced by rail or air. Canada's major bus lines – Greyhound Canada and Voyageur Colonial – offer a number of cost-saving travel passes and packages, and some local services participate in these programs.

Railways are good for both short and long distances, although trains take five days to travel the extensive 6,360 km (3,950 miles) from Halifax in the east to Vancouver in the west. VIA Rail, which is Canada's major passenger train service, offers a range of cost-saving package discounts and travel passes. Ontario and British Columbia also operate some passenger rail services.

For further information on bus and train routes, prices and timetables, contact:
Greyhound Lines of Canada Ltd, 877 Greyhound Way SW, Calgary, AB T3C 3V8. Tel: 1-800/661-4747.
Voyageur Colonial Bus Lines, 265 Catherine St, Ottawa, ON K1R 7S5. Tel: 613/238-5900.
VIA Rail, 2 Place Ville Marie, Montréal, PQ H3C 3N3. Or call toll-free 1-800/835-3037 in Canada, 1-800/561-3949 in US.

DRIVING

If general touring is on the agenda, it is usually straightforward to hir a car. Foreign drivers' licenses are valid in Canada and accident liability insurance is required. Driving is on the right and conventions are similar to those in the US. Highway speed limits are usually 100 kph (60 mph), but speed limits, seat-belt regulations and other laws differ slightly from province to province. Provincial regulations are usually summarized in tourism literature and on many official road maps. The Canadian Automobile Association is a good source for information, maps and driving regulations. Members of European automobile associations can write to:
Canadian Automobile Association, 1145 Hunt Club Road, Suite 200, Ottawa, ON K1V 0Y3. Tel: 613/820-0117.
www.caa.ca
    Gasoline prices range from around 55 cents to 70 cents per liter (there are 3.8 liters in a US gallon; 4.5 liters in a Canadian Imperial gallon), being somewhat lower in Alberta.

Rules of the Road

Besides remembering to drive on the right, there are few other safety considerations to keep in mind. As some traffic rules vary from province to province, ask your car rental company if you have any queries of this nature.
    While Canada has an extensive and modern system of highways, most of which are well numbered and clearly marked, at times it is very helpful to know your north from south and your east from west. Speed limits are posted in kilometers per hour (kph) and they vary from 30 to 50kph in built-up areas, to between 80 and 100kph on highways.
    To improve highway safety, some Canadian provinces and territories require vehicles to be driven with

headlights on for extended periods after dawn and before sunset. The headlights of most newer vehicles turn on automatically once the engine is started.
    In all Canadian provinces except Québec, you may turn right at a red traffic light, after coming to a full stop and making sure that the way is clear before you do so.
    School buses display flashing lights for around 500ft before stopping and 100ft after leaving a stop; drivers may only pass the bus at this time with caution. If the bus has stopped and is flashing its red lights, other drivers must stop behind that bus. Remember that pedestrians have right-of-way at all intersections without stoplights and crosswalks.

CAR RENTALS

Several car rental companies have offices throughout Canada and rentals can usually be arranged before arriving. Call the following firms, toll-free, from anywhere in North America, for information:

Avis Tel: 1-800/879-2847.
Budget Tel: 1-800/527-0700.
Hertz Tel: 1-800/654-3131.
National/Tilden Tel: 1-800/387-4747.
Thrifty Tel: 1-800/367-2277.

MOTOR HOMES

If you plan to rent a camper/RV in July and August, you should book 3 to 4 months in advance.

Canadream Campers
2508-24th Avenue NE,
Calgary, AB T1Y 6R8.
Tel: 403/291-1000. (Also in Vancouver, Whitehorse and Toronto.)
www.canadream.com
Cruise Canada
2980 26th Avenue,
Calgary AB T1Y 6R7.

Tel: 1-888/278-1736, 1-800/327-7799. (Also in Vancouver, Whitehorse, Toronto and Montréal.)
www.cruiseamerica.com

CAR FERRIES

There are numerous car ferries all over Canada which cross lakes and rivers large and small. Of the large ferries, the most notable are those operated by BC Ferries along the British Columbia coast, and Marine Atlantic's large ferries between Nova Scotia and Newfoundland and New Brunswick.

Province by Province

ALBERTA

By Air Calgary and Edmonton International Airports are served by a number of airlines from elsewhere in Canada and from the US, Europe and Asia. Call Air Canada in Calgary on 265-9555 and in Edmonton on 423-1222. Call Canadian International Airlines in Calgary on 235-1161 and in Edmonton on 421-1414.
By Rail VIA Rail has thrice-weekly services to Edmonton and Jasper on its transcontinental route. For more information call toll-free 1-800-835-3037 in Canada; 1-800/561-3949 in the US. Rocky Mountain Rail tours operate a seasonal two-day sightseeing service from Banff to Vancouver, with overnight stops at Kamloops BC, so as to ensure the most spectacular sightseeing in daylight hours. Tel: toll-free 1-800/665-7245.
By Bus Greyhound Bus Lines, (toll-free 1-800/661-8747), which has its Canadian headquarters in Calgary, and Red Arrow Express (1-800/232-1958) provide access to almost every Alberta community, while Brewster Transportation & Tours (toll free 1-800/661-1152) provides major bus services to the parks and other tourist locations.
By Car The speed limit is 100 kph (60 mph) on most highways, reduced to 90 kph (55 mph) at

night. The major car rental companies are all represented, as well as a number of camper/RV rental agencies. Taxis are readily available in Calgary, Edmonton, Banff and Jasper.

Calgary (403)
The Calgary Transit (Tel: 262-1000) operates buses and light rail transit (LRT or the C-Train). City bus tours can be arranged through the tourist information center at the Calgary Tower on Center Street, or through most hotels.

Edmonton (780)
Edmonton Transit (Tel: 496-1611) operates city buses and an efficient LRT line.

Area Codes

Telephone area codes are given in brackets after the place name.

BRITISH COLUMBIA

By Air Vancouver International Airport, located just south of the city on Sea Island, is western Canada's major air hub. It is served by major North American, European and Asian airlines. Many smaller airlines and charters also serve northern BC and the Yukon.

By Sea The British Columbia Ferry Corporation (tel: 1-888/BCFERRY in BC) is the province's major carrier, with 40 ships and services between Victoria, Vancouver, and other points along the coast. Of note is the "Inside Passage" as far as Prince Rupert (from Port Hardy on Vancouver Island): a scenic, day-long cruise through deep fjords and narrow channels. Booking is strongly recommended and essential if taking a vehicle. Write to BC Ferries at 1112 Fort St, Victoria, BC V8V 4V2 or contact Tourism BC for further information: toll-free 1-800/663-6000.

By Rail VIA Rail operates passenger services connecting Vancouver and Prince Rupert with Alberta and the

rest of Canada. It also has a service between Victoria and coastal towns on southeastern Vancouver Island. Tel: 1-800/561-8630.

BC Rail has passenger services from North Vancouver to Prince George with connections to VIA Rail.

The Royal Hudson train runs a day return in summer from North Vancouver to Squamish, with optional return via MV Britannia. Tel: toll free 1-800/663-1500

Rocky Mountain Rail Tours operates a seasonal two-day sightseeing service between Vancouver and Banff AB, with overnight stops at Kamloops BC. Tel: toll-free 1-800/665-7245.

By Bus Greyhound Lines of Canada, toll-free: 1-800/661-8747, offers services throughout British Columbia. Island Coachlines operates throughout Vancouver Island. Tel: 385-4411. There is also a number of regional bus lines and BC Transit provides services in most larger towns. Tourism BC can provide details.

By Car The speed limit on BC's major freeways is 100 kph (60 mph); on other major highways the limit is usually 80–90 kph (50–60 mph). Seatbelts are mandatory. All international car rental agencies have offices at the airport or in the city center hotels.

Vancouver (604)
BC Transit provides a mass-transit system, with buses and trolleys, the SkyTrain LRT service and SeaBus harbor ferries. For full transit information, tel: 521-0400.

Several tour companies including Gray Line (Tel: 879-3363) offer bus tours of Vancouver and environs, including Capilano Canyon and Grouse Mountain and as far as Whistler. Harbor cruises also run.

Taxis can usually be hailed on the streets. Companies include: Yellow Cabs (Tel: 681-1111) and Blacktop (Tel: 731-1111).

Victoria (250)
BC Transit (Tel: 382-6161) provides a bus service to Greater Victoria. A number of tour companies including

Hitchhiking

Hitchhiking is permitted in most of Canada, except on high-volume highways where stopping for passengers constitutes a danger. It is prohibited in certain municipalities, so prospective hitchhikers should check with tourist boards about local regulations.

Gray Line (Tel: 388-5248) offer several bus tours, some on British-built double-decker buses. For slower, more romantic sightseeing, hire a horse-drawn carriage on Belleville Street, near the Royal British Columbia Museum. Major taxi companies include Blue Bird Cabs (Tel: 382-4235) and Empress Taxi (Tel: 381-2222).

MANITOBA (204)

By Air The following major airlines serve Winnipeg International Airport: Air Canada (Tel: 943-9361), Canadian Airlines International (Tel: 632-1250) and Northwest Airlines (Tel: 1-800/255-2525). There are also a number of regional and charter carriers. Limousines, taxis, and city buses are available at the airport for the short ride downtown.

By Rail Winnipeg's Main Street station is on VIA Rail's transcontinental passenger service and is the terminus of the line to Churchill (tel: 944-8780, toll-free 1-800/561-8630).

By Bus Grey Goose Bus Lines (tel: 784-4500) and Greyhound Bus Lines serve Winnipeg through the terminal at 487 Portage Ave. Tel: 1-800/661-8747.

By Car Manitoba's speed limit is 90 kph (56 mph), unless otherwise posted. A reliable network of good paved roads extends across the southern part of the province and north to Thompson and Flin Flon. Several large car rental companies have offices in Winnipeg, both at the airport and downtown.

Winnipeg (204)
The Winnipeg Transit System has
an efficient bus system. For
information call Winnipeg Transit,
tel: 284-7190.
 Taxis can usually be hailed easily
downtown. You can also call Unicity
Taxi (Tel: 925-3131) or Duffy's
(Tel: 775-0101).

Area Codes

Telephone area codes are given
in brackets after the place name.

NEW BRUNSWICK (506)

By Air Air Canada (tel: Saint John
632-1500, Fredericton: 458-8561)
and Canadian Airlines International
(tel: toll-free 1-800/363-7530) both
offer flights into the major airports
at Saint John and Fredericton, with
connections via associated airlines
to smaller communities.
By Sea Saint John is connected via
Marine Atlantic ferry with Digby NS.
Within the province, ferries connect
Blacks Harbour to Grand Manan
Island and Deer Island to
Campobello.
By Rail VIA Rail passenger services
between Halifax and Montréal follow
two routes within New Brunswick:
three times a week via McAdam,
Saint John, Sussex and Moncton;
and three times a week via
Campbellton, Bathurst, Newcastle,
Moncton and Sackville. For details
call toll-free in Canada 1-800/835-
3037; in the US 1-800/561-3949.
By Bus Greyhound and Voyageur
offer routes into New Brunswick
and transfers to the province-wide
service provided by SMT Bus
Lines. Contact SMT within the
Maritimes, toll-free 1-800/567-
5151 or 506/859-5060 from
anywhere else.
By Car New Brunswick has excellent
highways. The speed limit on major
highways is 100 kph (60 mph), 80
kph (50 mph) elsewhere. (*See*
Getting Around, introduction, page
343, for toll-free numbers of car
rental companies.)

NEWFOUNDLAND AND LABRADOR (709)

By Air Air Canada and Canadian
Airlines International fly between the
Canadian mainland and
Newfoundland, and their associated
airlines service communities within
the island; they also fly in Labrador
from the main hubs at St John's and
Deer Lake.
By Sea The large ferries of Marine
Atlantic cross up to four times a day
in summer from North Sydney, Nova
Scotia, to Channel-Port aux Basques
(6 hour journey) and Argentia,
Newfoundland (18 hour journey).
Fares for two people plus a car on
the Channel-Port aux Basques
service are about $100 plus $105
for a private cabin if required. Fares
on the Argentia service for two
persons plus a car are $235 and
$144 for a cabin or $15 for two fairly
comfortable "dayniter" seats.
Marine Atlantic also operates
freight/passenger services from St
Antony and Lewisport to the
Labrador Coast. For more
information on these services,
contact: Marine Atlantic, 355 Purvis
Street, North Sydney, NS B2A 3V2.
Tel: 1-800/341-7981.
 In addition, a ferry service
operates between St Barbe and
Blanc Sablon, Que on the border
with Labrador. There are a number
of coastal ferries which carry a few
passengers. For more information
on these services, contact the
Newfoundland Department of
Tourism, Culture and Recreation.
(*see* Tourist Offices section pages
340–342).
By Bus DRL Bus Line connect the
Port aux Basques ferry docks with
St John's, a distance of some 905
km (562 miles). Tel: 738-8088 in
St John's.
By Car The major car rental
agencies are represented at St
John's and Deer Lake. Speed limits
are 100 kph (60 mph) on four-lane
highways and 90 kph (55 mph) on
other highways. Major highways are
paved, though a few secondary
roads are gravel surfaced. The 80

km (50 mile) stretch between the
Blanc Sablon, Que, ferry dock and
Red Bay, Labrador, is paved, but
Labrador highways are otherwise
largely gravel surfaced.

St John's
The city's **Metrobus system** is
efficient and inexpensive. It is often
difficult to hail taxis on the street,
so the best bet is to find one at a
downtown hotel or to call Bugden
taxi. Tel: 726-4400.

NORTHWEST TERRITORIES

By Air Canadian Airlines
International (Tel: toll-free 1-
800/426-7000) and Air Canada
(Tel: 1-800/422-6232) fly into
Yellowknife from Edmonton. From
Yellowknife you can travel elsewhere
in the Northwest Territories and to
the Yukon by a number of carriers
including First Air (Tel: toll-free 1-
800/267-1247) and Ptarmigan
Airways (Tel: 1-800/267-1247).
Numerous charter companies
located in the Yellowknife airport
can fly travelers to almost any
destination west of Hudson Bay.
By Bus Greyhound Bus Lines offer
services between Edmonton and
Yellowknife. Tel: 1-800/661-8747.
By Car The territory has three
highways, all hard-packed gravel.
The Dempster Hwy stretches from
Dawson City, Yukon to Inuvik on the
Arctic Ocean. The Mackenzie Hwy
runs between Edmonton, Alta, and
Yellowknife. The newest road, the
Liard Hwy, runs from the Alaska Hwy
near Fort Nelson, BC, to Fort Liard,
close to Nahanni National Park, and
then east to Yellowknife.
 For special precautions about
driving in the north, *see* the Yukon
Getting Around section (page 349).
Note that all three highways become
impassable during the spring thaw
and fall freeze-up (usually May and
November). Tel: toll-free 867/873-
7799 or 1-800/661-0751 for ferry
schedules and the latest road
information. Should visitors need to
rent a vehicle, several agencies are

available, but it is wise to reserve as far in advance as possible.

NOVA SCOTIA (902)

The CheckIn Reservation and Information Service also offers information on transportation. Call toll-free: 1-800/565-0000.

By Air Canadian Airlines International (Halifax, tel: 427-5500; Sydney, tel: 564-4545) and Air Canada (Halifax, tel: 429-7111; Sydney, tel: 564-8646) connect Halifax and Sydney with the rest of Canada as well as the eastern US.

By Sea A number of car-ferry services are available, ranging from one- to six-hour voyages to a more luxurious overnight special with cabins and entertainment.

For travel from Bar Harbor, Maine to Yarmouth, NS; Port aux Basques, Nfld to North Sydney, NS; Saint John, NB to Digby, NS, write to Marine Atlantic, Reservations, Box 250, North Sydney, NS B2A 3M3; or call toll-free 1-800/341-7981 from anywhere in North America.

For journeys from Prince Edward Island to Caribou, NS, contact Northumberland Ferries Ltd, Box 634, Charlottetown, PEI C1A 7L3. Tel: 485-6580 in Caribou NS, or 962-2016 in Wood Islands, PEI.

The Prince of Fundy sails from Portland, Maine, to Yarmouth, NS. For information about overnight cruises, tel: 1-800/341-7540.

By Rail VIA Rail provides service from Montréal to Halifax via Amherst and Truro. For schedules and fares call the Halifax office, tel: 429-8421 or 1-800/835-3037.

By Bus Acadian Lines Ltd operates daily throughout Nova Scotia (tel: 453-8912). Cabana Tours of Halifax (tel: 455-8111) is one of a number of tour companies which offer seasonal bus tours of the province.

By Car Nova Scotia highways are generally in very good condition, and the speed limit is 100 kph (60 mph) on the 100-series highways and 90 kph (55 mph) on the others. Cars can be rented in downtown Halifax, Yarmouth or Sydney, and at the two

airports. *See* Getting Around introduction (page 343) for toll-free car rental numbers or contact the Reservation & Information Service. Recreational vehicles can be rented through the province's accommodation reservation system (toll-free 1-800/565-0000).

Halifax

Metro Transit operates a bus system in the Halifax/Dartmouth area. The system's pedestrian ferry service between Halifax and Dartmouth is a truly delightful way to see the Halifax waterfront. Drivers will find that parking in downtown Halifax on business days can be difficult or expensive.

A number of tour companies, including Acadian Lines (tel: 454-9321) offer bus tours from the major hotels. However, the city is compact enough to explore on foot, either with a conducted group or on a self-guided tour, both of which are available from Tourism Halifax in the Old City Hall on Barrington Street. Taxis in Halifax are fairly inexpensive and easy to catch, as there are many cab stands.

NUNAVUT (867)

By Air Air Inuit, tel: 514/636-9445, Calm Air, tel: 204/778-6471, Canadian North, 867/669-4000, First Air, tel: 1-800/267-1247, Kenn Borek Air, tel: 867/979-1919, and Skyward Aviation, tel: 1-800/476-1873, all fly from Yellowknife, Edmonton, Winnipeg, Montreal and Ottawa to various points in Nunavut including Iqaluit, Rankin Inlet, Cambridge Bay, Resolute Bay, Nanisivik and Kangerlusssuaq. Within Nunavut, both the above-mentioned scheduled air services and six charter air services fly travelers in twin- or single-engine propeller aircraft. There are also five or six helicopter charter services.

By Road As there is no road connecting Nunavut to the south, and only one 21-km (13-mile) stretch of road within the territory, connecting the communities of

On Departure

Citizens of the United Kingdom may bring home, duty-free: 200 cigarettes or 50 cigars; 2 liters of wine and 1 liter of liquor; 50 grams of perfume; and additional goods totaling no more than $32.

Each American citizen who spends more than 48 hours in Canada may return with $400 worth of goods, duty-free. Some airports and border points feature duty-free shops, offering liquor and other goodies at bargain prices. Americans should direct their questions to any US customs office or on its website: www.customs.ustreas.gov while travelers from other countries should contact the customs office in their own country for information on what they can bring back.

A number of airports across Canada are now levying an Airport Improvement Fee (AIF) to all visitors departing from the airport. In most cases, the fee per person is paid at the airport; it sometimes varies according to destination. At Calgary International Airport, travelers are charged $10 on all flights, which is included in the purchase price of the airline ticket.

At Edmonton International Airport, the fee is $5 for flights within Alberta and $10 for out-of-province flights. At Montréal Dorval Airport, an AIF of $10 per person is levied on passengers who are originating their trip from that airport. (If, for example, a traveler has flown in from Vancouver or Ottawa and is continuing on another flight from Montreal, an AIF is not charged provided that a boarding pass or ticket from the previous flight is shown.) Ottawa and Winnipeg Airports charge $10 per person. At Vancouver International Airport, travelers are charged $5 for a flight within BC, $10 for a flight within North America, and $15 outside North America.

Arctic Bay and the mining town of Nanisivik, travel by bus or car is not an option.

ONTARIO (416)

By Air Lester Pearson International Airport, just 30 minutes northwest of Toronto, is served by nearly all the major Canadian airlines as well as international carriers. Useful numbers are as follows:
Air Canada.
Tel: 925-2311.
Canadian International Airlines.
Tel: 798-2211.
American Airlines.
Tel: 283-2243, toll-free 1-800/433-7300 in US and Canada.
Delta Airlines.
Tel: 1-800/221-1212
Pacific Western provides an Airport Express bus service (Tel: 905/564-6333) every 20 minutes from all three terminals to several downtown hotels (journey time 40 minutes). The service operates between 4.45am and 12.30am.
Ottawa's MacDonald Cartier Airport is located 15 minutes south of the city. Air Canada, tel: 613/247-5000.
Many of the province's northern hunting/fishing resort camps can be reached only by air. Usually, chartered air fare is included in a package deal. Ask Travel Ontario for its *Ontario Northern Trip Planner*.
By Rail Toronto's famous Union Station on Front Street is the city's main rail terminus, with direct access to the subway as well. VIA Rail (Tel: 416/366-8411 in Toronto, 1-800/361-1235 from elsewhere in Ontario, and a toll-free fax number from the US 1-800/304-4842 to request literature) can whisk you across Canada, including to and from US connections in Windsor and Niagara Falls. VIA Rail serves Ottawa from Toronto and Montréal. The station is located at 200 Tremblay Rd, near the Queensway.
By Bus Toronto's bus terminal is located at 610 Bay Street, close to City Hall and the Eaton Center. The major carriers include Greyhound

Lines of Canada (Tel: 367-8747), Trentway-Wager and Voyageur Colonial (Tel: 393-7911). Voyageur provides bus services to and from Ottawa, operating out of the Central Bus Station at 265 Catherine St (Tel: 613/238-6668). In all, over 30 bus lines operate in Ontario, offering service across the province.
By Car The speed limit on Ontario Highways is 100 kph (60 mph), unless otherwise posted. Remember that adults and children weighing over 40lb must wear seat belts. In Ontario drivers are in general allowed to turn right on a red traffic light, as long as traffic conditions are conducive to doing so.
Ontario's road network is among the best maintained in North America, so your car should leave the province in as good shape as it came. Unless, of course, you travel the dirt and gravel side-roads of northern Ontario, in which case a post-vacation underbody flush is appropriate. *See* Getting Around introduction for toll-free car rental numbers (page 343).

Toronto (416)

Toronto features an excellent system of mass-transit, including clean, efficient and safe subways, with connections to timely buses and trolley buses. For information, call the **Toronto Transit Commission** (TTC) at 393-4636. Route maps are often available at hotels.
Taxis are easily hailed on the street. Otherwise, call:
Diamond (Tel: 366-6868),
Metro Cab (Tel: 504-8294), or
Beck Taxi (Tel: 449-6911).
As in any large city, driving in Toronto can enervate the most patient of drivers, especially at rush hours. Parking, naturally, is expensive although less so in municipal lots marked with a large, green "P". Whenever possible, it's more pleasant to walk or take the subway. When a streetcar comes to a halt, stop behind it so that its passengers can exit through the right lane to the sidewalk.
Ferries leave for Centre Island daily every 30 minutes, every 15

minutes on summer weekends, from the foot of Bay Street, tel: 392-8193.
Gray Line Sightseeing (Tel: 594-3310) runs several daytime excursions which often include extended stops at the CN Tower, Royal Ontario Museum or Casa Loma. Moreover, Gray Line offers pleasant meandering bus tours to Niagara Falls.
To enjoy a harbor cruise call Toronto Harbour & Islands Boat Tours, tel: 869-1372, or wander through the Harborfront area, where smaller outfits and privately owned yachts run tour cruises.
Ottawa is served by OC Transpo (Tel: 613/741-4390). For taxis, call Blue Line, tel: 238-1111.

PRINCE EDWARD ISLAND (902)

By Air Air Canada (Tel: 892-1007) and Canadian Airlines International (Tel: 1-800/665-1177) fly into Charlottetown daily from numerous Canadian cities.
By Sea During the summer, ferries leave hourly from Caribou, NS, to Wood Islands, PEI, a 75-minute trip. The ferries are almost always crowded, with early morning and evening sailings having the shortest waiting lines.
By Bus Greyhound, under the auspices of SMT Bus Lines, provides services to the island. For information, call toll-free on 1-800/567-5151. There are few local bus services, but there are several taxi companies, including: Art's (tel: 894-5586), City (tel: 892-6567), and Star (tel: 566-6666).
Abegweit Sightseeing Tours (Tel: 894-9966) is one company that runs tours of Charlottetown, the North Shore beaches and other island attractions.
By Car Confederation Bridge, a recently-opened toll bridge now permits driving to the island from Cape Tormentine. NB: The island speed limit is 90 kph (55 mph). *See* Getting Around introduction (page 343) for toll-free rental car numbers.

By Bicycle Cyclists adore PEI's rural lanes. Rent a bike by the day or week from one of a number of agencies. MacQueen's Bike Shop and Travel, 430 Queen St in Charlottetown (Tel: 368-2453) will design a customized itinerary, arrange accommodation and provide all the equipment – even an emergency road service.

QUÉBEC

By Air Dorval International Airport (Tel: 514/394-7377) is on the outskirts of the city. It serves domestic, US flights and international flights. Mirabel International Airport (Tel: 514/394-7377 or toll-free 1-800/465-1213), some distance northeast of Montréal, handles mainly charter and cargo flights. All major Canadian airlines and numerous international carriers fly into Montréal. Call Air Canada, tel: 514/393-3333 or toll-free 1-800/361-6340. Canadian Airlines International can be reached at 514/847-2211 or toll-free 1-800/665-1177.

Visitors piloting private aircraft should check first with Transport Canada in Ottawa. Canadian Airlines International (Tel: 1-800/667-7000) in Québec City will fly you to northern Québec.

By Rail In Montréal, tel: 514/989-2626 or toll-free 1-800/835-3037; in Québec City, tel: 418/692-3940, for information on trains. Both Amtrak and VIA Rail run to the city.

By Bus Greyhound and Voyageur Lines serve Québec. In Montréal, tel: 514/842-2281. For Québec City call toll-free 1-800/661-8747.

By Ferry Many ferries offer year-round or seasonal service on the St Lawrence and other major rivers, and between the Îles-de-la-Madeleine and Prince Edward Island. A passenger/cargo ship connects the entire Lower North Shore between Havre-St-Pierre, Île d'Anticosti and Blanc-Sablon. Places on this ship should be reserved in peak season.

By Car Perhaps the best way to travel Québec is by automobile, which gives you the flexibility to explore, the freedom to stop and sample the local cuisine, and to meander through the exceptional provincial parks. While good maps are available from most service stations, north of the major population areas, the road may become increasingly unpaved and perhaps impassable in winter. The speed limit on autoroutes is 100 kph (60 mph) and drivers and all passengers must wear seat belts. Turning right on a red light is strictly prohibited in Québec unless there is an additional green arrow.

Speed Limits

Speed limits in Canada are posted in kilometers per hour and vary from 30 to 50 kph in built-up areas to between 80 and 100 kph on highways.

Montréal (514)

The City Transit System, STCUM, services the city with buses and its excellent Metro. You can use a bus transfer for admission to the subway and vice-versa.

If you drive, try to make overnight parking arrangements in advance with a hotel. Be prepared to pay $20 a day to park around the city. Taxis abound in Montréal. The base rate is around $3.00. For car rentals, try: Avis (Tel: 866-7096); Hertz (Tel: 842-8537) or Budget (Tel: 937-9121).

Québec City (418)

In the old city, walking is by far the easiest and most convenient way to get around. Woe to those who drive: parking is scarce and expensive (check with your hotel). You can avoid traffic snarls by renting a bicycle from Cyclo Services (Tel: 692-4052).

SASKATCHEWAN (306)

By Air Saskatchewan's two principal airports, situated in Regina and Saskatoon, are served by the following airlines: Air Canada (tel: 525-4711 in Regina; 652-4181 in Saskatoon or toll-free in Canada: 1-800/361-6340; Canadian Airlines International (tel toll-free: 1-800/665-1177); and Northwest Airlines, tel: toll-free 1-800/225-2525. There are also a number of regional and charter carriers offering flights across the area.

By Rail Saskatoon is on VIA Rail's transcontinental service with bus links to Regina. For information, call the railway (toll-free 1-800/561-8630 in Canada; 1-800/531-3949 in US).

By Bus The Saskatchewan Transportation Co and Greyhound Bus Lines serve the province from the Regina terminal at 2041 Hamilton Street, and the Saskatoon station at 50 23rd Street. For further information, tel: Regina 787-3340 or toll-free in Saskatchewan: 1-800/663-7181.

By Car The speed limit in Saskatchewan is 100 kph (60 mph). Free maps can be obtained from Tourism Saskatchewan or from any other travel bureau in the province. Budget, Dollar, and Hertz car rental agencies all have depots at the airports as well as downtown. (See Getting Around introduction, page 343, for toll-free numbers.)

Regina and Saskatoon (306)

Regina Transit (Tel: 777-7433) runs several bus routes through the city and to the airport. In Regina, taxis are readily available downtown; otherwise, Capital Cab (Tel: 781-7777) is a popular choice to call for a pick-up. Saskatoon also has a city bus service. Taxis are readily available, or call United at 652-2222.

THE YUKON

By Air Canadian Airlines International (Tel: 294-2054) runs direct flights to Whitehorse from Vancouver. Air North (tel 668-2228) offers services to Alaska and Alkan Air (toll-free 1-800/661-0432), operates within the Yukon with connections to BC and the NWT.

By Sea Most visitors arrive in the Yukon aboard cruise ships as part of a package tour. Independent travelers will find that Skagway, the nearby Alaskan port, has ferry connections with Prince Rupert BC. (See BC's Domestic Travel section, page 345)

By Rail There's a sightseeing rail service between Skagway and Lake Bennett, about half-way to Whitehorse, with connecting buses to complete the journey. However, it is a seasonal operation, and visitors would probably want to use the direct bus service for their return journey. For details, contact White Pass and Yukon Railway, tel: toll-free 1-800-343-7373.

By Bus Greyhound Bus Lines (Tel: toll-free: 1-800/661-8747) travels from Edmonton to Whitehorse and Alaska Highways through Yukon. Regional bus lines service the interior and connect with Alaska.

By Car Among the national car-rental agencies Budget and Tilden are represented in Whitehorse and there are also a number of local car and RV-rental companies. The speed limit is 90 kph (55 mph). Yukon roads are well maintained and all the major highways are paved. The Alaska Highway runs from Dawson Creek, BC, through Whitehorse and Haines Junction, the Yukon, and on into Alaska. The Klondike Highway commences in Skagway and cuts north from Whitehorse to Dawson. There it splits into the Dempster Highway which runs due north to Inuvik, the North West Territories and the Top of the World Highway, which drops west into Alaska.

Although these are open year-round, travel is recommended only between mid-May and mid-September. Service stations and campgrounds can be found at regular intervals. Any trek should be planned and undertaken with great care, following these recommendations:

● Headlights must remain on at all times.

● When journeying between October and April, make sure that the vehicle is properly winterized.

● Before starting, ensure that the vehicle is in good working order. Bring at least two spare tires.

● Refuel frequently.

For taxi bookings in Whitehorse, call the Yellow Cab at 668-4811.

Women Travelers

Canada is probably one of the safest countries in the world for women to travel alone. With the dramatic increase of women traveling on business, the majority of hotels and restaurants are fully accustomed to seeing women on their own and are becoming increasingly sensitive to safety issues. Provided a female traveler follows a common-sense-based code of conduct, the chances of running into a problem should be minimal.

Some city hotels have recently introduced "singles" tables in their dining rooms, at which hotel guests can ask to be seated – this is a civilized way to encounter other single travelers in a "safe" environment. The hotel's concierge is also likely to be a reliable source of information on suitable or safe places to go and acceptable routes to get there.

Children

North America generally, including Canada, is strongly oriented towards accommodating family travel. Many hotels have excellent packages for children that often include children under a certain age staying free of charge, and most restaurants will produce children's menus and a supply of paper and wax crayons to keep them happy.

Shopping malls and parks frequently have children's play areas. Restaurants and cinemas will also provide booster seats on hand for smaller children. Across the country there are hundreds of attractions geared towards children, from toddlers to teens.

Where to Stay

Although the rates quoted are for the lowest current rack rate at the time of going to press, ask about special packages and promotions when making a reservation. The prices indicated are based on double occupancy.

Price Codes

Addresses for accommodations are listed by province and thereafter by city. Hotels are divided into three categories:
$$$ – over $200 per room
$$ – $100–200 per room
$ – under $100 per room

ALBERTA

Bed and breakfasts are a popular alternative to hotels, with prices generally in the inexpensive to medium range. The following agencies represent B & Bs throughout Alberta. Bed & Breakfast Agency of Alberta (a no-fee reservation service) at 410-19th Avenue NE, Calgary, AB T2E 1P3. Tel: toll-free 1-800/425-8160. All members of the Alberta Bed & Breakfast Association have been inspected and approved by the association (www.bbalberta.com).

Alberta Tourism distributes a Accommodation and Visitors' Guide, a sampling of which is given below.

Banff (403)
Banff International Hotel
Tel: 762-5666 or toll-free: 1-800/665-5666. New hotel within walking distance of downtown Banff. Provides a complimentary downtown shuttle in the evening. **$$–$$$**

Banff International Hostel
Tunnel Mountain Rd.
Tel: 762-4122.
A mix of dormitories, single and
family rooms. **$**
Banff Springs Hotel
Tel: 762-2211 or toll-free in the US
and Canada 1-800/44-1414.
This resort is a town unto itself. Its
famous golf course is as scenic as it
is challenging. **$$$**
Irwin's Mountain Inn
Tel: 762-4566.
One kilometer from town centre,
newly renovated. Some suites
suitable for light self-catering. **$$**
Tunnel Mountain Chalets
Tel: 762-4515 or
toll-free: 1-800/661-1859.
2.5 km (1½ miles) from downtown
Banff. 75 chalets designed for
family accommodations; each
comes with full kitchen. **$$**

Calgary (403)
Calgary's Convention and Visitor
Bureau operates a free
"Accommodations Bureau" which
can make reservations from its list
of lodgings. Tel: 263-8510 or make
your own arrangements directly with
one of their residences listed below:
Calgary International Hostel
520-7th Avenue, on LRT line, 1 km
from downtown.
Tel: 269-8239.
Single rooms or dormitories. **$**
Glenmore Inn
2720 Glenmore Tr. SE
Tel: 279-8611 or
toll-free: 1-800/661-3163.
Modern, spacious rooms; exercise
and dancing facilities. **$–$$**
International Hotel
220-4th Avenue SW
Tel: 265-9600 or
toll-free 1-800/661-8627.
High-rise hotel features over 250
gorgeous suites. Good value for
families. **$$–$$$**
The Palliser Hotel
133-9th Avenue SW.
Tel: 262-1234 or toll-free (Canada
and the US): 1-800/441-1414.
Everything about this hotel is done
on a grand scale, including the
rooms. Deluxe suites are available.
$$–$$$

Travelodges
9206 Macleod Tr. S.
Tel: 253-7070; and
2750 Sunridge Blvd NE
Tel: 291-1260 or
toll-free: 1-800/578-7878.
Well-respected chain. **$$**
Holiday Inn Macleod Trail
4206 Macleod Tr.
Tel: 287-2700 or
toll-free: 1-800/830-8833
Floor for non-smoking guests and no
charge for children under 19 sharing
parents' room. Full breakfast and
evening glass of wine included.
Central location. **$–$$**
University of Calgary Housing
2500 University Dr NW
Tel: 220-3210.
Accommodations on this sprawling
campus are available during the
winter and summer holidays. **$**
Westin Hotel Calgary
320-4th Avenue SW
Tel: 266-1611 or
toll-free 1-800/228-3000
Very large hotel located in the
financial district; caters to the
business set. Reputedly the finest
accommodations in Calgary. **$$–$$$**

Drumheller (403)
Best Western Jurassic Inn
1103 Hwy 9S
Tel: 823-7700 or
toll-free: 1-888/823-3466
Spacious rooms with refrigerators
and microwave ovens. Indoor pool
and hot tub. **$$**
Newcastle Country Inn
1130 Newcastle Trail
Tel: 823-8356
Small inn for non-smoking guests,
close to downtown. Vegetarian
meals on request. **$**

Edmonton (780)
Alberta Place Suite Hotel
10049 103 Street
Tel: 423-1565 or
toll-free: 1-800/661-3982.
Comfortable suites come with
kitchenettes. **$–$$**
Delta Edmonton Centre Suite Hotel
10222, 102 Street
Tel: 429-3900 or
toll-free 1-800/268-1133
A unique city-center hotel, part of

Alberta's Guest Ranches

Alberta's "country vacation"
program provides the chance to
experience life on an Albertan farm
or ranch. Like other packages of
this sort, it's fun, inexpensive and,
if you choose, hard work. Unlike
other programs, you can select
from a list of accommodations
ranging from large cattle ranches
to small family farms. Full details
are supplied in Travel Alberta's
Accommodation Guide.

the Eaton Centre shopping mall.
$$–$$$
Edmonton International Hostel
1064 81st Avenue
Tel: 988-6837 or
toll-free: 1-877/467-8336
An attractively refurbished convent.
Mix of dormitories and doubles. **$**
The Macdonald,
10065 100 Street.
Tel: 424-5181 or
toll-free 1-800/441-1414.
Beautifully restored heritage hotel.
$$–$$$
Union Bank Inn
10053 Jasper Avenue
Tel: 780-3600 or
toll-free: 1-888/423-3601
Small charming inn with individually
designed rooms. **$$**

Jasper (780)
Jasper Inn
Tel: 852-4461 or toll-free in western
Canada 1-800/661-1933
Condominium-style accommodations
suitable for self-catering, with many
resort facilities. **$$–$$$**
Jasper Park Lodge
Tel: 852-3301 or
toll-free 1-800/441-1414
Elite resort with golf course and
many superior amenities; perhaps
the most beautiful of its kind in the
Rockies. **$$$**
Pine Bungalows
2 km (1 mile) east of Jasper Townsite
Tel: 852-3491
Open May–mid-Oct. Cabins, many
with fires, besides Athabascar River.
Groceries, laundry, gift shop. **$**

Camping in Alberta

For detailed information on
Alberta's campgrounds, request
a copy of the *Alberta
Campground Guide* from Tourism
Alberta. With five national parks,
more than 300 provincial parks
and recreation areas and over
460 privately or municipally
owned campgrounds, there is a
great choice. All have been
inspected and improved by
Travel Alberta. It's advisable to
book ahead. Prices are subject
to change.

Lake Louise (403)
Chateau Lake Louise
Tel: 522-3511 or
toll-free 1-800/441-1414
This famous, chateau-like resort
complex, set high in the Rockies,
offers all the luxury amenities. **$$$**
Lake Louise Inn
Tel: 522-3791 or
toll-free: 1-800/661-9237
Large estate offers a choice of
hostelry: rooms, kitchen
apartments, or inn-style
accommodations, some deluxe,
others moderately priced. **$–$$**

Mountaineer Lodge
3 km (2 miles) from Lake Louise
Tel: 522-3844
Open May-Oct. One- and two-

bedroom units, some with mountain
views. Whirlpool and steam room.
$$–$$$
Paradise Lodge and Bungalows
Tel: 522-3595
Rustic units just a short drive from
the lake. Closed in winter. **$$–$$$**

BRITISH COLUMBIA

Tourism BC publishes the *British
Columbia Accommodations Guide,*
which lists accredited motel, hotel,
B&Bs, resort accommodations and
campgrounds in the province. They
also book you into accommodation
at no extra charge. Listed below is a
selection of what's available.

Banff (403)
Johnston Canyon
Tel: 762-1581
26km (16 miles) west of Banff. 132
sites, all basic services. **$**
Tunnel Mountain Village
Tel: 762-1571
4 km (2½ miles) northeast of Banff
on Tunnel Mountain Road. 618 sites
with all basic services and an
interpretive amphitheater. **$**

Cardston (403)
Police Outpost Provincial Park
about 20km (12½ miles) southwest
of Cardston on Hwy 2
Tel: 653-8008
46 sites, open all year round.

Campground fee varies depending
on services provided.

Jasper (780)
Wapiti Campground
5km (3 miles) south of Jasper on
Hwy 93. Tel: 852-6176
366 sites, 40 equipped with power.
Open all year round.

Kelowna (250)
Manteo Beach Club & Resort
3766 Lakeshore Rd
Tel: 860-1031 or
toll-free 1-888/462-6836
Year-round resort complex; offers
lodgings of various sizes and prices.
$–$$$

Fairmont Hot Springs (250)
Fairmont Hot Springs Resort
Hwys 93 and 95
Tel: 345-6311 or
toll-free 1-800/663-4979
Open all year-round resort lodge and
cabins; great for skiing and golfing.
$–$$

Prince George (250)
Coast Inn of the North
770 Brunswick Street
Tel: 563-0121 or
toll-free 1-800/663-1144
Modern hotel close to center of
town. Indoor pool. **$$**
Connaught Motor Inn
1550 Victoria Street
Tel: 562-4441 or
toll-free: 1-800/663-6620
Comfortable motel, with indoor pool,
hot tub and sauna. **$**
Ramada Hotel Downtown
444 George Street
Tel: 563-0055 or
toll-free 1-800/830-8833
Downtown hotel with all facilities.
$–$$

Prince Rupert (250)
Coast Prince Rupert Hotel
118, 6th Street
Tel: 624-6711 or
toll-free 1-800/663-1144
Pleasant, comfortable lodgings with
views over the harbor. **$$**
Totem Lodge Motel
1335 Park Avenue
Tel: 624-6761 or

Accommodations

Canadian accommodations are
similar to those in the US in the
range of choices available, but
some lodgings in Canada are more
personalized and service-
orientated. Reservations are
essential in the busy summer
months. Hotels generally will hold
a room until 6pm, but if you plan to
arrive later, notify the
establishment in advance. If you
have not reserved, begin looking
for accommodations early in the
afternoon, particularly during the
summer when most
establishments (especially those

along highways) fill up quickly.
Almost all hotels, motels and
resorts accept major credit cards,
but it's a good idea to check in
advance, especially if you travel in
remote areas. Bed-and-breakfasts
and hostels are becoming
increasingly popular alternatives to
hotels. Generally cheaper and
more friendly, they are located
throughout the country. Another
practical and fun place to stay is in
one of Canada's 2,000
campgrounds, most of which
accommodate recreational
vehicles as well as tents.

toll-free 1-800/550-0178.
Pleasant motel near ferry docks. **$**

100 Mile House (250)
Best Western 108 Resort
4816 Telqua Drive (13 km or 8 miles
north of 100 Mile House)
Tel: 791-5211 or
toll-free: 1-800/667-5233
Lakeside golf and cross-country ski
resort. **$$**
Red Coach Inn
170 Hwy 97N
Tel: 395-2266 or
toll-free: 1-800/663-8422
Downtown location, with pool,
whirlpool and sauna. **$**

Revelstoke (250)
Daniel's Hostel Guesthouse
313 First Street East
Tel: 837-5530
Historic guest house with
dormitories and private rooms, and
a communal kitchen. **$**
Peak Lodge
Hwy 1, 5 km (3 miles) west of
Revelstoke
Tel: 837-2176
Alpine-style lodge in mountain
setting, some units with kitchen.
Outdoors hot tub. **$**

Quesnel (250)
Cascade Inn
383 St-Laurent Avenue
Tel: 992-5575 or
toll-free: 1-800/663-1581
Quiet downtown location with many
facilities. **$**

Vancouver (604)
Vancouver offers a wide variety of
places to stay.
Bosman's Motor Hotel
1060 Howe Street
Tel: 682-3171 or
toll-free 1-888/267-6267
Free parking and close to downtown.
$–$$
Four Seasons
791 W. Georgia Street
Tel: 689-9333 or
toll-free in Canada 1-800/268-
6282, in the US 1-800/332-3442
Mid-town hotel is one of Vancouver's
most luxurious. Attached to Pacific
Center Mall. **$$$**

Granville Island Hotel
1253 Johnston Street
Tel: 683-7373 or
toll-free: 1-800/663-1840
An elegant hotel in spectacular
setting amidst the action of
Granville Island. **$$$**
Hotel Linden
1176 Granville Street
Tel: 688-8701 or
toll-free: 1-888/654-6336
Centrally located boutique hotel,
close to Stanley Park. **$–$$**
Hotel Vancouver
900 W. Georgia Street
Tel: 684-3131 or
toll-free in Canada 1-800/441-1414
Spacious, old-fashioned rooms with
graceful touches. Houses several
fine lounges and restaurants in
heritage building. **$$$**
Hyatt Regency
Royal Centre, 655 Burrard Street
Tel: 683-1234 or
toll-free 1-800/233-1234
Cosmopolitan elegance, atop
fashionable shopping center. **$$$**
Sandman Hotel Richmond
3233 St Edwards Drive
Tel: 736-4388 or
toll-free: 1-800/726-3626
New hotel close to airport with
continuous airport shuttle and
indoor pool. **$**
Sandman Inn
180 West Georgia Street
Tel: 681-2211 or
toll-free: 1-800/726-3626
Downtown with some facilities. **$$**
Sylvia Hotel
1154 Gilford Street
Tel: 681-9321
Attractive old hotel overlooking
English Bay, adjacent to Stanley
Park. Surprising grandeur for the
price, hence very popular, especially
during the summer. **$–$$**

Prairie Farms

Farm vacations are a great way to
get a true sense of the prairies.
Lasting from one day to a week or
more, they offer a wide enough
variety of different activities to
suit almost any taste. For further
information, write to Manitoba
Country Vacations Association,
c/o Ernest Fraser, Fairfax, M ROK
DVD. Tel: 204/776-2176.
If you prefer to have a similar
kind of hospitality but in a more
urban setting, try contacting Bed
and Breakfast of Manitoba at
434 Roberta Avenue, Winnipeg,
MB R2K 0K6. Tel: 661-0300
(www.bedandbreakfast.mb.ca).

UBC Conference Centre
5961 Student Union Boulevard
Tel: 822-1010
Single and twin units on gorgeous
University of BC campus, offers
cheap rooms all year round. Access
to campus facilities. **$**
Waterfront Centre Hotel
900 Canada Place Way
Tel: 691-1991 or toll-free in North
America 1-800/441-1414
Modern glass tower with
tremendous views. **$$$**
Westin Bayshore
1601 W. Georgia Street
Tel: 682-3377 or
toll-free 1-800/228-3000
Airy rooms overlooking the harbor
and Stanley Park. Resort
ambience. **$$$**
YWCA Hotel
733 Beatty Street
Tel: 895-5830 or
toll-free in BC, Alberta and western
US 1-800/663-1424
Near BC Place Stadium.
Comfortable rooms;
accommodations suitable for
singles, couples and families. **$**

Victoria (250)
The Bedford Regency Hotel
1140 Government St
Tel: 384-6835 or
toll-free 1-800/665-6500
Small, pleasant, heritage hotel. **$$**

Chateau Victoria
740 Burdett Avenue
Tel: 382-4221 or
toll-free 1-800/663-5891
Pleasant, large rooms and central
location. **$$**

Edwardian Inn
135 Medana Street
Tel: 380-2411 or
toll-free: 1-888/388-0334
Small hotel in heritage home, quiet
residential area. **$**

The Empress
721 Government Street
Tel: 384-8111 or
toll-free 1-800/441-1414
Heritage hotel, spacious, subtly
decorated rooms, with service for
the discriminating traveler.
Afternoon tea a speciality. **$$$**

Harbour Towers Hotel
345 Quebec Street
Tel: 385-2405 or
toll-free 1-800/663-5896
Large rooms, each with a view of the
city or its inner harbor. **$$–$$$**

Royal Scot Inn
425 Quebec Street
Tel: 388-5463 or
toll-free 1-800/663-7515
Comfortable rooms and apartments
for long-stay visitors. **$$**

Hostels in BC

For complete information on
hostels in British Columbia, write
to **Hostelling International**,
Canada, BC Region, 402-134
Abbott Street, Vancouver, BC V6B
2K4. Tel: 604/684-7111 or toll-
free: 1-800/663-3153.

Whistler (604)
Chateau Whistler Resort
4599 Chateau Blvd
Tel: 938-8000 or
toll-free 1-800/606-8244
All that one expects of Canadian
Pacific Hotels, in a resort setting,
close to Whistler village and the ski
lifts. **$$$**

Delta Whistler Resort
4050 Whistler Way
Tel: 932-1982 or
toll-free 1-800/515-4050
Resort hotel favored by skiers;

much cheaper during the summer
months. **$$$**

Durlacher Hof Alpine Country Inn
7055 Nesters Road
Tel: 932-1924
Austrian hospitality in authentic pine
pension. Mountain views, sauna,
jacuzzi. **$$**

Hostelling International Whistler
5678 Alta Lake Road
Tel: 932-5492
Rustic lodge on shore of Alta Lake
with shared and private rooms for
budget travelers. **$**

MANITOBA

Winnipeg offers a variety of
lodgings, from old and grand to slick
and modern. Ask about weekend
packages. In Manitoba's small
towns, accommodations tend to be
modest, both in décor and price.
Travel Manitoba will provide its
annual *Accommodation and
Campground Guide* (a complete list
of places to stay in the province
including campgrounds) on request.

Brandon (204)
Canadian Inn
150-5th Street
Tel: 727-6404 or
toll-free 1-800/852-2712
Pool and other facilities, dining
room. **$**

Royal Oak Inn
3130 Victoria Avenue
Tel: 728-5775 or
toll-free 1-800/852-2709
Best in town, pool, sauna, good
lounge and dining room. **$$**

Flin Flon (204)
Victoria Inn
160 Highway 10N
Tel: 687-7555
Modern hotel with pool and other
facilities. **$**

Portage la Prairie (204)
Manitobah Inn
Hwy 16
Tel: 857-9791 or
toll-free 1-800/214-6655
Pleasant motor hotel with popular
dining room. **$**

Winnipeg (204)
Charter House
330 York Avenue
Tel: 942-0101 or
toll-free 1-800/782-0175
Good location downtown; large
rooms, restaurant, outdoor pool. **$$**

Crowne Plaza Winnipeg Downtown
350 St Mary Avenue
Tel: 942-0551 or
toll-free 1-800-2CROWNE
A first-class hotel, connected to the
Winnipeg Conference Center, with all
facilities, attractive rooms, most
with balconies. Near Convention
Center. **$$$**

Hotel Fort Garry
222 Broadway
Tel: 942-8251
toll-free 1-800/665-8088
Elegant rooms set in a late
19th-century French-style
château. **$$–$$$**

Ivey House International Hostel
210 Maryland Street
Tel: 772-3022
Kitchen and laundry facilities, a
sundeck and bike rentals. **$**

Guest House International Hostel
168 Maryland Street
Tel: 772-1272 or
toll-free: 1-800/743-4423. **$**

**Travelodge Hotel Downtown
Winnipeg**
360 Colony Street
Tel: 786-7011 or
toll free 1-800/578-7878
Budget hotel in a convenient
location. **$$**

The Lombard
2 Lombard Place
Tel: 957-1350 or
toll-free 1-800/441-1414
Large luxury hotel, with all facilities
and excellent dining room. **$$**

NEW BRUNSWICK

Tourism New Brunswick will provide
assistance with reservations for
accommodations throughout the
province at each of the five
Provincial Visitor Information
Centers. These are in:
Woodstock (tel: 506/325-4427),
St Stephen (tel: 506/466-7390),
Aulac (tel: 506/364-4090),

Campbellton (tel: 506/789-2367) and Saint-Jacques (tel: 506/735-2747). Campgrounds are listed in Tourism New Brunswick's annual *Travel Planner*.

Alma (506)
Fundy National Park Youth Hostel
Tel: 887-2216 or 902/425-5450 in the offseason
Ideal for exploring the park. $

Bathurst (506)
The Rosewood Inn
285 St Patrick Street
Tel: 548-2106
Seven minutes from the beach, the inn offers antiques, fireplaces and lobster suppers. $

Campbellton (506)
Aylesford Bed & Breakfast
8 McMillan Avenue
Tel: 759-7672
Victorian home with period antiques, a library and a billiard room. $
Howard Johnson Hotel
157 Water Street
Tel: 753-4133 or
toll-free: 1-800/446-4656
Standard North American motel, clean, functional, no surprises. $

Campobello (506)
Lupine Lodge
Tel: 752-2555
Open Jun–Oct. A maritime lodging and dining experience. $
Owen House
Tel: 752-2977
Historic oceanfront house with antiques, fireplaces. Convenient for golf, whale watching and hiking. Some shared bathrooms. $$

Edmundston (506)
Auberge-Hotel Wandlyn
919 Canada Road
Tel: 735-5525 or
toll-free: 1-800/561-0000
Offers sports, a pool and surprisingly good food. $$
Hotel Républicque City Hotel
919 Canada Road
Tel: 563-2489 or
toll-free: 1-800/563-2489
Recently renovated, offers sports, a pool and good food. $

Fredericton (506)
Lord Beaverbrook Hotel
659 Queen Street
Tel: 455-3371 or
toll-free: 1-800/561-7666
Besides the majestic St John River, walking trails and historical sites. $$
Sheraton Inn Fredericton
225 Woodstock Rd
Tel: 457-7000 or
toll-free: 1-800/325-3535
New luxury hotel overlooking Saint John River. Convenient for downtown. Indoor and outdoor pool. $$–$$$
Fredericton International Youth Hostel
621 Churchill Row
Tel: 450-4417. $

Price Codes
Addresses for accommodations are listed by province and thereafter by city. Hotels are divided into three categories:
$$$ – over $200 per room
$$ – $100–200 per room
$ – under $100 per room

Grand Manan (506)
Shorecrest Lodge
North Head
Tel: 662-3216
Attractive country inn with gourmet restaurant and lovely ocean view from the verandah. $
Swallowtale Inn
50 Lighthouse Road, North Head
Tel: 662-1100
Open May–Oct. Former lighthouse keeper's house, with ocean views from each room. $

Moncton (506)
Auberge Wild Rose Inn
17 Baseline Road.
Tel: 383-9751 or
toll-free: 1-888/389-7673.
Colonial country inn overlooking lakeside golf. $$
Colonial Inn
42 Highfield Street
Tel: 382-3395 or
toll-free 1-800/561-4667
Modern rooms in great locale; many facilities. $$

Delta Beauséjour
750 Main Street
Tel: 854-4344 or
toll-free: 1-800/441-1414
Moncton's finest hotel. $$

St Andrews (506)
Algonquin
184 Adolphus
Tel: 529-8823 or
toll-free 1-800/441-1414
Luxury resort hotel in the old style with numerous recreations, from golf to croquet. $$
Rossmount Inn
Hwy 127
Tel: 529-3351 or
toll-free:1-877/529-3351
Victorian-style inn on historic Rossmount Estate overlooking Passamaquoddy Bay. Hiking, spa, pool and driving range. $$
Treadwell Inn
129 Water Street
Tel: 529-1022 or
toll-free: 1-888/529-1011
Open May-Oct. Waterside property built circa 1820. $$

Saint John (506)
Inn on the Cove
Sand Cove Road
Tel: 672-7799
Overlooks Bay of Fundy, Irving Nature Park and Digby ferry. Best Heritage Inn Award. $–$$
Red Rose Mansion
112 Mount Pleasant Avenue
Tel: 649-0913 or
toll-free: 1-888/711-5151
Central and elegant 1904 mansion built for owner of Red Rose Tea company. Stately gardens. $–$$
Saint John Hilton
One Market Square
Tel: 693-8484 or
toll-free: 1-800/561-8282
This luxury hotel overlooks the harbor. $$

NEWFOUNDLAND AND LABRADOR

Finding good lodgings is not hard, and although few small-town hotels and motels are of the modern variety, travelers almost always find the rooms comfortable and the owners hospitable. There are also many B&Bs which provide excellent opportunities to meet the locals. As St John's becomes increasingly cosmopolitan, so do its hotels, which are generally more modern and pricey than those of Newfoundland's interior. The Department of Tourism, Culture & Recreation publishes an excellent *Travel Guide* which includes detailed lists of campgrounds. Note that lodgings carry a 12 percent provincial tax and 7 percent federal Goods and Service Tax.

Gander (709)
Albatross Motel
Trans-Canada Hwy
Tel: 256-3956, or
toll-free: 1-800/563-4900
Comfortable; fine dining room. **$–$$**
Country Inn Motel
315 Gander Bay Road
Tel: 256-4005
Comfortable rooms in quiet country setting. Very near downtown. **$**

Channel Port aux Basques (709)
St Christopher's Hotel
Caribou Road, west of ferry terminal
Tel: 695-7034 or
toll-free 1-800/563-4779
Pleasant lodgings, and a nice introduction to Newfoundland. **$**

St John's (709)
The Battery Hotel and Suites
100, Signal Hill
Tel: 756-0040 or
toll-free 1-800/563-8181
On historic site with lovely views of the harbor and city. All mod cons. **$$**
Memorial University Hostel
Tel: 737-7933
Open in summer only. **$**
Hotel Newfoundland
Cavendish Square
Tel: 726-4980 or
toll-free 1-800/441-1414
A Canadian Pacific Hotel in traditional style, often considered the city's downtown hotel. **$$–$$$**
Quality Hotel
2 Hill O'Chips. Tel: 754-7788
Great harbor location, medium-sized comfortable rooms. **$$**

The Roses Bed and Breakfast
9 Military Road
Tel: 726-3336
One of a number of superior B&Bs near the Hotel Newfoundland. **$**

Trinity Bight (709)
Peace Cove Inn
Tel: 464-3738 or 781-2255 in off-season
Open May–Oct. An original schooner shipper's home by the sea offers all modern amenities. **$**

Price Codes

Addresses for accommodations are listed by province and thereafter by city. Hotels are divided into three categories:
$$$ – over $200 per room
$$ – $100–200 per room
$ – under $100 per room

THE NORTHWEST TERRITORIES

Nearly every community has at least one inn or hotel, often an Inuit co-operative. Most have dining rooms or kitchenette facilities, and meals are very often included in the overnight price.

The amenities will vary: private bathrooms, radios and even TVs are not uncommon; however, room service is rare, bell-hops unheard of. Expect to pay $80–$250 for a double. Although there is no sales tax on lodgings here, the federal 7 percent Goods and Services Tax is payable. Summer reservations should be made the previous spring.

For a complete accommodations listing, contact Department of Tourist Development and Marketing, Suite 196, Box 1320, Yellowknife, NT X1A 2L9. Tel: toll-free 1-800/661-0788 for its latest *Explorers' Guide* which includes hotels, B&Bs and camps. The following is a representative sample of hotels.

Yellowknife (867)
Discovery Inn
Tel: 403/873-4151
Located downtown. **$$**

The Explorer Hotel
Tel: 403/873-3531 or
toll-free: 1-800/661-0892
Modern urban hotel with restaurant and other facilities. **$$**
Yellowknife Inn
Franklin Avenue
Tel: 873-2601 or
toll-free: 1-800–661-0580
Yellowknife's largest, on main street, connected to shopping mall, most facilities of a city hotel. **$$**
Eskimo Inn
Tel: toll-free 1-800/661-0725
Lounge and dining room. **$$**
Mackenzie Hotel
Tel: 777-2861
Central 33-room hostelry with café, bar and dining room. **$$**

Hayriver (867)
Ptarmigan Inn
Tel: 403/874-6781 or
toll-free: 1-800/661-0842
Comfortable rooms and suites. Good facilities for leisure and business travelers. **$$**

Fort Smith (867)
Pelican Rapids Inn
Tel 872-2789
Small modern hotel with suites from standard to luxury. **$$**

NOVA SCOTIA

Nova Scotia publishes its annual *Doer's and Dreamer's Complete Guide* which contains listings of lodgings and campsites throughout the province. Any of Nova Scotia's 70 visitor information centers will reserve accommodation for you, or call toll-free 1-800/565-0000. For information on hostels, contact Hostelling International Nova Scotia, P.O. Box 3010, South, 5516 Spring Garden Rd, Halifax, NS, B37 3G6. Tel: 425-5450.

Baddeck (902)
The resort town of Baddeck is the starting point for the world-famous Cabot Trail.
Inverary Resort
Hwy 205.Tel: 295-3500 or
toll-free 1-800/565-5660

Quiet and tranquil; has an excellent dining room, its own pool, and a private beach. **$$**

Telegraph House
Chebucto Street
Tel: 295-1100
A Victorian house that has become a Cape Breton favorite. **$**

Grand Pré (902)

Evangeline Motel & Guest House
11668 Hwy 1
Tel: 542-2703 or
toll-free: 1-888/542-2703
Historic house with 5 rooms, and renovated motel units nearby. Set in rock gardens and waterfalls. **$**

Halifax (902)

Hotel Halifax
1990, Barrington Street
Tel: 425-6700 or
toll-free: 1-800/441-1414
Service-oriented luxury hotel with pool and fitness centre. Connected to Scotia Square Shopping Mall. **$$**

Chebucto Inn
6151 Lady Hammond Rd
Tel: 453-4330 or
toll-free: 1-800/268-4330
Comfortable, quiet motel lodgings, on the outskirts of Halifax. **$$**

Citadel Inn
1960 Brunswick Street
Tel: 422-1391 or
toll-free 1-800/565-7162
Large and luxurious modern hotel across from Scotia Square. **$$$**

Delta Barrington
1875 Barrington Street
Tel: 429-7410 or
toll-free 1-800/268-1133
In the heart of the historic area, this modern hotel has all facilities. **$$**

Keddy's Halifax Hotel
20 St Margaret's Bay Road, Armdale
Tel: 477-5611 or
toll-free: 1-800/561-7666
Part of an Atlantic Canada chain, modestly priced, many facilities. **$**

Shelburne (902)

Cooper's Inn
36 Dock Street
Tel: 875-4656 or
toll-free 1-800/688-2011
Open Apr–Oct. A provincial heritage property (1785) on historic Dock

Street. Good food served in relaxed environment. **$$**

Yarmouth (902)

Rodd Grand Hotel
417 Main Street
Tel: 742-2446 or
toll-free: 1-800/565-RODD
138 rooms, a fitness centre and a dinner-theatre. **$$**

Victorian Vogue B&B
109 Brunswick Street
Tel: 742-6398
Old captain's house, Queen Anne-style. **$**

NUNAVUT

Cape Dorset

Kignait Inn
Tel: 897-8863
17 rooms, 8 with private bath, and laundry facilities available in evenings only and access to a pay phone. **$$**

Polar Lodge
Tel: 897-8335
8 rooms with TVs and telephones. Will coordinate cultural and sports activities with local guides. **$$**

Iqaluit

Discovery Lodge Hotel
Tel: 979-4433
E-mail: disclodge@nunanet.com
Centrally located, long established, with conference facilities for more than 100 people. **$$**

The Regency Frobisher Inn
Tel: 979-2222
E-mail: frobinn@nunanet.com
A 50-room hotel frequently used by corporate, government and tourist groups. Comfortable rooms and conference facilities. They even cater to anglers by freezing their catch. **$$**

ONTARIO

Travel Ontario includes details of accommodation in the *Ontario Discovery Guide* which list over 4,000 hotels, motels, resorts and fly-in camps. It's worth enquiring about weekend packages – many

hotels discount their rooms up to 50 percent if visitors stay on Friday and Saturday nights.

Try to book summertime resort accommodations at least a month in advance. Representing over 75 lodges and resorts. For more information and brochures contact: Resorts Ontario, P.O. Box 2148, Orillia, 29 Albert Street, ON L3V 6S1. Tel: 705/325-9115, or toll-free in Canada and the US at 1-800/363-7227. Visit their website – www.resorts-ontario.com – for further information.

B&Bs in Ontario

For Bed and Breakfast information throughout Ontario, write to the **Federation of Ontario Bed & Breakfast Accommodations**, PO Box 437, ON M5T 1R5. Tel: 416/964-2566. Budget travelers interested in hostelling can write to **Hostelling International** – Canada, 205 Catherine Street, Ste 400, Ottawa, ON K2P 1C3. Tel: 613/237-7884 (www.hostellingintl.com) or **Backpackers Hostels Canada**, 1594 Lakeshore Drive, Longhouse Village, PO Box 10-1, RR 13, Thunder Bay, ON P7B 5E4. Tel: 807/983-2042 E-mail: candu@microage-tb.com for more information.

Algonquin Park (705)

Arowhon Pines
Little Joe Lake
Tel: 633-5661
Legendary lodge and cottages. Canoeing, swimming, hiking and other outdoor facilities are available. A member of the Relais & Château chain of superior lodgings. **$$**

Blue Spruce Inn
Dwight
Tel: 635-2330
Cottages and motel rooms; great for all-season recreation. **$$**

Bracebridge (705)
Clevelands House
Minett. Tel: 765-3171 or
toll-free 1-888/567-1177
Historic lodge with modern
amenities on Lake Rosseau; full
summertime facilities, including
tennis, golf and water sports. **$$$**

Tamwood Resort
Lake Muskoka
Tel: 645-5172 or
toll-free 1-800/465-9166
A smaller resort, built of logs; offers
a full range of summer and winter
sports. **$$**

Collingwood (705)
Beaconglow Motel
RR3, Collingwood
Tel: 445-1674 or
toll-free 1-800/461-2673
Comfortable units of various sizes
some with fireplaces. **$**

Blue Mountain Inn
RR3, Collingwood
Tel: 445-0231 or 416/869-3799
Lodge located at the base of its
namesake; full summertime
facilities, but especially popular with
skiers. **$$**

Wasaga Beach (705)
Georgian Inn Resort
Box 105, 21 Spruce St
Tel: 429-2319
Lakeside property. Full range of
summer and winter packages. **$$**

Huntsville (705
Deerhurst Resort
1235 Deerhurst Drive
Tel: 789-6411 or
toll-free 1-800/461-4393
Large luxurious, lakeside resort on
the American Plan; caters to a young
clientele. **$$$**

Kingston (613)
Holiday Inn
1 Princess St
Tel: 549-8400 or
toll free 1-800/465-4329
Waterfront location, with pool,
lounge restaurant. **$$**

Hochelaga Inn
24 Sydenham St. S
Tel: 549-5534 or
toll-free: 1-800/267-0525

A bed-and-breakfast in this lovely old
home close to downtown. **$$**

Kitchener-Waterloo (519)
Riviera Motel
2808 King St E
Tel: 893-6641
Large, modern motel. **$**

Four Points Sheraton
105 King St E
Tel: 744-4141 or
toll-free: 1-800/483-7812
Pleasant; popular dining room and
lounge, close to Farmer's Market. **$$**

Niagara Falls (905)
Rates vary wildly with the season,
but are highest from late June to
late September, especially
weekends.

Sheraton Brock Hotel
5685 Falls Ave
Tel: 374-4444 or
toll-free 1-800/263-7135
Very popular hotel next to the
casino. Around three quarters of the
rooms overlook the Falls. **$$**

Honeymoon City Motel
4943 Clifton Hill
Tel: 357-4330 or
toll-free 1-800/668-8840
Pleasant lodgings for romantic
couples; outdoor pool. **$$**

Nelson Motel
10655 Niagara Parkway
Tel: 295-4754
Peaceful, family-run
accommodations up the river;
outdoor pool. **$**

Old Stone Inn
5425 Robinson St
Tel: 357-1234 or
toll-free: 1-800/263-6208
Sizable, modern hotel, but retaining
a rustic atmosphere. **$$$**

Niagara-on-the-Lake (905)
Oban Inn
160 Front St
Tel: 468-2165
Small inn featuring old-fashioned
comfort. **$$**

Prince of Wales Hotel
6 Picton St
Tel: 468-3246 or
toll-free: 1-888/669-5566
Replete with the grandeur one
expects in Niagara-on-the-Lake. Full

indoor recreational facilities,
excellent dining room, low-key disco
and exquisite lounge. **$$$**

**Niagara-on-the-Lake Bed &
Breakfast Association**
Tel: 468-0123
E-mail: admin@bba.notl.on.ca

Ottawa (613)
Capital Hill Hotel
88 Albert St
Tel: 235-1413 or
toll-free: 1-800/463-7705
Family-run lodgings of rooms and
suites, walking distance from
Parliament Hill. **$$**

Château Laurier
1 Rideau St
Tel: 241-1414 or
toll-free: 1-800/441-1414
An Ottawa landmark, renowned for
grandeur befitting its château-style
appearance. Spacious rooms. **$$$**

The Citadel Ottawa Hotel
101 Lyon St
Tel: 237-3600, or
toll-free: 1-800/567-3600
Renovated, high-rise hotel, with all
the amenities and a rooftop lounge,
Stop 26. **$$$**

Delta Ottawa Hotel & Suites
36 Queen St
Tel: 238-6000 or
toll-free: 1-800/268-1133
Beautiful rooms and a health club
complete with a 115ft indoor water
slide. **$$$**

Embassy Hotel & Suites
25 Cartier St
Tel: 237-2111 or
toll-free: 1-800/661-5495
Tastefully decorated and well-
equipped suites. Work-out center
and sauna. **$$**

Embassy West Hotel
1400 Carling Ave at Queensway
Tel: 729-4331 or
toll-free 1-800/267-8696
Bright, comfortable motel close to
museums and sights. **$**

Lord Elgin
100 Elgin St
Tel: 235-3333 or
toll-free 1-800/267-4298
A regal atmosphere; smallish, yet
modern rooms. Great value. Near
Parliament Hill and across from the
National Arts Center. **$$$**

Novotel Hotel-Ottawa
33 Nicholas Street
Tel: 230-3033 or
toll-free: 1-800/221-4542.
Comfortable hotel, well located
beside the Rideau Centre. **$$$**
Ottawa Bed-and-Breakfast
18 The Driveway,
Ottawa, ON K2P 1C6
Tel: 613/563-0161
An umbrella organization, listing and
licensing the city's B&Bs. **$**
Ramada Hotel and Suites
111 Cooper St
Tel: 238-1331 or
toll-free: 1-800/267-8378
This new hotel has all modern
facilities, including exclusive
executive suites with their own
kitchenettes. **$$**
Talisman Hotel
1376 Carling Ave, at the Queensway
Tel: 722-7600 or
toll-free 1-800/267-4166
Balconied rooms overlook Japanese
gardens, two pools; suburban golf
course nearby. **$$**

Stratford (519)
Check with the Theater Box Office
(see Performing Arts for address)
about bed-and-breakfast
accommodations during the festival.
Albert Place – Twenty-Three
23 Albert Place
Tel: 273-5800
Spacious modern rooms. **$$**

Budget Stays

For cheap, summertime lodgings
in Ottawa, book at one of the
following:

Carleton University
Tour and Conference Center,
1125 Colonel By Drive,
Ottawa, ON K1S 5B7
Tel: 520-5611.
Ottawa International Hostel
75 Nicholas St
Tel: 235-2595 or
toll-free 1-800/461-8585
In what was formerly the Carleton
County Jail (1862–1972), this is
an excellent downtown location
for budget accommodation.

Victorian Inn on the Park
10 Romeo St N
Tel: 271-4650 or
toll-free 1-800/741-2135
Spacious, elegant hotel.
Reservations a must during the
festival. **$$**

Sudbury (705)
Ambassador Motor Hotel
225 Falconbridge Rd
Tel: 566-3601 or
toll-free 1-800/859-4442
Motel with saunas, pool. **$$**
Ramada Inn Sudbury
85 St Anne Road
Tel: 675-1123 or
toll-free 1-800/272-6232
A city-center hotel, with an indoor
pool. **$$**
Travelway Inn
1200 Paris St
Tel: 522-1122, or
toll-free 1-800-461-4883
Spacious rooms all with a view, and
a minute's walk from Sudbury's
biggest attraction, Science North. **$$**

Toronto
Between an open-ended tourist
season and a large convention
market, there is constant demand
for Toronto hotel rooms. There is
accommodation to match every
budget, and the standards are high.
Tourism Toronto and the Hotel
Association of Metropolitan Toronto
offers a free year-round
reservations service seven days a
week. Tel: 203-2500.
Bond Place Hotel
65 Dundas St E
Tel: 362-6061 or
toll-free 1-800-268-9390
Small rooms, but the service and
furnishings are commendable. **$–$$**
Days Inn
6257 Airport Rd
Tel: 905/678-1400 or
toll-free: 1-800/387-6891
Pleasant, close to airport, with
indoor pool and health club. **$–$$**
The Delta Chelsea Inn
33 Gerrard St W (between Yonge
and Bay)
Tel: 595-1975 or
toll-free: 1-800/268-2266
Large hotel with upscale

Price Codes

Addresses for accommodations
are listed by province and
thereafter by city. Hotels are
divided into three categories:
$$$ – over $200 per room
$$ – $100–200 per room
$ – under $100 per room

accommodations in convenient
downtown location. Good programs
for children. **$$$**
Four Seasons Hotel
21 Avenue Rd
Tel: 964-0411 or toll-free in Canada
1-800/268-6282, or 1-800/332-
3442 from US location
Understated elegance, jet-set
clientele; spacious rooms with nice
views. **$$$**
Hilton Toronto
145 Richmond St W
Tel: 869-3456 or
toll-free in Canada: 1-800/267-2281
Opulent lobby; rooms have useful
extras including alarm clocks and
scales. **$$–$$$**
Inn on the Park
1100, Eglinton Ave E
Tel: 444-2561 or toll-free 1-
800/268-6282 in Canada; 1-
800/332-3442 in US
This sprawling complex overlooks
Wilket Creek Park. Resort-style
recreational facilities; gorgeous
landscaping, 15 minutes drive from
downtown. **$$**
Toronto Colony Hotel
89 Chestnut St
Tel: 977-0707or
toll-free 1-800/777-1700
A pleasant hotel behind City Hall
and close to Chinatown with fitness
center and supervised children's
play programs. **$$–$$$**
Le Royal Meridien King Edward
37 King St E
Tel: 863-9700 or
toll-free 1-800/543-4700
An old Toronto favorite. Marble
columns punctuate the lobby;
spacious rooms gracefully
decorated. **$$–$$$**
Park Hyatt Hotel
4 Avenue Rd (at Bloor)
Tel: 924-5471 or

Price Codes

Addresses for accommodations are listed by province and thereafter by city. Hotels are divided into three categories:
$$$ – over $200 per room
$$ – $100–200 per room
$ – under $100 per room

toll-free in Canada 1-800/977–4197 Old hotel, currently undergoing renovations. Its Roof Restaurant is favored by the literati. **$$$**
Regal Constellation Hotel
900 Dixon Rd
Tel: 675-1500 or
toll-free 1-800/268-4838
Has the class, charm and facilities of a downtown hotel, located near the airport. A favorite of prime ministers. **$$$**
Sheraton Centre Toronto Hotel
123 Queen St W (opposite City Hall)
Tel: 361-1000 or
toll-free in Canada: 1-800/325-3535
Over 1,300 rooms; walking distance to most downtown attractions; atop underground shopping, restaurants, cinemas. **$$–$$$**
SkyDome Hotel
1 Blue Jays Way
Tel: 341-7100 or
toll-free 1-800/341-1161
Literally part of SkyDome, it's the

B&Bs in Toronto

If you are having difficulty finding a B&B in Toronto, there are several associations that will help you with your search. Try the following for starters:
Bed-and-Breakfast Homes of Toronto
PO Box 46093, College Park PO
444 Yonge St,
Toronto ON M5B 2L8
Tel: 363-6362
Downtown Bed & Breakfast Association
PO Box 190
Station B, Toronto, ON M5T 2W1
Tel: 368-1420
Send stamped, self-addressed envelope for their brochures.

world's only sports-and-entertainment hotel. A dream for baseball fans. **$$$**
Sutton Place Hotel
955 Bay St
Tel: 924-9221 or
toll-free 1-800/268-3790
Elegant, low-key hotel, rising 17 stories above Bay Street. Intended to resemble the grand hotels of Europe, and a favorite of showbiz types. Rooms have nice touches. **$$**
Westin Harbour Castle
1 Harbour Square
Tel: 869-1600 or
toll-free: 1-800/228-3000
Plush decor; all rooms in the two towers offer a sparkling view of the harbor, especially the Lighthouse Restaurant on the 37th floor. **$$$**

Windsor (519)
Cadillac Motel
2498 McDougal Ave
Tel: 969-9340 or
toll-free: 1-888/541-3333
Large hotel with all the amenities. **$**
Windsor Hilton
277 Riverside Dr W
Tel: 973-5555 or
toll-free 1-800/HILTONS
Deluxe hotel overlooking the Detroit River. **$$$**

PRINCE EDWARD ISLAND

PEI's hotels, motels and resorts fill fast in the summer, so reservations should be secured as far in advance as possible. Write or call Tourism PEI, (see Tourist Offices section, page 342) for their annual Visitors Guide, or for help in making reservations. Once on the island, any Visitors Information Center can help to arrange accommodations. In addition to hotel, motel, campground and resort lodgings, visitor information centers can arrange stays at farm, tourist and vacation homes. For about $60 a day per person, visitors share meals, activities and sometimes farmwork with their hosts. Those who have experienced it often claim this is the best (and cheapest) way to get to know PEI and its inhabitants.

Charlottetown (902)
Canadian Hostelling Association
153 Mount Edward Road
Tel: 894-9696. **$**
The Charlottetown
Kent Street/corner of Pownal Street
Tel: toll free: 1-800/565-7633
Old-fashioned elegance with renovated rooms and facilities. **$$**
Islander Motor Lodge
146-148 Pownal Street
Tel: 566-1623
Recently renovated hotel in the town center with many facilities. **$$**
Prince Edward Hotel
18 Queen Street
Tel: 566-2222 or
toll-free 441-1414
Luxury waterfront hotel. Part of the long-established Canadian Pacific Hotels & Resorts. **$$–$$$**
Quality Inn on the Hill
150 Euston Street
Tel: 894-8572 or
toll-free 1-800/466-4734
Medium-priced motel-style property close to downtown. **$$**

Grand Tracadie
Dalvay-By-The-Sea
Tel: 672-2048
Luxury resort of Victorian inn and cottages, right next to PEI National Park. **$$$**

Montague
Lobster Shanty Motel and Restaurant
Tel: 838-2463
Rustic setting with river views. Some high-quality cottages, good restaurant. **$$**

Roseneath
Rodd Brudenell River Resort
Tel: 652-2332 or
toll-free 1-800/565-633
A hotel and 50 chalets rest on 1,500 acres. Facilities include a heated pool, shuffleboard, lawn championship golf course, tennis courts, bowling green, and canoeing. **$$$**

Summerside
Silver Fox Inn
61 Granville Street
Tel: 436-4033

Elegant B&B in historic late-19th-century villa. **$–$$**
Quality Inn Garden of the Gulf
618 Water Street E
Tel: 436-2295 or
toll-free 1-800/265-5551
Summerside's fanciest hotel features pool and beachfront swimming, restaurant, dinner theater. **$$**

Victoria (902)
Simple Comfort Bed & Breakfast & Bicycle Hostel
Hwy 2
Tel: 658-2963
Accommodation in an updated 1853 church manse or a renovated horse barn. **$**

Wood Islands (902)
Meadow Lodge Motel
Belle River
Tel: 962-2022 or
toll-free 1-800/461-2022
Country lodgings close to ferry dock, with restaurant nearby. **$$**

Summerside Motels

Two motels on Water Street offer comfortable rooms at low prices:
Cairns Motel
721 Water Street E
Tel: 436-5841. **$**
Sunny Isle Motel
720 Water Street E
Tel: 436-5665. **$**

QUÉBEC

Book lodgings as far in advance as possible. Large hotels often offer discounts on Friday, Saturday and Sunday nights, but resort areas will be crowded and therefore more expensive on weekends. If you reserve rooms with two double-beds, your child can usually stay free; if need be, rent extra roll-away beds at a low extra cost.

The hotel association Hôtellerie Champêtre-Québec Resorts & Country Inns offers charming country inns in beautiful locations. For their catalogue with prices, contact addresses and interesting

travel suggestions, please write to:
Hôtellerie Champêtre-Québec Resorts & Country Inns,
455 rue St-Antoine Ouest, Bureau 114, Montréal,
Qué, H2Z 1J1.
Tel: 514/861-4024 or
toll-free 1-800/861-4024.

Chicoutimi
Hôtel Chicoutimi
Tel: 549-7111 or
toll-free: 1-800/463-7930
Known for its fine Québécois cuisine. **$$**

Gaspé (418)
Quality Inn des Commandements
178 rue de la Reine
Tel: 368-3355 or
toll-free: 1-800/462-3355
An excellent base for exploring the peninsula. **$–$$**

Hull (819)
Holiday Inn Crowne Plaza de la Chaudière
2 rue Montcalm
Tel: 778-3880 or
toll-free 1-800/567-1962
Luxury accommodation with extra touches. **$$$**

Magog (819)
Auberge L'Étoile-sur-le-Lac
1150 Principale Ouest
Tel: 1-800/567-2727
Great location on Lake Memphremagog. Minutes from Mont Orford for hiking and skiing. **$$**

Mont Tremblant (819)
Auberge Château Beauvallon
Tel: 425-7275
One of the area's many small, cozy, New England-style resorts. Ask about their ski packages. **$$**
Station Mont Tremblant
Tel: 631-3000 or
toll-free 1-800/461-8711
Largest all-year-round resort in East Canada. **$$$**

Montréal (514)
Most hotels fall in the expensive to deluxe range, especially those downtown which, incidentally, rarely have swimming pools. Yet a full

Island Camps

Private and provincial campgrounds are scattered throughout the island. The fees range from $15 to $25 a night, depending on the services available. Note that camping anywhere other than on a designated campground is illegal.

range of accommodations is available, and most hotels have excellent restaurants.
Auberge de la Fontaine
1301 rue Rachel Est
Tel: 597-0166 or
toll-free 1-800/597-0597
Besides Parc Lafontaine in Plateau Mont-Royal neighborhood. **$$**
Delta Montréal
475 Président-Kennedy
Tel: 286-1986 or
toll-free 1-877/286-1986
Good facilities. **$$$**
Hilton Montréal Bonaventure
1 Place Bonaventure
Tel: 878-2332 or
toll-free: 1-800/HILTONS
Central location, first-class facilities and gloriously peaceful rooftop garden. **$$$**
Holiday Inn Montréal-Midtown
420 rue Sherbrooke Ouest
Tel: 842-6111 or
toll-free 1-800/387-3042
One of five Montréal Holiday Inns which vary in size and price. Health club and indoor pool. **$$$**
Hôtel du Parc
3625 Ave Parc
Tel: 288-6666 or
toll-free: 1-800/363-0735
One of four Ramadas, providing good service. **$$**
Hôtel Manoir des Alpes
1245 rue St-André
Tel: 845-9803 or
toll-free 1-800/465-2929
Modern rooms set in Gallic neighborhood. **$**
Hotel Montréal Crescent
1366 René-Lévesque
Tel: 938-9797 or
toll-free 1-800/361-5064
Small and intimate in heart of downtown. **$–$$**

Price Codes

Addresses for accommodations are listed by province and thereafter by city. Hotels are divided into three categories:
$$$ – over $200 per room
$$ – $100–200 per room
$ – under $100 per room

McGill University Residences
3935 rue University
Tel: 398-6367
Central budget accommodation during the summer. **$**
Montréal Youth Hostel
1030 Rue Mackay
Tel: 843-3317. **$**
The Queen Elizabeth
900 René-Lévesque Ouest
Tel: 861-3511 or
toll-free: 1-800/441-1414
Dependable comfort in prime location. **$$–$$$**
Ritz Carlton Montréal
1228 rue Sherbrooke Ouest
Tel: 842-4212 or
toll-free: 1-800/363-0366
Located amid the downtown shopping area. The Ritz caters to an élite clientele. **$$$**
Westin Mont-Royal
1050 rue Sherbrooke Ouest

Québec Farm Vacations

The Fédération des Agricotours du Québec and the Québec Ministry of Agriculture co-sponsor an inexpensive bed-and-breakfast farm vacation program which offers several possibilities. It's an interesting alternative for campers. For further details, contact:
Fédération des Agricotours du Québec, 4545 ave Pierre-de-Coubertin, Montréal, PQ H1V 3R2. Tel: 514/252-3138.
They publish a useful bilingual book, *Affordable Bed and Breakfast in Québec*, which can be purchased through the website www.agritours.qc.ca or at most Canadian bookstores.

Tel: 284-1110 or
toll-free 1-800/228-3000
Excellent location and fine facilities including a fitness center. Multilingual concierge. **$$$**

North Hatley (819)
Auberge Hatley
Tel: 842-2451
A Relais & Châteaux inn, overlooking Lac Massawippi. Mix of traditional French–Canadian, Provençal and English country decor. Superb dining room. **$$$**
Hovey Manor
Tel: 842-2421
An impressive lakeside mansion inspired by George Washington's Mount Vernon. Cozy English country-style decor, excellent dining. **$$$**

Alternative Accommodation

Montréal and Québec have both adopted the European system of staying in residents' homes. Tel: 514/289-9749 or toll-free: 1-800/267-5180 for B & B Downtown Network in Montréal. Tourism Québec publishes an excellent *Accommodation Guide* that includes bed & breakfasts, tourist residences (for 5 or fewer guests), youth hostels, resort villages and educational institutions.

Percé (418)
Hôtel-Motel La Normandie
Tel: 782-2112 or
toll-free 1-800/463-0820
Hotel overlooking Percé Rock with a pleasant restaurant and a gym. **$$**

Québec City (418)
Although a wide variety of accommodations can be found within the old city, Québec is renowned for its grand old hotels and modest, European-style guest homes. Visitors looking for larger or more modern lodgings may have to stay in the new city.
Auberge de la Place d'Armes
24 rue Ste-Anne
Tel: 694-9485
Simple but elegant rooms; excellent locale near city hall. **$**

Centre International de Séjour de Québec
19 rue Ste-Ursule. Tel: 694-0755
Sizable youth hostel featuring bed-and-breakfast lodgings. **$**
Château Frontenac
1 rue des Carrières
Tel: 692-3861 or
toll-free: 1-800/441-1414.
600-room castle set atop a cliff overlooking the St Lawrence river – worth seeing even if one doesn't stay overnight. **$$$**
Hôtel Château Bellevue
16 rue de la Porte
Tel: 692-2573 or
toll-free 1-800/463-2617
Within the old city, antique facade conceals ultramodern accommodation. Free parking. **$–$$**
Hôtel au Château Fleurs-de-Lys
15 ave Ste-Geneviève
Tel: 694-1884
Inside the old city walls. Wide selection of rooms, all prices include continental breakfast. **$$**
Hôtel Château Laurier
695 Grand Allée E
Tel: 522-8108 or
toll-free 1-800/463-4453
Old, but well-maintained; perfect location for Winter Carnival. **$$**
Hôtel Clarendon
57 rue Ste-Anne
Tel: 692-2480 or
toll-free: 1-800/463-5250
The city's oldest hotel. Centrally located, good value. **$$–$$$**
Hôtel La Maison Acadienne
43 rue Ste-Ursule
Tel: 694-0280
Quiet rooms just outside the city walls. **$**
Hôtel Manoir Ste-Geneviève
13 ave Ste-Geneviève
Tel: 694-1666
Like most small Québec hotels, the Ste-Geneviève offers a variety of charming, comfortable rooms. **$–$$**
Hôtel Manoir Victoria
44 Côte du Palais
Tel: 1-800/463-6283
Renovated hotel in heart of Old Quebec, with European ambience. **$–$$**
Québec Hilton
1100 boul. René-Lévesque
Tel: 647-2411 or

toll-free: 1-800/447-2411
Spacious rooms, recently
renovated; kids often stay free. **$$$**
Radisson Hôtel des Gouveneurs Québec
690 boul. René-Lévesque
Tel: 647-1717 or toll-free 1-888/910-111 (Canada and US) or 1-800/333-3333 (internationally)
Modern, tasteful accommodations a short walk from the old city. **$$$**

Ste-Adéle (450)
Hôtel L'Eau à la Bouche
3003 boul. Ste-Adèle
Tel: 229-2991
Cosy country lodge with international cuisine. **$$$**
Hôtel Le Chantecler
1474 chemin du Chantecler
Tel: 229-3555 or
toll-free 1-800/363-2420
Popular lakeside resort with a wide range of activities on and beyond the resort. **$$**

Ste-Agathe-des-Monts (819)
Auberge de la Tour du Lac
173 chemin Tour du Lac.
Tel: 326-4202 or
toll-free 1-800/622-1735.
Charming country inn on Lac des Sables. **$$**

St-Sauveur (450)
Hôtel Manoir St-Sauveur
246 Chemin du Lac Millette
Tel: 1-800/361-0505
Modern hotel in one of the Laurentian's most picturesque villages, only 45 minutes from downtown Montreal. Sports centre and fine dining. **$$**

Val David (819)
Auberge de Vieux Foyer
3167 montée Doncaster
Tel: 322-2686 or
toll-free 1-800/567-8327
Small, comfortable swiss-style inn. **$$**
Hôtel La Sapinière
1244 chemin de la Sapinière
Tel: 322-2020 or
toll-free 1-800/567-6635
La Sapinière is perhaps the finest luxury resort in Québec. Expensive, but full board included. Cottages are also available. **$$$**

Moose Jaw (306)
Temple Gardens Mineral Spa Hotel/Resort
24 Fairford Street East.
Tel: 694-5055 or
toll-free:1-800/718-7727.
In heart of historic district, with a geo-thermal mineral spa. Full facilities. **$$**

Saskatchewan Farm Vacations

There are farm vacations and then there are Saskatchewan farm vacations. Time and again, travelers return home with glowing accounts of their stay on a Saskatchewan farm: the hearty home-cooking, the fresh air, even sharing the chores, are often raved about. Camping on a farm can be arranged. Vacation farms are listed along with B&Bs in Tourism Saskatchewan's annual *Accommodation, Resort & Campground Guide*. For further information, write to Saskatchewan Country Vacation Association, 1308 Fifth Avenue North, Saskatoon, SK S7K 2S2. Tel: 306/664-3278.

SASKATCHEWAN

Regina (306)
Hotel Saskatchewan Radisson Plaza
Victoria Avenue at Scarth Street
Tel: 522-7691 or
toll-free: 1-800/333-3333
Elegantly restored heritage hotel with modern accoutrements. **$$$**
Plains Hotel
1965 Albert Street
Tel: 757-8661 or
toll-free: 1-800/665-1000
Quality accommodation in downtown location. Known for its Sunday brunch. **$**
Regina Inn
1975 Broad Street at Victoria Avenue
Tel: 525-6767 or
toll-free: 1-800/667-8162
Good rooms and suites. Piano bar, dinner theater, restaurant. **$$**

Saskatoon (306)
Comfort Inn by Journey's End
2155 Northridge Drive
Tel: 934-1122 or
toll-free 1-800/228-5150
Large well-kept family-sized rooms, few facilities. **$**
Delta Bessborough
601 Spadina Crescent. E
Tel: 244-5521 or
toll-free: 1-800/268-1133
Elegant riverside château-style hotel, where each room or suite is different; recreational facilities, bars and restaurants. **$$$**
Saskatoon Inn
2002 Airport Drive
Tel 242-1440 or
toll-free 1-800/667-8789
Pool, restaurant, nightly entertainment. Situated close to the airport. **$$**
Sheraton Cavalier
612 Spadina Crescent. E
Tel: 652-6770 or
toll-free 1-800/325-3535
Luxury downtown hotel; skytop lounge. **$$–$$$**

Prince Albert (306)
Marlboro Inn
67 13th Street East
Tel: 763-2643 or
toll-free 1-800/661-7666
Clean, comfortable rooms. Close to airport, bus station and shopping mall. **$$**

THE YUKON

The Yukon offers a good variety of lodgings. Make reservations early in the year for the crowded summer months, particularly July. As a general rule, the territory's hotels and motels equal those in southern Canada, but are more expensive. Tourism Yukon provides a complete list of accommodations in its *Official Vacation Guide*. Below is a representative sampling.

Dawson City (867)
Westmark Inn Dawson
Tel: 1-800/993-5542
Prestigious chain hotel connected with Holland America Cruise Line.

Numerous campgrounds, many with modern facilities and hook-ups, dot Yukon highways. Bring a tent, bring or rent a camper, or trailer. Contact Tourism Yukon for more details.

Downtown area, good dining room, also Klondike barbecue. **$$**
Dawson City Bunkhouse
Princess Street
Tel: 993-6164
Newly built, rustic setting, no-frills. **$**

Whitehorse (867)
Hawkins House
303 Hawkins Street
Tel: 668-7638
Luxurious Victorian home, now a highly recommended B&B. **$$**
River View Hotel
102 Wood Street
Tel: 403/667-7801
Though remodeled, hostelry dates to early days of territory. Large, tasteful rooms, overlooking Yukon River. **$$**
Westmark Klondike Inn
2288 2nd Avenue
Tel: 668-4747 or
toll-free: 1-800/999-2570
Modern hotel with nice touches, great view of the mountains. Cocktail lounge, dining room, cabaret on the premises. **$$**
Yukon Inn
4220 4th Avenue
Tel: 667-2527 or
toll-free: 1-800/661-0454
Modern, spacious rooms, some with kitchenettes. Lounges, dining room, hair salon. **$$**

Price Codes

Addresses for accommodations are listed by province and thereafter by city. Hotels are divided into three categories:
$$$ – over $200 per room
$$ – $100–200 per room
$ – under $100 per room

Where to Eat

Canada's culinary history is like a recipe made up of many ingredients, with each province having its own specialties. The Atlantic waters of the Maritimes dish up excellent seafood, while Québec's French roots, combined with the Native ways of eating, have created a unique cuisine. Ontario is known for its vegetables, fruits and wines; the Prairies produce wheat and choice beef; British Columbia is synonymous with salmon, and the Northern Territories with Arctic char.

Dining out in Canada's cities is every bit as sophisticated and varied as in any of the world's major cities. For the more casual eater, fast-food restaurants, diners and coffee shops, some open 24 hours, dot the landscape. Provincial sales tax (except in the Northwest Territories) and the national 7 percent Goods and Services tax apply to eating out.

ALBERTA

Alberta is cowboy country in the midst of fertile famland, producing some of the best grain-fed beef in North America. Not surprisingly, it's a steak-lover's paradise. French, Italian, Continental, and Asian cuisine are also well represented.

Banff (403)
Le Beaujolais
corner of Banff Avenue and Buffalo Street
Tel: 762-2712
French four-star restaurant in a pleasant setting. **$$$**
Caramba! Restaurante
Banff Ptarmigan Inn
337 Banff Avenue

Tel: 762-3667
A fun, laid-back atmosphere with open kitchen. Mediterranean-based dishes plus BC seafood, Alberta beef and Asian specialties. **$–$$**
Giorgio's Trattoria
219 Banff Avenue
Tel: 762-5114
Italian decor and menu. Pizza prepared in a wood-fired store. **$$**

Calgary (403)
La Brezza Ristorante
990 1st Avenue
Tel: 262-6230
Fine Italian cuisine in a cosily converted old house. Haunt of local celebrities. **$$**
El Sombrero
520 – 17th Avenue SW
Tel: 228-0332
A cheerful "el-cheapo" restaurant that dishes up substantial Mexican fare. **$**
Inn on Lake Bonavista
747 Lake Bonavista Drive SE
Tel: 271-6711
Lakeside patio, floor to ceiling windows. Continental health menu. Children's menu. **$$**
The Owl's Nest Dining Room
Westin Hotel Calgary
320 – 4th Ave SW
Tel: 266-1611
Continental cooking, interesting menu; extensive wine list. **$$$**
The Panorama Dining Room
Calgary Tower,
101 – 9th Ave SW
Tel: 256-7171
Spacious, sky-top, revolving restaurant features international fare. Beautiful view of Calgary and the Rocky Mountains. **$$$**
River Café
Prince's Island Park
Tel: 261-7670
Frontier decor, Canadian home-style menu, generous portions. Large wine list. Because it's on an island, be prepared to walk 500 meters. **$$**
Street Rose
2116 – 4th Street SW
Tel: 509-9111
California café food with emphasis on health-conscious eating. Salads and low-fat vegetarian dishes, burgers, stir-fries and fajitas. **$**

Santorini Greek Taverna
1502 Centre Street N
Tel: 276-8363
Greek decor and menu. Famous for its seafood platters. **$**

Edmonton (708)
Asian Hut
4620 – 99th Street
Tel: 438-1204
The place for Indian curries, prepared to every spice level. Wide selection of vegetarian dishes, including a vegetarian buffet on Tuesdays. **$**
Bistro Praha
10168 – 100A Street
Tel: 424-4218
Sober decor, heavy furnishings, antique lamps. Central European theme and menu. **$$**
Café Select
10018 – 106th Street
Tel: 423-0419
Low-light elegance. Superb beef and lamb, sinful desserts. **$$$**
The Crêperie
10220 – 103rd Street
Tel: 420-6656
French-style stuffed crêpes. **$$**
Jack's Grill
5824 – 111th Street
Tel: 434-1113
Considered by some to be Edmonton's best restaurant. Save room for the homemade bread pudding. **$$$**

BRITISH COLUMBIA

Pacific salmon reigns supreme, along with king crab and other shellfish, but lamb is also a great favorite here where English-style roasts – and afternoon teas and chocolate creams – reflect the British heritage. These days other ethnic cuisines have made a significant dent in that heritage. The lush Okanagan Valley produces apples, cherries, peaches and apricots, and out of its vineyards come choice wines.

Nelson (250)
All Season's Cafe
620 Herridge Lane
Tel: 352-0101
Delicious food in unusual combinations, combined with award-winning wine list mean reservations highly recommended. **$$$**
The Rice Bowl Sushi Whole Foods
542 Vernon Street
A sushi bar that also serves a wide variety of vegetarian and other oriental fare. **$$**

Prince George
Da Moreno
1493 3rd Ave
Tel: 564-7922
On main shopping street, decor is minimal, but the basic Tuscan menu lives up to its promises. **$$**
The Log House Restaurant
Hwy 16a, 10 km (6 miles) south of town
Tel: 963-9515
Pretty setting overlooking lake, interesting decor, good food. **$$**

Culinary Capital

One of Canada's cosmopolitan cities, Vancouver is not only influenced by the trends from California to the south, but has also experienced the huge Pacific Northwest culinary boom drifting north from Seattle, Washington. The result is that this gourmet-trendy city has some of the most avant-garde chefs and best restaurants in the country.

Vancouver
The Cannery
2205 Commissioner Street
Tel: 254-9606
West-coast style seafood, excellent service; among the top restaurants in Canada. **$$$**
Chartwell
Four Seasons Hotel, 791 W Georgia Street
Tel: 844-6715
Primarily French dishes, perfectly prepared and served. **$$$**
Diva
Metropolitan Hotel, 645 Howe Street
Tel: 687-1122
Flawless execution of international

Price Codes

The price of a meal is indicated is per person, excluding alcohol, taxes and tip. The categories are:
$$$ = over $40
$$ = under $40
$ = under $20

cuisine and a spectacular wine cellar. **$$$**
Grouse Nest Restaurant
6400 Nancy Green Way, North Vancouver
Tel: 984-0661
High above the city, reached via complementary Skyride lift. West coast menu. **$$**
William Tell
Georgian Court Hotel
765 Beatty Street
Tel: 688-3504
Swiss-continental cuisine in the Georgian Court Hotel. **$$**
Le Crocodile
909 Burrard Street
Tel: 669-4298
French-Alsatian menu and impeccable service. **$$**
Seasons in the Park Restaurant
Queen Elizabeth Park
Tel: 874-8008
Pacific Northwest menu, nice service and superb views of the beautiful park with the city as backdrop. **$$**
The Prow
Canada Place (northeast corner)
Tel: 684-1339
Waterside cafe with panoramic views of the harbor. Seafood, poultry, etc. **$$**
Tomato Cafe
3305 Cambie Street
Tel: 874-6020
Fifties-style diner serving wholesome, casual meals mixing Mexican, New Mexican and Thai cuisine with good selection of vegetarian dishes. **$$**

Victoria (250)
Dilettantes Cafe
787 Fort Street
Tel: 381-3327
Cozy cafe, voted one of the city's best vegetarian restaurants. **$**

Empress Room
Empress Hotel, 741 Government St
Tel: 389-2727
Primarily continental menu, with a
few added Northwest coast specials.
Lives up to CP Hotels' reputation for
tasteful elegance. **$$$**

Herald Street Caffe
546 Herald Street
Tel: 381-1441
Modest, but an excellent menu and
wide-ranging wine list. **$$**

Sooke Harbour House
1528 Whiffen Spit Road, Sooke
Tel: 1-800/884-9688
40 km (25 miles) out of town but
worth the journey, for fresh local
seafood and vegetables and
extensive wine list. **$$$**

**Spinnakers Brew Pub and
Restaurant**
308 Catherine Street
Tel: 386-2739
West Coast pub-style restaurant,
overlooking Inner Harbor, with in-
house brews. **$**

Whistler (604)

Grassroots Cafe
4295 Blackcomb Way
Tel: 938-0331
Popular with locals. Good range of
vegetarian fare on the menu. **$**

La Rua
4557 Blackcomb Way
Tel: 932-5011
One of Whistler's better restaurants,
with wide-ranging and imaginative
Mediterranean fare. **$$$**

MANITOBA

Selkirk whitefish and Winnipeg
goldeye are local delicacies in a
region that's dominated by beef.
Along with the other Prairie provinces,
Manitoba has a significant Ukrainian
population which has contributed
pierogies (ravioi-like crescent-shaped
pockets of cheese, cabbage or
potato), cabbage rolls and spicy
sausages to the local cuisine.

Flin Flon

Bakers Narrows Lodge
Tel: 687-7944
In Bakers Narrows. A favorite of

hunters and fishermen. (You may
like to stay here, too.) **$$**

Portage la Prairie

Bill's Sticky Fingers
210 Saskatchewan Avenue
Tel: 857-9999
Home style cuisine, children's
menu. **$**

Price Codes

The price of a meal is indicated is
per person, excluding alcohol,
taxes and tip. The categories are:
$$$ = over $40
$$ = under $40
$ = under $20

Winnipeg

Part of the Prairie Borscht Belt,
Winnipeg's Ukrainian heritage
coexists with a respectable number
of ethnic cuisines.

Amici
326 Broadway
Tel: 943-4997
Elegant Continental restaurant with
Italian leanings. A few blocks from
downtown. **$$$**

Le Beaujolais
131 Boulevard Provencher,
St-Boniface
Tel: 237-6306
In the French quarter, Winnipeg's
premier French restaurant, with
prices to match. **$$$**

Pasta La Vista
Eaton Place,
234 Donald Street
Tel: 956-2229
Despite its shopping center
location, this Italian restaurant
provides excellent value. **$$**

The Prairie Oyster
1 Forks Market Road
Tel: 942-0918
A wild mix of cuisine, from haute to
basic, but it's always good.
Frequently rated tops in the Prairies
for atmosphere, wit and service. **$$**

Restaurant Dubrovnik
390 Assiniboine Avenue
Tel: 944-0594
Balkan specialties; located in
renovated brick townhouse. **$$**

**Green Gates Country House and
Restaurant**
6945 Roblin Boulevard
Tel: 897-0990
A one-time farmhouse in spacious
grounds beside the Assiniboine
River. Nice country-style menu. **$$**

NEW BRUNSWICK

Lobster, Atlantic salmon, oysters
and clams are plentiful here as in all
the Maritimes, but this province is
particularly known for fiddlehead
greens, the shoots of an edible fern.
This delicacy is usually served
steamed, and can also be bought
pickled in jars.

Alma

Parkland Village Inn
Tel: 887-2313.
A must-stop, close to Fundy National
Park. Famous for its seafood platter
and its hummingbirds, although
fortunately these are not served on
a platter. Reserve ahead in July and
August. **$$**

Campobello Island

Friar's Bay Restaurant
Welshpool
Tel: 752-2056
Substantial, home-cooking at
modest prices. **$**

Fredericton

Brew-Bakers Cafe-Bistro Bar & Grill
546 King Street
Tel: 459-0067
Lively joint, said to have the best
wood-fired pizza in Atlantic Canada. **$**

Bruno's
Sheraton Inn, Fredericton,
225 Woodstock Rd
Tel: 451-7935
International cuisine. Overlooks the
St John River. **$$$**

Fifty Eight Prospect
58 Prospect St W (located in the
Auberge Wandlyn Inn near Trans-
Canada Hwy)
Tel: 462-4444
Canadian menu, children's menu. **$$**

Schade's Restaurant
536 Queen Street. Tel: 450-3340.
Good continental cuisine. **$$**

Kedgewick
La Vieille Gare
24 rue Jeanne D'Arc
Tel: 284-2804
Vegetarian meals served in an old train station by the New Brunswick Trail. Open May–mid-Oct. **$**

Moncton
Le Chateau a Pape
2 Steadman Street
Tel: 855-7273
Occupies an old house overlooking a tidal inlet. An Acadian-accented menu with an extensive wine list. **$$**
Gaston's
644 Main Street
Tel: 858-8998
Popular, modern bistro, interesting menu. **$$**
The Windjammer Dining Room,
Hôtel Beauséjour,
750 Main Street
Tel: 854-4344
Traditional dishes, extensive wine list; formal décor. **$$$**

Robertville
Auberge Les Amies de la Nature
Tel: 783-4793
Between Bathurst and Campbellton, this country restaurant has an extensive vegetarian selection, much of it produced in its own expansive organic gardens. **$$**

Sackville
Marshlands Inn
73 Bridge Street
Tel: 536-0170
Historic country inn with a guest book that reads like a chunk of Canadian history. Interesting seafood concoctions and excellent desserts. **$$**

Saint John
Grannan's Seafood Restaurant
Market Square
Tel: 634-1555
One of the city's most popular seafood restaurants, with locals and visitors alike. **$$**
Incredible Edibles
42 Princess Street
Tel: 633-7554
Fish and poultry, but vegetarian dishes are the specialty. **$$**

Saint John City Market
For Billy's Seafood Restaurant and a number of other excellent, inexpensive eateries. **$**
Taco Pico
96 Germain Street
Tel: 633-8492
A Guatemalan-Mexican menu, delicious sauces made from old family recipes. Fish-lovers, go on Fridays. **$**

Shediac
Chez François 93
Main Street
Tel: 532-4543
Menu emphasises seafood in this port town renowned for its lobster. Also a B&B. **$$**

St Andrews
Passamaquoddy Room
Algonquin Hotel
Tel: 529-8823
Energetic students serve bountiful buffet lunches and formal dinners.
Pansy Patch Tea Garden
59 Carelton
Tel: 529-3834
A turreted house oozing with whimsy and history. Seafood heavily featured on its 5-course dinners. **$$**

NEWFOUNDLAND AND LABRADOR

Fishing has always been the main industry here, especially cod, which is cooked in many ways from fish and chips to gratiné. The island is famous for local specialties with unusual names like brewis (cod), scrunchions and "seal flipper pie". Outside St. John's, the most reliable dining is usually in hotel dining rooms and motel coffee shops. As a general rule, expect the service to be cheerful, but on the slow side.

St John's
Bianca's
171 Water Street. Tel: 726-9016
Bulgarian owner/chef gives makes every dish a distinctively exotic creation. Open kitchen, large wine selection and even a room for cigar smokers. **$$**

Drinking Notes

Canadians are traditionally a beer-drinking nation, and fine beer is brewed at home where microbreweries now produce lagers, ales, pilsners and bock. Imports from Europe, Australia and Mexico are also popular. Canadian wines, mostly from Ontario and British Columbia, are very competitive – some excellent enough to win international aclaim, although restaurants still tend toward French, Italian and California wines. Liquor laws vary from province to province, and sales are heavily regulated. Alcohol can only be purchased in government stores and some special stores (usually of Canadian wines), except in Québec where alcohol can also be purchased in privately-owned convenience stores called *dépanneurs* (check the Yellow Pages). Most restaurants are licensed to serve alcohol, but it's best to check first. The legal age for drinking is 18 or 19.

Classic Cafe
364 Duckworth Street
Tel: 579-4444
The city's first all-night restaurant. Great breakfast dishes served all day. Bread, fishcakes and other local specialties all made on the premises. **$**
The Cabot Club
Hotel Newfoundland
Tel: 726-4980
St John's finest. Wonderful view of the harbor. **$$$**
Stella's
106 Water Street
Tel: 735-9625
Good, home-style cooking with varied menu. **$**

Witless Bay (709)
The Captain's Table
Hwy 10, 35 km (22mi) south of St John's
Tel: 334-2278.
Touted as serving the best fish and chips in Newfoundland. The

fisherman's platter is also spectacular, as are the largely homemade desserts. **$**

THE NORTHWEST TERRITORIES

Food is flown into the Territories and is mostly canned and packaged. The traditional Inuit and Dene (Northern Indian) ways of eating have largely been lost, but Artic char – similar to salmon but with a softer taste – is a regional delicacy.

Inuvik (867)
The Green Briar
Mackenzie Hotel, 185 Mackenzie Rd
Tel: 777-2861
Musk ox, caribou and Arctic char are its summer time specialties, along with a nice selection of homemade deserts. **$$$**

Yellowknife (867)
Factor's Club
Explorer Hotel
Tel: 403/873-3531
Surprisingly cosmopolitan dining with Greek influence; known for beef and seafood dishes. **$$$**
The Office
4915 50 Street
Tel: 873-3750
A comfortable restaurant which serves many southern staples as well as local caribou, musk ox and whitefish. **$$$**
The Wildcat Café
Wiley Road
Tel: 873-8850
Dating to pioneer times in the 1930s, it preserves the frontier atmosphere in a log house where strangers share tables. Menu includes caribou and musk ox meat and locally caught whitefish. **$$**

Price Codes

The price of a meal is indicated is per person, excluding alcohol, taxes and tip. The categories are:
$$$ = over $40
$$ = under $40
$ = under $20

NOVA SCOTIA

Clam chowder, lobster, Digby scallops, Lunenberg sausage are part of Nova Scotia's menu, particularly the clam chowder which Nova Scotians will goodhumoredly insist is superior to that of New England, their neighbor to the south. Here you'll also find delicious baked fruit puddings of Acadian origin.

There is no sales tax on food or restaurant meals, but the latter are subject to the 7 percent national Goods and Services Tax. Prices here are still 20 percent higher than in southern Canada.

Ingonish Beach
Keltic Lodge
Tel: 285-2880 or
toll-free 1-800/565-0440
This famous hotel's dining room is thought to serve the best fare on Cape Breton Island, and also the most expensive. Fabulous coastal views. **$$$**

Halifax
Hotel dining rooms are popular, but the following are representative of independent restaurants and cafés:
Cheelin
Brewery Market
1496 Lower Market Street
Tel: 422-2252
A family-run restaurant offering almost 100 innovative Chinese dishes that are constantly changing. 48-hours notice required for Peking duck. A great favorite with locals. **$$**
De Maurizio
in Old Brewery complex,
1496 Lower Water Street
Tel: 423-0859
Italian theme, excellent Mediterranean menu. **$$$**
Five Fishermen
1740 Argyle Street
Tel: 422-4421
A good seafood restaurant in historic building where Anna and the King of Siam once taught. **$$**
Old Man Morias
1150 Barrington Street
Tel: 422-7960
Warm atmosphere, Greek cuisine. **$**

Satisfaction Feast
1581 Grafton Street
Tel: 422-3540
A long-time fixture on the Halifax scene, and considered its premier vegetarian restaurant. Huge helpings and cheerful decor. **$**

Shelburne
Charlotte Lane Café
13 Charlotte Lane
Tel: 875-3314
Local produce, both seafood and vegetables, a strong feature, but Cajun and Italian grace the menu as well. **$$**

Yarmouth
Captain Kelley's Restaurant
577 Main Street
Tel: 742-9191
Good range of pub fare at the right price. **$**

NUNAVUT

Generally, visitors to Nunavut eat at their hotel, or the tour outfitters provide their meals.

Iqaluit
Grind and Brew
Tel: 979-0606
Specialty coffees and desserts.
Fantasy Palace
Tel: 979-3963
A popular coffee and dessert spot.
The Granite Room
Discovery Hotel
Tel: 979-4433
Limited menu reflects city's remote location, with three or four table d'hôte dinners nightly, one of which features local seafood. **$$$**

ONTARIO

In the last few decades, the province has progressed from a stodgy meat-and-potatoes heritage to a vibrant food culture. It is rich in cornfields, peach orchards and vineyards producing prize-winning wines, a flourishing cheese-making industry (Ontario cheddar is famous), and game bird farms.

Kingston (613)
Chez Piggy
68 Princess St
Tel: 549-7673
Inventive food including excellent soups. Set in former livery stable and courtyard at rear of building.
Hoppin' Eddy's
393 Princess Street
Lively, easy-going atmosphere featuring good Cajun fare and zydeco. **$$**

Niagara Falls
Skylon Tower Restaurant
5200 Robinson St
Tel: 356-2651
Continental menu; one pays, in part, for the phenomenal view. **$$$**

Ottawa (613)
Claire de lune
81B Clarence Street
Tel: 241-2200
Extraordinary creations of fusion-style cuisine, with a different *menu du jour* every night. **$$**
Coriander Thai
282 Kent St
Tel: 233-2828
Serves a beautifully presented range of classical Thai dishes. **$$**
Friday's Roast Beef House
150 Elgin St
Tel: 237-5353
Known for its steaks and ribs. Lunches are crowded, dinners on the expensive side. **$$**
Mamma Teresa's
300 Somerset St W
Tel: 236-3023
Delightful Italian dishes; very authentic. **$$**
Marble Works
14 Walter St
Tel: 241-6764
Medieval-style gluttony with wandering minstrels and hearty Canadian food. **$$**
The Mill Restaurant
555 Ottawa River Pkwy
Tel: 237-1311
Great seafood and steaks; overlooks the river. **$$**
Nate's Deli
316 Rideau St
Tel: 789-9191
An Ottawa landmark. **$**

Old Fish Market
54 York St
Tel: 241-4954.
Situated in historic Byward Market. Fresh fish; consistently good. **$$**
Romano's
309 Richmond Rd
Tel: 722-6772
A taste of Tuscany in a cheery neighborhood restaurant. **$$**
Something Fishy In Bells Corners,
194 Robertson Rd. Nothing but fresh fish in the café at the front of Lapointe's fish store. **$**
Japanese Village Steak & Seafood House
170 Laurier Ave W
Tel: 236-9519
Japanese cuisine, prepared at your table. **$$**
Le Café
National Arts Centre
Tel: 594-5127
Lovely setting beside Rideau Canal. Focuses on Canadian product and wines. **$$$**
L'Echelle de Jacob
27 Blvd Lucerne, Aylmer
Tel: 819/684-1040
Cozy French restaurant. **$$**
Le Jardin
127 York St
Tel: 241-1424
Award-winning international cuisine, set in an old Victorian home. **$$**

Stratford (519)
The Church Restaurant
70 Brunswick St
Tel: 273-3424
One of Canada's premiere dining experiences in a huge church with altar and organ pipes. Unequaled lamb, veal, trout and lobster are regularly on the menu. Reserve at least two weeks in advance, especially for a weekend visit. **$$$**

Toronto
There is almost no food or ingredient that can't be found in Toronto, however exotic. Thanks to massive immigration, in the last several decades the city has turned into a foodie's paradise, not just in its restaurants, numbering up to 5,000 at any given time, but also in its gourmet stores and countless

Toronto restaurants
Toronto is home to at least half a dozen world-class restaurants. Dinner for two, with wine, taxes and tip, will cost at least $150 in this category, although lunch often runs less than half that. Proper dress usually required; call ahead for reservations.
Avalon, 270 Adelaide St W. Tel: 979-9918. One of the most imaginative menus in the city. Wood-roasted chicken and wood-grilled sardines are both regular features. **$$$**
Centro, 2472 Yonge St. Tel: 483-2211. An exotic fusion of French technique and Canadian ingredients in gorgeous art deco surroundings. **$$$**

ethnic markets. The abundance of ethnic eateries also makes Toronto an exciting city in which to dine.
Amadeu's
184 Augusta Ave
Tel: 591-1245
Popular Portuguese seafood restaurant in heart of Kensington Market. **$$**
Boulevard Café
161 Harbord Street
Tel: 961-7676
A longtime Annex fixture, Peruvian decor and cuisine. Extensive wine list, largely from South America or Spain. Heated outdoors terrace. **$$**
Café Brussel
786 Broadview Avenue
Tel: 465-7363
Could almost be sitting in Brussels' Grand' Place, enjoying an intriguing selection of Old World classics. **$$$**
Canoe
66 Wellington St W
Tel: 364-0054
Great views overlooking Lake Ontario and downtown from 54th floor. Canadian is theme of both decor and food. **$$$**
Filet of Sole
11 Duncan St
Tel: 598-3256
Far-ranging menu with spicy overtones, served in former warehouse in Theatre District. **$$**

Price Codes

The price of a meal is indicated is per person, excluding alcohol, taxes and tip. The categories are:
$$$ = over $40
$$ = under $40
$ = under $20

Grappa
797 College St
Tel: 535-3337
An unpretentious restaurant in heart of Little Italy, with a superb, and reasonably-priced wine list. **$$**
Happy Seven
358 Spadina Ave
Tel: 971-9820
Large and tasty Cantonese and Szechuan dishes. **$**
Le Select
328 Queen St W
Tel: 596-6406
Hearty French fare at moderate prices; a popular spot for over 20 years. **$$**
Masa
205 Richmond St W
Tel: 348-9720
Painstakingly authentic Japanese cuisine. **$$**
Mövenpick
133 Yorkville Ave
Tel: 926-9545
Imaginative complex of Swiss restaurants and lounges. Provides something to suit all different tastes and budgets. **$$**
Queen Mother Café
208 Queen St W
Tel: 598-4719
Combination of Thai and vegetarian. No connection to royalty, but fun. **$$**
Rashnaa
307 Wellesley St E
Tel: 929-2099.
Based in tiny quarters, excellent, and mostly mild, Tamil-Sri Lankan fare is served. Friendly atmosphere and inexpensive. **$**
Sneaky Dee's
431 College St W
Tel: 603-3090.
Good, cheap Mexican food. **$**
Southern Accent
595 Markham St
Tel: 536-3211

Good Creole-Cajun vittles served in a renovated two-storey Victorian house. **$$**
El Palenque
653 St. Clair Ave W
Tel: 656-0725
Small, inexpensive Mexican eatery. Large servings and good Mexican beer. **$**
Jacques' Bistro du Parc
126A Cumberland St
Tel: 961-1893
California-styled cuisine with a Québec flavor served in attractive but narrow, second-floor walk-up space. **$$**
Le Paradis
166 Bedford Rd
Tel: 921-0095
Popular neighborhood bistro, solid French cuisine. **$$**
Little Tibet
81 Yorkville Ave
Tel: 963-8221
Delicious meals, with bold flavorings. **$$**
Madoka
252 Dupont St
Tel: 924-3548
A traditionally serene dining room, and a sushi bar that offers wide range of items. **$$**
Sultan's Tent
1280 Bay St
Tel: 961-0601
North African and Middle Eastern delights. **$$**

PRINCE EDWARD ISLAND

Prince Edward Island is best known for its delicious high-quality potatoes, with Malpeque oysters coming in a close second. Both are prized by the whole country. In summer, all-you-can-eat lobster suppers are traditional.

Charlottetown (902)
Cedar's Eatery
81 University Avenue
Tel: 892-7377
Basic surroundings but delicious Lebanese dishes. Very popular. **$**
Lobster on the Wharf
Prince Street Wharf
Tel: 368-2888

Great selection of reasonably priced seafood, overlooking the harbor. **$$**
The Selkirk Dining Room
Prince Edward Hotel, 18 Queen St
Tel: 566-2222
Expensive but sumptuous dining. **$$$**

Summerside
Brothers Two Restaurant
Water St E
Tel: 436-9654
Popular seafood and steaks. Features "Governor's Feast," a dinner-theater meal served by the cast. The building also houses Findley's pub. **$$**

Around the Island

Lobster Suppers: Civic groups sponsor traditional "Lobster Suppers" throughout the province in July and August. Expect to pay $20 to $25 per person for the evening, but they're usually "all-you-can-eat" dinners. Here are some popular ones:
New Glasgow Lobster Suppers
Rte 228, New Glasgow
Tel: 964-2870.
St Ann's Church Lobster Suppers
Rte 224
Tel: 621-6635 in Hope River.
St Margaret's Lobster Suppers
Tel: 687-3105.

QUÉBEC

Québec's French heritage includes a passion for good food and wine, and it's taken seriously whether it's in a gourmet restaurant or a modest bistro. French cuisine dominates but restaurants also offer local *habitant* cooking, a home-grown French provincial cuisine, such as the typical *tourtière*, game-and-potato pie, pea soup, and maple syrup desserts. Québec is Canada's maple syrup producer, and both the syrup and maple sugar candy are available everywhere.

Montréal (514)
More ethnically inclined than Québec City, Montréal rivals New

York for its delicatessen fare: Montréal smoked meat is famous, and its bagels are reputed to be the best. French and international cuisine are very well represented in its more than 5,000 restaurants, bistros and brasseries.

Ben's Delicatessen
990 boul. de Maisonneuve
Tel: 844-1000
Late night deli spot; Pierre Trudeau was known to stop by.

Le Caveau
2063 rue Victoria
Tel: 844-1624
Fine French food in a quaint, midtown locale. **$$**

Les Filles du Roy
415 rue Bonsecours
Tel: 849-3535
French-Canadian food in a 17th-century Québec setting. Reservations advised. **$$$**

Les Halles
1450 rue Crescent
Tel: 844-2328
This French restaurant is a Montréal institution. Known for its fresh fish, local lamb and enormous wine cellar. **$$$**

Laloux
250 avenue des Pins
Tel: 287-9127
A gay nineties decor and wonderful French food. One "must" is the foie gras, regardless of cost. **$$**

Le P'Tit Port
1813 rue St Catherine
Tel: 932-6556
A tiny restaurant where the fresh fish is cooked to perfection. A real find. **$$**

Québec City (418)
Québec City is gastronomy personified, and even fast food is a cut above the average. Service and atmosphere are very important, so only the best restaurants survive. Modest restaurants also reflect this dedication to excellence.

Aux Anciens Canadiens
34 rue St-Louis
Tel: 692-1627
Housed in one of the oldest houses in Québec, this hugely popular restaurant serves large helpings of delicious Québecois fare. **$$**

Le Commensal
860 St-Jean
Tel: 647-3733
Outside the walls, this popular vegetarian restaurant is packed, 7 days a week. **$**

Kyoto
560 Grande Allée Est
Tel: 529-6141
Japanese steak house. **$$**

La Marie Clarisse
12 Petit-Champlain
Tel: 692-0857
One of the city's best seafood restaurants, in the Lower Town. **$$$**

L'Omelette
66 rue St-Louis
Tel: 694-9626
Great selections of omelets, pancakes and quiches. **$**

Le Rétro Restaurant
1129 rue St-Jean
Tel: 694-9218
French cuisine and a sunny solarium. **$$**

La Ripaille
9 rue Buade. Tel: 692-2450

Québec Province

The hearty *habitant* cooking of rural Québec takes advantage of the fresh herbs, vegetables, fish, rabbit, mutton and other meats found bountifully in the province.

AIE ST PAUL (418)
Le Mouton Noir
43 rue Ste-Anne
Tel: 435-3075
Most of the produce from Québec, from wild boar sausages to Charlevoix snails. **$$**

GASPE (418)
La Maison du Pêcheur
155 Place du Quai (Percé)
Tel: 782-5331
Seafood lovers' delight located right on the pier, with a great view of the harbor (early May to mid-October). **$$$**

HULL (819)
Laurier sur Montcalm
199 rue Montcalm
Tel: 775-5030

French cuisine and seafood. Reservations advised. **$$$**

Le St-Amour
48 Rue Ste-Ursule
Tel: 694-0667
French cooking in quiet romantic setting. **$$$**

SASKATCHEWAN

Canada's wheat grows here, so not surprisingly grain-fed beef and grain-fed fowl such as partridge and duck are extremely good. Unique to the province is the blueberry-like Saskatoon berry.

Regina (306)
Bartleby's Dining Emporium and Gathering Place
1920 Broad Street
Tel: 565-0040
Pub-style atmosphere, heavy on antiques and memorabilia. Popular dishes, children's menu. Some Karaoke evenings. **$$**

One of the best restaurants in the Ottawa area, housed in an old railway station. Innovative cooking. Reservations a must. **$$$**

ILE D'ORLEANS (418)
Auberge le Canard Huppé
2198 chemin Royale
Tel: 828-2292
Elegant inn overlooking the St Lawrence. Specialises in regional dishes. **$$**

Le Moulin de St-Laurent
754 chemin Royal
St-Laurent
Tel: 829-3716 or toll-free 1-888/629-3888
Traditional Québecois fare served in a converted flourmill dating back to 1720. A fine restaurant. **$$**

VAL DAVID
La Sapinière
Tel: 322-2020
Prizewinning entrées join an exquisite wine list for a truly sumptuous dinner. **$$$**

The Diplomat
2032 Broad Street
Tel: 359-3366
Semi-formal in elegant surroundings. Large menu with selections for the health-conscious. Good wine list. **$$$**
Neo Japonica
2167 Hamilton Street
Tel: 359-7669
Japanese restaurant in a residential district. An ever-expanding menu includes 23 varieties of sushi. **$$**

Saskatoon (306)
It is said that Saskatoon's Broadway Avenue has more good small restaurants than any other single Canadian street.
Boomtown Café
Western Development Museum,
2610 Lorne Avenue S
Tel: 931-1910
Home cooking à la Saskatchewan. No license. **$**
Calories
721 Broadway Avenue
Tel: 665-7991
Famed locally for its customer loyalty with a carefully selected eclectic menu. Many say it's the city's best independent restaurant. **$$**
Cousin Nik's
110 Grosvenor Avenue
Tel: 374-2020
Colorful Greek decor. Greek and North American dishes. Come on Sunday and Monday evenings for a traditional Greek dinner. **$$**
Gotta Hava Java
112 Second Avenue North
Tel: 665-3336
A healthy menu with lots of wraps and muffins. Homemade soups and the best coffee in town. **$**
Taj Mahal
1013 Broadway Avenue

Tel: 987-2227
Lovely Indian decor, subtly flavoured Northern Indian cuisine. **$–$$**

THE YUKON

Arctic grayling, salmon and moose steak add some interest to what is otherwise a prosaic Canadian menu of hamburgers and pizzas. Outside Whitehorse, your best bet is usually a hotel or resort dining room.

Whitehorse (867)
Alpine Bakery
411 Alexander Street
Tel: 668-6871
Wholesome baking and cooking with organic ingredients. Also specializes in packing food for major expeditions. **$**
The Cellar Dining Room
Edgewater Hotel, 101 Main Street, opposite White Pass Rail Depot.
Tel: 667-2572
Good west coast with some local specialties. Good wine list. **$$$**
Chocolate Claim
305 Strickland Street
Tel: 667-2202.
European-style coffee bar. Soups, salads, desserts. **$**
Panda's Fine Dining
212 Main Street
Tel: 667-2632
Traditional European cuisine plus local seafood. **$$$**
Sam 'n' Andy's
506 Main Street
Tel: 668-6994.
Mexican bar and grill. **$$**

Outdoor Activities

Travel Packages

ALBERTA

With its huge cultural and geographic diversity, including five of Canada's 12 designated United Nations UNESCO World Heritage Sites, there is a wide variety of packages which take in some of the treasures of the Canadian West. Peace Island Tours offer guided wilderness trips in Peace River Country, from overnight to weeklong adventures. For more information, P.O.Box 5070, Peace River, AL T8S 1R7. Tel: 780/6224-4295 (www.peaceisland.ab.ca).

Trail rides, from one to 10 days for people with no riding experience to experts, are another way to experience Alberta's wilderness. Tourism Alberta's *Explore & Experience Planning Guide* lists about 50 outfitters, another 50 ranches and wilderness retreats including the well-known Black Cat Guest Ranch in Hinton at Tel: 780/865-3084 or toll-free 1-800-859-6840 (www.telusplanet.net/public/bcranch).

For walkers, there's a similar selection of hiking companies, including Canadian Mountain Holidays at Box 1660, Banff, AB T0L 0C0, tel: 403/762-7100 or 1-800/661-0252 (www.cmhhike.com), offering from one to six days of heli-hiking, walking or mountaineering holidays.

For water-oriented travel, there are kayaking, canoeing and whitewater rafting possibilities throughout the province. Hiking, fishing, rockhounding and photography opportunities are often part of the package. One of the most magical of all experiences is watching the Northern Lights. The further north you venture, the more exceptional the view. Fort McMurray is Alberta's northernmost city and offers the most spectacular viewing. Companies such as Can Tours, at tel: 780/452-5187, Magic Country Wilderness Adventures at 780/743-0766 or Ultimate Adventures at 1-800/581-2769, can customize packages to please.

BRITISH COLUMBIA

Whether exploring the province's untouched wilderness or the rich variety of its cultural offerings – from art galleries, museums and theaters to native heritage – the *British Columbia Vacation Planner* and the *Outdoor & Adventure Guide* both list travel packages across the province that have something for practically every interest. Amongst the many firms listed is Seaside Adventures, P.O.Box 178, Tofino, BC V0R 2Z0, tel: 1-888/332-4255 (www.seaside-adventures.com) that offers whale watching, fishing charters and hiking along Pacific Rim Wilderness Trails. Brewster Rail and Motorcoach Tours is one of the longest established firms with over 40 tour packages through the Canadian Rockies. Tel: 1-800/661-1152 or from outside North America call 1-403/762-6717 (www.brewster.ca).

Sea kayaking through the Queen Charlottes, Broken Group, and the Broughton Islands (no experience required) is offered by Pacific Rim Paddling Company, P.O.Box 1840, Department T, Victoria, BC V8W 2Y3. Tel: 250/384-6103 (www.islandnet.com).

Alpine hiking and backcountry skiing is offered by Golden Alpine Holidays at tel: 250/344-7273 (www.fiber.net/users/goalalpine).

MANITOBA

VIA Rail offers exciting, week-long treks to Churchill, via The Pas and Flin Flon. Contact VIA Rail, 104-123 Main St, Winnipeg, R3C 2P8, tel: 944-8780, but don't delay – the waiting list can be up to a year long. Churchill Nature Tours (Box 429, Erickson, MB R0J 0P0. Tel: 636-2968) is one of a number of Manitoba tour companies who can combine this tour with other northern destinations.

Adventure Junkie Tours (Box 2384, Winnipeg R3C 4A6. Tel: 487-0004) has year-round eco-adventure tours across central and southern Manitoba, from kayaking to hot-air ballooning and sled dog tours.

NEW BRUNSWICK

New Brunswick's *Travel Planner* includes details on more than a hundred Day Adventures, as well as multi-day adventures, in every corner of the province, ranging from action-oriented to historical explorations. For example, in the province's River Valley region, On The Pond, 20 Route 615, Jewett Mills. NB E6L 1M2. Tel: 506/363-3420 (www.onthepond.com) offers spa treatments and outdoor adventure packages.

In the Bay of Fundy, Cape Enrage Adventures, tel: 506/887-2273 (summer) and 506/856-6081 (off-season) or www.monctonlife.com/cape_enrage arranges guided rappelling on the 40-meter cliffs. Acadian Day Adventures include kayaking in seal country and learning about Mi'kmaq and Acadian cultures with Kayakouch Inc. tel: 506/876-1199 (www.kayakkkkouch.com) and learning the ropes with T & T Sail Charters, tel: 506/533-4878 (www3.ns.sympatico.ca/jean.tangu ay). Not surprisingly, fishing packages feature heavily on Day Adventures in the Miramichi region.

NEWFOUNDLAND AND LABRADOR

Newfoundland is a popular destination for those seeking exciting wilderness excursions. Canoeing, fishing, hunting and even dogsled tours are available into the recently charted depths of Labrador, but be prepared to pay above $200 per person a day for these. Coastal vessels based at Argentia and Lewisporte, which call at up to five or six isolated coastal villages a day provide a unique way of seeing the province. These vessels have very limited accommodation and do not carry cars. Reservations can only be made from within Newfoundland. Contact the Marine Atlantic Reservations Bureau, Box 520, Channel-Port aux Basques, NF A0M 1C0 or tel: 1-800/341-6866.

Follow the Viking Trail and cross to the Labrador coast for a 900-km (560-mile) return trip which takes in Gross Morne National Park, the L'Anse aux Meadows Viking settlement and Basque whaling station at Red Bay. You will rarely be out of sight of the sea and can expect to see lots of icebergs, probably whales as well. You can drive yourself, or arrange a tour.

Maxxim Vacations is one company which specializes in assembling tour packages of the island, which include customized itineraries, accommodation, car rentals, shipping reservations, and guide services if required. Their address is 11 Rowan Street, Churchill Square, St John's NF A1B 4J9, tel: toll-free 1-800/567-6666.

THE NORTHWEST TERRITORIES

Booking a package tour is a convenient way to visit NWT. These usually depart from Edmonton and entail flying to at least one – probably several – northern outposts, stopping to sample the local food, shop, meet the residents, go canoeing, watch the Northern Lights, etc.

Many visitors choose to stay for a week or two at one of the territories' wilderness hunting/fishing camps and lodges. Packages usually include meals, accommodations, transportation (usually by charter aircraft), guides, outfitting, etc., depending on what one wants and what is available.

A simpler excursion is to drive or fly to Fort Smith and visit Wood Buffalo National Park. For a better description of all the possibilities, contact the NWT Department of Tourism Development and Marketing (*see* Tourist Offices page 341).

NOVA SCOTIA

Outdoor adventure tours are detailed in Nova Scotia's *Complete Guide for Doers & Dreamers*, from companies that offer packages province-wide, including:
Freewheeling Adventures,
RR1, Hubbard, NS, B0J 1T0,
Tel: 902/857-3600
Offers cycling, hiking and ocean kayaking trips in coastal Nova Scotia.
Adventure Quest Expeditions,
Site 8, Box 40, RR1,
Elmsdale, NS B0N 1M0.
Tel: 902/883-1974
For cycling, walking, rafting, sea kayaking and sailing tours. Many more companies are listed in each of the province's tourist regions.

NUNAVUT

The only sensible way to explore the wonders of Nunavut is in the experienced hands of a northern tour operator or outfitter. Many are listed in the *The Arctic Traveler's Nunavut Vacation Planner* published by Nunavut Tourism, ranging from less demanding naturalist/cultural tours to a wide range of more physically demanding adventure packages.
Adventure Canada
Tel: 905/271-4000
www.adventure canada.com
Well established in selling packages to many of Canada's more remote areas, including Nunavut.
Elderhostel
308 Wellington Street, Kingston,
Ontario K7K 7A7
Tel: 613/530-222

Offering a range of educational tours that offer the chance to learn a little Inuktitut, land skills, culture and modern arctic life.

ONTARIO

Bus and train tours often originate from Toronto or Ottawa, lasting anywhere from a day to a fortnight. Common destinations include: Niagara Falls, Toronto, Ottawa, the Muskoka Lakes, 1000 Islands, Québec, Agawa Canyon, or Cochrane. Many excursions are seasonal, such as Fall Color tours, or jaunts to Ottawa for its glorious Tulip Festival.

A convenient and often inexpensive way to visit Toronto, Ottawa, Niagara Falls and other cities and regions, is to travel on a package, which usually includes transportation from the US border, accommodations, and sometimes meals. There are numerous recreation and wilderness packages, including whitewater rafting trips, snowmobiling safaris, yacht and houseboat vacations, bicycle treks and so on.

The major outfits are:
Canadian Wilderness Trips,
45 Charles Street E, Toronto,
ON M4Y 1S2.
Tel: 416/960-2298
www.cndwildernesstrips.com
Wilderness Tours,
Box 89, Beachburg, Ontario.
Tel: 1-800/267-9166 or 613/646-2241
www.wildernesstours.com
Offers whitewater raft trips from mid-May to mid-Sep on the Ottawa River, from 1 to 5 days.
VIA Rail Canada Inc.
Union Station, Toronto,
ON M5J 1E7.
Tel: 416/366-8411, 1-800/835-0337 from elsewhere in Ontario, and a toll-free fax number from the US 1-800/561-3949 to request literature.

The Polar Bear Express, a one-day and three/four train excursions from Cochrane to Moosonee on James Bay, has become famous for

good reasons. The train travels along a historic route through a virtually untouched wilderness, offering a unique opportunity to see northern Ontario. The longer packages make a few stops along the way to pick up/drop off geologists, hunters, aboriginal people, and so on, and are hence a little less touristy. They also afford greater time to explore Moosonee (some bring canoes), which is the air terminus for flights into Polar Bear Provincial Park.

For more details, contact:
Ontario Northland Railway,
Union Station, 65 Front St W,
Toronto, ON M5J 1E6.
Tel: 416/314-3750 or
toll free: 1-800/268-9281 from both Canada and the US.

If you would like to spend all or part of your Ontario vacation on a farm, write to:
Ontario Farm and Country Accommodation,
RR2, Vankleek Hill,
ON N0B 1R0.
Tel: 807/623-0497
www.countryhosts.on.ca

PRINCE EDWARD ISLAND

The gentle topography of Prince Edward Island lends itself more than that of most of the other provinces to unaccompanied pursuits. Nonetheless, there are many companies listed in the *Prince Edward Island Visitors Guide* that offer cycling, sailing, sea kayaking, seal watching, sport fishing, trail riding and walking activities.

QUÉBEC

Tourisme Québec and the regional Tourist Associations offer literally thousands of tours, excursions and packages. The three most northern Tourist Associations can arrange any number of similar excursions for travelers with a penchant for adventure but a distaste for crowds.
Duplessis,
Association Touristique de

Duplessis, 312 av. Brochu, Sept-Îles, PQ G4R 2W6.
Tel: 418/962-0808.
Northwest Québec, Association Touristique Régionale Abitibi-Témiscamingue, 170 avenue Principale, bureau 103, Rouyn-Noranda, PQ J9X 4P7
Tel: 819/762-8181 or toll-free 1-800/808-0706.
Tourism Baie-James, 166 Springer Boulevard, P.O. Box 1270, Chapais, PQ G0W 1H0.
Tel: 418/745-3969 or toll-free: 1-888/745-3969.

Montréal (514)

Guided Tours: The romantic can hire a horse-drawn *calèche* at Dominion Square, Pl. Jacques-Cartier, or Beaver Lake on Mount Royal.

For something different during the summer, sample a river/harbor boat cruise available from **Montréal Harbor Cruises**. Tel: 842-3871 or toll-free: 1-800/667-3131.

Québec City (418)

Guided Tours: Contact: **Maple Leaf**. Tel: 622-3677 for walking tours.

A *calèche* can be hired year-round at the Place d'Armes or on the rue d'Ateuil, call **Calèche du Vieux-Québec**, tel: 683-9222.

Various bus tours originate from the Place d'Armes, call the **Gray Line**, tel: 523-9722.

SASKATCHEWAN

The big landscapes of Saskatchewan yield themselves to a plethora of outdoors activities. Tourism Saskatchewan's *Saskatchewan Fishing and Hunting Guide* lists all outfitters as well as information on licensing requirements and regulations. For more independent explorations, one of Canada's main conservation organizations, Ducks Unlimited Canada, at P.O.Box 4465, 1606-4th Avenue, Regina, SK S4P 3W7. Tel: 306/569-0424, provides information on self-drive nature tours throughout the province. More

than 55 canoe routes have been well described in a series of Saskatchewan canoe route booklets, which can be obtained from the visitor information centre in La Ronge, from Sask Geomatics at 2151 Scarth Street, Regina, SK S4P 3V7. Tel: 306/787-2799, or from Environment and Resource Management offices throughout the north. In addition, the tour outfitters listed in the *Saskatchewan Vacation Guide* offer many packages from guided horseback trips in Cowboy Country to whitewater rafting, cycling, birdwatching and hiking.

THE YUKON

Most tourists arrive in the Yukon with package tours which include a cruise liner passage, accommodation, meals, ground transportation and side trips. (Holland-America and Princess are two such lines and travel agents can supply details). Packages for independent travelers arriving by air, bus or their own vehicle are available from:
Atlas Travel,
Box 4340, Whitehorse YT Y1A 3T5.
Tel: 867/667-7823.

Culture

Theaters and the Performing Arts

ALBERTA

Banff (403)

Banff Center for Fine Arts, St Julien Road. Tel: 762-6100 or toll-free: 1-800/4134-8368. This center is becoming a significant performing arts complex. Its two theaters offer dance, drama, film and concerts. The Banff Arts Festival in August highlights the summer season. Find current program information in the periodical, *Banff*, which is widely distributed throughout the area.

Calgary (403)

To find out what's happening on Calgary's increasingly sophisticated performing arts scene, check local newspapers or with visitor information sources.
Calgary Center for Performing Arts, 205 8th Avenue SE. Tel: 294-7455. A unique facility which houses one of the most accoustically perfect halls, Jack Singer Concert Hall. The complex is also the home of the **Calgary Philharmonic, Max Bell Theater, Theater Calgary, Engineered Air Theatre, Martha Cohen Theater** and **Big Secret Theater**.
Southern Alberta Jubilee Auditorium, 1415–14 Avenue NW. Tel: 297-8000. Calgary's cultural centerpiece, this beautiful modern performance hall houses the Calgary Opera and the Alberta Ballet Company.
Pumphouse Theater, Pumphouse Ave SW. Tel: 263-0079. A variety of performing arts groups can be found in this converted municipal pumphouse.

Edmonton (780)
Citadel Theater, 9828 101A Avenue. Tel: 425-1820. The city's largest theater complex.
Northern Alberta Jubilee Auditorium, 87 Avenue at 115 Street. Tel: 433-7741. This place houses the Alberta Ballet and the Edmonton Opera.
The Winspear Center 99 Street and 102 Avenue Tel: 428-1414 or toll-free: 1-800/563-5081 Home of the Edmonton Symphony Orchestra, and renowned for its superb acoustics.

BRITISH COLUMBIA

Vancouver (604)
With the possible exception of its theater life, Vancouver's performing arts scene is not quite in step with the city's growing wealth and prominence. Nevertheless, it is worth checking the daily papers to find out what's happening and where.
Arts Club Theater, 1585 Johnson Street, Granville Island. Tel: 687-5315. Features modern Canadian drama, both light and serious, on its two stages.
Orpheum Theater, 601 Smithe. Tel: 684-9100. This theater in the grand style is permanent home to the Vancouver Symphony Orchestra.
Queen Elizabeth Theater, Hamilton Street at Georgia. Tel: 280-3311. The spacious theater hosts concerts, dramas and musicals and other major cultural events. It is permanent home of the fine Playhouse Theater Company.
Vancouver East Cultural Center, 1895 Venables Street. Tel: 254-9578. Wide variety of cutting-edge events.

Victoria (250)
The Belfry, 1291 Gladstone Avenue. Tel: 385-6815. Professional comedy and music hall shows.
McPherson Playhouse, 3 Centennial Square. Tel: 361-0800 This restored old theater is the focus of Vancouver Island's regional

and professional presentations in musical comedy, opera and drama. Regular concerts at noon.
The Royal Theater, 846 Broughton Street. Tel: 385-9771. Home of the Victoria Symphony Orchestra, presents classical and pop music as well as theatrical performances.

There are also presentations at the University of Victoria Auditorium and outdoor concerts at Butchart Gardens, Beacon Hill Park and Centennial Square.

MANITOBA

Winnipeg (204)
Consult the *Winnipeg Sun* or the *Winnipeg Free Press* for information and a complete listing of performing arts events.
Centennial Concert Hall, within the Centennial Center at 555 Main St, is the major focus of Winnipeg's cultural scene. Aside from the **Museum of Man and Nature**, the Centennial Center houses:
The Royal Winnipeg Ballet. Tel: 956-0183. Canada's first ballet company is also among one of the best in the world. It performs at home in October, December, March and May.
Manitoba Opera. Tel: 942-7479. Presents three operas and one recital from November to April.
The Winnipeg Symphony Orchestra. Tel: 949-3950. This highly prestigious orchestra offers classical, contemporary and popular orchestral music from September to May.
Manitoba Theater Center Mainstage, 174 Market Ave. Tel: 942-6537. From October to May, the center, reputedly the finest in the prairies, presents a series of classics, comedies and modern productions. MTC's second stage, the Warehouse, offers more experimental theater.

In the heart of St-Boniface's French district, **Le Centre Culturel Franco-Manitobain** at 340 boulevard Provencher (tel: 233-8053) offers productions by Le Cercle Molière (Canada's oldest

continuously active theater group) as well as choral and dance groups.

NEW BRUNSWICK

Fredericton (506)
The Playhouse, 686 Queen Street. Tel: 458-8344. Houses **Theatre New Brunswick**, the province's premier theatrical company.

NEWFOUNDLAND AND LABRADOR

St John's (709)
Arts and Culture Center, Prince Phillip Drive. This is the province's cultural center and in addition to hosting formal theater, symphony orchestra and jazz concerts, it houses a library and the Memorial University Art Gallery, which exhibits modern Canadian artwork and sculpture. For more information and ticket reservations, tel: 729-3900.

NOVA SCOTIA

Halifax (902)
In the summertime, look for free concerts and shows on the streets of Historic Properties. Otherwise, daily local newspapers will give details of what's going on at these and other locations.
Neptune Theater, 1593 Argyle Street. Tel: 429-7300. This is home to Nova Scotia's oldest professional live repertory theater group.

Wolfville (902)
Atlantic Theatre Festival, 356 Main Street. Tel: 1-800/337-6661. Fine repertory productions of classical theatre from mid-June to September.

NUNAVUT

While there are no formal art centers, Inuit music is featured at numerous festivals throughout the summer. See Festivals section (*page 382*).

ONTARIO

Mississauga (905)
Living Arts Center, 4141 Living Arts Drive. Tel: 306-6100. Just a 20-minute drive west from downtown Toronto, the performing, visual and digital arts are presented in this dynamic center.

Niagara-on-the-Lake (905)
Set in one of the best preserved 19th-century small towns in Canada, the *Shaw Festival* is devoted to performing the works of George Bernard Shaw and his contemporaries. Expert productions with renowned actors draw large crowds, especially on weekends. Try to make prior arrangements and reservations as early as possible.

The festival runs from April through October. For more information, write to the Shaw Festival, Box 774, 200 Picton St, Niagara-on-the-Lake, ON L0S 1J0, or call (905) 468-2172 for the box office in Niagara-on-the-Lake, or toll-free 1-800/511-7429 from the rest of Canada and the US.

Ottawa (613)
National Arts Center, 53 Elgin St. Tel: (613) 947-7000. It is the focus of Ottawa's performing arts scene. The center has three auditoriums: the 2,300 seat opera house, home to the acclaimed National Arts Center Orchestra and guest performers; the theater seating 800 for its French and English-language plays; and the studio, a theater for experimental works, seating 300.

Ottawa Little Theater, 400 King Edward Ave, tel: (613) 233-8948, has a fine resident company.

Stratford
The annual **Stratford Festival** (from mid-May–November) draws over a half-million theater-goers from around the world to this town on the banks of the Avon river. Three fine theaters perform Shakespearean, classic and modern dramas.

Tickets go on sale in late February. Write to the Festival Theater Box Office, Box 520, Stratford, ON N5A 6V2 or call (519) 273-1600 in Stratford, or 1-800/567-1600 from elsewhere in Canada and the US.

Toronto (416)
To check out what's happening in Toronto, look in the daily (or better, the weekend) editions of the *Globe and Mail* or the *Toronto Star* or pick up a free copy of *Now* or *Eye* (both weekly). Toronto offers world-class performances year round.
Bloor Cinema, 506 Bloor St W. Tel: 537-6677.
Canadian Stage, 26 Berkeley St. Tel: 368-3110 has an emphasis on Canadian drama.
Carlton Cinemas, 20 Carlton St. Tel: 598-2309.
Elgin and Winter Garden Center, 189 Yonge Street. Tel: 872-5555. Beautifully restored to its original vaudeville era and now hosting a variety of musical shows and drama.
Factory Theater Lab, 125 Bathurst St, tel: 504-9971 produces experimental plays.
Ford Center for the Performing Arts, 5040 Yonge St. Tel: 872-2222 This state-of-the-art performing arts center has a main 1800-seat theater for major international musicals, a 1000-seat Recital Hall, and a 250-seat experimental studio theater.
Hummingbird Center, 1 Front St E (at Yonge). Tel: 872-2262. Aside from hosting visiting performers and companies, Hummingbird Center (formerly known as the O'Keefe Center) houses the superb Canadian Opera Company and the internationally renowned National Ballet of Canada.
Massey Hall, 178 Victoria St, at Shuter. Tel: 872-4255. Toronto's Victorian grande dame now plays second fiddle to Roy Thomson Hall, but still attracts international stars and musical groups to suit all tastes.
Molson Amphitheatre, Ontario Place. Tel: 260-5600. There's room for an audience of 16,000 here, with 2,000 under the canopy roof. Summertime rock, jazz and dance performances all take place here.

Pantages Theater, 244 Victoria Street. Tel: 872-2222. A 2,000-seat theatre restored to its original 1920s opulence. Home to *Phantom of the Opera* for the last ten years.
Princess of Wales Theater, 300 King Street West. Tel: 872-1212 or toll-free: 1-800/461-3333. A spectacular modern theatre designed to accommodate major international productions.
Royal Alexandra Theater, 260 King St W. Tel: 872-1212. The "Royal Alex", with its lavish baroque decor, hosts the latest plays from Broadway and London, as well as top local productions. Try to write ahead for tickets.
Roy Thomson Hall, 60 Simcoe St. Tel: 872-4255. Downtown Toronto's newest concert hall, opened in 1982, it is designed so that all 2,800 members of the audience sit within 34 meters (110 ft) of the stage. It is the winter home of the excellent Toronto Symphony and Mendelssohn Choir.
St Lawrence Center for the Arts, 27 Front St E. Tel: 366-7723. Just east of the Hummingbird Center, its modern theater showcases classic and contemporary drama, with an emphasis on Canadian playwrights and local talent. It is home to the Canadian Stage Company.
Second City, 56 Blue Jays Way. Tel: 343-0011. New home in the entertainment district for Toronto's well-known satirical comedy group.
Tarragon Theater, 30 Bridgeman Ave, tel: 531-1827 produces excellent works, with an emphasis on Canadian drama.
Theater Passe Muraille, 16 Ryerson Ave, tel: 504-7529, innovative or experimental productions.
Toronto Truck Theater, 94 Belmont St. Tel: 922-0084. This theater has been home to Agatha Christie's *The Mousetrap* for longer than anyone can remember.

Young People's Theater, 165 Front St E. Tel: 862-2222. Offers fine children's drama.

PRINCE EDWARD ISLAND

The Confederation Centre of the Arts, 145 Richmond Street, Charlottetown, tel: 628-1864 or toll-fre 1-800/565-0278, houses a museum, art gallery and theater. In summer, two theatrical productions are presented simultaneously (with some matinée performances), one of which is the perennial musical *Anne of Green Gables*. Summer stock is a tradition on the island with performances in a number of locations. Particularly noteworthy are the **Victoria Playhouse** in Victoria (tel: 658-2025) and the **Carrefour Theatre** in Georgetown (tel: 566-4242).

QUÉBEC

Québec offers limitless opportunities for cultural diversions and entertainment. To find out what's on, contact the local travel bureau, but newspapers can be helpful too. As a general rule, call ahead for program information, especially concerning movies and plays, the majority of which will be in French but some also in English.

Montréal (514)
The weekend editions of *Gazette* and *La Presse* are the two mainstream publications that update Montréalers on what's happening around town. For a wider range of alternative arts and entertainment listings, consult *Mirror* and *Hour* (both English) and *Voir* (French), all available free of charge throughout the city.
Centaur Theatre, 453 rue St-François-Xavier. Tel: (514) 288-3161. Performances in English from October to June only.
Saidye Bronfman Center, 5170 Chemin de la Côte Ste-Catherine. Tel: (514) 739-2301. Performances in English.

Place des Arts, corner of rues Ste-Catherine and Jeanne-Mance. Tel: 790-ARTS. Holds three halls, offering the finest in performing arts: **Salle Wilfrid-Pelletier**, home to the acclaimed Montréal Symphony Orchestra, Montréal Opera company and Les Grand Ballets Canadiens. **Maisonneuve Theater** features chamber music and plays. **Théâtre Jean-Duceppe** is home to a famous Québec drama group.

Québec City (418)
Grand Théâtre du Québec, 269 boul. René-Lévesque E. Tel: 643-8131. Two concert halls host classical concerts, variety shows, dance and theatre productions. **Théâtre Capitole**, 972 rue St-Jean. Tel: (418) 694-4444. Québec City's largest theatre. **Théâtre Petit-Champlain**, 78 rue du Petit-Champlain. Tel: 692-4744. A unique theater where patrons pay a cover charge to view French-language productions in a licensed café.

The Laurentians
In the summertime, this ski resort area hosts a number of theater productions, many outdoors. For information, write to: Association Touristique des Laurentides, 14142 rue de La Chapelle, RR1, St-Jérôme, PQ J7Z 5T4 or tel: (450) 436-8532. www.laurentides.com

SASKATCHEWAN

Regina (306)
Globe Theater
1801 Scarth Street
Tel: (306) 525-6400
In the converted former City Hall, this is home to Regina's professional acting company which features eight performances between September and April.
Saskatchewan Center of the Arts, within the Wascana Centre at 200 Lakeshore Dr. This is the home of the Regina Symphony and where Regina's major dance, theater and symphony performances are held. Box office, tel: 525-9999 or toll-free: 1-800/667-8497

Nightlife

ALBERTA

In Alberta's resort areas (and to a lesser extent, in Calgary and Edmonton), hotels generally offer the most popular hot-spots, but a little exploration can take visitors off the beaten path to watering holes which cater mainly to the locals. Some bars and "beer parlours" are laid-back, but many have a free-spirited (and sometimes raucous) Western atmosphere. The provincial drinking age is 19.

Calgary (403)
Dusty's Saloon, 1088 Olympic Way SE. Tel: 263-5343. Where country and western rules supreme, including free two-step lessons on Tuesday and Wednesday nights. **Kaos Jazz and Blues Bistro**, 718-17th Avenue SW. Tel: 228-9997 is a local favorite.
Mercury, 801B – 17th Avenue SW. Tel: 541-1175. Popular with the arty crowd, with creative drinks to match.
Oak Room, Palliser Hotel, 133-9th Avenue SW. Tel: 262-1234. Famous for its traditional martinis.
Ranchman's, 9615 MacLeod Trail South. Tel: 253-1100, Where the real cowboys hang out.
Señor Frog's, 739 2nd Avenue. Tel: 264-5100. Mexican atmosphere and food. Dancing for the over 25 crowd.
Sole Luna, 739 2nd Avenue S. Popular club with live bands. Often queues to get in Saturday nights.

Edmonton (780)
Stop at any hotel for a copy of *Billy's Guide*, a comprehensive, bi-monthly guide to what's happening in Edmonton, but here's a sampling:

Blues on White 10329-82nd Street. Tel: 439-5058. An R&B club.
Taps Brew Pub 3921 Calgary Trail South. Tel: 944-0523. Edmonton's first pub with an on-site brewery. Batches brewed in small amounts to maintain freshness and taste.
Yardbird Suite in old Strathcona Hotel, 10203-86th Ave. Tel: 432-0428. Edmonton's best and longest running jazz venue.

BRITISH COLUMBIA

British Columbia's legal drinking age is 19. Bars and cabarets may stay open until 1 or 2am.

Vancouver (604)
Among the city's numerous bars, discos, etc, many are located in hotels, including some listed.
Arts Club Lounge, 1515 Johnston Street. Tel: 687-1354. Popular Granville Island hangout with live bands on weekends. Waterside patio for cooling off.
Moomba, 3116 Broadway. Tel: 737-8980. Candle-lit version of Studio 54, with two dance floors and lots of gorgeous people.
Steamworks Brewery, 375 Water Street. Tel: 689-2739. Some of best beer in town served in convivial downstairs pub.
The Dover Arms, a British-style pub at 961 Denman.
Courtnall's at 118 Robson.

Victoria (250)
Perhaps due to the preponderance of retirees, Victoria's nightlife is rather quiet and hotel bars are possibly your best bet.
However, there is a year-round Jazz Hotline, tel: 658-5255 for up-to-date happenings at clubs and restaurants around town.

Harpo's, 15 Bastion Square. Tel: 385-5333 Dishes up jazz, live rock and blues.
Legends on Douglas, Strathana Hotel. Tel: 383-7137. Nightclub, dancing; part of an entertainment complex housing several discos and lounges.

Whistler
Garfinkel's Unit 1, 4308 Main Street. Tel: 932-2323. The best of many, as far as locals are concerned. Live bands and top 40.

MANITOBA

Minimum drinking age is 18.

Winnipeg (204)
Much of Winnipeg's nightlife can be found at the downtown hotels. Even the more staid hostelries offer lively watering holes.
Bailey's Lounge, 185 Lombard Avenue. Tel: 944-1180. A piano bar favorite with the 30s and up crowd.
Blue Note Café, 875 Portage Avenue. Tel: 774-2189. A fabulous jazz spot.
Die Maschine, 108 Osborne Street. Tel: 284-6766. From Techno-Gothic to swing, British rock and the Twilight Zone of rock, on two floors.

NEW BRUNSWICK

New Brunswick's legal minimum drinking age is 19. Most large hotels have bars and some have nightspots.

Fredericton (506)
Chestnut, 440 York Street. Tel: 450-1230. Dance music (sometimes live) and a games room.
The Hilltop Pub, 152 Prospect Street. Tel: 458-9057. Fun, cheap steaks, cheap beer.
Rockin' Rodeo, 546 King Street. Tel: 444-0122. Country rock.
Sweetwaters, 339 King Street. Tel: 444-0121, downtown Fredericton's hottest nightclub.

Moncton (506)
Caesar's, Hotel Beauséjour, 750 Main Street. Tel: 854-4344. Lounge with 1890s motif.

St John
Look for pubs in the Market Square area, or try:
Shuckers, Delta Brunswick Hotel, 39 King Street. Tel: 648-1981.

NEWFOUNDLAND AND LABRADOR

Newfoundland's legal drinking age is 19. In St John's, nightlife happens mainly in the Water and Duckworth Street areas, as well as in the bars of all major hotels. Outside the capital, hotels are usually the centers of nightlife.

St John's (709)
Scottish, English and (especially) Irish pubs abound, so explore and enjoy. Here are a few starting points:
Erin's Pub
184 Water Street.
Tel: 722-1916.
Popular and well-established, best of folk music – especially Irish.
The Ship Inn
265 Duckworth Street.
Tel: 753-3870.
Lively pub with jazz, blues, reggae, rock and roll.
Sundance Saloon
George Street at Adelaide.
Tel: 753-7822.
Crowded disco, thumping recorded music with some live bands.
Trapper John's
2 George Street.
Tel: 579-9630.
Down-home atmosphere, some live music.

THE NORTHWEST TERRITORIES

Northwest Territories' legal drinking age is 19, and bar time is 1am. Many native communities are completely dry by law (check first before flying anywhere with alcohol), but the rest of the territories more than makes up for them. In short, most watering holes are wild establishments. Licensed hotels generally sport a lounge. While in Yellowknife, visitors should take in the waterfront Pilot's **Brew Pub** on Wiley Road (opposite the **Wildcat Café**) if only to browse through the memorabilia, which includes the wing of a floatplane, now serving as the bar.

NOVA SCOTIA

Nova Scotia's watering holes stay open until midnight or 2am depending on classification, and the drinking age is 19. Most taverns in the province's small towns welcome travelers, but a word of caution: many have acquired a rough-and-tumble atmosphere unsuited to quiet drinkers.

Halifax (902)

Most nightlife is centered in the downtown area, with Argyle Street as its focus. The clubs can be crowded on weeknights and absolutely packed on weekends. Here is a selection:
My Apartment, 1740 Argyle Street. Tel: 422-5453. A busy club with live bands and a vibrating dance floor.
Lawrence of Oregano, 1726 Argyle Street. Tel: 422-6907. Popular live bands and DJ, good food and drink.
Granite Brewery, 1222 Barrington Street. A stylish English brew-pub with a wide variety of English and Irish imports.

ONTARIO

Ontario possesses a set of liquor laws that are, in part, remnants from its prohibitionist past. Many restrictions are being eased but:
● several small towns (and some neighborhoods within larger cities) are still completely dry.
● all carry-out alcohol is marketed through provincially owned outlets: **The Beer Store** for beer, and **Liquor Control Board of Ontario** (LCBO) stores for liquor, wine and specialty beers. Many are open seven days a week. Check the phone book for the nearest one.
● you may not go out in public with an open bottle of booze or opened case of beer.
● licensed establishments can serve liquor from 11am–2am seven days a week.
● The legal drinking age is 19. Though the old laws remain, Ontario has long since shed its

reputation for having a dull nightlife, as evidenced below.

Ottawa (613)

Ottawa's nightlife yearly becomes more vibrant, but the action often gravitates across to Hull, where quite literally "anything goes" until 3am. A plethora of discos, singles bars and clubs line two main strips – the Promenade du Portage and Boulevard St Joseph.
  Here are some starting points on the Ottawa side of the river.
Byward Market Area. Youngish crowd cruise and dance.
Blue Cactus Bar & Grill, 2 Byward Market. Tel: 241-7061.
Houlihan's, 110 York St. Tel: 241-5455.
Rainbow Bistro, 76 Murray Street. Tel: 541-5123. Great for blues on Sunday afternoons.
Stoney's, 62 York St. Tel: 241-8858.
Lieutenant's Pump, 361 Elgin St. Tel: 238-2949. English pub.

Toronto (416)

This entire book could be spent describing Toronto's nightlife. Yorkville and nearby Bloor St. clubs draw a younger, stylish crowd. Queen St E, out toward the Beaches area, is also trendy these days. The Yonge/St Clair and Yonge/Eglinton area bars cater to single, young professionals on the make. Yonge St south of Bloor is home to gay bars, and heavy metal emporiums. Post-New Wave dancing can be had around Queen St W. Downtown hotel lounges draw a youngish to middle-aged crowd, while the increasingly gentrified Annex neighborhood (immediately north and west of the University of Toronto) has sprouted a half-dozen imported English pubs. For listings of events, check *Now* or *Eye* free weekly newspapers. Here are a few samplers, by category.

English-Style Pubs
Duke of York, 39 Prince Arthur Ave, just north of Bloor St. Tel: 964-2441. A plush basement lounge popular with the "after work" crowd and young singles.

Duke of Gloucester, 649 Yonge St at Gloucester. Tel: 961-9704.
Duke of Kent, 2315 Yonge St, north of Eglinton. Tel: 485-9507.
Duke of Westminster, First Canadian Place. Tel: 368-1555.

Jazz
Chick 'n' Deli, 744 Mt Pleasant Rd. Tel: 489-3363.
Top O' the Senator, 249 Victoria Street. Tel: 364-7517. Considered to be one of the city's top jazz venues, it's the place to catch exciting new talent.

Quieter Lounges
Expect a dress code, usually "no jeans".
Parorama, Atop Manulife Center, 55 Bloor St W. Tel: 967-5225. Piano lounge, great midtown view.

Bars, Clubs and discos
Most of the major hotels have discos. Many are still somewhat flashy, and most cater to a mid-20s to mid-30s crowd. Try also:
Bamboo, 312 Queen St W. Tel: 593-5771. Live reggae, salsa and other Latin beats.
El Mocambo, 464 Spadina Avenue. Tel: 968-2001. Some of the world's most celebrated bands have played here over the years.
The Government, 132 Queen's Quay E. Tel: 869-9261. Huge dance floor and renowned for its hot Thursday night disco.
Gypsy Co-op, 817 Queen St W. Tel: 703-5069. The mishmash decor attracts a wide-ranging crowd, from suits to snakeskins.
Horizons, Atop CN Tower. Tel: 362-5411. An unequaled view of the city at night. A singles' haunt.
Joker, 318 Richmond Street W. Tel: 598-1313. Three floors thundering with rock, electronica and lasers.
Rivoli, 332 Queen St W. Tel: 596-1908. A Queen Street institution. An eclectic mix of live music, dance, readings and comedy in the back room.

Drink-and-Sink
Brunswick House, 481 Bloor St W, at Brunswick. Tel: 964-2242. Huge,

famous beer hall where matronly waitresses bring cheap draught by the trayload. Raucous, sing-alongs, contests – one not to be missed.
Imperial Pub Library, 58 Dundas Street East. Tel: 977-4667. Mainly a student crowd, fun atmosphere and cheap beer.
Morrissey Tavern, 815 Yonge St. Tel: 923-6191. Little atmosphere, but cheap beer. Draws a college crowd during the summer.

Gay Scene
Trax, 529 Yonge St. Tel: (416) 963-5196. Golden oldie.
Pope Joan, 547 Parliament St. Tel: 928-1495. A very popular lesbian bar.

PRINCE EDWARD ISLAND

PEI's legal drinking age is 19.

Charlottetown (902)
The Provinces Lounge, Charlottetown Hotel. Tel: 894-7371. Quiet, elegant establishment.
The Merchantman Pub, Queen and Water Streets. Tel: 892-9150. Located in a historic property, pub menu includes Thai and Cajun. Local and imported beers on tap.
Olde Dublin Pub, 131 Sydney Street. Tel: 892-6992. Sells imported draft beer from Scotland and Ireland, some live entertainment. Upstairs from the Claddagh Room.

Summerside
Crown & Anchor Tavern, 195 Harbor Street. Tel: 436-3333. Varied menu, weekend entertainment.

QUÉBEC

The drinking age in Québec is 18. Bars close at 3am.

Montréal (514)
The major hotels house lavish nightclubs which feature discos, cabaret shows, comedies and other entertainment. With the growth in popularity of micro brewery beers,

produced by small, independent breweries, there are many bars along the St-Laurent strip between Sherbrooke and Mont-Royal, as well as along Rue St-Denis to try the wide range of these beers available. Most clubs and bars are located in the downtown area, where explorers can sample the chic rue Crescent scene, rue Ste-Catherine's red-light district, or trendy rue Bishop.
Here are a few starting points:
L'Air du Temps, 191 rue St-Paul)uest. Tel: 842-2003. Intimate jazz hangout in Old Montréal.
Allegra, 3523A St-Laurent. Tel: 288-4883. Hops to live Latin music on Thursdays, world beat, R & B, funk and even swing on other nights.
Bar St-Sulpice, 1680 rue St-Denis. Tel: 844-9458. Converted house in the Latin Quarter.
Jello Bar, 151 Ontario Est. Tel: 288-2621. House specialty is the martini.
La Cervoise, 4457 St-Laurent. Tel: 843-6586. Beer brewed on the premises.
Shed Café, 3515 St-Laurent. Tel: 842-0220. Popular, especially in summer, with its outside patio.
Winston Churchill Pub, 1465 Crescent St. Tel: 288-3814.
For a panoramic view while drinking, dancing and dining, try **Restaurant Tour de Ville**, on the 30th floor of the Radisson Hôtel des Gouverneurs (777 rue University, tel: 879-1370). This is the only revolving rooftop restaurant in the city, so worth the few extra dollars. If you just want a drink, there is a non-revolving piano bar on the floor immediately below the restaurant.

Québec City (418)
The city sports few clubs, but many small cafés and bars. Stroll rue St Jean to find sidewalk cafés, while rue Ste-Anne offers rather more expensive fare.
Bar l'Arlequin, 1070 St-Jean. Tel: 694-1422. Rock club that features many local bands.
Le Bistro Plus, 1063 rue St-Jean. Tel: (418) 694-9252. Disco.

Le Sacrilège, 477 St-Jean. Tel: 649-1985. Continuing party on a terrace that's open till 3am.

SASKATCHEWAN

There are a number of night-spots in the province, particularly in Regina and Saskatoon, but in most cases, meals figure as prominently as entertainment. In smaller towns, the nightlife tends to center around the hotels and resorts. Saskatchewan's drinking age is 19.

Regina (306)
Elephant & Castle, Cornwall Center, 11th Ave at Scarth Street. Tel: 757-4405. English-style pub.
The Pump, 61 Victoria Avenue. A Country and Western venue.
Gerry Lee's, 1047 Park Street. A lively R & B club.

Saskatoon (306)
Amigos Cantina, 632 10th Street. Tel: (306) 652-4912. Mexican decor and food. Eclectic live music several times weekly ranges from blues to reggae.
The Bassment, 245 – 3rd Avenue S. Tel: 683-2277. The city's premier jazz club, featuring the best of local and touring jazz.

THE YUKON

The drinking age is 19; bar-time is 2am. Most hotels sport licensed restaurants and lounges, and in the summer, when Yukon swells with visitors, the nightlife resembles that of southern Canada.
One locale of special note is in Dawson City. Named after a gold rush belle of questionable repute, **Diamond Tooth Gertie's Gambling Hall** on Queen Street was Canada's first legal gambling casino. The action starts at 7pm sharp, but the stakes stay pretty low most of the time. The decorations and entertainment are pure Klondike. Open daily, May– September; closed Sunday.

Festivals

ALBERTA

July and August (Banff)
Festival of the Arts
Professional dance, opera, and music presented by artists from around the world, as well as showcases of the visual arts.

July 1
Canada Day, Provincial holiday.

First weekend of July (Vegreville)
Ukrainian Pysanka Festival
A folk fair in this center of Ukranian settlement. Camp in the shadow of the world's largest easter egg, standing over 10 meters (30 ft) tall.

Second Week of July (Calgary)
Calgary Exhibition and Stampede
This is deservedly the most famous annual Canadian event – 10 days of raucous western showmanship and celebration with rodeo events, chuck-wagon racing and much more. Make hotel reservations well in advance for this one (by some estimates, Calgary's population doubles at this time), and book tickets for main events as soon as possible. Write to:
Calgary Exhibition and Stampede, Box 1860, Station M, Calgary, AB T2P 2K8.
Tel: toll-free in North America 1-800/661-1260.

Late July (Edmonton)
Klondike Days
For 10 festive days, the entire city reverts imaginatively to Edmonton's gold rush era. Well worth planning a trip around. Make hotel reservations far in advance.

BRITISH COLUMBIA

January–February (alpine areas)
Skiing Competitions
Witness expert downhill skiers showing their stuff.

First Week in July (Williams Lake)
Williams Lake Stampede
Five thousand spectators come to watch top contenders in what is regarded as one of Canada's best rodeo events.

July 1
Canada Day, Provincial holiday
Folk Music Fest
Multicultural dancing, food and exhibits, held throughout Vancouver.

Mid-July (Vancouver)
Sea Festival
With the famous Nanaimo-Vancouver bathtub race.

Mid-July (Kimberley)
Julyfest
A Bavarian celebration of folk dancing and entertainment, set in "Canada's highest city." Try the beer-filled glass boots.

Last two weeks in July (Penticton)
Peach Festival

Late August (Vancouver)
Labour Day
Pacific National Exhibition
Features parades, exhibits, sports, entertainment and logging contests.

MANITOBA

February (St Boniface)
Festival du Voyageur
The lively francophone community celebrates the early fur traders.

July 1
Canada Day, Provincial holiday

Mid-July (Birds Hill Park, near Winnipeg)
Winnipeg Folk Festival
The internationally-acclaimed folk music festival is held over four days in this nearby provincial park, featuring bluegrass and gospel music of yesteryear.

End of July (Austin)
Manitoba Threshermen's Reunion and Stampede
Antique tractor races, sheep-tying and threshing contests draw participants from throughout the North American prairies.

August (Dauphin)
National Ukrainian Festival
Music, fun and games galore for all.

First Week in August (Gimli)
Icelandic Festival
The town people of Gimli take this opportunity to celebrate their heritage in this, the largest Icelandic community outside of Iceland.

August (Winnipeg)
Folklorama
This two-week, city-wide festival features the food, dancing, crafts and culture of 40 different ethnic groups.

NEW BRUNSWICK

July 1
Canada Day
Provincial holiday

Mid-July (Saint John)
Loyalist Days
Parades, dancing, and sidewalk festivities celebrate the landing of the Loyalists.

Early July (Shediac)
Lobster Festival

Late July–early August (Edmundston)
Foire Brayonne
The most popular festival in this area of New Brunswick, the mythical République du Madawaska. The local French-speaking population engages in three days of celebrations. Visitors enjoy the local food and the weaving and other crafts.

End of July–Early August
(Newcastle)
Miramichi Folk Song Festival
Offers a fascinating introduction to the exuberant local ballads.

First Monday in August
New Brunswick Day

Mid-August (Caraquet)
Acadian festival
This festival is opened with prayers for the fishing fleet. Food, music, dancing, etc.

Mid-September (Fredericton)
Harvest Jazz and Blues Festival
Musicians from across Canada turn Fredericton into New Orleans of the North, playing jazz, blues and Dixieland.

NEWFOUNDLAND AND LABRADOR

June (St John's)
Newfoundland Kite Festival
Kites of all sorts on a windy plain by Signal Hill.

June 24 (St John's)
St John's Day Celebrations
Colorful street festival on the town's anniversary.

July 1
Canada Day
Provincial holiday.

July 1 (St John's)
Canada Day Folk Festival
Folk groups from all over the province gather together to play Scottish and Irish folk music.

First Wednesday in August
(St John's)
Royal St John's Regatta
The regatta on Quidi Vidi Lake is the oldest sporting event in North America, but get up early – the rowing's over before breakfast. The city closes down and general festivities continue for the rest of the day. (If it rains, the race – and festivities – will be postponed until the following week.)

NOVA SCOTIA

May–June (Annapolis Valley)
Apple Blossom Festival
Dancing, parades, and entertainment celebrate the blossoming apple trees.

July 1
Canada Day
Provincial holiday.

Mid-July (Antigonish)
Highland Games
This action-packed Scottish festival features caber tossing (log throwing) and a continuous display of Highland dancing with hundreds of marching bagpipers.

Mid-August (Lawrencetown)
Annapolis Valley Exhibition
Nova Scotia's largest agricultural fair; sheep rodeo, ox pulls and horse pulls.

Late August (Lunenburg)
Nova Scotia Fisheries Exhibition and Fishermen's Reunion
Parades, contests, dory races and sumptuous seafood (including lobster specials) are the highlights of this exhibition.

Mid-September (Dartmouth)
Shearwater International Air Show
Flying and static displays of military and civilian aircraft.

THE NORTHWEST TERRITORIES

Late March (Yellowknife)
Caribou Carnival
This three-day festival celebrates spring, such as it is, in the Arctic, featuring Inuit and Dene northern games, ice sculpting, and the Annual Canadian Championship Dog Derby, a three-day, 143-mile (230-km) dog-sled race.
For information on this and other festivals, write to the Territory's tourism authority (see Tourist Offices pages 341/242) for further information.

June 20 (Yellowknife)
Raven Mad Daze
Celebration of the summer solstice with entertainment in the streets.

June 20 (Inuvik)
Midnight Madness
Celebrates the summer solstice with traditional music and dance.

July 1
Canada Day
Territorial holiday.

Early July (Yellowknife)
Midnight Classic Golf Tournament
Uproarious journey at the Yellowknife Golf Club takes advantage of the midnight sun.

Mid-July (rotates yearly)
Northern Games
Dene and Inuit come from Yukon, NWT and Alaska to compete in sport, dance and crafts. The "Good Woman" contest features Inuit women competing at seal skinning, sewing and so on.

NUNAVUT

Third weekend in May
(Cambridge Bay)
Omingmak Frolics
A popular festival that appeals to all age groups, and includes northern games, snowmobile races and a-memorable community feast.

July 1
Canada Day
Celebrated in most communities with parades, Inuit games and feasts and square dances.

July 9
Nunavut Day
Inuit traditions such as tea-boiling contests and traditional games, and honoring the Elders fill the day.

Mid-August
Arviat
Inummarit Music Festival
Traditional and contemporary Inuit music in a town famous for its musicians including singer Susan

Aglukark who has made her mark at concerts around the world.

ONTARIO

February (Ottawa)
Winterlude
Extravagant carnival features ice-sculpting, snowshoe races, ice-boating, and other wintertime fun.

May (Ottawa)
Canadian Tulip Festival
Over three million tulips highlight this festival, which also offers parades, regattas, craft shows, etc.

May (Toronto)
International Children's Festival
Over 100 performances including street mime and juggling.
Tel: 416/973-3000 for more information.

May–October (Niagara-on-the-Lake)
Shaw Festival
See section on Performing Arts, page 377.

Last week in June (Toronto)
International Caravan
Ethnic celebrations in pavilions all over Toronto, featuring over 60 "international cities".

First Sunday in July (Toronto)
Queen's Plate
Oldest stakes race in North America, held at the Woodbine Race Track.

Late July–Early August (Toronto)
Caribana
The city's West Indian community celebrates with singing, dancing and parades, mostly on Toronto Islands, creating a Mardi Gras atmosphere.

Early August (Maxville)
Glengarry Highland Games
Canada's second-largest Highland gathering.

First three weekends in August (Brantford)
Six Nations Native Pageant
Iroquois tribes celebrate and exhibit their culture and history.

Mid-August (St Catharines)
Royal Canadian Henley Regatta
The largest rowing regatta in Canada draws competitors and spectators from throughout the continent.

Mid–August to Labor Day (Toronto)
Canadian National Exhibition
The largest and oldest exhibition of its kind in the world, featuring air shows, big-name entertainment and all sorts of exhibits. All this takes place for three weeks at Exhibition Place on LakeShore Boulevard.

September (Oakville)
Canadian Open Golf Championship
Glen Abbey Golf Club hosts one of golf's top five tournaments.

October (Kitchener/Waterloo)
Oktoberfest: This famous Bavarian celebration attracts yearly over a half-million festive party-goers to the area's 30-odd beer halls and tents.

First Monday in August
Civic Holiday.
Provincial holiday.

PRINCE EDWARD ISLAND

Mid-June to Labour Day (Charlottetown)
Charlottetown Festival
The Confederation Center hosts a very fine series of concerts, theater and film.

July 1
Canada Day
Provincial holiday.

Mid-July (Summerside)
Summerside Lobster Carnival
Five days of fairs, parades and lobster suppers.

Early August (Tyne Valley)
Tyne Valley Oyster Festival
Fiddling, dancing and oyster-shucking contest. Oysters, presented all sorts of different ways, are featured on the menus of the Oyster Suppers.

QUÉBEC

Late January (Québec City)
Québec International Bonspiel
This is where world-class curling takes place.

Early February (Québec City)
Carnaval de Québec
Québecois engage in 11 days of revelry, heightened somewhat by the ubiquitous "Cariboo", a concoction of whisky, sweet red wine and other surprises. There's a parade, ice-sculpture contests, and even a canoe race on the frozen St- Laurent.

Early February (Montréal)
La Fête des Neiges
Winter carnival, including costume balls, ice sculptures and outdoor sport events held on the islands in the river.

Mid-February (Chicoutimi)
Carnival Souvenir de Chicoutimi
Winter carnival featuring wonderful historic costumes.

February (Lachute to Hull)
Canadian Ski Marathon
Cross-country skiing marathon.

February (Gatineau Provincial Park)
Keskinada Loppet (formerly Gatineau 55)
International cross-country skiing competition.

Early April (Province-wide)
Sugaring-off Parties
Festivities accompany the collection of maple tree sap.

June (Montréal)
Grand Prix Molson
Formula 1 auto-racing.

June 24
St-Jean-Baptiste Day
Provincial holiday.

Late June (Matane)
Shrimp Festival
A great time to feast on excellent shrimp and salmon at low prices.

June–August (Mont Orford)
Festival Orford
Performances of the Jeunesses Musicales du Canada draw international talent and are presented throughout the summer in Mont Orford park's music center (Tel: 819/843-3981 or toll-free 1-800/567-6155.)

July (Québec City)
Québec City Summer Festival
Free concerts and lively shows throughout the city.

July (Montréal)
Montréal International Jazz Festival
A mammoth jam, with over 300 free shows, besides the ticketed events.

Late July/early August (Mont St-Pierre)
Fête du Vol Libre
Hang-gliding and kite festival.

July (Péribonca to Roberval)
Traversée Internationale du Lac St-Jean
International swimming marathon across Lake St Jean.

Late August/Early September
Montréal World Film Festival
Over 350,000 people flock to this event every year.

SASKATCHEWAN

Mid-July (Saskatoon)
Saskatoon Exhibition
This is a popular, week-long fair of contests, historical displays, horse racing and livestock exhibitions. For information, contact: Tourism Saskatchewan.

July 1
Canada Day
Provincial holiday.

Mid-July (Battleford)
Saskatchewan Handicrafts Festival
One of Canada's premier crafts shows which attracts 150 handicraft exhibitors from the region and beyond. For more information

contact: Saskatchewan Craft Council, 813 Broadway Ave, Saskatoon, SK S7N 1B5. Tel: 653-3616.

First weekend in August (Regina)
Buffalo Days Exhibition
This seven-day exhibition harks back to the "pioneer days" when bison roamed the prairies. Beard-growing contest, livestock judging, horse racing, and grandstand entertainment are just some of the events on the itinerary.

THE YUKON

Last week in February (Whitehorse)
Sourdough Rendezvous
Native-born Yukoners call themselves "sourdoughs" after the famous biscuits. However, sourdoughs are not necessarily native-born. To qualify as a sourdough, you must have spent one winter in Yukon. Their rendezvous is a week-long bash celebrating the Klondike days. It includes such local traditions as dog-sled races, dressing up in 1898 costumes and drinking heavily at the nightly cabarets.

July 1
Canada Day
Territorial holiday.

Third Monday in August
Discovery Day

Third weekend in August (Dawson)
Discovery Day
Parades, dancing, races and general merriment to celebrate the anniversary of the discovery of gold near Dawson City.

Shopping

Province by Province

ALBERTA

Handicrafts stores in Edmonton and Calgary as well as Banff, Jasper and other tourism centers offer a range of Western and Northern specialities including furs, and wood and stone carvings made by native peoples. A number of tourist information centers around the province offer garments designed and made in Alberta.

In Calgary, **Cottage Craft Gifts** (6503 Elbow Drive SW. Tel: 252-3797), offers a large collection of Indian and Inuit artifacts. Otherwise, the pedestrian mall along 8th Avenue is the site of three large shopping centers. In Banff, **Western Outfitters** (103 Banff Avenue. Tel: 762-0335) features a sizable array of cowboy outfits and accessories.

BRITISH COLUMBIA

Vancouver
For chic galleries, boutiques and import shops, head to Gastown or Robson Street, the former for antiquities and bookshops, the latter for casual designer clothes, as well as souvenirs, including authentic and hence pricey North American native handiwork. Underground shopping malls proliferate downtown, offering countless specialty stores.

Victoria
The emphasis for visitors is on specialty shops which offer Canadian handicrafts as well as goods imported from Britain and the Orient. Government Street is lined

with interesting shops, and leads to Trounce Alley, Market Square and Bastion Square, which together offer a wide range of arts and crafts. The Inuit soapstone carvings and Vancouver Islanders' elaborately-worked wooden masks may be beyond most pockets, but the Cowichan knitware made by local native people are more affordable. **The Bay**, the modern department store descendent of the original Fort Victoria trading post, carries Cowichan sweaters along with its famous Hudson's Bay blankets.

MANITOBA

If it's sold in Manitoba, chances are it can be bought in Winnipeg. Wander through Osborne Village (behind the Legislative Building) to find artisan and specialty shops. **The Forks Market** at the junction of the Red and Assiniboine rivers, is where vendors sell ethnic foods, produce and baked goods. It is also very popular for crafts and jewellery. There are a number of ethnic snack bars and some good restaurants.

NEW BRUNSWICK

Fredericton's highly respected New Brunswick College of Art and Design is one reason for this province's high-quality crafts, including yarn portraits, blown glass, wood sculptures, pottery and pewterware. These goods are readily available in St John and Moncton, while Fredericton is especially well-known for such pewter shops as **Aitkens Pewter**, 680 Charlotte St and **Pewtercraft** in suburban Harvey Station. Tourism New Brunswick (see Tourist Offices page 341) can supply a directory of crafts stores.

NEWFOUNDLAND AND LABRADOR

Aside from the run-of-the-mill handicrafts, Newfoundland is famous for its Labradorite jewelry,

seal-skin products and Grenfell cloth parkas. For a huge variety of shops browse along Duckworth and Water Streets in St John's. Note that sales taxes here are the highest in the country, so prices for everyday goods and services will be slightly higher here than on the mainland.

NORTHWEST TERRITORIES

The territory's Dene and Inuit people operate co-operatives which produce soapstone sculptures, ivory carvings, delicate tapestries and intriguing prints, as well as beaded parkas and mukluks (sealskin boots). These are all available at lower prices than elsewhere in Canada, since there are no shipping costs and the lowest taxes, although genuine items are still pretty expensive.

Reputable outlets can be found in Yellowknife's shopping malls, while the **Northwest Trading Company**'s store on Bryson Drive has a good selection of native arts and crafts.

NOVA SCOTIA

Nova Scotia is known for its crafts, and Tourism Nova Scotia will send a booklet containing the names and addresses of outlets on request.

Halifax

Halifax is the largest retail center east of Montréal. Scotia Square and other shopping malls contain representatives of most Canadian retail chains, along with local businesses. The Historic Properties district houses numerous craft shops, while outlets in the Spring Garden Road area offer a variety of regional goods and imports from Britain and elsewhere.

NUNAVUT

The Inuit's long history in art and crafts has been well documented and their sculptures, prints, jewelry and ceramics can be seen in

museums, art galleries and stores throughout Canada. **Cape Dorset** is one of the main centers for this activity and much can be seen at the **West Baffin Eskimo Co-operative Store**. Tel: 867/897-8997. Soap stone carvings, paintings and other crafts are also sold in numerous stores in Iqaluit, including **Arctic Creations** tel: 979-1841, **DJ Sensations**, tel: 979-979-0650 or 1-888/979-0650 and **North Country Arts**, tel: 979-0067.

ONTARIO

For craft shopping, check out the **Shaw Village Gift Shoppe** in Niagara-on-the-Lake, Canada's Four Corners in Ottawa, or the Cornerstone artists' cooperative in Kingston. There is an extensive, although pricey, collection of Inuit art and handicrafts, at the **Isaacs/Inuit Gallery** in Toronto.

For antiques browse Queen St (East and West), Markham Village, Yorkville or the Harborfront in Toronto. Sunday flea markets in Burlington and Hamilton also offer some good finds. In Hamilton, visit the restored specialty shops in Hess Village and browse through some rare displays.

Ottawa

Some very classy gift stores are to be found here, perhaps catering to the international diplomatic corps as well as to regular tourists. **Canadian Geographic**, a long-established and much revered institution, recently opened a store in the Rideau Center with numerous items of interest for naturalists. **The Snow Goose** specializes in Inuit and Indian arts and artifacts.

Ottawa has at least three commendable shopping areas. **Sparks Street Mall** is a central, pedestrian-only stretch lined with specialty shops and assorted vendors. The **Rideau Center** also lies downtown. Its three floors offer over 200 stores, including the major department stores. Cross the walkway to **Byward Market**, a former farmers' market, which also houses several fascinating artisan shops and is worth a visit.

Toronto

Stories have been told of travelers who came to Toronto and stayed for months browsing through the city's myriad shops, stores, boutiques and stalls. A word to the wise: bring a good pair of walking shoes with you.

Yorkville Village and **Bloor St W** offer the latest in European and North American fashion. The trendy cafes and chic boutiques are pricey, but surprisingly unintimidating.

Walk south from Bloor along eclectic Yonge St to find bookstores, army surplus retailers, audio/video outlets, jewelry stores and more. This trek leads to the famed **Eaton Center**, whose about 300 stores of variety stretch from Dundas to Queen St. (Eaton's recently filed for bankruptcy. The name of the Eaton Center will certainly change, and may depend on which retailer takes over the Eaton's store.)

From Queen Street south lie the skyscrapers of the downtown core, underneath which winds a subterranean maze of interconnected shopping centers where you can find everything from the practical (florist, liquor and drug stores) to the stylish (hair salons, fashion boutiques). Interesting furniture stores, antique shops, cafes and secondhand clothiers dot Queen St West to Bathurst.

Moving north again, you'll find **Village-by-the-Grange**, a cobble-stoned, European-style complex on McCaul St. Venture west through bustling **Chinatown** to **Kensington Market**, just north of Dundas and west of Spadina. It's a lively area, where the narrow streets are lined with produce vendors, European butchers, West Indian music shops and secondhand dealers.

Trek north to **Honest Ed's** (Bloor St W at Bathurst), a raucous discount department store with a garish three-story, brightly-lit sign announcing its presence – especially at night. Owner Ed Mirvish has created a more sedate shopping area next door on Markham St south of Bloor: **Mirvish Village** is a renovated Victorian mews lined with galleries, bookstores and restaurants.

Of note outside the downtown area are some good shopping malls: **Yorkdale, Scarborough Town Center, Fairview Mall** and **Sherway Gardens**. All are accessible by mass transit; Scarborough Town Center by subway and then LRT (Light Rapid Transit).

PRINCE EDWARD ISLAND

The island offers little in the way of fashion goods, but its crafts – including leatherwork, wood carvings, weaving and pottery – never fail to please its visitors. The Prince Edward Island Crafts Council (156 Richmond St, Charlottetown, C1A 1H9. Tel: 892-5152) gives detailed information on PEI handicrafts and where to find them. Two of the larger outlets are **Islands Craft Shop**, 156 Richmond Street, Charlottetown, tel: 892-5152 and **The Dunes Studio Gallery**, Brackley Beach, tel: 672-2586, which also has a fine restaurant.

QUÉBEC

Québécois crafts such as patchwork quilts and Inuit carvings and drawings are traditionally popular items, but shop around and ask questions to be sure that what you buy really is genuine. Price is often a good indicator: authentic crafts tend to cost more than the mass-produced variety.

The major department stores of cosmopolitan Montréal and Québec City will carry the latest continental fashions, and the smaller shops and boutiques will offer an intriguing range of styles and merchandise to the persistent browser.

Shopping hours vary with the season or locale.

Montréal

The Underground City, a sprawling system of subterranean passages linking business complexes, offers theaters, cinemas, hotels, restaurants and shops, all underground and connected to the Métro. Rue Ste-Catherine is home to the major department stores, while Sherbrooke Street features high fashion outlets. Smaller or more specialized boutiques dot the downtown area, both above ground and below.

Visitors in search of handicrafts should visit any of **Le Rouet** stores, or the **Canadian Guild of Crafts**, at 2025 Peel St. Tel: 514/849-6091.

Québec City

Although Montréal offers substantially more shopping opportunities, a sizeable antiques district has formed around rue St Paul in the recently restored Basse-Ville. For the right price, dealers will part with Victorian furnishings, Québec furniture and various colonial objects.

THE YUKON

Unique native arts and crafts, including moose-hair tufting, and locally-made jewelry crafted from gold nuggets are available from hotel-lobby crafts stores. Other than the federal Goods and Services Tax, there are no sales taxes in the Yukon. For detailed information, contact Tourism Yukon.

Sport

ALBERTA

Skiing
Alberta is internationally renowned for its excellent alpine skiing. The season runs from November to May, the best months being January and February. Although slopes can be found throughout the Rockies, the major ski areas are Nakiska in Kananaskis Country, Marmot Basin in Jasper National Park, and Sunshine Village, Mount Norquay and Mystic Ridge in Banff National Park.

Water Sports
Water sports thrive here. **Canoeing** and **rafting** opportunities abound throughout the provincial and national parks. Rocky Mountain Raft Tours (Tel: (403) 762-3632) offer river excursions for those who like to "rough it".

Fishing
Alberta is a fisherman's fantasyland. Certain species can be caught year-round, but a license is required. (The national parks have their own regulations.) For details, and a sport-fishing guide, contact Alberta Environmental Protection, Fish and Wildlife Services, 9920 108 St, Edmonton, AB T5K 2M4. Tel: 944-0313.

Hunting
Hunting of any kind is prohibited in Alberta's national and provincial parks. In other specified areas, goose, waterfowl and some big game can be hunted, but check with the Environmental Protection Fish and Wildlife Service (address above). Alberta Tourism is also helpful.

BRITISH COLUMBIA

Golf
In summer, golf courses should not be hard to find, but Victoria's mild climate allows golfing year-round.

Mountaineering/Hiking
British Columbia's mountain ranges are a perennial challenge to climbers, who should check with the provincial and national parks for details. Hikers will find that provincial and national park authorities maintain well-marked trails which are often used in winter by cross-country skiers and snow-shoers.

Water Sports
Water sports opportunities abound in BC, both in the interior and on the ocean. Contact Victoria or Vancouver tourism offices or local yacht clubs for advice on renting boats for **deep-water fishing** or **sailing**. **Canoeing** and **sea-kayaking** are highly popular; contact Tourism BC for rental and route information. The Sunshine Coast region between North Vancouver and Powell River, and the lower east coast of Vancouver Island lay claim to some of the warmest **sea-water swimming** in Canada. More great swimming and **boating** can be had in the Okanagan Valley Resort areas.

Fishing/Hunting
For fishermen, British Columbia's lakes and streams offer bass, char, perch and trout. BC is famous for its salmon, caught in its rivers or from charter boats offshore. The halibut fishing around Prince Rupert is unparalleled. Many rivers yield the famous fighting steelhead, and interior lakes can produce mammoth trout.

Hunters come to BC in search of moose, caribou, deer, mountain goat, grizzly and black bear, and waterfowl. Secluded resort camps around Prince George reward those who make the long drive with excellent fishing and hunting. Fly-in camps farther north offer still better opportunities. Required non-resident hunting and fishing licenses can be obtained from local outfitters or through park rangers. For more information contact: Environment, Lands and Parks, 10334 152A Street, Surrey BC V3R 7P8. Tel: 1-800/665-7027.

Skiing
Excellent ski slopes dot BC from the Coast Mountains to the Rockies. The major resort areas include Big White and Silver Star in the Okanagan Valley; Red Mountain in the Kootenays; the Panorama in the Rockies; and Forbidden Plateau on Vancouver Island. Cypress Bowl, Grouse Mountain, Hemlock Valley and Mount Seymour lie near Vancouver, as do the superb Whistler and Blackcomb Mountains, at Garibaldi Provincial Park. A complete list of downhill and cross-country skiing locations is available from Tourism BC.

MANITOBA

Write to Travel Manitoba, (address, *see* Tourist Offices see page 340) for complete information on the sports and recreation activities listed below.

Summer Sports
Golf and **horseback riding** are popular in the summer, as is nearly every conceivable water sport. Provincial authorities have cleared several challenging **hiking trails**, including the exciting "Amisk" trail in Whiteshell Provincial Park.

Fishing/Hunting
Manitoba offers both summer and winter fishing seasons for those in pursuit of trout, northern pike, walleye and arctic grayling. Hunters come to Manitoba in search of black bear, deer and moose. To obtain a license and find out about other requirements (and opportunities), contact Department of Natural Resources, Box 22, 200 Salteaux Crescent, Winnipeg, MB R3J 3W3. Tel: toll-free 1-800/214-6497.

Winter Sports

Manitoba is increasing its wintertime recreational facilities. Many of Manitoba's provincial park trails are utilized for **cross-country skiing**. Growing numbers of resorts offer **tobogganing, snowmobiling**, and of course, **skiing** opportunities.

NEW BRUNSWICK

Tourism New Brunswick provides the most extensive information on sports and recreation in the province.

Golf/Boating

In the summer, New Brunswick's 30-plus golf courses are rarely too crowded. Boating is popular, both out on the ocean and on the gorgeous, if tame, St John River.

Fishing/Hunting

In the more remote areas of northern New Brunswick, hunting for deer and small game can be arranged, with the proper licensing. Deep-sea fishing charters usually originate from Caraquet, while the rivers of the Miramichi and Restigouche valleys are renowned for their Atlantic salmon fishing. Tourism New Brunswick can provide more specific information (*see* Tourist Offices page 341)

Winter Sports

For winter sports enthusiasts, **alpine and cross-country ski trails** can be found in New Brunswick's parks, both provincial and national. **Snowmobiling** is also popular.

NEWFOUNDLAND AND LABRADOR

The province has laid out over 20 **canoeing** routes and special tours/rentals are available (contact the Department of Tourism, *see* Tourism Offices page 341). Newfoundland is a **fisherman's** paradise unequaled in eastern Canada, although the province has stringent regulations and bag limits. Pike, bass, salmon and trout abound in inland rivers and lakes, while offshore tuna fishing can be great. For experienced **hunters**, with a licensed guide, Newfoundland has moose and caribou seasons. The Tourism Department will put you in touch with the right authorities.

THE NORTHWEST TERRITORIES

Water Sports

Canoeing and **rafting** in the Northwest Territories can be an adventure. Only expert canoeists should attempt such rivers as the Dubawnt or South Nahanni; nevertheless, most lakes and tamer rivers are suitable for beginner or intermediate paddlers. Remember the scourge of the north, black flies and mosquitoes. When planning a canoe trek, bring plenty of repellent, netting and sunblock, as well as warm, waterproof clothing.

Many lodges and camps offer canoe vacations and packages, usually supplying all the needed equipment and supplies. Otherwise, travelers can bring their own, or rent a canoe locally.

The Tourism Department offers complete information about canoeing in the Territories. (*see* Tourist Offices page 341)

Fishing/Hunting

Although hunting is above-average, fishing is the favorite pastime in Northwest Territories.

Northern pike, arctic grayling, trout, and the delicious arctic char are major sport fish. Although one can fish from the roadside or canoe, serious anglers stay at fishing camps or lodges, or make arrangements with an outfitter and air charter. (Even so, fish mature so slowly in these cold northern waters, that many outfitters follow a "catch and release" program where fish are set free after being weighed and photographed.)

Hunters come to the Northwest Territories in search of big game: moose, caribou, black, brown, grizzly and polar bear (fortunately for the

---

Participant Sports

Canada's vast outdoors is perhaps its finest attraction. Consult the individual provinces for more details about the activities listed below.

● **HIKING** All over Canada, particularly on provincial and national park trails.
● **RAFTING AND CANOEING** Every province, especially Ontario, BC, Yukon and the Northwest Territories.
● **SAILING** Throughout Canada, especially on the coasts and Great Lakes.
● **DIVING** The Broken Islands Group and Sunshine Coast in BC, the Nova Scotia coast and Georgian Bay, Ontario.
● **GOLF** Every province, especially southern BC and Ontario.
● **TENNIS** All of Canada, but especially in resort areas.
● **FISHING AND HUNTING** Throughout Canada, but regulations, licensing and seasons differ between provinces. Fishing is permitted, but hunting is prohibited in most provincial and national parks.
● **MOUNTAIN CLIMBING** Alberta, BC, Yukon.
● **ALPINE SKIING** Alberta, BC, Québec, Ontario.
● **CROSS-COUNTRY SKIING** Throughout Canada, particularly in the provincial and national parks.
● **SNOWMOBILING** All over Canada, especially in Ontario, Québec, the Yukon, the Northwest Territories and Nunavut.

Other possible recreation activities include skating, snowshoeing, ice-fishing, hang gliding, sky diving, horseback riding, windsurfing, water skiing, nature study and photography.

animals most hunters merely photograph their prey). Licensed guides must accompany non-resident hunters. Check in the

Explorer's Guide about season, limits, outfitters and guides.

Winter Sports

In late spring and early fall, cold-weather sports of all kinds can be enjoyed. **Ice-fishing, snowshoeing, skiing** and **dog-mushing** (sledding) are especially popular. Equipment can be rented from local outfitters. Many lodges and resorts stay open year-round. Incidentally, the Territories are among the best places in the world to view the magical Aurora Borealis (Northern Lights) and winter is the time to do it, giving winter sports enthusiasts an added bonus.

NOVA SCOTIA

Winter sports enthusiasts will probably head for neighboring provinces for their abundant wintertime sporting opportunities, but the province comes into its own in summer. Tourism Nova Scotia's *Doer's and Dreamer's Complete Guide* gives details of what is available. **Canoeing** enthusiasts hold Nova Scotia's rivers, both tame and wild, in high regard and the more sheltered coastline is great for **sea-kayaking**.

Fishing/Hunting

Fishing and hunting are highly controlled, but it is well worth buying a license. Salmon and trout fishermen enjoy the rivers, while others pursue bigger prizes, particularly bluefin tuna, out on the ocean. A variety of game is available to hunters, including bear, white-tailed deer, rabbit, pheasant, duck and grouse. For detailed information on Nova Scotia's sports opportunities, contact Sports Nova Scotia, 5516 Spring Garden Road, South Halifax, NS B3J 1G6. Tel: 425-5450.

NUNAVUT

With winter lasting from October to June, snow season adventures for the snow enthusiast abound. **Dog sledding**, either mushing the dogs and caring for a team, or just enjoying the ride is one way to experience Nunavut. **Snowmobiling** is also a popular way to travel on a wildlife-spotting trip. In the spring, **cross-country skiing** in Nuvavut's parks offers opportunities to see caribou or arctic hares.

Water Sports: Every activity should be arranged through one of Nunavut's outfitters. There is **sea-kayaking** around icebergs in the fiords of Baffin Island, **canoeing** and **rafting** on rivers such as Baffin Island's **Soper River** or the **Coppermine River**, with its wildlife, fish and archeological sites to wonder at.

Fishing is an angler's dream, since the fish are abundant and large. No ultrasonic lures are needed here. High oxygen levels in Nunavut's waters mean that large fish feed near the surface in relatively shallow waters. There are lodges and tent camps for experienced anglers, day trips for interested novices.

Hikers have miles of trails to explore in Nunavut's various parks, from the mountains of Auyuittuq National Park to the willow forest of Katannilik Park. One option is to trace the steps of the Franklin expedition when searching for the Northwest Passage.

Two of the main attractions for **mountaineers** flocking to Nunavut over the past few years are the 1,000-meter (3,280-ft) west face of Mount Thor and the 800-metre (2,624ft) west face of Mount Asgard, both in Auyuittuq National park, although there are many other challenging mountains in this park and elsewhere in Nunavut, including around Sam Ford Fiord/Clyde River area on north Baffin Island.

ONTARIO

Travel Ontario's three *Trip Planners* for South Central, Eastern and Northern Ontario list **canoeing, whitewater, survival sports, hiking**

and **rock-climbing expeditions** and package tours. Some useful addresses are:
Ontario Travel, Queen's Park, Toronto, ON M7A 2E9. Tel: toll-free in Canada and the US 1-800/668-2746.
Ministry of Natural Resources, National Resources Information Center, Macdonald Block, Room M1-73, 900 Bay St, Toronto, ON M7A 2C1. Tel: 314-2000.
Sports Alliance of Ontario, 1185 Eglinton Ave E., North York, ON M3C 3C6. Tel: 426-7000.
Resorts Ontario, 29 Albert Street, Orillia, ON L3V 5JP. Tel: 705/325-9115 or toll-free in Canada and the US 1-800/363-7227.

Hiking

Over a dozen magnificent trails slice through Ontario. The most famous is the Bruce Trail, which winds 740 km (460 miles) along the Niagara Escarpment, from near Niagara Falls to the Bruce Peninsula. Contact: Bruce Trail Association, Box 857, Hamilton, ON L8N 3N9. Tel: 905/529-6821 or 1-800-665-HIKE.

Algonquin Park offers many **wilderness trails**. The most beautiful ones are the Western Uplands Trail, divided into three lengths – 32, 55 and 82 km (20, 34 and 51 miles) – and the Highland Trail, divided into two – 19 and 35 km (12 and 22 miles). Contact: Ministry of Natural Resources, Box 219, Whitney, ON K0J 2M0. Tel: 705/633-5572.

The Rideau Trail follows the Rideau Canal for 250 miles (400 km) from Kingston to Ottawa. Contact: Rideau Trail Association, Box 14, Kingston, ON K7L 4V6, or phone 613/545-0823.

Trails of various length meander their way through most Ontario provincial parks. Pukaskwa National Park, on the north shore of Lake Superior has rugged paths which are not for novices.

Fishing/Hunting

A spate of regulations await anglers and hunters in Ontario, but the rewards are plentiful. Although most

North American freshwater fish can be found in Ontario, the province is known particularly for its muskellunge, bass, walleye, pike and trout. Hunters come in search of animals including deer, moose, pheasant and black bear.

Hunting and fishing are seasonal. For maps and more information about licensing and outfitters, contact the Ministry of Natural Resources Information Center, 300 Water Street, P.O.Box 7000, Peterborough, ON K9J 8M5. Tel: 314-2000 in Toronto, or toll-free 1-800/667-1940 from elsewhere.

True aficionados charter a plane and pilot to fly to a northern locale, where the fishing and hunting are unparalleled. Contact: Travel Ontario for a list of fly-in services. Resorts Ontario also lists fishing packages.

Water Sports
With access to one-third of the world's fresh water, including over 400,000 lakes and innumerable rivers and streams, Ontario is a water sports heaven. Canoeing enthusiasts can enjoy Ontario's rivers and lakes from mid-May to October. The best known, albeit still remote, routes lay in Algonquin and Quetico Provincial Parks. The Ottawa River and some provincial parks lay claim to excellent whitewater canoeing and rafting, which grow yearly in popularity.

For a list of outfitters, contact the Ministry of Natural Resources Information Center.

Lake Huron's Georgian Bay, the Muskoka Lakes, 1000 Islands, and the Trent-Severn Waterway are all excellent boating areas. Many marinas rent motorboats, sailboats and water skiing equipment.

Ontario's beaches offer excellent opportunities for swimming. Of note are the "cottage country" lakes of central Ontario and Georgian Bay (especially Wasaga Beach).

Other Summer Sports: Ontario has nearly 400 **golf courses**, many open to the public. **Horseback riding** is also a favorite, while one of the best ways to see Ontario is from a

bicycle. **Scuba divers** love Georgian Bay, a graveyard of sunken vessels (equipment can be rented from outfitters in Tobermory). For more details on everything from **table tennis** to **skydiving**, contact the Ontario Sports Center in Toronto.

Skiing
A popular downhill skiing haunt in southern Ontario is the Blue Mountain range near Collingwood. Otherwise, try the northern slopes around Sault Ste Marie and Thunder Bay. The latter is known for its titan ski jumps.

Ottawa is blessed with three **alpine and cross-country skiing** areas less than 32 km (20 miles) away in Québec: Mont Cascades (Tel: 819/827-0301), Camp Fortune (Tel: 819/827-1717) in Gatineau Park, and Edelweiss Valley (Tel: 819/459-2328). More challenging slopes await at Mont Ste-Marie (Tel: 819/467-5200 or toll-free 1-800/567-1256), 100 km (60 miles) north. Remember: Ottawa is but a short drive from the Laurentians.

The Ontario Ski Resorts Association (110 Saunders Rd, Unit 10, Barrie, ON L4M 6E7. Tel: 705/727-0351) and Travel Ontario can help with accommodations and packages. For the latest snow conditions, tel: 1-800/ONT-ARIO or, for a recorded message, 416/314-0998. For information about cross-country skiing, tel: 1-800/ONT-ARIO or, for a recorded message, 416/314-0960. Information on snow conditions for snowmobiling tel: 1-800/ONT-ARIO.

Cross-country skiers will find superb trails throughout the province. Tel: toll-free 1-800/461-7677 or 705/457-1640.

Other Winter Sports: **Snow-mobiling** was invented in this part of the world and remains immensely popular here. Trails crisscross the Georgian Bay and Muskoka/Algonquin Park regions, but can be found all over the rest of the province as well. For anglers who can't wait for warm weather, Ontario has an **ice-fishing** season. The

province's hiking trails are often suitable for **snowshoeing**.

QUÉBEC

Each of the 19 tourist regions has a list of sports and recreation activities, including **skiing, boating, hunting** and **fishing**. Write to: Tourisme Québec (see Tourist Offices, page 342).

Spectator Sports

Hockey is Canada's favorite sport. Children start playing it as soon as they can skate, so the country is filled with organized leagues. Canadians avidly follow their National Hockey League teams, including the Vancouver Canucks, Calgary Flames, Winnipeg Jets, Edmonton Oilers, Toronto Maple Leafs and Montréal Canadiens. The season lasts from October to the end of May.

Canadian football, very similar to the American variety, is very popular. Inquire with a hotel concierge or local travel bureau on how to go about obtaining tickets, sometimes a hard task.

In summer, you'll find professional **baseball** is also popular. The Montréal Expos have been long-time contenders, and in 1992 (but not since!) the Toronto Blue Jays won the World Series. Games in both cities can be exciting events.

Other sports are popular too. Canada's national sport is **lacrosse**, a hard hitting native American game. For another glimpse of Canadiana, try **curling** (a bit like bowling on ice), where only the rocks are hard hitting. **Basketball** and volleyball draw more interest yearly. **Cricket** and **soccer** have their adherents and **rugby** is played vigorously in some parts. In summer, central BC and Alberta become **rodeo** country.

Summer/Winter Sports

Canoeing and **hiking** are popular in the summertime, particularly in the lake-strewn forests of the Canadian Shield. **Canoeists** will find that provincial parks offer the best excursions. Québecois have also cleared over 1,200 trails for **cross-country skiing** and **snowshoeing**, and 30,000 km (18,600 miles) for **snowmobiling**.

Fishing/Hunting

Québec's rivers and lakes are renowned for their excellent fishing. It is claimed that there are more fish in Québec than in any other country! Deep-sea excursions and trips to northern fly-in camps are popular with aficionados. Tourisme Québec can provide details of licensing, seasons, limits and packages.

Skiing

An average of 200 cm (78 inches) of snow falls on Québec's downhill slopes between October and April, making the province a skiers' paradise. Enquire at resorts about weekend or week-long packages which often include lodgings, meals, lift tickets, lessons and more.

THE EASTERN TOWNSHIPS

Skiing

Mont Orford is the place to ski. Call or write Magog-Orford Tourist Information, 55 Cabana, Magog, PQ J1X 2C4 (tel: 819/843-2744 or toll-free 1-800/267-2744) to plug into a highly organized network of facilities that offering a variety of accommodations and packages.

From Québec City, skiing approx. 1,000-meter (3,050-ft) high Mont Ste-Anne can be a one-day excursion by bus or car. Call the Parc du Mont Ste-Anne (Tel: 418/827-4561) for details of the well-groomed downhill and cross-country trails just 40 km (25 miles) from the Old City walls.

The Laurentians

Just northwest of Montréal, this region offers a plethora of superb

hotels and resorts, which, incidentally, are the favorite of the **golf** and **tennis** set in the summer.

Mont Tremblant

The largest complex here, by far, is Station Touristique de Mont Tremblant. Tel: 819/681-2000 or toll-free 1-800/461-8711. For complete information on the whole area, write to the Bureau touristique de Mont-Tremblant, C.P.240, 140 rue du Couvent, Mont-Tremblant, PQ J0T 1Z0. Tel: 819/425-2434.

Ste-Adèle

For general information you can call the Bureau touristique des Pays-d'en Haut. Tel: 1-800/898-2127, or write the Tourist Information office at 333 Boul. Ste-Adèle, PQ J0R 1L0, tel: 514/229-5399. Le Chantecler, tel: 450/229-3555 or 1-800/363-2420, is a very popular ski resort.

SASKATCHEWAN

For details on sports and recreation, contact Saskatchewan Environment and Resource Management, 3211 Albert St, Regina, SK S4S 5W6. Tel: 306/787-2300.

The people of Saskatchewan love **curling**, and nearly every small town has a *bonspiel* in January/February. **Hiking** and **cross-country skiing** are popular, especially through parks.

Water Sports

Saskatchewan has more than 100,000 lakes, so water sports are a favorite. Among them, **canoeing** is probably the best. The province has laid out more than 50 canoe routes, for amateur and veteran alike. Canoe outfitters can put together a package to suit any need by arranging the necessary lodgings, food and equipment rentals. Contact Tourism Saskatchewan (address, *see* Tourist Offices page 342) for more details about canoe vacations and a list of tours and outfitters.

Fishing/Hunting

Hunters will find large game as well as several species of wildfowl

available in Saskatchewan. For fishermen, the province's northern lakes and streams offer an abundance of catch, including: trout, northern pike, walleye, and arctic grayling. For information about fly- or drive-in camps, outfitters, licenses, etc., contact Environment and Resource Management (for address see above.)

THE YUKON

Canoeing

Yukon is a haven for canoeists of intermediate level or better. The Stewart and Yukon Rivers are fairly tame. The Klondike and Big Salmon, conversely, can be challenging and treacherous. In any event, non-residents must register with the RCMP for safety reasons, and they will be required to show they have adequate equipment and supplies.

Hiking

Hiking is popular, though Yukon's jagged terrain means that this often entails rock or mountain climbing as well. Kluane National Park is a favorite for this, but Tourism Yukon can give more detailed information about hiking and climbing throughout the territory.

Fishing/Hunting

Essentially a wilderness, Yukon is perfect for fishing and hunting. Obtain a license from an outfitter, find a suitable spot, then cast for trout, arctic grayling, salmon and northern pike. Some of the best fishing spots lie just off the main roads although some people prefer to fish at the more obscure fly-in camps and lodges.

The *Yukon Vacation Guide* has details of fishing and fishing lodges. Big game and bird hunting is possible during the prescribed season (usually in fall). Non-resident hunters must be accompanied by a licensed guide. For further information on regulations, seasons, limits and outfitters, write to the Director of Game, Box 2703, Whitehorse, Y1A 2C6.

Language

English

Though officially bilingual, English is the language of choice throughout most of Canada outside Québec and some relatively small sections of the Atlantic provinces, Ontario and Manitoba. Canadians speak with their own distinct accent, but written Canadian English is very similar to that of Great Britain. Americans will note the British spellings: often in such words as "labour" and "centre"; and usage: such as "railway" instead of "railroad".

Newfoundland English

Newfoundlanders speak a dialect all their own. The accent is vaguely Irish, but the idioms and expressions are truly unique:

"Go to the law with the devil and hold court in hell"/the odds are against you

"To have a noggin to scrape"/an extremely difficult task

"Pigs may fly but they are very unlikely birds"/a vain hope

"in a hobble"/not worrying

"he is moidering my brains"/he is disturbing me

"Long may your big good jib draw"/good luck

French

PRONUNCIATION

Even if you speak no French at all it is worth trying to master a few simple phrases. The fact that you have made an effort is likely to get you a better response.

Pronunciation is key; they really will not understand if you get it very wrong. Remember to emphasise each syllable; not to pronounce the last consonant of a word as a rule (this includes the plural "s") and always to drop your "h"s. Whether to use "vous" or "tu" is a vexed question; increasingly the familiar form of "tu" is used by many people. However, it is better to be too formal, and use "vous" if in doubt. It is important to be polite; always address people as Madame or Monsieur, and address them by their surnames until you are confident first names are acceptable.

Learning the pronunciation of the French alphabet is a good idea and, in particular, learn how to spell out your name.

Montréal claims to be the second-largest French-speaking city in the world, after Paris. Some 65 percent of the city's residents and 70 percent of those in the metropolitan area are French-speakers (francophones), with 12 percent and 15 percent English-speakers (anglophones), respectively. Despite nationalistic insistence, the province's French has never been pure. After 300 years of separation from the motherland, how could it be? Québecois and French visitors struggle to find words in common. Over the past decades, as Montréalers acknowledge differences and gain confidence, this is amusing rather than disconcerting.

Unique to Montreal is joual, a patois whose name is garbled French for horse: cheval. The earthy dialect flourishes among the city's working class and in the work of playwright Michel Tremblay.

Pronunciation of mainstream French also differs. Accents distinguish French in Québec from French in Paris or Marseilles. Québec's francophones form sounds deep in the throat, lisp slightly, voice toward diphthongs, and bend single vowels into exotic shapes. It has also incorporated some English words, such as "chum", as in mon chum, or ma chumme, and blonde, for girlfriend,

while le fun is a good time.

Even if you don't speak much French, starting a conversation with 'Bonjour,' is likely to evoke a positive response. Indeed, some shopkeepers hedge, with an all-purpose: 'Hi-bonjour.'

The Inuit Language

There is little available literature on the Inuktitut Inuit language, largely because the Inuits don't want "the whites" to take their language away. The best guide to the language and culture is *The Inuit of Canada*, published by The Inuit of Taparitsat, 170 Laurier Avenue West, Suite 150, Ottawa, Ontario K1P 5V5. Tel: (613) 238-8181.

French words and phrases

How much is it? *C'est combien?*
What is your name? *Comment vous appelez-vous?*
My name is... *Je m'appelle...*
Do you speak English? *Parlez-vous anglais?*
I am English/American *Je suis anglais/américain*
I don't understand *Je ne comprends pas*
Please speak more slowly *Parlez plus lentement, s'il vous plaît*
Can you help me? *Pouvez-vous m'aider?*
I'm looking for... *Je cherche*
Where is...? *Où est...?*
I'm sorry *Excusez-moi/Pardon*
I don't know *Je ne sais pas*
No problem *Pas de problème*
Have a good day! *Bonne journée!*
That's it *C'est ça*
Here it is *Voici*
There it is *Voilà*
Let's go *On y va. Allons-y*
See you tomorrow *A demain*
See you soon *A bientôt*
Show me the word in the book *Montrez-moi le mot dans le livre*
At what time? *A quelle heure?*
When? *Quand?*
What time is it? *Quelle heure est-il?*
● Note. The French generally use the 24-hour clock.

Emergencies

Help!	Au secours!
Stop!	Arrêtez!
Call a doctor	Appelez un médecin
Call an ambulance	Appelez une ambulance
Call the police	Appelez la police
Call the fire brigade	Appelez les pompiers
Where is the nearest telephone	Où est le téléphone le plus proche?
Where is the nearest hospital	Où est l'hôpital le plus proche?
I am sick	Je suis malade
I have lost my passport/ purse	j'ai perdu mon passeport/ porte-monnaie

yes *oui*
no *non*
please *s'il vous plaît*
thank you *merci*
(very much) *(beaucoup)*
you're welcome *de rien*
excuse me *excusez-moi*
hello *bonjour*
OK *d'accord*
goodbye *au revoir*
good evening *bonsoir*
here *ici*
there *là*
today *aujourd'hui*
yesterday *hier*
tomorrow *demain*
now *maintenant*
later *plus tard*
right away *tout de suite*
this morning *ce matin*
this afternoon *cet après-midi*
this evening *ce soir*

On Arrival

I want to get off at... *Je voudrais descendre à...*
Is there a bus to the Place d'Armes? *Est-ce qui'il ya un bus pour la Place d'Armes?*
What street is this? *A quelle rue sommes-nous?*

Which line do I take for...? *Quelle ligne dois-je prendre pour...?*
How far is...? *A quelle distance se trouve...?*
Validate your ticket *Compostez votre billet*
airport *l'aéroport*
train station *la gare*
bus station *la gare routière*
Métro stop *la station de Métro*
bus *l'autobus, le car*
bus stop *l'arrêt*
platform *le quai*
ticket *le billet*
return ticket *aller-retour*
hitchhiking *l'autostop*
toilets *les toilettes*
This is the hotel address *C'est l'adresse de l'hôtel*
I'd like a (single/double) room... *Je voudrais une chambre (pour une/deux personnes) ...*
...with shower *avec douche*
...with bath *avec salle de bain*
...with a view *avec vue*
Does that include breakfast? *Le prix comprend-il le petit déjeuner?*
May I see the room? *Je peux voir la chambre?*
washbasin *le lavabo*
bed *le lit*
key *la clé*
elevator *l'ascenseur*
air conditioned *climatisé*

On the road

Where is the spare wheel? *Où est la roue de secours?*
Where is the nearest garage? *Où est le garage le plus proche?*
Our car has broken down *Notre voiture est en panne*
I want to have my car repaired *Je veux faire réparer ma voiture*
It's not your right of way *Vous n'avez pas la priorité*
I think I must have put diesel in the car by mistake *Je crois que j'ai mis le gazole dans la voiture par erreur*
the road to... *la route pour...*
left *gauche*
right *droite*
straight on *tout droit*
far *loin*
near *près d'ici*
opposite *en face*
beside *à côté de*

car park *parking*
over there *là-bas*
at the end *au bout*
on foot *à pied*
by car *en voiture*
town map *le plan*
road map *la carte*
street *la rue*
square *la place*
give way *céder le passage*
dead end *impasse*
no parking *stationnement interdit*
motorway *l'autoroute*
toll *le péage*
speed limit *la limitation de vitesse*
petrol *l'essence*
unleaded *sans plomb*
diesel *le gazole*
water/oil *l'eau/l'huile*
puncture *un pneu crevé*
bulb *l'ampoule*
wipers *les essuies-glace*

Shopping

Where is the nearest bank (post office)? *Où est la banque*

On the telephone

how do I make an outside call?	Comment est-ce que je peux téléphoner à l'exterieur?
I want to make an international call	Je voudrais une com-munication pour l' étranger
local call	une com-munication locale
dialling code	l'indicatif
I'd like an alarm call for 8 tomorrow morning	Je voudrais être réveillé a 8 heures demain matin
who's calling?	Qui est à l'appareil?
Hold on, please	Ne quittez pas s'il vous plaît
The line is busy	La ligne est occupée
I must have dialled the wrong number	J'ai dû faire un faux numéro

Poste/PTT la plus proche?
I'd like to buy Je voudrais acheter
How much is it? C'est combien?
Do you take credit cards? Est-ce que vous acceptez les cartes de crédit?
I'm just looking Je regarde seulement
Have you got? Avez-vous...?
I'll take it Je le prends
I'll take this one/that one Je prends celui-ci/celui-là
What size is it? C'est de quelle taille?
Anything else? Avec ça?
size (clothes) la taille
size (shoes) la pointure
cheap bon marché
expensive cher
enough assez
too much trop
a piece of un morceau de
each la pièce (eg ananas, $3 la pièce)
bill la note
chemist la pharmacie
bakery la boulangerie
bookstore la librairie
library la bibliothèque
department store le grand magasin
delicatessen la charcuterie/le traiteur
fishmonger's la poissonerie
grocery l'alimentation/l'épicerie
tobacconist tabac
market le marché
supermarket le supermarché
junk shop la brocante

Sightseeing

town la ville
old town la vieille ville
cathedral la cathédrale
church l'église
mansion l'hôtel
hospital l'hôpital
town hall l'hôtel de ville/la mairie
nave la nef
stained glass le vitrail
staircase l'escalier
tower la tour
walk le tour
museum le musée
art gallery la galerie
exhibition l'exposition
tourist information office l'office du tourisme

free gratuit
open ouvert
closed fermé
every day tous les jours
all year toute l'année
all day toute la journée
swimming pool la piscine
to book réserver

Dining out

Note: Garçon is the word for waiter but never used directly; say Monsieur or Madame to attract their attention.
Table d'hôte (the "host's table") is one set menu served at a set price.
Prix fixe is a fixed price menu. **A la carte** means dishes from the menu are charged separately.

breakfast le petit déjeuner
lunch le déjeuner
dinner le dîner
meal le repas
first course l'entrée/les hors d'oeuvre
main course le plat principal
made to order sur commande
drink included boisson compris
wine list la carte des vins
the bill l'addition
fork la forchette
knife le couteau
spoon la cuillère
plate l'assiette
glass le verre
napkin la serviette
ashtray le cendrier

BREAKFAST AND SNACKS

baguette long thin loaf
pain bread
petits pains rolls
beurre butter
poivre pepper
sel salt
sucre sugar
confiture jam
miel honey
oeufs eggs
...à la coque boiled eggs
...au bacon bacon and eggs
...au jambon ham and eggs
...sur le plat fried eggs
...brouillés scrambled eggs

False Friends

Words that look like English words but mean something different.

coach	car
car, or railway carriage	voiture
bus driver	le conducteur
change	la monnaie
money/silver	l'argent
to stay	rester
hiring/renting	location
memory	un souvenir
"person" or "nobody" in different contexts.	personne
doctor	le médecin

tartine bread with butter
yaourt yoghurt
crêpe pancake
croque-monsieur ham and cheese toasted sandwich
croque-madame ...with a fried egg on top
galette type of pancake
pan bagna bread roll stuffed with salad Niçoise
quiche tart of eggs and cream with various fillings
quiche lorraine quiche with bacon

FIRST COURSE

An amuse-bouche, amuse-gueule or appetizer is something literally to "amuse the mouth", served before the first course
anchoiade sauce of olive oil, anchovies and garlic, served with raw vegetables
assiette anglaise cold meats
potage soup
rillettes rich fatty paste of shredded duck rabbit or pork
tapenade spread of olives and anchovies
pissaladière Provençal pizza with onions, olives and anchovies

MAIN COURSE

La Viande/Meat

bleu rare

à point medium
bien cuit well done
grillé grilled
agneau lamb
andouille/andouillette tripe sausage
bifteck steak
boudin sausage
boudin noir black pudding
boudin blanc white pudding (chicken or veal)
blanquette stew of veal, lamb or chicken with creamy egg sauce
boeuf à la mode beef in red wine with carrots, onions, mushroom and onions
boeuf en daube beef stew with red wine, onions and tomatoes
à la bordelaise beef with red wine and shallots
à la Bourguignonne cooked in red wine, onions and mushrooms
brochette kebab
caille quail
canard duck
carbonnade casserole of beef, beer and onions
carré d'agneau rack of lamb
cassoulet stew of beans, sausages, pork and duck, from southwest France
cervelle brains (food)
chateaubriand thick steak
choucroute Alsace dish of sauerkraut, bacon and sausages
confit duck or goose preserved in its own fat
contre-filet cut of sirloin steak
coq au vin chicken in red wine
côte d'agneau lamb chop
dinde turkey
entrecôte beef rib steak
escargot snail
faisan pheasant
farci stuffed
faux-filet sirloin
feuilleté puff pastry
foie liver
foie de veau calf's liver
foie gras goose or duck liver pâté
gardiane rich beef stew with olives and garlic, from the Camargue
cuisses de grenouille frog's legs
grillade grilled meat
hachis minced meat
jambon ham
langue tongue
lapin rabbit

lardon small pieces of bacon, often added to salads
magret de canard breast of duck
médaillon round piece of meat
moelle beef bone marrow
mouton navarin stew of lamb with onions, carrots and turnips
oie goose
perdrix partridge
petit-gris small snail
pieds de cochon pig's trotters
pintade guinea fowl
porc pork
pot-au-feu casserole of beef and vegetables
poulet chicken
poussin young chicken
rognons kidneys
rôti roast
sanglier wild boar
saucisse fresh sausage
saucisson salami
veau veal

Local choice

● For Canadian specialities, see Food and Drink chapter, page 117

Poissons/Fish

amoricaine cooked with white wine, tomatoes, butter and cognac
anchois anchovies
anguille eel
bar (or *loup*) sea bass
barbue brill
bigorneau sea snail
Bercy sauce of fish stock, butter, white wine and shallots
bouillabaisse fish soup, served with grated cheese, garlic croutons and *rouille*, a spicy sauce
brandade salt cod purée
cabillaud cod
calmars squid
colin hake
coquillage shellfish
coquilles Saint-Jacques scallops
crevette shrimp
daurade sea bream
flétan halibut
fruits de mer seafood
hareng herring
homard lobster
huître oyster
langoustine large prawn

limande lemon sole
lotte monkfish
morue salt cod
moule mussel
moules marinières mussels in white wine and onions
oursin sea urchin
raie skate
saumon salmon
thon tuna
truite trout

Legumes/Vegetables

ail garlic
artichaut artichoke
asperge asparagus
aubergine eggplant
avocat avocado
céleri remoulade grated celery with mayonnaise
champignon mushroom
cèpe boletus mushroom
chanterelle wild mushroom
cornichon gherkin
courgette zucchini
chips potato crisps
chou cabbage
chou-fleur cauliflower
concombre cucumber
cru raw
crudités raw vegetables
épinard spinach
frites chips, French fries
gratin dauphinois sliced potatoes baked with cream
haricot dried bean
haricots verts green beans
lentilles lentils
maïs corn
mange-tout snow pea
mesclun mixed leaf salad
navet turnip
noix nut, walnut
noisette hazelnut
oignon onion
panais parsnip
persil parsley
pignon pine nut
poireau leek
pois pea
poivron bell pepper
pomme de terre potato
pommes frites chips, French fries
primeurs early fruit and vegetables
radis radis
roquette arugula, rocket
ratatouille Provençal vegetable stew of aubergines, courgettes,

tomatoes, peppers and olive oil
riz rice
salade Niçoise egg, tuna, olives, onions and tomato salad
salade verte green salad
truffe truffle

FRUIT FRUIT

ananas pineapple
cerise cherry
citron lemon
citron vert lime
figue fig
fraise strawberry
framboise raspberry
groseille redcurrant
mangue mango
mirabelle yellow plum
pamplemousse grapefruit
pêche peach
poire pear
pomme apple
raisin grape
prune plum
pruneau prune
reine claude greengage

SAUCES SAUCES

aioli garlic mayonnaise
bearnaise sauce of egg, butter, wine and herbs
forestière with mushrooms and bacon
hollandaise egg, butter and lemon sauce
lyonnaise with onions
meunière fried fish with butter, lemon and parsley sauce
meurette red wine sauce
Mornay sauce of cream, egg and cheese
Parmentier served with mashed potatoes
paysan rustic style, ingredients depend on the region
pistou Provençal sauce of basil, garlic and olive oil; vegetable soup with the sauce.
provençale sauce of tomatoes, garlic and olive oil.
papillotte cooked in paper

PUDDING DESSERT

Belle Hélène fruit with ice cream and chocolate sauce
clafoutis baked pudding of batter and cherries
coulis purée of fruit or vegetables
gâteau cake
Ile flottante whisked eggs whites in custard sauce
crème anglaise custard
pêche melba peaches with ice cream and raspberry sauce
tarte tatin upside down tart of caramelised apples
crème caramel caramelised egg custard
crème Chantilly whipped cream
fromage cheese

Drinks

drinks *les boissons*
coffee *café*
...with milk or cream *au lait* or *crème*
...decaffeinated *déca/décaféiné*
...black espresso *express/noir*
...American filtered coffee *filtre*
tea *thé*
...herb infusion *tisane*
...camomile *verveine*
hot chocolate *chocolat chaud*
milk *lait*
mineral water *eau minérale*
fizzy *gazeux*
non-fizzy *non-gazeux*
fizzy lemonade *limonade*
fresh lemon juice served with sugar *citron pressé*
fresh squeezed orange juice *orange pressée*
full (eg full cream milk) *entier*
fresh or cold *frais, fraîche*
beer *bière*
...bottled *en bouteille*
...on tap *à la pression*
pre-dinner drink *apéritif*
white wine with cassis, black-currant liqueur *kir*
***kir* with champagne** *kir royale*
with ice *avec des glaçons*
neat *sec*
red *rouge*
white *blanc*
rose *rosé*
dry *brut*

sweet *doux*
sparkling wine *crémant*
house wine *vin de maison*
local wine *vin de pays* **Where is this wine from?** *De quelle région vient ce vin?*
pitcher *carafe/ pichet*
...of water/wine *d'eau/ de vin*
half litre *demi-carafe*
quarter litre *quart*
mixed *panaché*
after dinner drink *digestif*
brandy from Armagnac region of France *Armagnac*
Normandy apple brandy *calvados*
cheers! *santé!*
hangover *gueule de bois*

Where to Eat

● For where to eat in French Canada, *see* page 364

Numbers

0 *zéro*
1 *un, une*
2 *deux*
3 *trois*
4 *quatre*
5 *cinq*
6 *six*
7 *sept*
8 *huit*
9 *neuf*
10 *dix*
11 *onze*
12 *douze*
13 *treize*
14 *quatorze*
15 *quinze*
16 *seize*
17 *dix-sept*
18 *dix-huit*
19 *dix-neuf*
20 *vingt*
21 *vingt-et-un*
30 *trente*
40 *quarante*
50 *cinquante*
60 *soixante*
70 *soixante-dix*
80 *quatre-vingt*
90 *quatre-vingt-dix*
100 *cent*
1000 *mille*
1,000,000 *un million*

Days of the Week

Days of the week, and months are not capitalised in French.
Monday *lundi*
Tuesday *mardi*
Wednesday *mercredi*
Thursday *jeudi*
Friday *vendredi*
Saturday *samedi*
Sunday *dimanche*

Seasons

Spring *le printemps*
summer *l'été*
autumn *l'automne*
winter *l'hiver*

Months

January *janvier*
February *février*
March *mars*
April *avril*
May *mai*
June *juin*
July *juillet*
August *août*
September *septembre*
October *octobre*
November *novembre*
December *décembre*

Further Reading

Generall

Canada has a strong literary tradition (*See* Art and Performance chapter, page 99). Among the best-known writers are Robertson Davies, Margaret Atwood and Mordecai Richler. For those who want a taste of the wild, Jack London's books, *The Call of the Wild* and *White Fang* are classics.

Other books to look out:
The Shipping News, by E. Annie Proulx
The Apprenticeship of Duddy Kravitz by Mordecai Richler
The Nunavut Handbook: Travelling in Canada's Arctic edited by Marion Soublière
Random Passage by Bernice Morgan
I Married The Klondike by Laura Beatrice Berton and Pierre Berton
A Peculiar Kind of Politics by Desmond Morton
Roads to Remember: The Insiders Guide to New Brunswick by Colleen Whitney Thompson
Home Sweet Home – My Canadian Album, by Mordecai Richler
The Two Solitudes, by Hugh MacLennan
The Canadians, by Andrew H. Malcolm
The Penguin History of Canada, by Kenneth McNaught.

Insight Guides

There are a number of **Insight Guides** to North America. Titles include Montréal, Vancouver and Alaska. There are also 32 titles on the USA. **Insight Pocket Guides**, with special routes chosen by local authors, cover British Columbia, Montréal, Québec and Toronto. There are **Insight Fleximaps**, with clear cartography, travel information and a laminated finish, for Montréal, Toronto and Vancouver.

ART & PHOTO CREDITS

Anthony Blake Photo Library 121
Archives Canada 16/17, 22, 27, 33, 35, 90
D.L. Aubry 42, 44
Axiom/Chris Coe 85, 87L, 134/135, 143, 145, 155T, 160, 174T, 184, 194, 208, 212T, 224L&R, 226, 235, 236, 236T, 241, 260/261, 276T, 280, 280T, 294L&R, 320T
Ottmar Bierwagen back flap bottom, 80, 81, 139, 139T, 140R, 141L, 142T, 144, 144T, 169
Bodo Bondzio 2/3, 267, 297
Dirk Buwalda 167, 181T
Canada House 52/53, 62, 64, 68, 99, 100, 101, 105, 110, 111, 113, 115, 159, 168, 172, 230
Canadian Pacific Railway 2
Canadian Tourism Commission 102
Pat Canova 240, 244L&R, 247, 248, 249, 256/257, 316
Maxine Cass 23, 282
Stuart Dee 272
Winston Fraser 332, 335
Government of Québec 28, 87R, 114
Blaine Harrington 140L, 157, 158T, 181, 183L&R, 196T, 198, 254, 264T, 265, 266, 274T, 289, 291, 292T, 293, 299, 301, 307, 308T
Robert Harris/Archives Canada 50
M. Hetier 122/123, 199, 212, 225, 246
C.W. Jeffreys/Archives Canada 32, 34, 43, 49R
C. Kreignoff/Archives Canada 36, 37, 38
Joris Luyten/Cephas 118
Nancy Lyon 184
Chris Mack 179, 253
Mary Evans Picture Library 19, 40, 47, 51, 57, 60, 163
Metropolitan Toronto Library 56
Darien Murray 195, 197, 211T, 242
NHPA 202T, 333
Nova Scotia Tourism 231
Office de Tourisme Canadienne de la Communauté Urbaine de Québec 41
Ontario Archives 24, 25, 46, 48L&R, 49L, 54/55, 58, 59, 61, 91
Ontario Ministry of Tourism 173L, 175
Paramount, Charles Bush 112
Province of British Columbia 6/7, 276R
Carl Purcell 12/13, 86, 107, 178, 187

Leanna Rathkelly/Whistler Resort Assn 4/5, 281
Raven Images 147
D. Richard 226T, 232
Charles Shugart back cover center, 8/9, 275, 279, 304
David Simson 69
Société Régionale de Développement de Portneuf 18
Ted Stefanski/Cephas 117
Joe Terbasket front flap bottom,20
Yves Tessier/Productions Tessima Itée 203
Tony Stone Worldwide spine top, 88, 95, 268/269
Topham Picture Point 65L, 98, 104, 106, 137, 141R, 142, 146
Tourism British Columbia 273, 274
Joe Viesti front flap top, spine center & bottom, back cover left, bottom & center right, back flap top, 10/11, 14, 39, 66, 67, 72/73, 74, 75, 76L&R, 77L&R, 78L, 79L&R, 82, 83, 84, 96/97, 103, 124/125, 126/127, 136, 148/149, 150, 151, 153, 154, 155L&R, 161, 162R, 164, 165, 166, 170, 171, 173R, 174, 176/177, 182, 186, 190, 191, 200, 201, 204, 205, 206/207, 210, 213, 215, 216, 220, 221, 223, 227, 228, 229, 237, 243, 245, 262, 263, 277, 278L, 283, 286/287, 288, 290, 292, 295, 298, 302L&R, 303, 305, 306, 308, 310, 311, 312, 313, 314, 315, 326, 329, 336
Voscar 65R, 70, 119, 132, 156T, 200T, 202, 211, 214, 217, 218, 219, 228T, 233L&R, 234L&R, 238, 239, 242T, 246T
Harry M. Walker back cover top right,

78R, 89, 92, 93, 94, 116, 128, 258, 278R, 296, 301T, 321T, 323T, 318, 319, 321, 322, 330, 331
Werner Forman Archive 334
D. Wilkins 162L, 169, 250, 252, 255, 309
Young/Vancouver Public Library 30/31

Picture Spreads

Pages 70/71 *Left to right, top to bottom:* Voscar; Design Archive/Robert Burley; CIBPR; Robin Armour; CIBPR; Axiom /Chris Coe; Tourism British Columbia; James Dow; Canadian Museum of Civilization
Pages 108/109 *Left to right, top to bottom:* Canadian Museum of Civilization (2); Werner Forman Archive; Canadian Museum of Civilization; Werner Forman Archive (2); Canadian Museum of Civilization; Werner Forman Archive (2)
Pages 188/189 *Left to right, top to bottom:* Mike Hewitt/Action-Plus Dan Smith/Allsport; Harry M. Walker; Image Bank; Bob Winsett; Mike Hewitt; Image Bank; Ben Radford/ Allsport; Didier Givois/Allsport
Pages 238/239 *Left to right, top to bottom:* Topham Picture Point; Voscar; Peter Newark's Pictures (2); T. Kitchin & V. Hurst/NHPA; Voscar (3)
Pages 284/285 *Left to right, top to bottom:* David Middleton/NHPA; Stephen Krasemann/NHPA; Harry M. Walker (2); Kevin Schafer/NHPA; Harry M. Walker; John Shaw/NHPA; Harry M. Walker; David Middleton/NHPA; Stephen Krasemann/NHPA
Pages 324/325 *Left to right, top to bottom:* Harry M. Walker; Valérie Richard/Vandystadt Agence de Presse; John Shaw/NHPA; B & C Alexander/NHPA; Harry M. Walker (2); B & C Alexander/NHPA; Allsport/ Vandystadt; Rod Planck/NHPA

Map Production Polyglott Kartographie, Berndtson & Berndtson Publications, Huber Kartographie
© 2000 Apa Publications GmbH & Co. Verlag KG (Singapore branch)

INSIGHT GUIDE
Canada

Cartographic Editor **Zoë Goodwin**
Production **Mohammed Dar**
Design Consultants
Klaus Geisier, Graham Mitchener
Picture Research **Hilary Genin**

Index

Note: illustrations are indicated by page numbers in *italics*.

y

☀ INSIGHT GUIDES

The world's largest collection of visual travel guides

A range of guides and maps to meet every travel need

Insight Guides

This classic series gives you the complete picture of a destination through expert, well written and informative text and stunning photography. Each book is an ideal background information and travel planner, serves as an on-the-spot companion – and is a superb visual souvenir of a trip. Nearly 200 titles.

Insight Pocket Guides

focus on the best choices for places to see and things to do, picked by our local correspondents. They are ideal for visitors new to a destination. To help readers follow the routes easily, the books contain full-size pull-out maps. 120 titles.

Insight Maps

are designed to complement the guides. They provide full mapping of major cities, regions and countries, and their laminated finish makes them easy to fold and gives them durability. 60 titles.

Insight Compact Guides

are convenient, comprehensive reference books, modestly priced. The text, photographs and maps are all carefully cross-referenced, making the books ideal for on-the-spot use when in a destination. 120 titles.

Different travellers have different needs. Since 1970, Insight Guides has been meeting these needs with a range of practical and stimulating guidebooks and maps